JOHN DONNE
AND THE RHETORICS OF
RENAISSANCE DISCOURSE

JOHN DONNE
AND THE RHETORICS OF
RENAISSANCE DISCOURSE

JAMES S. BAUMLIN

UNIVERSITY OF MISSOURI PRESS
Columbia and London

5   4   3   2   1   95   94   93   92   91

Library of Congress Cataloging-in-Publication Data

Baumlin, James S.
  John Donne and the rhetorics of Renaissance discourse / James S.
Baumlin.
      p.   cm.
  Includes bibliographical references and index.
  ISBN 0–8262–0768–5
  1. Donne, John, 1572–1631—Criticism and interpretation.
2. Rhetoric—1500–1800.   I. Title.
PR2248.B38   1991
821′.3—dc20   90–25375
                                                                          CIP

∞™ This paper meets the requirements of the
American National Standard for Permanence of Paper
for Printed Library Materials, Z39.48, 1984.

Designer: Liz Fett
Typesetter: Connell-Zeko Type & Graphics
Printer: Thomson-Shore, Inc.
Binder: Thomson-Shore, Inc.
Typeface: Palatino

TO TITA

CONTENTS

PREFACE

Decades ago, in her influential *Elizabethan and Metaphysical Imagery: Renaissance Poetic and Twentieth-Century Critics*, Rosemund Tuve implicitly criticized the New Critics—perhaps the liveliest and most resourceful generation of readers Donne's poetry has enjoyed—for neglecting historical context. Seeking to reconstruct the rhetorical theory Donne's contemporaries would themselves, presumably, have espoused (and rightly assuming that theories of rhetoric provide models of reading), she chose to interpret his poetry against a Ramist background. In the main, readers have since followed her lead, dressing their critical vocabularies in recognizably Renaissance garb. Beyond Ramism, scholars have fashioned theories of reading from a range of contemporary sources, including school logic, classical poetics, biblical hermeneutics, and Protestant typology, the word-magic of Hermeticism, and the Ciceronian rhetoric of Continental humanism. These historical theories have taught us much about the verbal practices and possibilities of meaning in the Renaissance. In contrast, lacking obvious coordinates in Donne's own intellectual milieu, our more modern critical methods—specifically those informed by structuralist and poststructuralist theories of language and meaning—remain suspect in the eyes of many. Have these modern methods nothing, in turn, to teach us about Donne? Earlier in this century his poetry was among the New Criticism's touchstones; it would seem time for Donne to be questioned, in depth, by a newer criticism still.

Certainly our understanding of rhetoric has progressed beyond Tuve's study; through the following chapters I hope both to record and extend this progress, outlining a history of rhetoric that opens a space, as it were, for this newer criticism. I have sought to reconstruct a number of theories available to Donne, theories that would inform contemporary practices of interpretation as well as composition. In fact I outline a system of competing rhetorics, each of which has its origins in classical or early Christian discourse. Still, it may appear to some that I have simply shanghaied Donne from his own time and culture. I have no wish to make him a spokesman for modernism; if anything, though, his poetry demonstrates the extent to which modernism is itself prefigured by the Renaissance—if by modernism we mean a reawakening of historical consciousness, a recognition of cultural difference, a growing sense of the problem of language and meaning, and an awareness of the conflictual nature of discourse. These are among the many characteristics of modernism; are they not the prior discoveries of Donne's own age?

Finally, the following chapters reinterpret the nature and scope of Renaissance rhetoric per se. I have applied this revisionary theory of discourse to a reading of the *Satyres* and, in greater depth, to the *Songs and Sonets;* arguably, it should apply to other of Donne's works and, indeed, to Renaissance literature generally. This thesis, of course, remains to be tested. The Prelude and Coda provide a theoretical frame for the work as a whole; the Prelude is especially rigorous, however, and perhaps the most difficult of access. Readers may seek respite, then, in the opening section of Chapter 8, which recapitulates earlier arguments and illustrates them directly from Donne's poetry. Beyond this trick, I hesitate to give directions. Subject to reading, after all, the book ceases to be one's own.

I wish to express my gratitude to the presses and journal editors who have given permission to reprint the following material. Chapter 3 revises and expands a previously published essay, "Donne's 'Satyre IV': The Failure of Language and Genre" (*Texas Studies in Literature and Language* 30 [1988]: 363–87). Chapter 5, similarly, presents an expanded version of my article, "Donne's Poetics of Absence" (*John Donne Journal* 7 [1988]: 151–82). While their arguments remain faithful to these previous incarnations, other chapters assume a freer and, at times, more critical relation to earlier work. Chapter 2 combines and substantially alters material from two essays: "Generic Contexts of Elizabethan Satire: Rhetoric, Poetic Theory, and Imitation," in *Renaissance Genres: Essays on Theory, History, and Interpretation* (Harvard English Studies 14, ed. Barbara Kiefer Lewalski [Cambridge, Mass.: Harvard University Press, 1986], pp. 444–67), and "Donne as Imitative Poet: The Evidence of 'Satyre II'" (*Explorations in Renaissance Culture* 11 [1985]: 29–42). Chapter 4 reshapes material from two essays as well: "Donne's Christian Diatribes: Persius and the Rhetorical Persona of *Satyre III* and *Satyre V*," in *The Eagle and the Dove: Reassessing John Donne* (ed. Claude J. Summers and Ted-Larry Pebworth [Columbia: University of Missouri Press, 1986], pp. 92–105), and "From Recusancy to Apostasy: Donne's 'Satyre III' and 'Satyre V'" (*Explorations in Renaissance Culture* 16 [1990]). As I have suggested, these chapters occasionally overturn my earlier arguments; while I do not claim to know better now, I at least think differently. Finally, as footnotes shall indicate, several scattered paragraphs of Chapter 8 are drawn from three essays: "Decorum, *Kairos*, and the 'New' Rhetoric" (*Pre/Text* 5 [1985]: 171–83), "Persuasion, Rogerian Rhetoric, and Imaginative Play" (*Rhetoric Society Quarterly* 17 [1987]: 33–43), and "*Psyche/Logos:* Mapping the Terrains of Mind and Rhetoric" (coauthored with Tita French Baumlin, *College English* 51 [1989]: 245–61).

I have two more acknowledgments. To my friend and mentor, Jim W. Corder, and to my wife and colleague, Tita: for conversation and constant encouragement, I offer humble thanks.

ABBREVIATIONS

Essays in Divinity   Simpson, Evelyn M., ed. *Essays in Divinity.* Oxford: Clarendon Press, 1952.

Letters   Hester, M. Thomas, ed. *Letters to Severall Persons of Honour* (1651). Delmar, N.Y.: Scholar's Facsimiles and Reprints, 1977.

Life and Letters   Gosse, Edmund. *The Life and Letters of John Donne.* 2 vols. Gloucester, Mass.: Peter Smith, 1959.

Paradoxes and Problems   Peters, Helen, ed. *John Donne: The Paradoxes and Problems.* Oxford: Clarendon Press, 1980.

Satires   Milgate, Wesley, ed. *John Donne: The Satires, Epigrams, and Verse Letters.* Oxford: Clarendon Press, 1967. Donne's *Satyres* are quoted from this edition.

Selected Prose   Gardner, Helen, and Timothy S. Healy, S.J., eds. *John Donne: Selected Prose, Chosen by Evelyn Simpson and edited by Helen Gardner and Timothy Healy.* Oxford: Clarendon Press, 1967.

Sermons   Potter, George R., and Evelyn M. Simpson, eds. *The Sermons of John Donne.* 10 vols. Berkeley: University of California Press, 1953–1961.

The *Elegies* and the *Songs and Sonets* are quoted from Helen Gardner, ed., *John Donne: The Elegies and the Songs and Sonnets* (Oxford: Clarendon Press, 1965).

Readers should note that when quoting from older texts I have written out orthographical abbreviations, normalized i/j and u/v to conform to modern practice, and on occasion added terminal punctuation. Translations, unless otherwise noted, are my own.

JOHN DONNE
AND THE RHETORICS OF
RENAISSANCE DISCOURSE

PRELUDE

Rhetoric and Form in Donne's Poetry

The Renaissance was perhaps the first age to glimpse fully, if fleet-ingly, the rhetorical dimension of culture, the way language provides the primary instrument of politics, science, philosophy, and religion as well as literature, the way language indeed constitutes these fields. The growing nationalism of Renaissance Europe, the consciousness of a national identity, rests squarely on each people's growing lin-guistic consciousness, and control of one's language brings with it cultural, economic, political power; hence the need for a laureate to "illustrate" (illumine, make resplendent) the vernacular on the prince's behalf. The various "defenses" and "illustrations" of the mother tongues, whether by Dante, DuBellay, or Puttenham, are all in a very real sense attempts to empower the vernacular and, by extension, the nationalist policies of one's prince. The Renaissance poet's gift to the nation is thus a renovated or, rather, a recovered language. For na-tionhood and a prince's claims to legitimacy of rule demand a myth of origins for the nation's language as well as its people, a cultural identity located within a heroic or "classical" linguistic past. The poet of *The Shepheardes Calender* ennobles—and in a sense enables, em-powers—the vernacular by archaizing it, valorizing it vis-à-vis the dead and venerated classical languages; in a word, the shepherd poet classicizes English, elevating it to the status of a classical language by uncovering its quasi-mythic past and exhuming its ancient vocabu-lary. The "native strengths" and beauties of this "classical" English become a source of cultural pride and translate, ultimately, into self-legitimizing political power—ample compensation for the fact that the shepherd poet's language is as dead, as far from the living spoken vernacular, as the classical languages it emulates.

1

The development of the New Science has an equally intense relationship to the age's linguistic consciousness. Premised upon an
empiricist epistemology, one that attempts an adequate and accurate description of the real world, this science could not mature
without first purifying the language of its discourse. It is not simply
that the *verbum* clouds the *res* or that abstract words substitute for
concrete reality; more serious is the fact that habits of language
constrain experience and perception. Vocabulary gives shape to the
world: what exists is what has a name. Epistemology being intimately, inseparably linked to verbal practice, it became apparent to
Francis Bacon and the later founders of the Royal Society that an
empiricist science was impossible so long as an equally empiricist
language, nominalist and unambiguous, remained unavailable to
create and sustain it. Modern science itself thus derives from an
intense reflection upon a language whose reform became the Royal
Society's first major undertaking. (And what is the Royal Society if
not a second aristocracy or "court," ruling over this nascent science
by determining its status as language? Like its political counterpart,
the Royal Society gains power, and legitimizes itself, by controlling
the discourse of its field.)

What aspect of Renaissance culture is not shaped by a similar
reflection upon language? Can we not describe humanism, with its
educational reforms and emphasis on literary culture as literally a
revolution in rhetoric? The recovery of ancient texts, the development of philology and modern editing techniques, advances in pa-
leography and historical linguistics and, above all, the invention of
printing: all are monumental achievements, and all bring language
to the fore. The consequences of this linguistic scrutiny are incal-
culably great, including Petrarch's "discovery" of history (historical
consciousness is again an effect of linguistic self-consciousness) and
Erasmus's discovery of cultural relativism and linguistic change—of
change in principle. We might add that classical and biblical schol-
arship proceed simultaneously: the historical study of Scripture, its
editing and analysis *as text*, unites the activities of the scholar and
the theologian. More significantly, the Reformation itself arises at
least in part out of the age's reinterpretation of Scripture, a reinterpretation often enabled by humanist philology. Developments in
theology, then, are instigated by the age's growing linguistic consciousness; the Reformation becomes no less than a crisis of language—and John Donne, certainly, was born into this crisis. But if
Donne's age is in its essence the (re-)nascence of linguistic consciousness, is its rhetorical theory (or our own, for that matter)

sufficient to describe the totality of its discourse? Recent philosophers have reinscribed culture *as discourse,* asserting the textuality of all human activity, all ideology and production.[1] Can traditional theory similarly comprehend Renaissance culture without violent distortion or reductiveness? Can it embrace rhetorical culture in all its complexities, conflicts, contradictions?

We typically speak of rhetoric as if it were a unified, stable system outlining the generative/structural principles of discourse. And though the theory of rhetoric has evolved through history we presume, nonetheless, that its principles are both finite in number and universal in application. It appears equally appropriate, however, to speak of each age, each institution, indeed each text as manifesting its own unique rhetoric, one rising out of assumptions discourse necessarily (if only implicitly) makes concerning the nature of language, being, and human understanding. The varying aims and shapes of discourse reveal an equal variety of distinct, *manifested* rhetorics. Thus when we ask, "what *is* rhetoric?" or "what is *classical* or *Renaissance* rhetoric?" the questions themselves are likely to mislead. For each anticipates a singular, univocal, definitive answer when in fact a multeity of rhetorics gives shape to the discourse of each age. Particular versions and practices of rhetoric may dominate at any one time; never, at least since Babel, has there existed one unifying practice, encompassing the whole of an age's discourse. Plato's theory is demonstrably not Gorgias's. Montaigne's or Erasmus's is not Luther's. The different epistemologies and language theories assumed by each of these writers, the different assumptions they make concerning human nature and the powers of intellect necessarily yield distinct versions of rhetoric. Each philosophy current in the Renaissance, each religious sect, each political or cultural institution develops its own vocabulary, its own tropology, its own interpretive and argumentative procedures to match its unique view of physical nature, human nature, and human communication. One could proceed inductively, therefore, describing the verbal practice of individual texts, their unique *manifestation* of rhetoric, rather than construct a generalizing and abstract theory. And perhaps one *should* dwell in the actual, emphasizing the uniqueness of each text rather than its participation in some abstract system or ideal conception. For no text fully embodies the ideal de-

---

1. See, for example, Michel Foucault, *The Order of Things: An Archaeology of the Human Sciences;* and Paul Ricoeur, *Hermeneutics and the Human Sciences: Essays on Language, Action, and Interpretation.*

scribed by any one theory, and no theory in the history of discourse has encompassed all manifestations of rhetoric, describing them fully and without distortion. Yet theories only claim rather than achieve absolute descriptive power; the range and variety of historical theories testifies, in fact, to the range and diversity of discourse itself. Different theories, then, describe the different rhetorics potentially resident within any text; they are capable of doing so because each major theory in the history of rhetoric articulates a distinctive verbal epistemology that texts of different aims and authors may make manifest.[2] Thus only the totality of theories, theories considered in their complementarity as well as combativeness, can hope to encompass the totality of discourse.

As I have suggested, the classical theories of discourse are in each case grounded upon carefully articulated theories of being and language—though Plato, for one, describes the sophistic rhetoric of Gorgias and Protagoras as a theory without an adequate epistemology, a knack or "routine" incapable of yielding knowledge (though quite capable, as Plato argues in the *Gorgias*, of creating deceptions).[3] At least from this perspective, sophistic rhetoric becomes an instrument of self-serving flattery and falsehood, a practice antithetical to the universal, eternal truths of Plato's own idealist philosophy. But can one trust Plato's evaluation of an opponent's rhetoric? What, rather, is Gorgianism . . . to Gorgias himself? Though no longer extant, Gorgias's textbook (cited in Aristotle's *Rhetorica*) has a practical exemplar in his own "Encomium of Helen," a self-conscious speech about the powers and effects of persuasive language— a speech, actually, about the possibility of its own composition, its own speaking-into-being. There Gorgias admits freely that persuasion deceives, that "all who . . . persuade people of things do so by molding a false argument."[4] Is this then a speaker's self-serving defeat of truth and reality? Or does such an admission proceed

2. On the concept of verbal epistemology see Marcia L. Colish, *The Mirror of Language: A Study in the Medieval Theory of Knowledge,* pp. 1–5. Hers is a seminal study of the relations between rhetoric and knowledge, though other studies are worth noting, such as Richard Rorty, *Philosophy and the Mirror of Nature;* Richard A. Cherwitz and James W. Hikins, *Communication and Knowledge: An Investigation in Rhetorical Epistemology;* and Walter H. Beale, *A Pragmatic Theory of Rhetoric.*

3. "This then I call a form of flattery," Socrates says of the sophist's discourse, "because it aims at what is pleasant, ignoring the good, and I insist it is not an art but a routine, because it can produce no principle in virtue of which it offers what it does, nor explain the nature thereof. . . . And I refuse to give the name of art to anything irrational" (*Gorgias,* in *The Collected Dialogues of Plato,* p. 247).

4. "Encomium of Helen," p. 52.

instead from a radically skeptical epistemology (outlined elsewhere, in his treatise *On Nature*)? Gorgias would himself observe that in the absence of sure knowledge all argument becomes irrational, an appeal to belief and action rather than a discovery or affirmation of some singular, stable truth. In fact Gorgianism, the great model of sophistic rhetoric, is as firmly grounded in a theory of being and language; its epistemology, simply, is at odds with Plato's, whose own verbal epistemology is developed in such dialogues as the *Meno, Thaetetus, Cratylus, Gorgias,* and *Phaedrus.* And to be different in philosophy from Plato is—of course, to Plato—to have no philosophy at all. Simply put, Plato rejects sophistic rhetoric precisely because he rejects its underlying epistemology, whose critique of knowledge threatens to relativize not only all argument but all perception, choice, action, and value. The "purified" rhetoric that Plato outlines in the *Gorgias* and particularly the *Phaedrus* thus takes shape from a unique description of the world and of language; so, too, does the rhetoric of Gorgias, Isocrates, and every major classical theorist.[5]

The point is that the ancient Greek texts are very much aware of the simultaneously epistemological and linguistic grounds of rhetorical theory. Renaissance theorists are also cognizant (often more so than we moderns) of these shifting epistemological grounds: for them, to speak or write is at once to speak about the possibility of speaking and to assert either the possibility or impossibility of knowledge. Modern theory must follow their lead, rediscovering the ways rhetoric articulates the premises, as much as the structures, of discourse. Of course these premises or orientations need not be strictly identified with any one philosopher's systematizations of being and knowing; often they conform to the natural attitudes we assume toward the world in our own lived experience. It so happens that philosophy has traditionally reflected on these natural attitudes and reduced them to method, in the same way that rhetorical theory has abstracted from natural, living discourse its most typical aims and shapes. We need not use the term epistemology in any specific philosophical sense, then; rather, we shall use it to describe the choice of an orientation each text necessarily makes toward being and knowledge. But, to the extent that the philosoph-

5. We might observe, in passing, that Aristotle attempts to mediate these differing positions, turning his *Rhetorica* into a rich though unstable synthesis of Platonic and sophistic theory. On the indebtedness of the *Rhetorica* to both traditions see Friedrich Solmsen, "The Aristotelian Tradition in Ancient Rhetoric"; and Forbes I. Hill, "The *Rhetoric* of Aristotle."

ical theories of epistemology derive from careful observation and interpretation of natural attitude (that is, of lived experience), it stands to reason that the major theories, from those of the pre-Socratics, to Plato, to Augustine, to Aquinas, to Descartes, to the modern phenomenologists, will find their foundations reflected, *as versions of rhetoric,* in some portion of the totality of discourse: a theory of knowledge, like rhetorical theory, offers no less than a systematic description of the Actual or Manifested.

I have suggested that modern rhetorics, particularly textbooks of composition, rarely demonstrate an awareness of their epistemological premises. Many, the "current-traditionalist" texts especially, are essentialist and dogmatic, quite the opposite of the worldview described by the Theory of Relativity and the Heisenberg Principle. Contemporary rhetoric is often, therefore, at odds with the reigning epistemology—which is not to say that contemporary science *should* determine or dominate a writer's view of the world: the danger lies simply in being unconscious of the way epistemology informs both the theory and practice of discourse. Teachers of writing continue to prize clarity and correctness in language and the stability—the accessibility—of a singular truth when current instruments of science and philosophy advise a more tentative, skeptical attitude toward truth and the powers of language. Thus any modern rhetoric, if it is to represent an advance over current (or Renaissance) texts, must make explicit its assumptions concerning epistemology and language attitude and be able to describe how those assumptions impact on the structural elements of discourse. Rhetorics always involve themselves in such premises about reality and language, though contemporary discussions are, again, often less conscious of this involvement than their forebears. But as I shall suggest, this broadening of rhetoric's purview is only apparently novel: Augustinian and Thomistic and Platonic and even pre-Socratic rhetoric proceed from fully articulated philosophical systems, their differing theories of knowledge giving shape to their unique theories of discourse. Moreover, the power of literature especially rests in its ability to redescribe reality and thus to sharpen, exceed, and reshape a reader's orientation. Classical theories of *mimesis* notwithstanding, no text is ever an innocent reflection or image of the Real; always more, and less, than description, texts are an inscription claiming some problematic relation with being, articulating or drawing-out some shape of the world.

Like the rhetorics it fosters, then, epistemology is never simply one thing; as the dialectic between Platonic and Gorgianic theories demonstrates, different texts manifest a range or repertoire of orientations toward their ideological and material culture (in a word, toward reality). But how shall we study a thing that does not stand still? Modern science teaches that the orientations of an observer should be as diverse as the phenomena observed. Physicists rely on the dual perspective of particle and wave; a multiplicity of perspectives and orientations deepens the scientist's understanding of a complex physical reality. The same with an author's or audience's relationship to the socioideological realm of discourse: different orientations deepen and diversify meaning. We might often wish this were not the case, desiring instead a consistency of thought and attitude; a text (or its author, or its reader) may for some reason feel a need to assert the absolute validity of a single orientation—of idealism, say, or empiricism, of dogmatism or relativism. And yet "lived experience," as Edmund Husserl teaches us, differs dramatically (though typically unconsciously) from "thought" experience: consciously we may espouse the epistemological relativisms of Einstein's and Heisenberg's (or Gorgias's) universe, but most of the time we still live very much in a Newtonian (or indeed, Platonic) universe of stable forms. Vincent Descombes describes the problem: "since astronomers have adopted the Copernican solution, we *live* in one world in which we both see and say that 'the sun rises', and we *think* in another, where we know that the earth revolves around the sun. Conflict exists between the lived world (*Lebenswelt*) and the known world, between the *percipio* and the *cogito.*"[6] In her academic research, then, a linguist might espouse nominalism as the underlying principle of discourse; in her private life she might participate in a religious ritual claiming essentialist powers for its language of sacrament. Unconsciously shifting orientations or epistemologies are a fact of lived experience and discourse alike. Yet each perspective, like each alternative rhetoric, asserts its absolute validity over consciousness, reducing the world (if temporarily) to its own partial, fragmented vision. In such cases, lived experience seems to be coterminous with reality itself, whereas reality is precisely what the *premises* of one's discourse—one's models and orientations (in a word, the dominant rhetoric)—allow it to be. Dominated (though never fully possessed) by any one orientation, each text attempts to remake the world after its own image, and some, historically, have achieved great authority in the attempt; yet no text in itself shall ever fully comprehend or encompass the world, for

6. *Modern French Philosophy,* p. 61.

this only the totality of perspectives and orientations (that is, discourse taken as a whole, unfolding throughout time and projected to the end of time) can ever hope to achieve. Needless to say discourse has not achieved this yet.

Thus there is, in practice, a range of attitudes toward language and knowledge and value, attitudes that once again determine the largely unique character of each text. All discourse nonetheless takes as a premise some ratio among competing epistemologies and language theories, and tends for this reason toward one of four extreme shapes. Within an incarnational rhetoric, for example, truth is presumed to be singular, accessible to reason, and fully expressible in language; within a transcendental rhetoric this same truth, though singular and stable, retreats from language at the same time that it defeats or transgresses formal logic and the palpable realities of the senses; within a skeptical rhetoric, language fails altogether to express a truth that is presumed to be unstable and ultimately unknowable; and yet, while assuming this same instability, sophistic rhetoric compensates by claiming to invent truth, to create a world out of words.[7] Throughout the following chapters, therefore, I shall argue for the utility of four major rhetorical perspectives. Arguably, each reading in the interpretive history of Donne's poetry has situated itself within at least one of these perspectives; this book is a study in their dynamic interplay, though I recognize that any model threatens to do violence to the variety of manifested rhetorics, distorting instead of delineating some of the shapes discourse actually takes. I offer the following, then, as no more than a description of tendencies inherent in discourse. And though texts in some sense move toward these "pure" or extreme versions, we shall discover that discourse in almost all cases manifests an impurity in its rhetoric (or manifests, rather, a mixture of rhetorics and an internal tension between the various meanings and effects of language). Not only are there multiple rhetorics; these rhetorics typically intersect and cohabit the same textual space, complementing as much as combating each other, multiplying as well as destabilizing the meanings of discourse. Any text, in other words, can become a scene of

7. In his article, "Rhetoric, Sophists, and the Possible," John Poulakos describes three ontologies implicit in classical rhetoric, the "real world" of Aristotle, the "ideal world" of Plato, and the "possible world" of Gorgias; these correspond to the rhetorics of incarnationism, transcendence, and sophism (which I have just outlined), and I would add to his list a fourth ontology, the mutable and ultimately unknowable world of Pyrrhonist skepticism. See also Victor Vitanza, "Critical Sub/Versions of the History of Rhetoric."

conflict between competing rhetorics and their enabling vocabularies, each attempting to impose its unique vision and attitude
upon the reading consciousness (see figures 1–3).

It is with trepidation that I offer a visual schema. To do so risks
pigeonholing oneself as structuralist or, worse(?), a sort of Ramist—
both schools having fallen, of late, rather far out of fashion. To anticipate the almost inevitable charges of over-simplification (charges
to which practically any model, I suspect, falls prey), I should state
that my intention is *not* to represent discourse as a static system or
structure but rather to chart certain dynamic relations among four
textual/interpretive strategies. A text may or may not orchestrate all
four in its unfolding argument; all four, in other words, may not be
consciously exploited *in the writing*. All four, nonetheless, are present as orientations of reading and response. A text or interpretation
may thus be said *to move through* the various rhetorics, much as a
musical composition modulates keys. When read clockwise, for example, the third figure charts a typical movement, one that I explain,
briefly, below; further explanation must await my final chapter,
whose arguments I can only anticipate now and partially rehearse.

The sophistic moment in any text conjures a world into being
(that is a world-of-*words*, a "counterfait Creation" [*Sermons* 4:87],
the skeptic would say), and it does so against a ground of doubt; dynamically, then, a moment of skepticism often precedes and prepares
the way for the sophist, whose world-of-words seeks ambitiously (if
also naively) to be deemed truth itself—that is, to be believed. From
that moment on, such discourse seeks to move beyond persuasion,
literally to embody that "truth" that it will now celebrate, sustain,
and defend through language. Here, clearly, sophism modulates into
a rhetoric of incarnationism. At crucial moments, however, the incarnationist text discovers realms of experience closed to language, at
which time it may turn from public celebration to a self-effacing language of transcendence. The next passage, from transcendence to
skepticism, is typically violent, and yet the germ of skepticism is
already planted in any text that admits its inadequacy to affirm experience—particularly when experience and reality itself are said to lie
beyond the bodily senses. Of course the skeptic questions the very
possibility of transcendent experience, subjecting all such affirmations to a withering doubt. But in this moment of doubt, one that
destroys belief in a stable, eternal (if ineffable) reality, we are brought
full circle: in the wake of destroyed faith one is left to fashion a new
world (again, of words). From skepticism we return to a moment of
sophism.

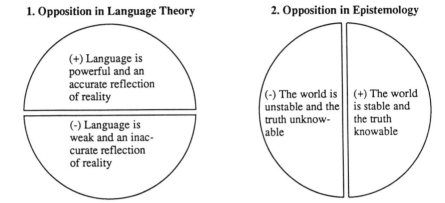

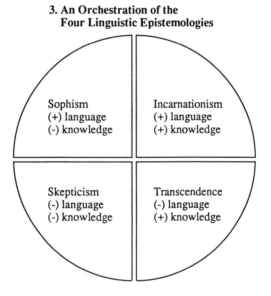

Figures 1-3

This by no means exhausts the possible itineraries of argument; other movements (indeed, oscillations and even reversals) are common. Note, in addition, the implicitly theological character of the four rhetorics as I have just described them. Certainly Donne's writing assumes a range of secular vocabularies, voices, and intentions; still, in his own age, each theory of language will invoke an underlying theology of language, and many of the poet's verbal performances will be subsumed, typologically as it were, within the priest's celebration of the "word incarnate," the mystic's *via negativa*, the agnostic's doubt, and the creator god's *fiat lux* (corresponding, albeit broadly, to the rhetorics of incarnationism, transcendence, skepticism, and sophism). Though controversial in its own right, this point, too, awaits clarification in later chapters.

Donne's poetry provides an appropriate test case for such a theory. Shall we read "The Exstasie," for example, as a poem whose language incarnates being and thus celebrates, in a sacramental, liturgical sense, the communion of lovers in their union of flesh and spirit? And if not as epideixis or celebration, shall we read "The Exstasie" as a poem whose language seeks persuasion through the sophist's verbal deceptions? (For persuasion, in Greek sophistic rhetoric, rests wholly on *apate* or deliberate falsehood: does the poet tell the truth, or *make* the truth, or simply lie about the nature of love as he attempts to redefine the relations between flesh and spirit, lover and beloved?) And if not as the sophist's persuasion or (less nobly described) a seduction poem, shall we read "The Exstasie" as the enactment of a negative or Augustinian rhetoric, a poem that denies language the power to express transcendent experience, thus effacing itself in silence? (For who has *heard* the "dialogue of one"? The souls are said to "speak" in unison, but does the poem allow for an audience outside of the souls themselves?) In short, is the experience of *extasis* that occasions this poem even capable of inscription? Is a language of transcendence *sharable,* accessible or in any way meaningful to anyone beyond the poet and his beloved? Again these diverse language attitudes, each with its unique epistemology or worldview, generate the multiple rhetorics whose intersection in a text simultaneously enriches and complicates reading.

In its broadest scope, then, this book is a study in the ways literary form is simultaneously enabled, sustained, and destabilized by the multiplicity of rhetorics potentially resident within each text, and the ways these different rhetorics offer alternative perspectives or orientations for reading: one and the same work ("The Exstasie," once again; "The Dreame"; or "The Canonization") can be read within an incarnationist rhetoric, a skeptical rhetoric, a transcendent rhetoric, or a sophistic rhetoric, orientations that, though distinct theoretically, rarely work in isolation. The first chapter of Part I describes the problems these multiple rhetorics have brought to the interpretive history of Donne; as a reading of others' interpretations, it simultaneously complements and complicates their more orthodox, unified readings by asserting the very terms they seek to refute—the equal claims of skepticism and fideism in Donne's epistemology, the continuing influence of Roman Catholicism upon an Anglican's writings, a consummate rhetor's mistrust of rhetorical argument, a gifted writer's radical questioning of literary-discursive form. One might object that such a chapter (and perhaps the book as a whole) gives unusual attention to Donne's more recent and influential readers, quoting other critics at such currently unfashionable length; in fact the meanings of Donne's poetry reside nowhere but in their continually unfolding interpretive history. And since the present work attempts to uncover the many oppositions (generic, rhetorical, ideological) that enable, complicate, and multiply interpretations, it stands to reason that Donne criticism becomes itself a subject of reading. Of course, in the broadest sense, rhetorical theory searches not for "the" meaning or "my" meaning so much as for what makes any meaning or interpretation possible. It is, after all, one thing to note the variety of readings and the fact of their divergence; it is another thing entirely to work out some structural or rhetorical or dialectical explanation of this fact.

With occasional glances at Donne's *Sermons* and *Essays in Divinity,* Part I (Chapters 1–4) reads Donne's early prose and the *Satyres* as documents in the competing rhetorics of Reformation theology, poems whose self-conscious assertions of skepticism continually question, test, and strain their literary-discursive form. Turning to Donne's more mature lyrics, the *Songs and Sonets,* Part II describes the historical theories and Donne's practice of these rhetorics in greater depth. Chapter 5 explores the linguistic theology of the valedictory poetry especially, observing the ways skepticism time and again undermines the poet's incarnationist arguments; Chapter 6 examines the theological basis of Donne's transcendent rhetoric (the second alternative to the poet's failed incarnationism); Chapter 7 describes the movement from skepticism to sophism, while Chapter 8 attempts to orchestrate all four rhetorics in a perspectivist reading of selected lyrics. The reigning assumption, then, is that these four perspectives are dialectically related. A rhetoric of skepticism (dominant, say, in "A Valediction: of my Name in the Window") deconstructs incarnationist argument, resting in an attitude of doubt, while a rhetoric of transcendence provides an alternative refuge (as in "The Canonization"), resting in an attitude of prayerful silence; in contrast, a rhetoric of sophism (given rein in "A Lecture upon the Shadow" and, perhaps more brilliantly, in "The Sunne Rising") aspires literally to an act of creation, the construction of possible worlds through language—indeed, sophism would describe itself as the creative moment within incarnationism itself, an originary *fiat lux*. In its most common (and negative) sense, sophism is often reduced to verbal deception and manipulation, an utterance of deliberate falsehoods for a speaker's advantage; in its positive and truly creative sense, sophism seeks to incarnate its desires, "to make dreames truth; and fables histories," as Donne would himself put it ("The Dreame," 8). Thus the movement from sophism to incarnationism seeks to transform the world and self by means of *logos*, and we shall find that the four rhetorics assume a theological character, modeling themselves upon the speech-acts of the priest-celebrant, the mystic, the agnostic, and the creator-god. We need only remind ourselves that *pistis*, the Greek philosopher's term for persuasion, is appropriated by Christian theology; now denoting one's faith in Christ, *pistis* remains, nonetheless, a fundamentally rhetorical event, the crisis of faith having become a crisis of interpretation and response.[8] And this points to the fundamental hermeneutic problem of Donne's poetry, the *Songs and Sonets* especially. Articulating their unique theologies of language, Donne's lyrics invite the reader into a world of private faith, one created, sustained, and celebrated by the poet-priest; whether we as readers choose to dwell within this same sacred space or to deny it, whether we choose to believe the poet's words or to doubt and refute them, we are at once immersed in the same crises of faith that history, in the guise of the Reformation controversy, presented to Donne the poet—who will, in fact, turn priest (though of the Anglican, not the Catholic Communion).[9] Perhaps Donne sought in poetry a place

8. See James L. Kinneavy, *Greek Rhetorical Origins of Christian Faith: An Inquiry,* pp. 33–55.

9. I have suggested that poetry provides the sacred space; in a letter to Henry Goodyer, Donne compares his "Litanie" to earlier Catholic models that Popes had "commanded . . . for publike service in their Churches," though his own "is for lesser Chappels, which are my friends" (*Selected Prose,* p. 131). As "temples of God," Donne's coterie readers are called literally to incarnate the discourse, giving themselves physically to such a prayer, becoming the psychic if not sacred space in which the poet-priest's words come to life. Setting aside

where the language and, arguably, the spirit of an older faith could be kept alive; perhaps his lyrics lament the *loss* of Catholic modes of worship and belief; perhaps, finally, they ironize and deliberately undercut their allusions to hagiography, relic worship, intercession, and the Roman liturgy and sacraments. Again, are we to doubt or believe, participate or deny? Poignantly, it is left to the reader to choose among these alternatives. Though rarely an explicit subject of these lyrics, the competing theologies of the Reformation have left an indelible mark upon the language of the *Songs and Sonets*; our task is to chart their complex interrelations.

I offer the following, finally, not as a definitive study of Donne's rhetorical and generic practice (and certainly not as a refutation of earlier readers) but rather as a series of directions new readings might take. The multiple rhetorical bases of his poetry, for which this book provides a theoretical outline, offer new bases for interpretation, demonstrating the logic and perhaps even the orderliness of polysemy, the ways that readings simultaneously complement and compromise one another, multiply and intersect. The dialectic among these disparate, competing rhetorics again figures throughout Part I, and will emerge as the explicit subject of Part II; the point to make here, though, is that polysemy discovers its own organization and systematic operation, each text containing within itself the potentialities of alternative, competing systems of rhetoric. And having described, if only partially, these multiple rhetorical bases, we might ask what effects their intersection and play have on literary-discursive form. Given the presence of skepticism particularly, can genre ever remain an entirely stable vessel of emotion, structure of knowledge, or instrument of persuasion? Does it not turn in against itself, succumbing to a text's own self-questioning and self-criticism?

Such is a reigning premise of the chapters on the *Satyres*, though *Biathanatos*, written during Donne's brief career as a satirist, offers an immediate illustration from among his early prose. For it is a

the boldly incarnationist assumptions of this argument, let me emphasize the *privacy* of such poetic devotion, the way readers, though "lesser Chappels," are called to worship by means of the poetic text. Donne adds that "neither the Roman Church need call it defective, because it abhors not the particular mention of the blessed Triumphers in heaven; nor the Reformed can discreetly accuse it, of attributing more than a rectified devotion ought to doe" (p. 131). Granted, he defends its Protestant orthodoxy. *By means of poetry*, though, Donne here reappropriates the Catholic liturgy of his youth; such, at any rate, is the implication, which following chapters explore.

work of casuistry that "explicitly criticizes the casuistical approach"—
criticizes, that is, its own discursive form, as Camille Wells Slights
observes. It "condemns the tortuous legalism of casuists 'applying
the rules of Divinitie to particular cases: by which they have made
all our actions perplex'd and litigious,'" and for this reason, she
suggests, the work as a whole fails: the "combination of serious
moral analysis with satire of an inadequate casuistical method is not
wholly successful, in spite of Donne's acute grasp of casuistical
procedures and his considerable satiric skill, because his central
argument relies too heavily on the methods he condemns."[10] The
intrusion of skepticism thus undermines the conclusions one would
hope to reach by means of casuistry. The text's rhetoric, in other
words, defeats its own discursive form. But we must ask: Is this an
unfortunate, perhaps unforeseen effect of *Biathanatos* or its very
subject and substance? In other words, is the text an exercise in
casuistical form or an exercise in self-criticism, in a rhetoric of skepticism that ultimately refutes casuistry? Proceeding from an assumption that human powers of judgment are too weak to attain,
much less confirm truth, Donne's systematic doubt denies the existence of adequate criteria for belief or grounds for moral action. As
Slights herself notes, "repeated attacks on the certainty of judgment have the further effect of suggesting the impossibility of clear
perception or sure judgment by the individual conscience."[11] As a
defense of self-murder, *Biathanatos* may not be successful. But as a
self-ironizing, self-reflexive exploration of its own form it succeeds
remarkably—though its success, paradoxically, lies precisely in its
refusal to validate the logic of moral argument. Far from "clearing
the doubt" about self-murder, it demonstrates only the doubtful-
ness of a method that can make "all our actions perplex'd and
litigious." As in the *Satyres,* Donne points up the inadequacies from
within. By pushing the method to its breaking point, by relying
"too heavily," as Slights remarks, on casuistry, Donne turns *Biathanatos* into an exploration of its own discursive form.

Similar effects may be observed in perhaps Donne's earliest writings, the *Paradoxes and Problems,* whose many puns, ambiguities of
reference and breaches of strict logical form are like so many mirrors that fragment and redouble reality: what one reads is not a
faithful representation of truth and experience so much as the infi-
nitely reflecting surfaces of language itself. And Donne's poetry, the

10. *The Casuistical Tradition in Shakespeare, Donne, Herbert, and Milton,* p. 141.
11. Ibid., pp. 139, 144.

Songs and Sonets especially, is typically no different. Though some lyrics assert confidence in their logic and in the strength, stability, and integrity of their form, yet an equal number become self-consuming artifacts—in a phrase, "paradoxes and problems," the forms themselves refusing to yield coherent and stable meaning, refusing in the process to perform or enact themselves (that is, to succeed in the traditional aims of their genre, whether these be praise or blame, instruction, or some manner of persuasion). Casting doubt upon their own epistemological and linguistic premises, the skeptical rhetoric of such works weakens from within the vessels that it relies on for its own expression, criticizing what it cannot abandon: its own literary form. Of course, in a prose letter to Henry Goodyer, Donne refers to his *Paradoxes and Problems* as "evaporations" (*Selected Prose*, p. 132), suggesting on the one hand their light, trifling nature and on the other their tendency to self-destruct. Donne elaborates in yet another letter, this time to Henry Wotton:

> Only in obedience I send you some of my paradoxes: I love you and myself and them too well to send them willingly for they carry with them a confession of their lightnes, and your trouble and my shame. But indeed they were made rather to deceave tyme than her daughter truth: although they have beene written in an age when any thing is strong enough to overthrow her. If they make you to find better reasons against them they do their office: for they are but swaggerers: quiet enough if you resist them. If perchaunce they be pretyly guilt, that is their best for they are not hatcht: they are rather alarums to truth to arme her than enemies: and they have only this advantadg to scape from being caled ill things that they are nothings. Therefore take heed of allowing any of them least you make another. (*Selected Prose*, p. 111)

Donne writes "in an age when any thing is strong enough to overthrow" truth. Surely the New Science and the Reformation controversies contribute to an older truth's overthrow (the overthrow, that is, of the medieval Catholic-Scholastic worldview), and it seems that argument itself—the very material of which this paradox is composed—does equal damage. As "alarums to truth," then, Donne's paradoxes seek "to arme her" by compelling the reader to struggle against their often skeptical, often sophistic rhetoric and pseudo-logic.

Of course, modern readers tend to think of rhetoric as a means to persuade, to gain an audience's trust and assent; even when we question the motives of a discourse, accusing it of deception and manipulation, still we assume that persuasion, gaining a reader's belief or assent, is its aim. Donne, however, invites a more complex response, turning the activity of reading into a game of belief *and* doubt, appealing to both attitudes, typically in one and the same work. Thus Donne's paradoxes demand that their readers "resist them" and "find better reasons against them," though anyone in the least acquainted with this poet knows the difficulty of such refutation. There is "a false thread, but not easily found" in all of his youthful, paradoxical writing.[12] Like contemporary readers of *Biathanatos*, we find ourselves similarly trapped—and resistant, the way of reading here described becoming at once combative and self-defensive, precisely the sort of reading fostered by the polemical warfare of the Reformation.

Admittedly, many of Donne's texts assert the dominance of a particular attitude toward language, or at least make claims for its dominance, as the "Valediction: forbidding Mourning," for example, asserts the power of language to preserve love in the physical absence of the beloved. Underlying such a poem is an incarnational rhetoric, one grounded in a linguistic theology that claims for the poet-priest's language a power of sacramental presence, of invoking the poet and his beloved within the textual space; in so doing, of course, such a poem becomes implicitly a self-critical study of its own ability to make such claims or assume such premises about language. For all discourse proceeds from a set of propositions about language and reality that are simultaneously its premises and that which needs to be proved. Can such a text perform itself, in other words? Can it do or be what it says? No text, it appears, fully escapes or resolves this anxiety over its own validation or performance. Thus such poems as "The Undertaking" and "Negative Love" emphasize not truth (or being, or knowledge) but the partiality of its expression in language, and they do so by means of a transcendent rhetoric, an Augustinian "rhetoric of silence." In isolation, though, either of these rhetorics ignores—or represses?—a text's oscillation between the truthfulness (or clarity, or efficacy) of language and the incompleteness of that truth.

Donne's epigram "Niobe" illustrates, in miniature, the problematic natures of performative language and poetic form: "By childrens birth, and death, I am become / So dry, that I am now made my owne tombe." As Niobe turns to stone, so the genre of epigram

12. Such is Donne's own report to Robert Ker, on presenting him with the manuscript of *Biathanatos*. It is, he continues, "upon a misinterpretable subject" as well as "a Book written by Jack Donne, and not by Dr. Donne" (*Selected Prose*, p. 152).

turns into funereal epigraph, an inscribing (of the poem itself) upon the tomb that is the speaker's own transformed body. Thus the poem attempts to literalize the Horatian metaphor of poem-as-monument, claiming for its language the power to metamorphose literary and human forms alike, turning the speaker into a statue and the epigram into epitaph. But the funereal inscription (again, the poem itself) records at one and the same time the death of the speaker and the death of spoken language in writing. In an act, seemingly, of self-composition, the writing turns the poet's speaking presence into stone, a self-representation that shall ever maintain "a most majestic silence," as Plato's *Phaedrus* describes the written text.[13] And yet "Niobe" asserts at least the possibility that genre *can* perform and validate itself; rarely, though, do Donne's lyrics assert so confident (or naive?) a solution to their anxiety of validation. Consider how the argument of "Niobe" is overturned by "The Paradox," where the poet claims "once" to have

> lov'd and dyed; and am now become
> Mine Epitaph and Tombe.
> Here dead men speake their last, and so do I;
> Love-slaine, loe, here I lye.
> (17–20)

Presumably the last line, echoing the hic jacet of funereal inscription, would metamorphose the lyric itself into the speaker's epitaph. And like "Niobe," the argument as a whole seems peculiarly resistant to counterargument or rebuttal; far from an awareness of their problematic assertions, such lines exude an absolute confidence in their self-sufficiency (absolute, indeed, to the point of brashness). But how sound, really, how "well wrought" is this urn for the love-slain poet's ashes? Cracks appear early on, as preceding lines assert nothing but the falsehood of lovers' words:

> I cannot say I lov'd, for who can say
> Hee was kill'd yesterday?
> . . . .
> We dye but once, and who lov'd last did die,
> Hee that saith twice, doth lye.
> (5–6, 9–10)

Such observations refute, point by point, the later connections between loving and dying, lyric and epitaph. The poet himself denies

13. Plato, *Collected Dialogues*, p. 521. I shall explore this issue at greater length in Part II, Chapters 5 and 6.

efficacy to the argument: to say the impossible, that he is "love-slain," is indeed to "lye"—not in the ground, but in the throat. A "paradoxical undoing of the whole discourse," as Arthur F. Marotti suggests,[14] the pun undermines the Petrarchan convention of the scorned lover's death, reflecting at the same time on the sincerity and efficacy of poetic language. Failing to transform itself into a *monumentum aere perennius*, "The Paradox" becomes instead a self-critical, self-consuming artifact.

There is thus a further assault upon the poet's incarnationist aims, one explored in Chapters 5 and 6 on Donne's valedictions (and one that puts the question to all assertions concerning the adequacy of literary genre). Though speech might claim a living relation to its speaker, audience, and subject, a poem's status as writing brings all such claims to a point of crisis, offering but a *simulacrum* of living, breathing presence. The *Songs and Sonets* make continuous reference to their own status as writing, describing themselves as so many books, legends, chronicles, contracts, autobiographies, testaments, letters, libretti, lectures, messages, curses, charms, emblems, hieroglyphs, and signatures; self-consciously, they continually address their own problematic relation to the poet's living voice and presence. "Before I sigh my last gaspe, let me breath, / Great love, some legacies" ("The Will," 1–2): thus the poet equates breath, life, and speech, deliberately suppressing the written nature of his text, his Last Will. And in many instances, death and writing are the twin themes; as in "A Valediction: of my Name in the Window," writing becomes both a preservative against death and the cause of death, an attempt both to invoke the poet's living presence and to substitute for him, inscribing his will and epitaph. Then again, whether the poem or *written* word succeeds or fails to give substantial, dialogic presence depends, I shall argue, on its relation to some conception of sacramental theology; so conceived, the act of reading aspires to a sacramental event, the reader himself affected by the poem as if by a second consciousness, entering into a dialogic relationship with it, questioning and receiving answers from it, hearing words unwritten though present, nonetheless, in the text's sacred space, offering his own mind and body as the place where inscription may reunite with the living word or psyche. Communion, then, whether of poetic language or of more traditionally liturgical modes of sacrament, is inherently dialogic and intersubjective; among Donne's love lyrics "The Exstasie"

14. *John Donne, Coterie Poet*, p. 87.

seeks to enact this insight in its "dialogue of one," perhaps the poet's boldest assertion of an incarnationist, soul-body rhetoric. But "Verse embalmes vertue," the poet writes elsewhere, "and Tombs, or Thrones of rimes, / Preserve frail transitory fame, as much / As spice doth bodies from corrupt aires touch" ("To the Countesse of Bedford At New-yeares Tide," 13–15). Though the sentiment is conventional, does this not, implicitly, toll the death of incarnational rhetoric? For even as "fame" is preserved, the poem is itself turned into a monument—to one's memory, to death. Given the poet's recognition of the proximity of death and of the failure of language to perform its presencing, preservative function, Donne's love lyrics rarely resort to incarnationist arguments without a self-criticism that leads, finally, to a rhetoric of skepticism.

Not all of Donne's writing is so explicitly self-consuming, and yet the potential for conflict resides within each text, each needing to argue against some implication or potential within itself; each text struggles to suppress the counterargument that its own argument enables, to kill that to which, paradoxically perhaps, it gives birth. Dialectically, all argument generates its antithesis, and in so doing confirms the proposition that *logos* or rational argument devolves from the binary oppositions of *dissoi logoi*.[15] Reflecting similar complexities in his biography, Donne's writing continually oscillates between the theologies of the Catholic and Reformed Churches, between rationalist and skeptical modes of argument, between a dogmatic conservatism and an iconoclastic libertinism, between a quest for certainty and a recognition of doubt. And though the reader may privilege one thought or term over another (skepticism, say, over rationalism or dogmatism) in the interpretation of any work, it is the very presence of opposition that becomes a text's condition of possibility: both terms together are its parents, though the text is born more of their strife than attraction. They are mutu-

15. We might observe, in passing, the remarkable similarity between the ancient skeptic's *dissoi logoi* and the deconstructionist's (or modern skeptic's) concept of "double antithetical patterns," whose presence and oscillation in a text destabilizes univocal meaning. J. Hillis Miller describes these patternings: "Far from being a chain which moves deeper and deeper into the text, closer and closer to a definitive interpretation of it, the mode of criticism sometimes now called 'deconstruction,' which is analytic criticism as such, encounters always, if it is carried far enough, some mode of oscillation. In this oscillation two genuine insights into literature in general and into a given text in particular inhibit, subvert, and undercut one another. This inhibition makes it impossible for either insight to function as a firm resting place, the end point of analysis" ("The Critic as Host," p. 252).

ally enabling and parasitic—neither can exist without the other. A literature of skepticism, for example, feeds off dogmatism as off its host; conversely a literature of dogma, asserting confidence in man's reason and in the accessibility of truth, argues itself into existence against a background of doubt and disbelief, constantly protecting itself from a skepticism lurking within the discourse itself—dogma must discover its own antidote, its own best argument, as it were, against the counterargument that is its parasite. And it would seem, finally, that a multiplicity of rhetorics serves to multiply and destabilize meaning; with this in mind, we might make suggestions regarding the reading of Donne's poetry *as collections* or as exemplary of (presumably) unified generic traditions.

□   □   □

Recent readings of the *Satyres* vary in details but largely agree on a number of points. The satiric persona is ostensibly the same throughout the collection, a singular, unified voice whose identity unfolds throughout and, indeed, deepens and grows in self-knowledge, much like a dramatic character. And the collection itself, though of disparate poems, is organically and thematically unified, forming a progression, in fact, each poem deepening in its understanding of the nature of satire. Read this way, the *Satyres* recount the speaker's own exploration of his literary form: the story told in each is of the poet learning, through insight and error, to become a Christian satirist. Granted, thematic unities may legitimately be discovered within the collection. It remains a question, though, whether the speaker learns to be a better satirist from one poem to the next. Emphasizing their meta-narrative unity, such a reading tends to downplay other intertextual relations—relations to the classical models, for example—realms of imitation that necessarily call into question the collection's presumed unity of voice. Does the second satire's imitation of Juvenal create a voice or personality that can in any way be identified with the Horatian personality of the first? Yes . . . and no, of course not, for the dialectic of classical imitation problematizes the relation of each poem not only to its Latin model but to other poems in the collection. So if a story does unfold in this collection, that story, I suggest, will be the poet's increasing recognition of the problem of writing satire, a problem for which he attempts five more or less distinct solutions. Rather than as meta-narratives, I have chosen to read these poems as studies in contrast, works that explore the problems of rhetoric and

Reformation theology, each returning to the problematic relation between traditional literary form and social *re*form. And for this reason the chapters immediately following offer a double reading of the *Satyres,* attending first to their thematic involvement in the Reformation controversy and then, perhaps more importantly, to the effects of this controversy on the language and genre.

We must attend, in other words, to the dynamic interplay between past form and present exigency—in the case of Donne's *Satyres,* between the decorum of his classical models and the demands of his unique historical circumstances. It is in fact the tension between the formal and the rhetorical, the decorous and the kairotic, that most thoroughly marks imitative poetry, and this tension, for the satirist especially, focuses squarely on the problem of competing authorities. For decorum, we might observe, is one of the most naive, and powerful, and problematic concepts invoked in the creation of genre. Asserting the timelessness of classical forms, a theory of imitative decorum treats models as ideal forms or even, indeed, as Platonic Ideas within which the new poet's work strives to participate. The new text thus arises from an idealized past and within a tradition whose forms were, presumably, perfected in antiquity. Differences in vernacular, culture, and spirit are subsumed within a typology of formal resemblances; in a sense, decorous imitation creates a secular typology, a literary system in which the new text recapitulates or completes its model in the same manner that the Christian antitype completes the Old Testament types that prefigure it—as a literary antitype, the Renaissance text derives meaning and value precisely from its participation in the meanings and structures of the original textual event. For the type alone, the classical model, offers an inviolate literary authority; there can be no new writing without a model to stabilize structures, styles, and meanings.[16]

16. See Dennis Quint, *Origin and Originality in Renaissance Literature: Versions of the Source,* pp. 1–31. And we might ask whether the major texts of Renaissance poetic theory (Jonson's *Timber* comes at once to mind, as does Puttenham's *Arte* and Scaliger's *Poetices*) are designed simply to teach critical reading or creative composition as well? Modern criticism tends to forget that, say, the *Ars Poetica* of Horace offers precepts for the aspiring writer and only incidentally provides observations on esthetic evaluation and response. Renaissance theorists, in the manner of Horace, describe a system of literary production as much as a methodology of critical analysis, a means of generating texts through the creative reinterpretation of the ancient models. And since their primary goal is to form or fashion an author, it becomes obvious why so many Renaissance theorists offer relatively little textual criticism, focusing instead on the generalized fea-

As Thomas Greene observes, "Valla wrote of the Latin language as a *magnum sacramentum,*" suggesting a version of literary history that is at foundation *"reproductive* or *sacramental,"* one that "celebrates an enshrined primary text by rehearsing it liturgically, as though no other form of celebration could be worthy of its dignity." Imitation thus becomes "analogous to ritual," where "the model or subtext is perceived as a fixed object on the far side of an abyss, beyond alteration and beyond criticism, a sacred original whose greatness can never be adequately reproduced despite the number of respectful reproductions."[17] Here Greene describes both the "ceremonial veneration" of decorous imitation (that is, imitation as a liturgical, almost eucharistic celebration of an ancient text) and the imitative poet's sense of the inadequacy of the reproduction. This second point becomes problematic, though. More than celebration, such reproduction aims at *participation* within the model; a decorous or sacramental conception of imitation seeks to reenact, and not simply echo or commemorate, the model in the new text. Decorous imitation claims, in fact, to celebrate the model's virtual presence within the new text, the text's own conversion, as it were, into the originary voice of its model. And yet Renaissance imitation—surely Donne's—rarely rests with invocation or self-conversion. Perhaps unwittingly, Ben Jonson illustrates this point: a "requisite in our *Poet,"* he writes, is *"Imitation,"*

> to bee able to convert the substance, or Riches of an other *Poet,* to his owne use. To make choise of one excellent man above the rest, and so to follow him, till he grow very *Hee:* or, so like him, as the Copie may be mistaken for the Principall. Not, as a Creature, that swallowes, what it takes in, crude, raw, or undigested; but, that feedes with an Appetite, and hath a Stomacke to concoct, devide, and turne all into nourishment.[18]

Initially, the imitative poem provides the scene of a poet's own conversion into the voice of his model. "Till he grow very *Hee":* the repetition of the pronoun emphasizes the achievement of identity.

---

tures of each poet: they offer the description of a model's decorum—a model for imitation in the vernacular—rather than a reading of specific classical texts.

17. Thomas M. Greene, *The Light in Troy: Imitation and Discovery in Renaissance Poetry,* p. 38. Greene's study of Renaissance imitation theory nearly exhausts an already well-explored subject, and the following is indebted to his terms. Other recent discussions include G. W. Pigman III, "Versions of Imitation in the Renaissance"; and Stephen Orgel, "The Renaissance Artist as Plagiarist."

18. *Timber, or Discoveries* (1641), in *The Works of Ben Jonson,* 8:638.

In the second instance, though, such aspiration reduces to mere forgery—"or, so like him as the Copie may be mistaken for the Principall." With this qualifying remark, in itself little more than an aside, Jonson casts doubt upon the very premise of decorous imitation. As forgery, all imitation becomes but a mis-taking, a parroting or parodying that misappropriates another's voice. Significantly, then, Jonson follows up this denial of the poet's self-conversion with yet another kind of conversion: not the poet into the ancient model, but the model into the new poet. A classical, in fact Senecan commonplace, this digestive metaphor points to the potential violence of the imitative poem in dismembering, ingesting, consuming the original, in turning the model's sinews and strength, the "flesh," as it were, of his language, bodily into this new text. Sacramental imitation becomes a kind of sacrifice, the dismemberment and reconstitution—as Jonson puts it, the "division" and "concoction"—of an ancient text.[19] This emulative impulse attempts literally to incorporate and consume the model in its quest for poetic supremacy, inviting explicit critical comparison between text and model.

Thus authors are at the same time to "follow and emulate the ancients" (*veteres sequi aemularique*), as Donne advises in his Latin verse to Jonson (*Amicissimo et meritissimo Ben. Jonson In Vulponem*, 3, in *Satires*). The prefatory letter to *Metempsychosis* describes a similar reappropriation of models, though Donne plays variations upon Jonson's metaphors, turning consumption into purchase and incorporation into extraction: "Now when I beginne this booke, I have no purpose to come into any mans debt . . . if I doe borrow any thing of Antiquitie, besides that I make account that I pay it to posterity, with as much and as good: you shall still finde mee to acknowledge it, and thanke not him onely that hath digg'd out treasure for mee, but hath lighted mee a candle to the place" (*Metempsychosis*, in *Satires*, p. 26). Calling explicit attention to the presence and play of subtexts, the preface invites an intertextual reading, the kind of critical reinterpretation of sources that the poem itself performs upon Lucian and Menippean tradition, Spenser and Du Bartas, the

19. Miller, similarly, describes the poetic text as "that ambiguous gift, food, host in the sense of victim, sacrifice. It is broken, divided, passed around. . . . The previous text is both the ground of the new one and something the new poem must annihilate by incorporating it, turning it into ghostly insubstantiality, so that the new poem may perform its possible-impossible task of becoming its own ground. The new poem both needs the old texts and must destroy them" ("Critic as Host," p. 225).

romance epics of Renaissance and classical predecessors. As Donne practices it, then, imitation may begin in decorous invocation of models; inevitably it ends in emulation, rivalry, and revisionism.[20] Though it begins as a faithful rehearsal or reproduction of the ancient model, the new poem's acts of critical revision are carried to the point of sacrilege (not that these terms operate in isolation, sacrilege being a ritual dismemberment or disfiguring of that Presence which sacrament invokes). A theory of poetry that combines imitative and emulative strategies becomes at once the ritual presencing and sacrifice of the ancient model. Though antithetical in nature, imitation and emulation, decorum and *kairos* become mutually enabling perspectives, operant within one and the same imitative text. For in establishing its own derivative nature, all emulative poetry must pass through an initial invocation to a moment of iconoclasm, of dismemberment and consumption.

The problem of imitation does not end, however, with the new poet's sacrificial actions against his source, for the ancient model, as Greene suggests, acts in turn upon the new text: even as it attempts to "expose the vulnerability of the subtext," the new text exposes itself "to the subtext's potential aggression." At its most subtle, then, imitation creates "a two-way current of mutual criticism between authors and between eras." The ancient model, in other words, is far from a willing sacrifice. And the new text is never simply an act of self-effacing invocation or of self-assertive violence: though it would be the altar of a model's sacrifice, the new text becomes instead "the locus of a struggle between two rhetorical or semiotic systems that are vulnerable to one another and whose conflict cannot be easily resolved."[21] Donne's re-creation of a model's decorum thus grants him a literary authority, asserting his right to be read or heard. It does not, however, guarantee him a persuasive moral authority in his own culture—and in many ways, Donne's *Satyres* explore their own *lack* of authority. For even as the poet

20. Donne, by the way, is not the first to link these terms dialectically. "Aemulatio semper cum imitatione conjuncta sit," Pietro Bembo writes in *De Imitatione ad Picum* (1513), "Let emulation always be a part of imitation" (printed in Giovanni Pico della Mirandola, *Opera Omnia*, 2:200), advice that Giraldi Cinthio echoes in his *Discorsi Intorno al comporre dei Romanzi* (1554), addressing young poets in the vernacular: "let imitation always have emulation as its companion" ("et vuole la imitation haver sempre compagna l'emulazion; laquale non è altro, che un fermo desiderio di avanzare colui, che l'huomo imita." Quoted in A. J. Smith, "Theory and Practice in Renaissance Poetry: Two Kinds of Imitation," p. 216).

21. Greene, *Light in Troy*, pp. 45–46.

questions the efficacy of his pagan models he reveals his own perilous marginality and voicelessness, reveals that he is as much an
alien within the dominant religious and political forces of his culture as the classical satirists whom he invokes and criticizes. For
Donne's poems are not about the making of a Christian satirist so
much as they are explorations of the conflicts between religious
authorities per se, explorations of the dangers that arise when one
theology (or any form of ideology) robs another of its worldview, its
self-sustaining voice, and its enabling vocabulary. The *Satyres* reveal their own vulnerability to mutual criticism; put simply, it
achieves little to supplant the paganism of the classical satirists with
a rhetoric whose efficacy relies, as I shall argue, on the sacramental
theology of Roman Catholicism and its traditional mechanisms of
spiritual reform—that is, of priestly confession and penance ("Satyre I"), of good works ("Satyre II"), of the necessary freedom and
sufficiency of will ("Satyre III"), of the Mass and such sacraments as
communion and extreme unction ("Satyre IV"). In each case, the
vulnerability points to the dominant culture's (specifically, the Protestant court's) intolerance toward competing ideologies and belief-
systems. And thus, as Donne writes to Henry Wotton, "to my satyrs there belongs some feare" (*Selected Prose*, p. 111). Of what would
this fear consist, if not of their pro-Catholic sentiments, putting
them at odds, politically as well as doctrinally, with a Protestant
monarchy? And while the fifth satire seeks to identify with the
court's authority, must it not do so at the expense of private conscience? Tantamount to an act of apostasy, "Satyre V" explicitly
repudiates the poet's earlier Romanist views. So if the first four
satires fall, they fall along with their classical models—and for the
same reason, their inability to assert a persuasive or self-validating
moral authority. Capitulating to their own admissions of skepticism, they render their own genre powerless.

  For satire, if it is to have any claim to efficacy, must weigh specific
actions, events, and individuals against a stable firmament or background of shared cultural values. The satirist must address or literally create an audience that shares his valuation of the world,
though his peculiar task, as taught by the Roman models, is to
observe the ways society falls short of its own values. Since antiquity, then, the efficacy of satire has traditionally been premised
upon a shared vocabulary and community of belief; the satirist
becomes a public moralist who speaks on behalf of his readers,
affirming the values of his society and maintaining them through
his invective—a railing and ridicule aimed at any deviance from

such values. Again, society may as a whole fall short; this does not deny the ideal of agreement between poet and reader, regardless of the reading audience's resistance to self-reformation. For since reading is a voluntary act, is a reader not invited, if implicitly, to collaborate with the text, agreeing at least to understand it (if such understanding lies within his or her power) and to entertain, if not entirely espouse, its valuation of the world? Indeed, within so optimistic and naive a view of the relations between readers and a writer's rhetorical intentions, the satirist resembles the pulpit orator or homilist addressing his congregation: by its very presence before him a congregation affirms its willingness to listen and, if at all possible, to agree with the preacher's arguments and the values they inculcate. What, however, when the poet or preacher maintains values and beliefs different from those of his immediate audience? Surely such discourse ceases to be a conservative moral force, becoming heretical (to the audience, that is) and perhaps even treasonous, should it speak against the dominant political culture. We should consider carefully, therefore, the way Reformation controversy complicates the poet's relationship to his subject matter and reading audience, calling into question his capacity to praise and blame, persuade and reform. The Reformation and its consequences, political and religious, are a thematic presence in the *Satyres*; to say that the Reformation is a subject of this collection would not be farfetched, nor is it farfetched that these poems seek, and largely fail, to enact a different sort of "reformation," the reforming of classical satire.

For once again Elizabethan poetry, its satire in particular, rarely contents itself with the decorous invocation and rehearsal of its models; the more subtle works inevitably establish an emulous, critical relation. Each poet's ultimate preference for a particular model (Hall and Marston favoring Juvenal; Wyatt, Lodge, and Jonson choosing Horace; Donne, we shall find, adapting Persius) is proof enough that their imitations as often sacrifice as sacramentalize their sources. Often these poets explore reasons why one or other of the Romans falls short as a model—why Persius, whom Donne uses to such advantage, fails Hall and Marston, and why Horace, who proves so amenable to Lodge, fails Donne.[22] We can

22. As I have suggested, imitation begins with an invocation of the model's decorum, requiring that one strive for the most characteristic effects. It would seem, then, that imitation necessarily generalizes features of a model, searching out effects that are typical while ignoring those elements that occur rarely or contradict other, more dominant features. The tendency to look for essential,

observe the critical relation of the new text to tradition, the ways it invokes only to annihilate its model; but given the new text's initial identification with its precursor, we discover that its criticisms are inherently self-referential. For the imitative poem incorporates a model's structures and discursive instruments precisely to test their efficacy. Paradoxically, then, Donne's *Satyres* critique their models by an act of self-criticism, the strange logic of imitation requiring that the new poem share its model's fate: if the model fails, the imitation, too, falls—prey, that is, to its own criticism. Of course, literature based on classical imitation, literature so highly conscious of its nature *as text*, never fully escapes self-reference. The Renaissance text, indeed, is often painfully aware of its own derivative nature and of its need literally to steal structures and materials from a heroic literary past. Typically, then, the Renaissance text acknowledges its need for a model, its need to become or enact a genre, and thus tells a story about its own generic derivation. Donne's *Satyres* bring to a crisis this radical reflection on genre, asserting their need for formal models even as they question the moral authority and rhetorical efficacy of their precursors in this new cultural setting. The first, second, and fourth satires explore the vulnerability of the poet's present circumstances obliquely through their own explicit criticisms of the classical models, sacrificing the models and their idiosyncratic discursive procedures without, however, discovering a new or better language of reform. And this disablement of the model's rhetoric does not enable or empower his own; once again, given their lack of self-validating authority, the imitations fall along with the models. And while "Satyre III" is perhaps Donne's most successful adaptation of a Roman (specifically Persian) model, the fifth, I shall argue, is no less than the third satire's retraction, a rewriting—or rather, unwriting—of its politically dangerous polemic. An implicit subject of Donne's *Satyres* is thus their own self-

---

defining features of a model and overlook the nuances marks Elizabethan imitation in all genres, but is most pronounced in the imitation of classical satire. And sixteenth-century criticism of the Romans contributes to this by keeping the stylistic bounds between them artificially distinct. The Renaissance critics and imitators of satire thus wink at the fact that Horace uses elements of Stoic diatribe as well as *sermo* and that Juvenal at times modulates his bitter invective to gentler strains of ridicule. Renaissance critics and satirists alike thus emphasize to the point of exaggeration those features they judged essential to the decorum of each model; nonetheless these and similar descriptions form the basis of Renaissance criticism of the Roman satirists, delineating them as three distinct personae—and thus three distinct models—for imitation in the vernacular.

criticism, particularly their concern with the efficacy of form. One can never, therefore, fully isolate their meaning from their dialogic encounter with the Roman satirists, works that provide subjects, styles, and strategies, and that the new poet criticizes at his own peril.

If readers tend to project some thematic or narrative unity upon the *Satyres*, there is perhaps an equally great urge to schematize and arrange the *Songs and Sonets* into orderly tonal and thematic groupings. After all, the tradition of lyric collections from antiquity to the Renaissance stresses an encompassing unity, such titles as Statius's *Silvae* ("forest," echoed in the titles of Jonson's *Forrest* and *Underwood*) emphasizing the greater whole, of which discrete lyrics form the constituent parts. Evidently, the metaphor describes the process of reading as well, whose temporal dimension compares in some naive sense to a forest walk: where one enters the woods and the direction one takes affects the experience. Immediate context also determines the effect of reading, since one's pleasure and discovery of meaning in an individual lyric (like the discovery of an exotic in the woods, a mimosa among maples) lies, at least partially, in the immediate surroundings. The publishing history of Ovid's *Amores* or Horace's *Sermones* reveals in each case an author's careful arrangement of poems for particular local effects; with Petrarch's *Rime*, moreover, whose songs and sonnets form a quasi-narrative in their arrangement, the Renaissance inherits an even greater urge toward sequence and contextuality. In fact the reader's expectation of thematic and narrative sequence becomes so strong after Petrarch that subsequent collections seem to demand biographical interpretations, no matter how tenuous the evidence or justification. The critical history of Shakespeare's sonnets demonstrates only too well, perhaps, that the reading experience, being necessarily temporal and sequential, projects its own temporality and sequentiality—in a word, its own narrativity—onto otherwise discrete lyrics and their meanings. Similarly with Donne: it is to the 1635 editor, and not to the poet himself, that we owe the collection now called *Songs and Sonets*, and ever since this generic reordering, editors and readers alike have sought ways to regulate not simply the canon but the reading experience. Some, like C. S. Lewis and Nancy Andreason, group the lyrics thematically, according to tone and their varying attitudes toward love; others, like Herbert Grierson and Helen Gardner, attempt autobiographical as well as tonal groupings. Yet the unity of such a collection remains forever problematic, and it is, apparently, not just an editor's concern; it falls to the reader as well, and interpretations of Donne's lyrics (like those of Shakespeare's sonnets) follow from the ways readers contextualize them, projecting their own versions of unity over and above the thematic, generic, and rhetorical variety of these poems.

For, though discrete, each individual lyric comments on and reinterprets previous lyrics even as it, in turn, is revised by the rest. Thus, when the eclectic intermixing of the 1633 edition yields to the broad generic divisions of 1635, certain local effects are emphasized even as others are lost: no longer are the sacred, the secular, and the autobiographical (the hymns, love lyrics, and verse letters) so thoroughly intertextualized. Later editors—Helen Gardner for example, who calls the arrangement of early editions "wholly irrational"— attempt to reduce further the range of local effects, stressing coherence over variety and contrast. As she writes of her own ordering of the *Songs and Sonets*, "I hope it will be to the reader's convenience to find the poems sorted here in a more reasonable way, and that even those who are not convinced by my arguments as to their probable dates will be glad to find, for instance, 'Air and Angels' followed by 'Love's Growth' rather than by 'Break of Day.' "[23] Why? Must we eat all the carrots on our plate before we eat the green beans? Actually, her attempt at rearrangement is not only arbitrary but misconceived, an attempt not so much to order the poems as to banish conflict from the reading experience, stratifying the collection in ways that protect the "serious" poems (which Gardner seems to prefer) from the ridicule and refutations of their libertine counterparts. It is an attempt to keep the good sheep from the bad. Her arrangement, in short, is not "more reasonable," as she suggests; rather, it suppresses the dialogic or intertextual relations among these many poems.

Of course, the manuscript tradition provides an imperfect record of canon and arrangement, one subject to copyists' own interests and vagaries. So unless we choose to privilege a particular manuscript or edition as being authorially intentioned, we can only despair of an "official" entry into and itinerary through Donne's lyrics. Yet the fact that we can enter the collection in so many places allows meaning to be more dynamic, even kaleidoscopic. Perhaps then, as Tilottama Rajan argues, "Donne deliberately randomized the arrangement of his poems in order to challenge the conventional assumption of the reading process as a linear movement in which a 'truth' is progressively explored and consolidated as the reader moves forward." For while it might seem that the poems of mutual

23. Gardner, Preface, *John Donne: The Elegies and the Songs and Sonets*, p. vi.

love "are overturned by profane and libertine poems . . . the point is rather that the *Songs and Sonets* are continuously self-reversing":

> The reader can no more find a resting place in the worldly cynicism of the profane poems than in the neo-platonic romanticism of the poems of mutual love. The poems as they stand mutually qualify each other within a larger structure which cannot be grasped in its entirety from the standpoint represented by any one poem. Moreover, individual poems are themselves binary in form, and if they do not stand as Janus in the field of knowledge, they are at least incipiently self-questioning, and point to the need for other poems to overturn their conclusions, and beyond that to the need for a higher standpoint to overturn the cycle as a whole.[24]

Sensitive to the problems of reading and intertextual relations, hers is a valuable corrective to much traditional Donne criticism. And yet it, too, is easily carried to extremes, for complete randomness, implying entropy—the loss of system, the loss of meaning—must be distinguished from dynamic relation. There are readers for whom the fluidity and creativity (the apparently infinite potentiality) of structure implies no structure at all. Theirs is an unnecessary nihilism. A collection or system of discourse, like the kaleidoscope, may be threatened by chaos, by the randomness of meaning asserted and embraced, with apparent heroism, by such critics as Paul de Man; it is equally threatened by stasis, its completion into some singular, fixed meaning. Yet it is in the nature of discourse forever to change its shape—and forever to have shape. The continuously shifting crystals of a kaleidoscope create images not of chaos but rather of structures that are constructed, deconstructed, and reconstructed with each view or turn of the scope. A thousand turns, a thousand patterns, a thousand meanings, a thousand worlds, each self-generating, each fleeting. Discourse never fully escapes from or loses structure, for its flight is never from structure per se but from one structure to another, in accordance with a reader's own shifting perspectives. Utter randomness and absolute determinacy of meaning stand at the unreachable extremes; interpretation itself, forever unfolding, forever incomplete, stands in between. The generative power of discourse lies in this double condemnation: it is forever compelled to mean, and to change in its meaning.

Like the *Satyres*, then, the *Songs and Sonets* frustrate attempts to regulate meaning through some quasi-narrative or thematic se-

---

24. Tilottama Rajan, " 'Nothing Sooner Broke': Donne's *Songs and Sonets* as Self-Consuming Artifacts," pp. 823, 822.

quence. For intertextual relations, as Rajan suggests, reach beyond a poem's immediate surroundings in a collection (and indeed, reach beyond the collection itself to embrace Petrarchan, Provençal, Ovidian, and Anacreontic traditions); such rhetorical relations reveal the radically fragmented, the radically *dialectical* nature of lyric, where meaning is never the possession of any text in itself but resides, rather, in the relations between texts, traditions, and readings. The companion pieces and thematic counterparts among the *Songs and Sonets* give ample evidence of the collection's own self-reflexiveness, the ways each poem provides a context (or pretext, as it were) for the rest. On rare occasions, poems may complement or extend the arguments of their companion pieces; "The Calme" and "Storme" for example, much in the manner of Milton's "L'Allegro" and "Il Penseroso," wonderfully harmonize in their alternative descriptions of experience. On other equally rare occasions, one poem proceeds from and utterly displaces another; *The Second Anniversary* is just such a work, completing its precursor, *The First Anniversary,* much as the Old Testament prophecies find their fulfillment in the New. Among the *Songs and Sonets,* however, poems do not complete or complement each other so much as compete for meanings and effects that never achieve finality or closure. It would be naive to assume that the aubade, "Breake of Day," is self-contained in its meaning; other poems, "The Good-morrow" and "The Sunne Rising" especially, return to the same scene and thematic genre, questioning and revising its rhetorical procedures. Similarly, the four valedictions and such emblem poems as "The Relique" and "The Funerall" seem intent to war among themselves, each enabling and undermining the other's argument, each incapable of claiming the full or final victory.

Again, the rhetorical complexities of Donne's lyrics complicate the reading experience. "Wee are thought wits, when 'tis Understood," writes Jasper Mayne, attesting to the difficulty of reading Donne's poetry (specifically *The First Anniversary*),[25] while Donne's own Preface to *Metempsychosis* seeks to "have no such Readers as I can teach," that is, no readers who would misinterpret him. Marotti ascribes this deliberate obscurity to Donne's participation in a coterie tradition; a majority even of his contemporaries would have difficulty reading works intended for a restricted audience, an audience that alone, presumably, would be in possession of the codes and contexts necessary for their interpretation. Doubtless there is

25. "On Dr. Donnes Death," cited in Marotti, *Coterie Poet,* p. 23.

truth in such an observation. And yet, does his poetry not enact a
crisis of interpretation for all its readers? Donne's biographers often
describe his life as a crisis of faith; his writing, in fact all writing, the
text that "I" am now writing, that "you" are now reading, enacts a
similar crisis in its appeal to an audience, its need to be believed, to
be enacted, *to be read or heard*. All discourse, in other words, engages
its readers in acts of discrimination, bringing them continuously to
question their beliefs as well as understanding, turning the activity
of reading into a crisis of faith and will.[26] Even for Donne's contemporaries, one is neither worthy nor adept *before* one reads; reading
becomes itself a test, which not all, perhaps, can pass. And though
the poet of *Metempsychosis* disclaims the desire to "teach" his reader,
in practice he teases, strains, and critiques his reader, attempts even
to construct an ideal reader, specifying his or her capacities and
requisite knowledge. And thus Donne "seems," as Marotti suggests, "to have created a kind of double relationship with his readers, alternately adversarial and intimate."[27] The poetry of skepticism, "Womans Constancy," for example, and such sophistries as
the elegy, "Natures Lay Ideot" and "The Flea" are indeed adversarial, while "The Exstasie" and "The Canonization," are intimate,
in contrast, and even celebratory of the (love-)relations they seek to
establish with their readers. Yet Donne's relationship with readers is
more complex even than this, for his poetry, the *Songs and Sonets*
especially, proposes different theories of reading, in accordance
with its divergent rhetorics. As later chapters demonstrate, some of
the poems provoke a combat of wills and words, while others engage their readers in a game of courtship, inviting the reader's
assent and active, imaginative participation—while others still seek
to tease their readers out of thought entirely, leading them to some
transverbal insight or transcendent vision. Some poems deliber-

26. A "central assumption of the humanist rhetorical tradition," as Victoria
Kahn describes it, is that "reading is a form of prudence or of deliberative rhetoric" (*Rhetoric, Prudence, and Skepticism in the Renaissance*, p. 11). She elaborates:
"For the humanists, the prudence that is the intellectual virtue of right judgment about our actions applies to the author's and reader's acts of interpretation
as well. Indeed, some humanists go further and suggest that insofar as deliberation, judgment, and writing involve the will, they can themselves be construed
as actions. In either case, the fifteenth- and sixteenth-century debates about the
nature and possibility of prudence and free will are also concerned with the
nature and possibility of correct interpretation" (p. 21). Thus Kahn asserts in
recognizably Renaissance terms the rhetorical nature of reading, which
becomes an act of moral deliberation as well as of imaginative participation.
27. *Coterie Poet*, p. 23.

ately restrict their readership, their paradoxical arguments becoming so many ciphers to exclude the "layetie" ("A Valediction: forbidding Mourning," 8) from participation in their "mysteries," while others enlarge their readership, seeking to ensure their fame and perdurance as public works. Some test their readers, some exclude their readers, some seek to define and ultimately construct their readers; notions of coterie can carry one only so far in appreciating the ways Donne explores the notion of readership per se.

Of course, as so many readers have observed, the influence of Donne's early thought continues throughout his career, the Sermons and Holy Sonnets displaying habits of wit and ratiocination first formed in the earliest secular writing. Yet Donne's attitudes toward literary form apparently change from the earliest to the last works, and the distinction between secular and religious forms is the least important of the differences. Excepting "The Litanie," some of the Holy Sonnets, and his familiar letters, Donne's later writings are public and largely orthodox affirmations of faith that seek out (and, arguably, at times achieve) unity, certitude, closure—the perfection and closure of the circle being a central structuring device of La Corona. The religious poetry tends to be conservative in form, seeking to validate its arguments by enacting its lyric genres. The earliest secular works, in contrast (I speak particularly of the Juvenilia, Biathanatos, the Satyres, Metempsychosis, and many of the Songs and Sonets) tend toward iconoclastic parody, questioning the validity of their literary forms, yielding deliberately cracked generic vessels. While the late works seek to rest in church authority or the certitudes of an accepted truth, these early works become arguments against religious and political authority, their skepticism enacting a radical critique of language, literary genre, and cultural value. In arguing they call into question the very power of argument, the ability to discover truth or certainty through discursive language and logical form. The later dogmatic works seek peace, consolation, and certitude in the truths they espouse; the early works, in contrast, discover nothing but the impossibility of knowing the truth fully and with complete certitude.

With some reason, then, readers may associate Jack Donne with a rhetoric of skepticism, Dr. Donne with a rhetoric of dogmatic assertion. The former, recalling the response of Catholic Pyrrhonists on the Continent to the controversies of the Reformation, dominates in the early prose and such classical imitations as the Satyres and Elegies. His later dogmatism, largely affirming the Anglican position in matters of faith, in turn dominates in many of the sermons and the divine poems. We can make such associations between Jack and skepticism, the Doctor and dogmatism, but we must keep in mind that these two versions of personality, much like the rhetorics of dogma and doubt, constitute a larger pair, an oppositional pair as it were, of versions of the self. Both are present throughout Donne's career: self-fashioning images of the conservative scholar-recluse appear as early as "Satyre I," while the funeral sermon to Sir William Cockayne attests to the continuing presence of the skeptic, even in the years after Donne's ordination. At any time one version of rhetoric, one version of the self may be privileged over and dominate the other; yet the minor term is always present, always providing the enabling ground for the dominant argument itself. And in their interplay, doubt and belief may, paradoxically, turn into one another, as skepticism (in "Satyre III," for example) becomes the way to faith.

Again, the early writings are dominated largely by the image of Jack Donne, the libertine skeptic; over the later writings reigns the conservative, dogmatic Doctor. In the center of his career, however, the poems belong to neither voice entirely. The two *Anniversaries* and the more serious (some would argue, the maturer) of the *Songs and Sonets* are pivotal in Donne's intellectual and literary career, works in which the poet explores the full range of belief, experience, argument, and attitude. Oscillating between skepticism and faith, the language attitudes of such works continuously shift in accordance with their differing epistemologies, nominalism and a linguistic pessimism alternating with an essentialist language, one of incantation, curse, and charm. The kaleidoscopic range of attitudes toward love, for which Donne's lyrics have received great praise, is thus matched by an equally kaleidoscopic range of rhetorics. Indeed, that they are of different lyric and thematic genres is less significant than their divergent attitudes toward truth and language, differences that bring some of these poems to claim a victory of argument even as others destruct under the strain of their own self-criticism. In short, the *Songs and Sonets* become a field where competing epistemologies and language theories intersect, works in which the rhetorics of doubt and certitude wage continuous warfare, neither emerging entirely victorious, neither remaining fully repressed, neither becoming forever dominant. In them the many oppositions are exploited fully and explicitly; little wonder they are regarded as Donne's masterpieces. Before we treat the love poetry, though, we must first consider the role Reformation controversy plays in articulating these multiple rhetorics, paying careful attention to the problems this controversy has raised in the interpretive history of Donne's works.

PART I

Skepticism and Faith in the *Satyres*

1

Reading the Theologies of Language

In *Panegyricus,* the sophist Isocrates claims the power "to discourse on the same subject matter in many different ways—to represent the great as lowly or invest the little with grandeur, to recount the things of old in a new manner or set forth events of recent date in an old fashion."[1] Such claims are far from innocent. Do the speaker's words make reality, as Isocrates suggests, or do they offer anything more than appearance, "a new guise" to things? Though words "can make great things humble and endue small things with greatness," do great things remain so humbled after the speech has ended? Do small things, made greater by language, lose their greatness when the spell of words wears off? Longinus, himself a sophist, is curiously willing to deflate Isocrates' encomium to *logos*:

> Isocrates fell into unaccountable puerility through his ambition to amplify everything. The theme of his *Panegyric* is that Athens surpasses Sparta in her benefits to Greece. But at the very outset he puts this: "Moreover words have such power that they can make great things humble and endue small things with greatness, give a new guise to what is old and describe recent events in the style of long ago"—"Why Isocrates," says someone, "do you intend by this means to change the roles of the Spartans and the Athenians?" For his praises of the power of words have all but published a prefatory advertisement to the audience that he himself is not to be believed.

"Perhaps then," he concludes, "the best hyperbole is the one which conceals" its verbal artifice—conceals, that is, "the very fact of its being a hyperbole."[2] What Longinus observes about the figure might be said about the sophist's language in general. Words must conceal themselves, their motivations and intentions, or else the

---

1. 1:123–25.
2. Longinus, "On the Sublime," p. 231. Though Brian Vickers would perhaps disagree with my interpretation, he has led me to this passage. See his *"Songs and Sonets* and the Rhetoric of Hyperbole," p. 140.

very act of reflection, of *looking* at one's language, disables it as persuasion and, perhaps, even as communication; no longer about the world, the language now speaks about itself. Ironically, then, Isocrates' encomium to *logos* casts doubt upon the sincerity of its own discourse—as if truth and persuasiveness can be claimed only by the naive text, one that dreams of its own power and persuasive authority, of its ability to speak things-into-being, creating stable realities. In contrast, the self-conscious text awakens in embarrassment to its own status as language, shocked into the recognition that it simply speaks words. Does Longinus attempt, much like a postmodernist critic, to embarrass the text of the *Panegyricus* by revealing its sheerly rhetorical basis? Perhaps; but far from concealment, the oration in fact celebrates its rhetoricity, asserting its power not only to change minds but to change reality itself. Indeed, the *Panegyricus* begins not simply by celebrating but by ritually invoking *logos*, as if such rituals of language were magic formulas, capable of wielding persuasion— as if persuasion were itself a divine force, over which the rhetorician claims mastery. The *Panegyricus* is not itself embarrassed, then, or deceived by its status as language. Yet it is (at least, so Longinus asserts) a failed attempt to deceive and persuade its Athenian audience.

For it seems that the force of language is inherently problematic; one can, and cannot, persuade. And thus "language," as one modern sophist, Harold Bloom, writes, "can be conceived in two valid ways. . . . Either one can believe in a magical theory of all language, as the Kabbalists [and] many poets . . . did, or else one must yield to a thoroughgoing linguistic nihilism, which in its most refined form is the mode now called Deconstruction." "But these two ways," Bloom adds, "turn into one another at their outward limits."[3] It seems that magic and nihilism, conviction and skepticism meet in the same author and often, one finds, in one and the same text. In a brief sermon passage John Donne makes similar observations, simultaneously asserting two differing, in fact antithetical conceptions of the powers and functions of discourse:

> How empty a thing is Rhetorique? (and yet Rhetorique will make absent and remote things present to your understanding) How weak a thing is Poetry? (and yet Poetry is a counterfait Creation and makes things that are not, as though they were). (*Sermons*, 4:87)

Which shall it be? Is rhetoric "empty" or a means to give things presence—to "make absent and remote things present"? Is poetry

3. "The Breaking of Form," p. 4.

"weak" or a "counterfait Creation"—mere words or a brave new world? As in Longinus (and Bloom), there is a powerfully ambivalent or, rather, oxymoronic quality to this and the majority of Donne's observations on language. Language can, and cannot, carry out its author's aims since the relationship of words to experience remains forever unsettled, the words yearning for, though never achieving, complete clarity and fidelity; an element of distortion, of incompleteness, of opacity resides in all language-use. Like oxymoron, then, which holds antithetical terms in tense suspension, all discourse enacts within itself the conflict of its partial truth, its partial effectiveness and partial success as an instrument of knowledge and communication. Poetry, Donne writes, is a "counterfait Creation," a making that is but a feigning, a creation that must announce its falseness, its status as counterfeit, even before it can claim status as creation. Similarly, rhetoric may claim to make present that which is "absent and remote." But what is an absent presence? What truth can a simultaneously "empty" and "presencing" language express? The balanced clauses themselves seem to confirm the equal claims of contrasting arguments (known to the ancient sophists as *dissoi logoi*) and, indeed, the very syntax charts the conflict between skeptical and sophistic conceptions of discourse. Rhetoric, Donne the skeptic would observe, is "empty" because language cannot comprehend being, because words are not the things they represent; "and yet," as Donne the sophist would say, rhetoric gives mental presence to things, imparting a psychological reality to that which is otherwise "absent and remote." Poetry, similarly, is too "weake" to transcend its own problematic status as language; "and yet" it becomes an imaginative "Creation," figuring forth not that which is so much as that which *is possible* in human belief, value, emotion, and action. "Imaginative presence" (what the sophists Gorgias and Isocrates would call *enargeia*) and the Gorgianic *dynaton* or assertion of "the possible" are the means by which sophistic rhetoric works its persuasions upon an audience. By ascribing such powers to language, therefore, Donne would seem to impute—to the sophist's words, at least—a power to overcome skepticism's paralysis of action and belief.

As the references to Gorgias and Isocrates might testify, expressions of the powers and problems of language are unique neither to Donne nor to modern criticism, but are as old as Western rhetorical tradition. In Plato's dialogue *Cratylus*, for example, the speaker by that name outlines one of Western culture's first essentialist theories of language, one in which words embody the truth and reality of things, faithfully figuring forth the nature of being. Endowed with magic property, each name expresses the essence of its object, sharing in its reality and powers. In contrast Hermogenes, Cratylus's opponent in the dialogue, presents one of the earliest outlines of nominalism. Far from establishing a magical or sacramental union with things, words remain but conventional counters and tokens, elements of a linguistic system designed to render intelligible an otherwise silent reality. And though words serve humanity, nonetheless they are of human manufacture, arbitrarily applied, and, worst of all, liable to misapplication and misuse, mixing falsehood and truth together. In an attempt to mediate the discussion, Socrates introduces the concept of *mimesis*, where words represent their objects in the same partial, imperfect manner that the objects themselves imitate the transcendent, changeless Ideas. Though rarely convincingly, Socrates's arguments from etymology assert the logic behind *res/verbum* relations, each word imitating the sound, shape, or effect of its object. And yet, by grounding these relationships in imitation, he implicitly denies language an epistemic function—never more than mimetic in function, words are never constitutive or creative of knowledge. Socrates argues similarly in *Ion:* language (poetic language especially), thrice-removed from the ideal forms, is incapable of yielding knowledge. At best, words may perform a commemorative function, reawakening the truth dwelling within the soul; more likely they will lead the soul away from its own self-knowledge, immersing their users in a world of illusions and false resemblances. Thus "no man of sense," Socrates concludes in the *Cratylus*, "will like to put himself or the education of his mind in the power of names. Neither will he so far trust names or the givers of names as to be confident in any knowledge which condemns himself and other existences to an unhealthy state of unreality."[4]

In the Renaissance especially, readers of the *Cratylus* typically ignore one half of this double argument, turning the dialogue into a defense of but one position, either an extreme realism or nominalism. Either choice, however, flies in the teeth of a text that ultimately cannot decide on the powers and functions of discourse. Socrates himself oscillates between both attitudes, although his mistrust of words, recounted in the above passage, leads him to advise a flight from language entirely. The ambivalence is striking: once again one can, and cannot, speak. In *Essays in Divinity,* Donne,

4. Plato, *Collected Dialogues,* p. 474.

too, meditates on the properties of "names," which are intended "to avoid confusion, and distinguish particulars." And yet, "every day begetting new inventions, and the names often overliving the things, curious and entangled Wits have vexed themselves to know, whether in the world there were more things or names." "Or else," in contrast with such nominalism, "names are to instruct us, and express natures and essences," something "*Adam* was able to do" with his own language, though "an enormous pretending Wit of our nation and age undertook to frame such a language, herein exceeding *Adam,* that whereas he named every thing by the most eminent and virtuall property, our man gave names, by the first naked enuntiation whereof, any understanding should comprehend the essence of the thing, better then by a definition" (*Essays in Divinity,* p. 23). Thus Donne describes the major language theories explored in the Platonic dialogue *Cratylus,* at the same time identifying an extreme realism or essentialism with the language of Adam— a pre-lapsarian language traditionally presumed to enjoy a perfect congruence with reality, "a complete, point-to-point mapping of language" onto nature, as George Steiner suggests, where "each name, each proposition was an equation, with uniquely and perfectly defined roots, between human perception and the facts of the case." Post-lapsarian speech, in contrast,

> interposes itself between apprehension and truth like a dusty pane or warped mirror. The tongue of Eden was like a flawless glass; a light of total understanding streamed through it. Thus Babel was a second Fall, in some regards as desolate as the first. Adam had been driven from the garden; now men were harried, like yelping dogs, out of the single family of man. And they were exiled from the assurance of being able to grasp and communicate reality.[5]

Lost to fallen humanity is the possibility of an immediate, certain knowledge of the world, for language, no longer tied to being, loses its heuristic power; lost as well is the means for faithful communication and social connectedness, for the ambiguities and warps within language corrode its communicative efficiency. Not only does the human soul need to be saved; with the tower's fall human speech, too, falls in need of redemption and renewal.

For Donne, similarly, human discourse finds itself balanced perilously between two crucial moments in providential history, the one speaking its absolute dearth and loss, the other its plenitude

5. *After Babel: Aspects of Language and Translation,* pp. 58–59.

and participation in God's own divinity (between "a magical theory of all language," as Bloom puts it, and "a thoroughgoing linguistic nihilism"). Of course, the very notion of providential history sets Christianity apart from the classical Greek (and postmodernist) philosophies of language. From God's *fiat lux* and creation of man, to man's seduction and fall, to the fall of the tower, to the giving of the Law, to the prophets, to the Incarnation, to the Crucifixion and Resurrection, to Pentecost, all events of providential history impact upon the soul—and its texts. Human discourse, therefore, remains thoroughly an aspect of creation and a reflection of its own fallen (or, at best, partially redeemed) nature; in this radical sense, rhetoric is always, we shall find, no less than a theology of language, and Renaissance theological controversy is itself implicated in the conflict among competing rhetorics. But for the moment, let us lay aside matters of theology to focus on conflict per se and the problems it poses to reading. How are we to interpret the texts of a fallen and only partially restored humanity? Situated somewhere between absolute dearth and plenitude, can such texts ever claim full truth or persuasiveness? And what of Donne's work particularly? Given that his own writings are so thoroughly divided against themselves, one might wonder whether a singular, consistent, unified reading is even possible. Many readers, nonetheless, expect more than Donne himself is willing, or able, to give.

Among Donne's contemporaries, Francis Bacon warns of the "contract of error" writers (and critics, apparently) make with their audience, "for he that delivereth knowledge, desireth to deliver it in such form as may be best believed, and not as may be best examined; and he that receiveth knowledge, desireth rather present satisfaction, than expectant inquiry; and so rather not to doubt, than not to err: glory making the author not to lay open his weakness, and sloth making the disciple not to know his strength."[6] Similar contracts often prevail in readings of Donne, particularly when the focus becomes in even the slightest degree biographical or suggestive of possible interrelations between the poet's life, mind, and art. Attempts to describe Donne's thought typically reveal the reader's own desire for consistency and unity, a weakness of critical perception reflecting Bacon's idol of the tribe (for "the spirit of man . . . doth usually suppose and feign in nature a greater equality and uniformity than is in truth").[7] The need to describe a psychological

6. *The Advancement of Learning* (1605), p. 141.
7. Ibid., p. 133.

consistency (in Bacon's words, an "equality and uniformity") in an author has often led readers to impose a rhetorical and ultimately an ideological consistency upon his writings, as if inconsistencies in argument imperil the personality itself. Of course we allow for a change of mind: we allow Donne to turn from Catholicism to Anglicanism, to turn from a ruined political career to ordination in the Established Church, to turn from Jack to the Doctor. Changes of mind can be explained, after all, by the sheerly literary conventions of conversion narrative, the Augustinian myth of personality development with which Donne himself identifies in much of his later prose. But change in a life, we often presume, necessarily represents a triumph of one ideology over another and the banishment of previous thought-systems, with their enabling rhetorics, from subsequent texts (as, indeed, from the changed personality). We demand that the individual speak with one voice—to speak in tongues is a sign of divinity or madness—and we tend still to identify that voice with the living personality.

And yet modern theory has only begun to perceive the multeity of voices and vocabularies, the multiplicity of rhetorics and the diversity of value-systems that inhabit one and the same textual space even as they constitute the intellectual, economic, religious stratifications of a culture. For "language," Mikhail Bakhtin suggests,

> is not an abstract system of normative forms but rather a concrete heteroglot conception of the world. All words have the "taste" of a profession, a genre, a tendency, a party, a particular work, a particular person, a generation, an age group, the day and hour. Each word tastes of the contexts in which it has lived its socially charged life; all words and forms are populated by intentions.[8]

It is necessary, then, "that *heteroglossia* wash over a culture's awareness of itself and its language, penetrate to its core, relativize the primary language system underlying its ideology and literature and deprive it of its naive absence of conflict."[9] Similar in conception to Bakhtin's *heteroglossia*, a multeity of rhetorics invades discourse, shattering its claims to unity or univocity, making each text the originating ground of its own counterargument (if not its own refutation). Is it Donne the man, therefore, that we confront, or rather the ideological conflicts of his age, controversies that pulse through the writing?

8. *The Dialogic Imagination: Four Essays*, p. 293.
9. Ibid., p. 368.

And is it any wonder that there are so many versions of Donne himself? The vocabulary is never strictly his own; always the language is "populated with intentions," echoing the past voices of religious and political conflict. And one might observe, simply, that biography, ideology, and poetry become at some point indistinguishable; like his poetry, Donne's life and beliefs rest perilously upon a reader's interpretive choices. The names of authors, nonetheless, have in themselves "no substantial value," as Jacques Derrida writes, indicating "neither identities nor causes."[10] The name stands for (stands in the place of) a collection of texts that are themselves orphaned from their originating consciousness. And yet "each proper name," G. C. Spivak suggests, seems to establish "a sovereign self against the anonymity of textuality," pretending to be "the origin and end of a certain collocation of texts that may be unified" under its aegis.[11] Perhaps the most problematic signifier is that of the author, whose own name transfers from a life to a text. Biography, indeed, is only and always textual, our lives, our very identities in some sense constituted by the stories told of us. By "Donne," then, we refer metonymically to a body . . . of texts. Donne the man becomes a verbal trace whom we seek as their ghostly inhabitant. But as this trace unfolds, Donne turns from the author or originator to an effect of the writing: in the place of *bios* we discover *ethos*, the author reduced to a textual trace. In the act of writing Donne stands on the outside of the text, pen in hand; yet we seek him within. Perhaps it is only as a text—or rather, as a version of texts, as an interpretation—that the poet's life is in any way recoverable and meaningful.

Donne's writings, then, present not a unified system of value and thought but rather a discursive field where opposing ideologies fight for a temporary supremacy, compelled continually to play out the warring rhetorics of their time and culture. Ideologies Donne himself at any time identified with can only be inferred from texts that continually repeat the same battles, the same verbal strategies, the same ideological conflicts. Donne may turn to orthodox Anglicanism, but the language of Roman Catholicism remains a continuous, if subversive, presence in his writing. Donne may consciously espouse fideism and even the certitudes of established dogma in later years; his writing continues, nonetheless, to struggle against

10. *Of Grammatology*, p. 99.
11. Translator's preface, ibid., p. liv.

skepticism and destabilizing doubt. We cannot describe the shape of a unified, singular, or consistent personality from any text—certainly not from any canon or collection of texts as diverse as Donne's—because its heteroglot language, giving rise to multiple rhetorics, necessarily reenacts the ideological conflicts of the European Renaissance.

◻   ◻   ◻

As the preceding suggests, most dangerous is the penchant to throw a conceptual blanket over the whole of Donne's writings, making him always thoroughly Protestant or else crypto-Catholic in attitude, forever either a rationalist or a skeptic dyed-in-the-wool. For when one banishes or attempts too neat a resolution of contradiction, whether by arguing away, trivializing, or simply ignoring the evidence against any unified interpretation, one reduces and thereby distorts an ideologically complex set of texts to a singular worldview—to a singular rhetoric. And yet such either/or thinking sustains some of the more hotly contested critical debates. Questions concerning epistemology provide an example, Terry G. Sherwood, for one, asserting "reason's primary role" in Donne's theology: "Donne's conviction of reason's dominant powers lies at the heart of his thought. Reason erects the strategies of argument; it is the operative faculty in Donne's wit; it is 'our connexion / Of causes' that comprehends the relationships between God and creation; it is the 'doore of faith' (*Sermons*, 9:360), achieving the wisdom that establishes the foundations for the will's several steps." And thus, according to Sherwood, "a long view of his writing reveals consistent principles that reach fruition in the mature religious prose." Donne's entire canon, from the earliest paradoxes to the last sermon, forms "a consistent whole."[12] There is a price for consistency, though. To assert the complete dominance of reason demands that the rhetorics of fideism, sophism, and above all skepticism—however insidious, explicit, or necessary to a text's unfolding in discourse—be trivialized if not banished altogether from one's interpretation. Paradoxical argument, often otherwise treated as the enactment or consequence of skepticism, comes rather to the aid than the defeat of reason:

12. *Fulfilling the Circle: A Study of John Donne's Thought*, pp. 15, 3, 18.

> Deliberate fallaciousness seeks fulfillment, not only in the bedevilment of its own chop logic, but also in the concurring dialectic with the reader's counterargument. The final truth played in the intellectual game is not necessarily a mocking parody of reasoning, but reasoning's defence against itself as well as its own pleasure. Such a defence recognizes that reasoning is a continuing activity in time that corrects the misuse of reason.

Finally, the skepticism that refuses to be argued away is simply ascribed to one of Donne's "shifting personae."[13] These observations are at least partially valid—within an incarnational rhetoric, that is, the rhetoric that Sherwood outlines and identifies as the singular dominant shape of discourse in Donne. To appreciate the strengths as well as the limitations of his reading, then, we must first outline its underlying rhetoric.[14]

Though historians note its early Christian development in St. Augustine, the rhetoric of incarnationism is perhaps most characteristic of St. Thomas, who grounds his sacramental theology of language upon an essentially Aristotelian epistemology. Rejecting both Protagoras's skepticism and Plato's transcendent philosophy of dual worlds, Thomas, like Aristotle before him, describes a world that is both knowable (that is, fully accessible to human thought) and capable of complete, faithful expression in speech. The fact that words or signs may at times mislead does not dampen his confidence in the denotative, referential capacities of language. Ambiguity and the possibility of linguistic error arise, as Marcia Colish suggests, "simply because men have a tendency to misinterpret and to abuse signs, or because signs may refer to things which are themselves dubious; it does not indicate any inability on the part of signs to correspond satisfactorily to objective reality."[15] Confident

13. Ibid., pp. 24–25, 22. And "these several faces," Sherwood adds, "lend support to the view that Donne is a poseur responding variously to a refracting external reality. We can allow that this tendency is present without having to concede that it defines his essential nature, since some faces emerge more forcefully than others" (p. 22).

14. Raman Selden, by the way, offers a partial description of this rhetoric in an article, "John Donne's 'Incarnational Conviction.' " See also Malcolm Mackensie Ross, *Poetry and Dogma: The Transfiguration of Eucharistic Symbols in Seventeenth Century English Poetry.*

15. *Mirror of Language*, p. 10. Like Sherwood, Colish emphasizes the Augustinian elements of Thomas's sign theory; she observes, nonetheless, that most commentators "place Thomas in Aristotle's epistemological universe, and do not shrink from attributing to Thomas Aristotle's unbounded confidence that the world is totally intelligible and that the human mind is perfectly adequate to

in its capacity for clear, truthful expression, much of Donne's own writing assumes (and often explicitly asserts) this same linguistic theology, whose great archetype, the Christian Incarnation or Word made Flesh, allows human speech, however partially, to participate in the same divine reality. For "the dogma of the Incarnation," as Malcolm Mackensie Ross suggested some years ago, is "the fixed star at the centre of the Christian firmament," a conception that not only enables but demands a "sacramental vision of reality" in which "the flesh, the world, things, are restored to dignity" and "made valid again." The discourse arising from this sacramentalism thus "celebrates the actual kinship that obtains between man and things, between subject and object,"[16] to which we might add the sheerly rhetorical relations of *verbum* and *res*. Ross has, in fact, described a sacramental rhetoric, one proceeding from an explicitly Catholic-sacramental theology of language. Where in Donne's writings might we look for this same rhetoric? And how stable is it in his writings?

The encomium to *logos*, an orator's praise of the beauties and civilizing powers of speech, is a traditional prose genre originating with Gorgias and, as we have seen, with Isocrates; in the following passage from the *Devotions Upon Emergent Occasions*, Donne Christianizes the form, writing an encomium, rather, to the divine *Logos*. As its first and best practitioner, God Himself baptizes classical rhetoric:

> My *God*, my *God*, Thou art a *direct God*, may I not say a *literall God*, a God that wouldest bee understood *literally*, and according to the *plaine sense* of all that thou saiest? But thou art also (*Lord* I intend it to thy *glory*, and let no *prophane misinterpreter* abuse it to thy *diminution*) thou are a *figurative*, a *metaphoricall God too: A God* in whose words there is such a height of *figures*, such *voyages*, such *peregrinations* to fetch remote and precious metaphors, such *extentions*, such *spreadings*, such *Curtaines* of *Allegories*, such *third Heavens* of *Hyperboles*, so *harmonious eloquutions*, so *retired* and so *reserved expressions*, so *commanding perswasions*, so *perswading commandements*, such *sinewes* even in thy *milke*, and such *things* in thy *words*, as all *prophane Authors*, seeme of the *Serpent*, that *creepes*, thou art the *Dove*, that flies. O, what words but thine, can expresse the inexpressible *texture*, and *composition* of thy *word*; in which, to one man, that *argument* that binds his faith to beleeve that to bee the Word of God, is *the reverent simplicity* of the Word, and to another, the

---

it" (p. 118). "The effect of this point of view," Colish adds, "is to produce an interpretation of Thomas's signs in which they have full cognitive powers but no cognitive limitations. In some instances scholars have gone so far as to claim that Thomistic signs are identical with their significata."

16. *Poetry and Dogma*, pp. 9–10, 11.

> *majesty* of the Word; and in which two men, equally pious, may meet, and one wonder, that all should not understand it, and the other, as much, that any man should. . . . The *stile* of thy works, the *phrase* of thine *actions*, is *metaphoricall*. The *institution* of thy whole *worship* in the *old Law*, was a continuall *Allegory; types* and *figures* overspread all; and *figures* flowed into *figures*. (*Selected Prose*, p. 102)

The passage is itself a virtuoso performance, a rhetorical display-piece calling attention to its own artifice. Observe the balanced, chiastic phrasing and the Gorgianic pairing of antitheses ("so *commanding perswasions*, so *perswading commandements*, such *sinewes* even in thy *milke*"), the epithets and apostrophes ("thou art the *Dove*, that flies. O what words but thine"): all celebrate God's eloquence by attempting to match it—indeed, the flying dove gives a literal and peculiarly Christian reference to an otherwise metaphoric concept, the soaringly high style. And Donne's own attempt to match this eloquence (perhaps even to emulate it, adding his own words to God's) argues implicitly for the power of priestly/poetic language, for its renovation by means of participation in the divine *Logos*. The passage is itself an enactment of incarnationism.

But there is actually much inner tension here, as we might expect, due to the confluence of competing rhetorics. While God's words enact a sacramental union between *res* and *verbum* (there being "such *things*" in His "*words*"), one finds in them an opacity or element of inexpressibility—and the foundation, then, of a second rhetoric, a rhetoric of transcendence. "O, what words but thine, can express the inexpressible *texture*, and *composition* of thy *word*": only God can express Himself fully and faithfully—humanity cannot find adequate words. In the radical untranslatability of scriptural language lurks the potential, moreover, for misreading. If interpretation entails the substitution of a reader's "inner word" for the external markings of a text, and if human language becomes an inadequate substitute or supplement, then the words of Scripture are condemned to repeat themselves liturgically—and tautologically, as scriptural language remains always itself, unsupplemented by the words of humankind. And in this opacity lies the central hermeneutic problem of Reformation theology, one that gives rise, ultimately, to skepticism: the lack of a sure criterion for interpreting scriptural language. The fact that God writes in a "figurative, metaphoricall style" (a point that Donne makes elsewhere, at even greater length) must complicate more than clarify the sense.[17] Evidently,

17. "There are not so eloquent books in the world, as the Scriptures," Donne

a rhetorical understanding will not regulate the meaning of Scripture so much as increase the potential for polysemy. Clearly this diverges from an orthodox Protestant understanding of scriptural interpretation, an understanding encapsulated by Luther's motto, "one word, one meaning," where the figurative substitutes for the literal, becoming the singular, univocal sense; indeed, in *Essays in Divinity* Donne recognizes that "that also is not the literall, which the letter seems to present, for so to diverse understandings there might be diverse literall senses" (p. 40).

From a perhaps more Catholic than Protestant perspective, then, the author of the *Devotions* allows for and in fact celebrates the polysemy of scriptural language, observing its *"Curtaines of Allegories,"* its *"retired"* and *"reserved expressions,"* in which *"figures flowed into figures."* Donne elaborates elsewhere, comparing Genesis to Revelation: "in the first Book of Scriptures, that of Genesis, there is danger in departing from the letter; in this last book, this of the Revelation, there is as much danger in adhering too close to the letter" (*Sermons*, 6:62). What is the two-fold "danger" just described, if not a consequence of the preacher's own acute rhetorical consciousness, one that complicates more than clarifies the sense? The passage is certainly indebted to Augustine, though not to *De Magistro*, where spiritual understanding rests upon the transverbal illuminations of our Inner Teacher, but rather to *De Doctrina Christiana*, where charity becomes the sole criterion of interpretation. Therefore, "in the figurative exposition of those places of Scripture . . . that Expositor is not to be blamed, who not destroying the literall sense, proposes such a figurative sense, as may exalt our devotion, and advance our edification" (*Sermons*, 6:63). "So doth that preacher well also," Donne adds, "who to the same end, and within the same limit, makes his use of both, of all those expositions; because all may stand, and it is not evident in such figurative speeches, which is the literall, that is, the principall intention of the Holy Ghost." And thus, having asserted the polysemy of Holy Writ, Donne further complicates meaning by making the "literall" or "principall" sense undecidable. For again, the Reformation empha-

---

writes: "Accept those names of Tropes and Figures, which the Grammarians and Rhetoricians put upon us, and we may be bold to say, that in all their Authors, Greek and Latin, we cannot finde so high, and so lively examples, of those Tropes, and those Figures, as we may in the Scriptures: whatsoever hath justly delighted any man in any mans writings, is exceeded in the Scriptures. The style of the Scriptures is a diligent, and an artificial style" (*Sermons*, 2:170–71).

sizes for participants on each side the radically linguistic basis of theology. "No garment," Donne writes, "is so neer God as his word: which is so much his, as it is *he*" (*Essays in Divinity*, p. 39). Yet no language, not even God's, yields clear and unambiguous meaning to our frail human understanding. So Donne suggests in his *Devotions:* "to one man, that *argument* that binds his faith to beleeve that to bee the Word of God, is *the reverent simplicity* of the Word, and to another, the *majesty* of the Word; and in which two men, equally pious, may meet, and one wonder, that all should not understand it, and the other, as much, that any man should" (*Selected Prose*, p. 102). And how does one account for the fact of controverted meaning, the fact that two men, "equally pious," may arrive at so radically different understandings? The disagreement among theologians becomes, we shall find, not only the historical ground of Reformation controversy but a ground for the poet's own Pyrrhonist skepticism, the philosophical position informing the rhetoric, say, of "Satyre III."

Like Isocrates' encomium, then, is Donne's encomium to *Logos* so thoroughly subject to self-questioning? Is there no logic to regulate discourse, protecting the poet's assertions from the insidious intrusions of skepticism? Must all language prove so weak? Regardless of our own human weakness, surely God's discourse is grounded in a faultless logic, for God is Himself "*Logos, speech* and *reason*," as Donne observes, "He declares his will by his *Word*, and he proves it, he confirms it; He is *Logos*, and He proceeds *Logically*" (*Sermons*, 5:103). Thus Donne preserves the dual meaning of the Greek *logos*, variously translated as *oratio* (or *verbum*) and *ratio*, speech and reason.[18] Throughout the history of rhetoric *logos* has implied a tense union of diverse elements, never simply *ratio* or *oratio* (that is, thought without speech) but rather thought realized in and through speech; indeed, to reduce *logos* exclusively either to signification or to thought would resolve the tension that gives the term its distinctive character. But while the divine *Logos* effects such a *conjunctio oppositorum*, what shall we say of human discourse? Does it, too, unite *ratio* and *oratio*, right reason with the faculty of persuasive speech? Of itself, Donne suggests, our speech is but a "*Sophistry*, which as farre as concernes our owne destruction, frustrates His

18. "For *Logos*," Donne writes, "is *Ratio*, and not only *Verbum*, as it is ordinarily translated" in the biblical texts (*Sermons*, 4:119). See Samuel Ijsseling, "Isocrates and the Power of *Logos*," in *Rhetoric and Philosophy in Conflict: An Historical Survey*, p. 20.

Logique" (*Sermons*, 5:103), though he would add that human discourse is redeemed by the Incarnation, for "Christ is Reason, rectified Reason" (*Sermons*, 4:119)—and faith in Christ, supported by grace, remakes human speech. *In principle,* and only in part. For reason, we must remember, is a faculty belonging to "Naturall man," its capacity for rectification remaining imperfect. In fact a conflict remains between the faith that seeks to remake or rectify reason and the very faculty of reason itself, which threatens continuously to reflect back upon the language of faith, questioning the latter (and thereby exceeding its own bounds, seeking continually to turn the subjectivities of faith into objective knowledge). The relation between reason and faith is never stable in Donne's writing, reflecting less on his own capacities and consistency than on the tension this binarity necessarily creates in Christian theology. For the Christian is possessed of both reason and faith, and both only partially, imperfectly; while faith and reason *can* support each other, while they are *supposed* to support each other, they do not always do so. Each speaks or inscribes a different language, articulating its unique rhetoric.

There is simply no reconciling this opposition, even in one and the same text; while faith and reason often support each other, at some crucial moment they draw apart. "Mysteries of Religion," Donne writes in a sermon, "are not the less believ'd and embrac'd by Faith, because they are presented, and induc'd, and apprehended by Reason." "But," he immediately continues, "this must not enthrone, this must not exalt any mans Reason so far, as that there should lie an Appeal, from Gods Judgements to any mans reason: that if he see no reason, why God should proceed so, and so, he will not believe that to be Gods Judgment, or not believe that Judgment of God, to be just: For, of the secret purposes of God, we have an Example what to say, given us by Christ himself, *Ita est, quia complacuit; It is so, Father, because thy good pleasure was such*" (*Sermons,* 1:169). Reason has its place, so long as it supports faith and the authority of the Church (in this case, the Anglican Church) in matters of doctrine; faith itself takes priority, though, ruling against reason where reason would question "the secret purposes of God." Here and in the following passage, reason carries one only so far; as the typical movement of Donne's theological arguments reveal, faith must carry to completion what reason leaves unfinished.

> I would faine be able to prove to my selfe that my redemption is accomplished, and therefore I search the Scriptures . . . and I growe to

> a religious, and modest assurance, that those marks are upon me. I
> finde reasons to prove to me, that God does love my soule; but why
> God should love men better then his own Son, or why God should love
> me better then other men, I must end in the reason of the text, *Quia
> complacuit,* and in the reason of Christ himself, *Ita est, quia,* It is so, O
> Father, because thy good pleasure was it should be so. (*Sermons,*
> 4:284–85)

Donne makes much of the show of logic, of the fact that his sermon
text claims the syllogistic force of a *quia* or "therefore." And it is an
argument of sorts, an argument from authority. Placed in the service of a religion that is, as Donne defines it, simultaneously a
"matter of faith" and a "matter of obedience, to lawfull Authority,"
reason must either offer itself in the service of the Established
Church (and in acquiescence to God's inscrutable will), or else run
the risk of "schisme, and sedition, and distraction" (*Sermons,* 6:318).
Dogmatic assertion, in short, looks to a rhetoric of faith for its completion; otherwise, of itself, reason proves too weak, falling prey to
skepticism and counterargument.

Yet another sermon demonstrates this convincingly (if unwilling-
ly) in its description of "Gods Method," which is "to make us
understand, certainely those things which belong to our Salvation."
These, Donne reasons, "are not *In-intelligibilia,* not In-intelligible,
un-understandable, un-conceivable things," for "the Articles of
Faith are discernible by Reason":

> For though Reason cannot apprehend that a Virgin should have a Son,
> or that God should be made Man and dye, if we put our Reason pri-
> marily and immediately upon the Article single, (for so it is the object
> of faith only) yet if we pursue Gods Method, and see what our under-
> standing can doe, we shall see, that out of ratiocination and discourse,
> and probabilities, and very similitudes, at last will arise evident and
> necessary conclusions; such as these, That there is a God, that God
> must be worshiped according to his will, That therefore that will of
> God must be declared and manifested somewhere, That this is done in
> some permanent way, in some Scripture . . . And when our Reason
> hath carried us so far, as to accept these Scriptures for the Word of
> God, then all the particular Articles, a Virgins Son, and a mortall God,
> will follow evidently enough. (*Sermons,* 9:355)

Of itself, "reason cannot apprehend" the Christian paradoxes, which
must be taken as the "object of faith onely." But besides for the
blatant circularity of the argument, Donne reduces "Gods Method"
to a travesty of adequate evidence: since Scripture *must* be true, it is
reasonable to believe it. Though the passage claims to demonstrate
the rational basis of belief, it reveals little more than the preacher's

will to believe, premised on the authority of the Church's interpretation of Scripture. For "God must be worshiped according to his
will": from this all else, presumably, follows—all subsequent argument becomes argument from authority. Then again "there is not so
wholsome a thing," Donne suggests elsewhere, "*Quam ut Rationem
praecedat authoritas,* Then still to submit a mans owne particular
reason, to the authority of the Church expressed in the Scriptures"
(*Sermons,* 6:282). Preceding and directing reason, the authority that
affirms and supports belief lies outside of the individual. Tradition,
not one's own powers of reason and interpretation, offers the safest
course: "Take heed of *Opinions,*" the preacher thus advises, "that
begin in thy selfe" (*Sermons,* 6:285).

Time and again, therefore, we find that dogmatic assertion erodes
into pseudo-logic, skepticism, or a self-conscious recognition of the
inadequacy of language; in the sermon passages just quoted, such
appeals to authority, similarly, announce the failure of rational argument and the preacher's mistrust, ultimately, of human reason itself. How, then, are we to understand the rhetorical (not to mention
the theological) relations among reason, doubt, and faith? In *Essays
in Divinity,* Donne terms reason "our Sword," and faith "our Target" or shield: "With that we prevail against others, with this we
defend ourselves: And old, well disciplined Armies punished more
severely the loss of this, then that" (p. 16). The language, perhaps,
is ambivalent in spite of itself; while faith shields and protects the
individual, reason becomes an offensive weapon, evincing "the
reach and violence of Argument" (*Essays in Divinity,* p. 16). And
while we might assume that Donne would chart a middle ground
between the Protestant emphasis on faith and the Catholic on good
works, or between the utter depravity and sufficiency of will, the
following in fact pleads for a suspension of argument over these
issues. Rather than "cleare the doubt" ("Satyre II," 102) over matters of doctrine, "contentious spirits" are themselves responsible
for controversy: "Of these two lights, *Faith* and *Grace,* first, and
then *Nature* and *Reason,* we said something before, but never too
much, because contentious spirits have cast such clouds upon both
these lights, that some have said, Nature doth *all* alone, and others,
that Nature hath *nothing* to do at all, but all is *Grace:* we decline
wranglings, that tend not to edification" (*Sermons,* 3:365). Here
Donne laments the *fact* of controversy in religion, the fact that "such
wranglings . . . tend not to edification." The poet of *Metempsychosis*
agrees, seeking to disarm such wranglings through ridicule and a
refusal to engage in argument. There the "curious Rebell" who "dis-

putes" (103) the meaning of God's will and "writ" (109) does so in vain; his

> reasons, like those toyes
> Of glassie bubbles, which the gamesome boyes
> Stretch to so nice a thinnes through a quill
> That they themselves breake, doe themselves spill:
> Arguing is heretiques game, and Exercise
> As wrastlers, perfects them; Not liberties
> Of speech, but silence; hands, not tongues, end heresies.
> (114–20)

"Arguing is heretiques game"—a telling critique of the Reformation controversy and the polemical practices of Donne's own age, the best (and perhaps only) cure of which is "silence," the repudiation of argument entirely.

Surely, then, Sherwood errs in describing a thoroughly rationalist Donne, and it would seem that his critical idol lies in the Thomist-incarnationist theology of language which he so privileges that all other rhetorics are ignored or actively suppressed. Readings such as his view the existence and accessibility—in fact, the possibility—of truth and logical certitude as a premise rather than the very subject of the writer's search. But as Donne himself observes in *Biathanatos*, "We must as well dispute *de veritate*, as *pro veritate*" (p. 30). In contrast to this confident dogmatism, John Carey describes Donne's writings as symptoms of his age's "crisis of reason," a result of the poet's own internal religious conflict and an "onrush of scepticism":

> The precarious and provisional role allotted to reason in Donne's poems is to be ascribed largely to his personal mental development, and that was determined in turn by his retreat from Catholicism and from the logical certitude which it encouraged. However, Donne's private history was in this respect . . . only a more compressed and intense version of a development in European thought. He was fortunate as an artist (though no doubt it caused him considerable distress as a man) to experience within the confines of his own acute sensibility that onrush of scepticism which was to transform, within half a century, the intellectual orientation of the Western world. What is odd about his poems is that they retain a relentless passion for arguing, yet treat argument with patent disrespect. They are, in this sense, fiercely schizoid—and that is what we might expect from a poet whose early habits of ratiocination, instilled by his educators and intertwined with his most basic beliefs, had met, when he came to manhood, the withering and liberating blasts of limitless doubt.[19]

19. *John Donne: Life, Mind, and Art*, pp. 231–32.

Where in Donne's writings shall we find this "limitless doubt"? In criticism of Pyrrhonist skepticism and its suspension of all claims to knowledge, Donne preaches that "ignorance . . . is not our Usher into this presence, *to shew us the face of Christ Jesus.* . . . That knowledge was a help to salvation, the Ancients thought: but that is a new Doctrine, that men should make a title to God, by being ignorant" (*Sermons*, 4:119). In a later sermon, though, we learn that "there is as much strength in, and as safe relying upon some ignorances, as some knowledges" (*Sermons*, 6:188).

Again, which shall it be? Even when Donne writes on behalf of knowledge he cannot simply argue away doubt; skepticism proves too strong, leading the following passage, though an invective against ignorance, to deconstruct of its own.

> Ignorance is not only the drousinesse, the sillinesse, but the wickednesse of the soule: Not onely dis-estimation in this world, and damnification here, but damnation in the next world, proceeds from ignorance. And yet, here in this world, knowledge is but as the earth, and ignorance as the Sea; there is more sea than earth, more ignorance than knowledge. (*Sermons*, 8:255)

"And yet." Ignorance remains our human condition: "It is so in naturall, in morall, in civill things; we are ignorant of more things than we know." Scripture, too, reveals this weakness of understanding: "it is so in divine and supernaturall things too; for, for them, the Scripture is our onely light, and of the Scripture, S. *Augustine* professes, *Plura se nescire quam scire*, That there are more places of Scripture, that he does not, then that he does understand" (*Sermons*, 8:255–56). Certainly the passage expresses a desire for understanding; it is not, however, by any means an assertion of the force or the reliability or even the possibility of knowledge. The argument collapses in upon itself, incapable of moving beyond the object of its own criticism. Throughout his writings, then, Donne wavers between two possible solutions to the problem of knowledge, one an absolute orthodoxy and conformity to established authority, the other a mode of fideism premised on a thoroughgoing doubt and devaluation of human reason.

We often assume that doubt and dogma stand at opposite poles. If this is the case, how does Donne move so easily between them? One answer, of course, is that acquiescence in authority is often itself the consequence of doubt, a suspension of one's own responsibility to choose (and choose right, or risk the hazard of choosing wrong, as Donne suggests in "Satyre III"). Paradoxically, doubt can prepare for one's embrace of authority as a *solution* to the lack of knowledge; where reason cannot lead, faith—in established practice, in the tradition and beliefs of one's "father" ("Satyre III," 71)—becomes one's best support and guide. The sermons, too, turn as often to skeptical as to apodictic argument in their quest for orthodoxy: casting idolatry and schism and even one's own powers of reasoning into doubt, the Articles of Faith and the teachings of the Established Church become one's safest refuge. The irony, however, is that these very arguments, used by an older Donne in support of the Anglican Church, are the same arguments that the more youthful Donne (and others in his time) marshalled in support of the Old Faith, Roman Catholicism. The *Satyres* demonstrate this convincingly: argument, whether dogmatic or skeptical, serves other masters than orthodoxy and the dominant political culture. Thus the Reformation controversy would convince Donne of the fact that arguments, and lives, are susceptible to mistaking. And willful misinterpretation, the exploitation of controversy for political or private aims, becomes a major theme in much of his writing, the *Satyres* offering its deepest and most sustained exploration. In the passage quoted earlier from the *Devotions*, for example, Donne finds a need to defend his figuralist interpretation of Scripture: "(Lord I intend it to thy *glory,* and let no *prophane misinterpreter* abuse it to thy *diminution*) thou are a *figurative,* a *metaphoricall God.*" In evident fascination with the very thing that he most suspects, Donne simultaneously exploits and undermines argument, revels in and repudiates rhetoric, appeals to and frustrates a reader's sympathetic understanding, though some of the most celebrated of his poems go so far as to remake argument, fashioning modes of logic that might enable belief and work their world-building persuasions upon an audience. What Donne most suspects, he most boldly uses; what he most fears in his own life and reputation—the possibility of mistaking or misinterpreting his language and actions—he embraces as an aspect of writing itself. And thus Donne, perhaps the age's most argumentative poet, views argument with ambivalence, turning his poetry into a self-conscious exploration of its own rhetorical procedures and of the problems of interpretation, a questioning of the possibility of communication and persuasion, of meaning, truth, knowledge—of the possibility of poetry itself.

Astutely, Carey has identified significant features of Donne's early classical imitations and the "libertine" poems, all of which exploit formal logic's inadequacy before the onslaught of skepticism. And he takes these observations a step further, rooting Donne's skepticism in his "retreat from Catholicism," which is also, Carey notes, a retreat from "logical certitude," the collapse of Roman Catholicism across Europe heralding the collapse of medieval scholasticism as well, its epistemological underpinning. He is right; the course of Renaissance skepticism is in fact intricately interwoven with the developing conflicts in Reformation theology, particularly in the attack against (and defense of) Catholicism.[20] In a famous passage from *Pseudo-Martyr* Donne describes his personal involvement:

> They who have descended so lowe, as to take knowledge of me, and to admit me into their consideration, know well that I used no inordinate hast, nor precipitation in binding my conscience to any locall Religion. I had a longer worke to doe than many other men; for I was first to blot out, certaine impressions of the Romane religion, and to wrastle both against the examples and against the reasons, by which some hold was taken; and some anticipations early layde upon my conscience, both by Persons who by nature had a power and superiority over my will, and others who by their learning and good life, seem'd to me justly to claime an interest for the guiding, and rectifying of my understanding in these matters. And although I apprehended well enough, that this irresolution not onely retarded my fortune, but also bred some scandall, and endangered my spiritual reputation, by laying me open to so many mis-interpretations; yet all respects did not transport me to any violent and sudden determination, till I had, to the measure of my poore wit and judgement, survayed and digested the whole body of Divinity, controverted betweene ours and the Romane Church. (*Selected Prose*, pp. 49–50)

Note the author's "wrastl[ing] against the examples and against the reasons" or doctrine of Romanism, "by which some hold was taken" on his conscience. The combativeness of such language is remarkable: another man's reasons, even one's own, need to be wrestled against and often defeated, indeed, destroyed. And skepticism would provide the means. Having "survayed and digested the whole body of Divinity, controverted between ours and the Romane Church," the youthful Donne must have soon recognized skepticism's awe-

---

20. Calling "all in doubt" (*The First Anniversary*, 205), the "new Philosophy" is often named a source of Donne's skepticism, and yet the shifts in scientific paradigms do little more than confirm a habit of skepticism forged in the heated controversies of Reformation theology. See Richard H. Popkin, *The History of Scepticism from Erasmus to Descartes;* and Margaret L. Wiley, *The Subtle Knot: Creative Scepticism in Seventeenth-Century England.* For discussions of Donne specifically, see Marius Bewley, "The Mask of John Donne"; Robert G. Collmer, "Donne and Charron"; and Louis I. Bredvold, "The Naturalism of Donne in Relation to Some Renaissance Traditions."

some power to undermine argument. For the systematic doubt of Pyrrhonist philosophers provided a battery of discursive weapons to both sides of the Reformation controversy, weapons Donne learned to wield in his own writings, secular as well as theological. Continually throughout his writings, therefore (but most fully in "Satyre III"), Donne restates the Pyrrhonist arguments that fuel the religious controversies of his age: the problem of interpretation, the insufficiency of reason and, above all, the partial truth of language.

"Except demonstrations (and perchance there are very few of them) I find nothing without perplexities." Taken from one of Donne's letters, this remark is often quoted. Typically neglected, though, is the passage immediately following, which articulates the linguistic basis of his cognitive skepticism: "I am grown more sensible of it by busying myself a little in the search of the Eastern tongues, where a perpetual perplexity in the words cannot choose but cast a perplexity upon the things. Even the least of our actions suffer and taste thereof" (*Life and Letters*, 2:16). The "perplexity" or uncertainty of language is "perpetual," and this perplexity casts its shadow "upon the things" themselves, confusing them in the Babel of discourse. And this same perplexity of language infects all human endeavor: the ability to comprehend "even the least of our actions" suffers from the language-boundedness of human perception, our need to translate experience into the shadowy perplexity of words. The floodgates of skepticism were thus opened during Donne's own age, fragmenting discourse into combative rhetorics, none of which proves capable of adequately accommodating or even comprehending the other's worldview: Babel, that is to say, linguistic and epistemological difference, becomes itself the originary ground of schism—in this sense, the Reformation is the institution of a second Babel, this time in the language of theology (or rather, the theology of language). And is the interpretive history of Donne's writing not, in its own way, a third Babel? Even now Donne's "irresolution" (admitted, as we have seen, in the Preface to *Pseudo-Martyr*) leaves him "open to so many mis-interpretations," his personal conflicts with the warring theologies having become interpretive conflicts for modern readers.[21] Of course, the question

---

21. Not surprisingly, though, Donne is himself more immediately concerned with his contemporary readership. "I am brought to a necessity of printing my Poems," Donne once wrote to Henry Goodyer, and while he did not, in fact, oversee their publication, he did "apprehend some incongruities in the resolution; and I know what I shall suffer from many interpretations" (*Selected Prose*, p. 144).

of Donne's skepticism or rationalism has never remained simply a literary issue, but has been tied continually to biography and to the poet's broader historical circumstances. In fact Carey follows an earlier tradition that links the skepticism to a crisis of faith, reading it either as a symptom of Donne's continued Catholic sympathy or, more poignantly, as a consequence of his apostasy; in contrast, arguments for Donne's rationalism are traditionally made in defense of his orthodox Anglicanism (or, as Barbara K. Lewalski reads Donne, of a more Calvinist theology).[22] Like the opposing rhetorics of Reformation theology, Carey's skepticism opposes Sherwood's dogmatic rationalism as if across a chasm, both claiming to describe Donne's life, mind, and art.

But is Donne ever fully represented in such either/or terms? Might Thomas O. Sloane's outline of "controversial thinking," the epistemic foundation of humanist rhetoric, provide an adequate alternative? *Controversia* and "literary culture" are the hallmarks of Renaissance humanism itself, the former "involving the acknowledgment, even the exploitation, of contraries, the latter involving modes of persuasion that do not depend upon reason alone."[23] And the "correlative of *controversia*," as Sloane observes, is the *via media* or "middle ground," the systematic attempt to resolve controversy by means of compromise. This search for a rhetorical and ideological middle ground becomes, presumably, a search Donne enacts in his personal life as well as his writing; reacting against the doctrinal extremes of Roman Catholicism and the more radical Protestant sects, Donne turns to Anglicanism, "and his restless, controversial thought seemed to bring him there as a compromise, one that he would pursue as a pragmatic solution to a long, intensely personal but legalistic battle." Thus Sloane finds repeated throughout Donne's life and art "a typically Donnesque, typically controversial pattern," where "two alternatives are counterpoised" only to be "rejected in favor of a third, which is actually a *via media*."[24] Certainly it would not surprise if a maturer Donne, confirmed and ordained into the Anglican faith, sought refuge from the doctrinal extremes of Rome and Geneva, nor would it surprise if Donne thought of preaching as a haven from religious polemic—from "wranglings,

22. *Protestant Poetics and the Seventeenth-Century Religious Lyric*, pp. 253–82. For seminal discussions of Donne's Catholicism see Dennis Flynn, "Donne's Catholicism"; Bewley, "Mask of John Donne"; and Carey, *Life, Mind and Art*, pp. 15–59.

23. Thomas O. Sloane, *Donne, Milton, and the End of Humanist Rhetoric*, p. 83.

24. Ibid., pp. 193, 198.

that tend not to edification." A congregation after all, as he describes it, is a community of believers who "speake one anothers language, and preach to one anothers conscience" (*Sermons,* 5:51); indeed the congregation, as P. G. Stanwood and Heather Ross Asals suggest, is a *linguistic* community that speech, the defining characteristic of humankind, thoroughly pervades and in fact constitutes, since "speech is the glue, the Cyment, the soul of Conversation, and of Religion too" (*Sermons,* 8:338).[25] In this sense, Donne's sermon art becomes quite literally a mode of conversation or *sermo,* a different mode of discourse entirely from polemic and debate. But even here the competing theologies of language leave their mark, claiming radically different powers and functions for the preacher's words.

Following Catholic tradition, the preacher might perhaps aim at persuasion, leading those of little or no faith to conversion and belief. After all, "it is not . . . the Gospell meerly," as Donne writes, "but the *preaching* of the Gospell" that wins souls, and "*Spiritus sacerdotis vehiculum Spiritus Dei;* The spirit of the Minister . . . is the chariot, the meanes, by which God will enter" individuals in the congregation (*Sermons,* 5:545). In a recent discussion Samuel Ijsseling takes this view to its logical extreme, describing the preacher's words as "constitutive of God's existence for man" and terming faith "a firm conviction (*doxa*) which only exists by virtue of preaching (*logos*)."[26] In fact the early Christian term for religious faith, *pistis,* is in its origins a *rhetorical* term designating the effect of persuasion upon an audience. As Donne writes elsewhere, though, from a more obviously Protestant perspective, "God shall send Prophets, Trumpets, and Trumpetors, that is, preachers of his word, and not the word of men" (*Sermons,* 2:169). What, then, is the relation between God's word and man's? When does the preacher cease preaching God's, to speak his own? Is the preacher's language but a "Trumpet" or proclamation, incapable in itself of saving without God's prior gift of grace to auditors? Taking this opposite extreme, George Kennedy argues that Christian preaching is "not persuasion, but proclamation, and is based on authority and grace, not on proof. . . . Its truth must be apprehended by the listener, not proven by the speaker."[27] Within this implicitly Calvinist interpretation of Christian rhetoric, the reader's or audience's response depends

25. P. G. Stanwood and Heather Ross Asals, ed., *John Donne and the Theology of Language,* p. 265.

26. "Sacred Eloquence," in *Rhetoric and Philosophy in Conflict,* pp. 76–77.

27. "Judeo-Christian Rhetoric," in *Classical Rhetoric and Its Christian and Secular Tradition from Ancient to Modern Times,* p. 127.

entirely on God's gift of grace and understanding; the speaker is himself "incidental," and neither his character, nor the logic of his argument, nor the capacities of his audience is sufficient in itself. Persuasion rather, as Kennedy suggests, "takes place when God is ready," not before.[28] The Calvinist might add, indeed, that God often hardens the heart of an audience, defeating the preacher's words by rendering his audience intransigent, even incapable of belief.

Once again, persuading and proclaiming are the extreme versions of conflicting theologies of language, and most writers of Donne's age would try to walk a middle ground. Even the Calvinist—for whom preaching was a proclaiming rather than persuading, and for whom a congregation's salvation depended entirely on God's grace—would allow some limited role for sermonic language, particularly as it edified an audience, guiding them in the interpretation and application of Scripture. Similarly, the preacher who believed his words wielded persuasion would still recognize the necessary role God plays in softening man's hard heart; auditors often fail to heed the preacher's words, after all, though the sermon is preached to everyone. Nonetheless the middle ground, in theology as in rhetoric, remains the most unstable ground of all; surely the Anglican church learned this in its attempt to mediate or follow the *via media* between Calvinism and Catholicism. At critical moments—in any discourse, whether poetic, polemical, or homiletic—the middle ground shifts and dissolves, revealing that it was not so much a compromise as a holding in suspension of warring attitudes toward language and belief. Put simply, one can, and cannot, persuade. One can, and cannot, speak.

We observe a similar opposition in the very faculty that preaching and persuading address: that is, the will. From an apparently Romanist standpoint, for example, Donne writes that "there is nothing in grace, that was not first in nature, so farre, as that grace always finds nature, and naturall faculties to work on . . . and therefore *let us cleanse our selves from all filthiness,* says the Apostle; There is something which *we ourselves* may doe" (*Sermons,* 5:176–77). But we can "banish all self-subsistence," Donne writes elsewhere, "all attributing of any power, to any faculty of our own, either by preoccupation, in any naturall or morall disposing of our-

28. Ibid., p. 122. And apparently, where God's own will works upon the beliefs of an elect, there the preacher's words bear witness to the silence of grace and belief, his own words being empty of persuasive power.

selves, before Gods preventing grace dispose us" (*Sermons*, 8:369).[29]
Where is there room for compromise? All one can say is that Donne
is capable of arguing on either side—that at times he apparently
needs to argue on a different side than he had before—and that the
fashioning of a stable middle ground is a rarer occurrence than
Sloane admits. Doubtless it would be unfair to base our criticism
solely on an opposition between sermon texts separated by some
years and addressed to different audiences; nonetheless compromise, particularly on matters of faith, is forever a perilous enterprise. Is not the *refusal* of such compromise an argument of "Satyre
III"? The theological inconsistencies of Donne's *Sermons* suggest,
rather, that an ideological middle ground is the most unstable ground
of all, that dogmatic assertion serves to destroy compromise, proving but the impossibility of escaping the competing claims of contrasting *logoi*. And let me add that the religious movement eventually to be termed Latitudinarianism is not compromise so much as
the admission of difference into the Anglican Communion; the *via
media*, in other words, is to be distinguished from an attitude of
tolerance, which would embrace and celebrate the difference that
compromise seeks to efface. It is for this very reason that the Anglican reforms proved dissatisfactory to Puritan and Papist alike. To
either side, Anglicanism seemed a religion that wavered *between*
two competing theologies rather than a religion with its own distinctive character. The subsequent history of Anglicanism has borne
this out: the struggle between High and Low Church is no less than
an internal struggle between two systematic theologies, each with
its distinctive attitude toward the sacraments and church ritual.

It is, however, contradiction not between but within individual
works that most concerns us as readers. And I shall argue that
Donne's poetry (the *Songs and Sonets* especially) dwells in contradiction, that contradiction is, indeed, its condition of possibility, and
that its attempts to resolve contradiction are largely unsatisfactory.
Often, as in "The Prohibition," the attempt at compromise seems
deliberately to fail, turning into a comedy of ineffectual argument;
equally often, as in "A Lecture upon the Shadow," the poet turns to
the deceptions of sophism (that is, to the *apate* that suppresses counterargument, denying rather than resolving the contradictory *logoi*).
Rarely, then, does Donne's writing assume the prior existence of a

---

29. In her article, "John Donne and the Problem of Religious Authority:
'Wranglings that Tend Not to Edification,'" Elizabeth Tebeaux points out the
inconsistencies in the two sermon passages (p. 140).

singular, stable truth; every text, rather, even the most orthodox and dogmatic, must seek to win an immediate victory for its argument, and this victory must be won within the space of the text itself. Even the most confident of texts must literally argue truth into existence, inscribing it against a ground of uncertainty, winning, if at all, only a temporary and partial victory against an ever-present and equally powerful counterargument. We have noted Donne's mistrust of argument, and yet his poetry is among our language's most argumentative for this very reason: truth and certitude are never taken for granted, never taken as an easy premise, but must be fought for in the act of composition. Total victories are apparently impossible, however, for the skepticism is never fully argued away, never shorn of its refutatory, deconstructive potential. And it is easy to speculate why Donne so rarely asserts a singular, absolute, certain truth. His readings in the Reformation controversy as well as his own early writings (in prose especially: the *Paradoxes and Problems, Pseudo-Martyr,* and *Biathanatos*) must have suggested the expediency if not the necessity of doubt.[30] Surely his own writings demonstrate all too clearly how the mind falls prey to fallacy, how illogic and equivocation appear as persuasive as formally valid reasoning, how belief lies beyond the powers of reason to prove, while reason itself proves unable to defend itself from skeptical counterargument. And, as we have seen, Donne's later religious prose is no less conscious of the ways doubt invades and destabilizes discourse. Skepticism thus becomes a powerful (though, certainly, a dangerous) philosophy for the poet to admit into his literary and intellectual habit of mind. Like a brushfire it consumes all certitude and all rational argument it meets. And when the skepticism is sparked by a critical imagination as strong as Donne's, all beliefs and received truths become dry tinder indeed.

As we turn to the *Satyres,* we shall put these many observations to the test. Above all, we must ask what impact this habit of skepticism has upon the classical genre. Are these early poems confident, dogmatic assertions and attempts at social reform? Or are they explorations of the problematic nature of their own rhetoric, works that

---

30. Should this surprise us? In *The Dynamics of Faith,* Paul Tillich describes Christian experience as a continual alternation between "participation" and "separation," concluding that "neither faith nor doubt can be eliminated" from human experience: "Out of the element of participation follows the certainty of faith; out of the element of separation follows the doubt in faith. And each is essential for the nature of faith. Sometimes certainty conquers doubt, but it cannot eliminate doubt" (pp. 100–101).

question their very capacity to reform and persuade? And what relation does skepticism have to the religious controversies that these poems continually, if obliquely, address? Is it the classical form only, or is it the nature of faith that these works question and explore? In other words, is this systematic doubt in any way a reflection of the poet's own involvement in the Reformation controversy? If so, is it an expression of his continued Catholic sympathy or, indeed, of his apostasy? Such questions as these shall direct our reading of the poems.

2

Satire and "Self-Guiltinesse"

Perhaps the most famous of his satires, Horace's *Sermo* 1.9 provides the dramatic situation and stylistic model of Donne's "Satyre I." Out for a walk, Horace meets a social-climbing acquaintance who "insists on accompanying him, hoping through closer intimacy to secure an introduction to Maecenas," the poet's patron. And though he seeks to shake him off, "it is only when the man's adversary in a lawsuit appears on the scene—a genuine *deus ex machina*—that Horace is rescued from his unhappy position."[1] Granted, the boor's importunity provides Horace with an occasion to praise the virtues and cultural values of the Maecenas circle, which the poet's own good manners reflect: modest behavior and polite conversation become refinements of coarse nature, elegant expressions of one's true thoughts and feelings. Yet in the boor's world—the world outside of this group, one marked by personal discontent, insincerity, and opportunism—"polite" language and behavior quickly become affected. So while the boor's importunity offers Horace an occasion to celebrate the social values of this circle, his inability to deal with the boor illustrates how frail these values are when confronted by hypocrisy and a self-serving language of flattery. For the satirist's own sense of social decorum works humorously against him: his own good manners prevent him from dismissing the boor outright—and the boor, an opportunist to begin with, takes advantage by continuing to dog him. Horace's politeness turns next to irony and the gap grows between his language and intentions, his

1. Horace, *Satires, Epistles, and Ars Poetica*, trans. H. Rushton Fairclough (p. 103). The Horatian influences upon Donne's "Satyre I" and "IV" have been discussed briefly by Raman Selden, *English Verse Satire, 1590–1765*, pp. 63–64, and in greater depth by Howard Erskine-Hill, "Courtiers out of Horace: Donne's *Satyre IV*, and Pope's *Fourth Satire of Dr. John Donne, Dean of St. Paul's, Versifyed*." For an alternative view—one arguing for Persius as Donne's thematic and structural model—see Y. Shikany Eddy and Daniel P. Jaekle, "Donne's 'Satyre I': The Influence of Persius's 'Satire III.'"

words deliberately understating his emotional disturbance, his actions greatly exaggerating it: "As he kept dogging me, I break in with, 'Nothing you want, is there?' But he: 'You must know me; I'm a scholar.' To this I say, 'Then I'll esteem you the more.' Dreadfully eager to get away I now walk fast, at times stop short, then whisper a word in my slave's ear, while the sweat trickled down to my very ankles."[2] The dialogue is surely humorous, but the humor is at the satirist's own expense. And on its more serious side, such a passage finds the poet and adversarius playing a game of mutual hypocrisy.

In Horace this may be but an undercurrent; in Donne the hypocritical use of polite conversation becomes an explicit focus. Of course, self-revelation and the expression of individual personality are hallmarks of the *Sermones*, and the satirist's own characterization, with all his likes, dislikes, strengths, and weaknesses, becomes part of his subject matter—so, indeed, does the poet's language and behavior. Like his model, then, Donne's satirist becomes an ironist rather than a railer, allowing the adversarius to condemn himself through his own language and actions; in the Horatian manner he strives "to tell the truth with a smile,"[3] and the smile seems apt, given that vanity and inconstancy are his explicit themes. "Satyre I" thus invokes the stylistic decorum of Horace, who "sportingly never leaveth until he make a man laugh at folly, and, at length ashamed, to laugh at himself, which he cannot avoid, without avoiding the folly."[4] And yet for Sidney, the author of this last passage, it is the reader who is "at length ashamed, to laugh at himself"; for Donne the shame belongs to the satirist. Since self-deprecation is an attribute of the Horatian persona we should not be surprised that, in "Satyre I," much of the irony and implied criticism reflects upon the poet himself. Yet complications arise, we shall find, when Donne's satirist proves unable to laugh at his own inconstancy.

Presenting himself as a young scholar-recluse, Donne's satirist allows a friend to lure him from his study to the pageantry of the city street, a parade of soldiers, justices, puritans, prostitutes, youths,

2. "Cum adsectaretur, 'num quid vis?' occupo. at ille, / 'noris nos,' inquit; 'docti sumus.' hic ego, 'pluris / hoc,' inquam, 'mihi eris.' misere discedere quaerens / ire modo ocius, interdum consistere, in aurem / dicere nescio quid puero, cum sudor ad imos / maneret talos" (Horace, *Sermo* 1.9.6–11). This and other translations of Roman satire are taken from the Loeb editions. References are to book, poem, and line.

3. "Ridentem dicere verum" (Horace, *Sermo* 1.1.24).

4. Sir Philip Sidney, "An Apology for Poetry," p. 165.

courtiers, fools. But the satirist is hardly objective in his narrative. Details are humorously exaggerated and usually more descriptive of his own interests, fears, and prejudices—all of which suggests that the satirist, from the beginning, is himself involved in the world and its follies. Though he commands his friend, the "fondling motley Humorist," to "Leave mee, and in this standing woodden chest, / Consorted with these few bookes, let me lye / In prison, and here be coffin'd, when I dye" (1–4), we cannot help but observe the ambivalence of the description: if his study is a prison to him, he should *want* to escape from it. And even as he admonishes his flighty companion, his mind is far away from deeper studies, especially of the "grave Divines" (5) with whom he keeps company. Thus the critical relation between text and model begins to emerge: more than a rehearsal or rehashed version of the Horatian plot, "Satyre I" makes for its complete inversion, Horace's importuning stranger here becoming the poet's intimate friend. And while Horace hopes for nothing more than to be rid of his adversarius, Donne's speaker goes so far as to make his friend swear *not* to abandon him on the street, even though he should meet "some more spruce companion" (16). Finally, the reader of the *Sermones* may fault Horace's speaker for enduring the boor's importunities, and yet their meeting and walk together is inadvertent; having himself chosen to accompany his friend, Donne's speaker lacks even this excuse for his city stroll, making him all the more culpable. "*Amici vitia si feras facis tua,*" Donne writes elsewhere: if you tolerate a friend's vices, you make them your own (*Letters*, p. 30).

But at this point the poet neither recognizes nor admits his personal involvement. Indeed, with an air of complete self-righteousness, he utters warnings against three possible rivals for the Humorist's companionship, a captain, a courtier, and a justice:

> First sweare by thy best love in earnest
> (If thou which lov'st all, canst love any best)
> Thou wilt not leave mee in the middle street,
> Though some more spruce companion thou dost meet,
> Not though a Captaine do come thy way
> Bright parcell gilt, with forty dead mens pay,
> Nor though a briske perfum'd piert Courtier
> Deigne with a nod, thy courtesie to answer,
> Nor come a velvet Justice with a long
> Great traine of blew coats, twelve, or fourteen strong,
> Wilt thou grin or fawne on him, or prepare
> A speech to court his beautious sonne and heire.

> For better or worse take mee, or leave mee:
> To take, and leave mee is adultery.
>   (13–26)

In sermon, a more mature Donne would return to the symbolism of dress: "How naked soever we came out of our mothers wombe, thus we came all apparelled, apparelled and invested in sin; And we multiply this wardrobe, with new *Habits*, habits of customary sins, every day" (*Sermons*, 2:101). The pun on "habit" (as both dress and behavior) identifies a theme that will run throughout the *Satyres:* language and clothing alike reflect one's spiritual state.[5] And yet we might wonder whether the satirist's attention to dress is given fully for his friend's edification or reflects the poet's own fascination with wealth and power. It is hard to read such lines without discovering some measure of attraction mixed in with the expressions of revulsion, some tincture of jealousy in the condemnation. Of course the poet himself wears "course attire" (47) and, *perhaps* proudly, calls attention to it, his humble clothes proclaiming his difference from the typical courtier and his repudiation of such vain display. At the same time, however, this coarseness dooms him from the beginning to abandonment. For he does not possess the wealth society prizes; his friend "hate[s] vertue," after all, because it is "naked, and bare" (41). And upon meeting such a suitor the Humorist would "with enquiring eyes / . . . search, and like a needy broker prize / The silke, and golde he weares, and to that rate / So high or lowe . . . raise thy formall hat" (29–32): clothing, like polite behavior, has become a means both to court and to display affluence. The justice, for example, advertises his own political power by the velvet he wears, claiming for himself the value of that cloth even as his followers are dehumanized, reduced to the synecdoche of "a long / Great traine of blew coats" (21–22)—to the cloth they wear on their backs for the sake of another man's self-aggrandizement.

Ironically these vignettes, intended as social criticism, serve only to whet his friend's desire for such influential companionship. Though the reader recognizes the criticism in the speaker's words,

5. We might recall Jonson's *Discoveries:* "Wheresoever, manners, and fashions are corrupted, Language is. It imitates the publicke riot. The excesse of Feasts, and apparell, are the notes of a sick State; and the wantonness of language, of a sick mind" (*Works*, 8:593). Such observations on language read like a gloss on Donne's Horatian imitations, the first and fourth satires. And dress, we might also observe, is among Donne's favorite metaphors for religious difference per se; he writes, for example, of those "which are religious in other clothes then we" (*Letters*, p. 30), an image he explores throughout "Satyre III."

the Humorist sees only the glitter and the prospects for pleasure. The poet's claim that his words have brought repentance to his friend is therefore either thoroughly naive or thinly veiled sarcasm:

> But since thou like a contrite penitent,
> Charitably warn'd of thy sinnes, dost repent
> These vanities, and giddinesses, loe
> I shut my chamber doore, and 'Come, lets goe.'
> But sooner may a cheape whore, that hath beene
> Worne by as many severall men in sinne,
> As are black feathers, or musk-colour hose,
> Name her childs right true father, 'mongst all those:
> . . . .
> Then thou, when thou depart'st from mee, canst show
> Whither, why, when, or with whom thou wouldst go.
> But how shall I be pardon'd my offence
> That thus have sinn'd against my conscience?
>   (49–56, 63–66)

Of a sudden the poet's prison-study has become a confessional: playing priest-confessor to his friend, the satirist demands both an oath of constancy and an act of contrition. So he "forgive[s]" the Humorist (and the reader might imagine him blessing his companion, making the sign of the cross as a stage direction in this quasi-dramatic parody of confession), and yet the poet finds himself lacking in priestly powers, incapable of freeing his friend—indeed, incapable of freeing himself—from sin. Sister Mary Geraldine notes the poet's many references to the Fall, his wistful glance, for example, at man's "first blest state" (45) and his observation, though tinged with humor, that "till our Soules be unappareled / Of bodies, they from blisse are banished" (43–44).[6] Such references evidence his ever-growing awareness of humanity's fallen nature, his own included. "Satyre I" thus recounts the satirist's discovery both of man's need for moral guidance and of his own limitations as just such a "Shepherd" or guide—for the Humorist, upon leaving him, shall become the poet's "lost sheep" (93).

Of course the Humorist has no capacity for repentance; this the poet implies in the prophecy that his friend *will* abandon him, since a prostitute could more easily name "her childs right true father" than the Humorist could explain "Whither, why, when, or with whom" he would go. Even after this mock-absolution, then, the Humorist remains subject to his own whims and passions. Actu-

6. "Donne's *Notitia:* The Evidence of the *Satires,*" p. 26.

ally, his friend is like a child lacking powers of moral choice and self-reflection; the satirist cannot say the same of himself, though, nor can he approach his own inconstancy—his own yielding to the allurement of the city street—with such tongue-in-cheek expressions of spiritual understanding. For the sportful and slightly blasphemous tone suddenly darkens when the satirist reveals, frankly and poignantly, his own spiritual conflict: "But how shall I be pardon'd my offence / That thus have sinn'd against my conscience?" Unlike his adversarius, he has a conscience that demands "Whither, why, when," and "with whom." After all, "our sins are our *own*," Donne writes in a sermon, and yet "we have a covetousnesse of more; a way, to make other mens sins ours too, by drawing them to a fellowship" (*Sermons*, 2:101)—which describes exactly the poet's own perilous spiritual state. So on the one hand the poet makes a mockery of absolution by playing priest-confessor over his weak-willed and obviously unpenitent friend; on the other hand he despairs of his own absolution by knowingly yielding to temptation.

In his typically candid and casual manner, Horace's own satirist proclaims himself "free from vices which bring disaster, though subject to lesser frailties such as you would excuse."[7] In such a passage Horace himself distinguishes between tragic vice and comic folly, the former deserving of hate and severe reprehension, the latter of more gentle techniques, laughter and mockery. In such a passage Horace also adopts a deliberate strategy of witty self-deprecation; as Antonio Sebastiano Minturno describes it, even as he criticizes an individual "he will at the same time win over with jests the person whom he reprehends."[8] As we have seen, this same sly jesting and insinuation lies at the heart of Sidney's brief discussion of the satiric poet, who "sportingly never leaveth until he make a man laugh at folly . . . who, while '*circum praecordia ludit*,' giveth us to feel how many headaches a passionate life brings us to."[9] When successful, the techniques Sidney describes are not so much a teaching as an entangling of the audience, an indirection that Horace himself notes: "Why laugh? Change but the name, and the tale is told of you."[10] Minturno, in comparison, suggests a simpler aim: to gain the good will of the reader as well as the person criti-

7. "Ego sanus ab illis, / perniciem quaecumque ferunt, mediocribus et quis / ignoscas vitiis teneor" (*Sermo* 1.4.129–31).

8. "Cum jocis eum, quem reprehendit, conciliaverit" (*De Poeta*, p. 424).

9. "Apology," p. 165. He quotes from Persius, who had already acknowledged Horace's subtle use of friendly insinuation.

10. "Quid rides? mutato nomine de te fabula narratur" (*Sermo* 1.1.69–70).

cized, which accounts for one other aspect of Horace's satiric persona, his self-effacement or *deprecatio*. "Doubtless," Minturno writes, "it is a skillful and witty shrewdness to attribute to himself another's vices, so that he might criticize others" even as he seems to speak of himself.[11] Such observations have relevance, at least on the surface, to Donne's imitation. "Part of the irony" of the first satire, as Nancy Andreason writes, "derives from the fact that the protagonist, aware of the inconstancy of the young man's friendship, goes off with him anyway." In so doing "he admits that he too sins, he establishes himself as an honest and human man, a man who can be believed and whose charitable warnings should go heeded, all the more because they grow out of his own experience of sin."[12] This technique, I would add, characterizes the Horatian model, and is one that Donne could have learned from a critic like Minturno or from his own reading of Horace. I do not mean to imply that the expression of personal guilt is made simply in imitation of his classical model. Donne is, after all, a Christian satirist (and perhaps Catholic at the time of writing), a poet whose introspectiveness and sense of conscience presumably surpass the pagan and philosophically eclectic (though typically epicurean) Horace. The Roman may wryly fault himself, but these same weaknesses, in a Christian poet, become sinfulness.

How dark, then, is Donne's admission of culpability in comparison to Horace's self-deprecation? In his most significant revision of the model, Donne turns Horace's ironies into an expression of conscience too dire for laughter. For "we come to sin Rhetorically, perswasively, powerfully," Donne would preach to his congregation:

> and as we have found examples of our sins in History, so we become examples to others, by our sins, to lead and encourage them, in theirs; when we come to employ upon sin, that which is the essence of man, Reason, and discourse, we will also employ upon it, those which are the properties of man onely, which are, To speake, and to laugh; we will come to speake, and talk, and to boast of our sins, and at last, to laugh and jest at our sins; and as we have made sin a recreation, so we will make a jest of our condemnation. (*Sermons*, 1:225–26)

As in satire, here in sermon Donne rejects the entire ethical foundation of Horace's comic satire, redefining as sin his model's "lesser frailties" and folly. Thematically, then, "Satyre I" describes the fail-

---

11. "Nimirum perita facetaque calliditas est, sibi aliena vitia tribuentis, ut alios, vafre in sua quidem persona carpat" (*De Poeta*, p. 426).
12. "Theme and Structure in Donne's *Satyres*," p. 66.

ure of penitence in the satirist's world, perhaps even the loss of Catholic-sacramental penance. And this failure of penance and "charitable warning" points to a larger failure, one of importance to the collection as a whole: the failure to find, or fashion, an efficacious rhetoric of reform. "Satyre I" is well placed in the collection for this reason: it reveals the reason classical satire (specifically Horation satire) fails *as a theology of language.* As Donne's contemporary, Henry Peacham, writes, "it committeth a great offence against pietie, when the occasion of mirth & laughter is taken from ye abuse of reverend matters, as the holy scriptures, the judgements of God."[13] Such offense may, however, be ineluctable in this genre if ridicule and rebuke alike, the major techniques of the pagan satirists, remain sins against charity. Unable to distinguish between comic folly and "tragical vice,"[14] Horace's ethical relativism is no longer possible for a satirist with a Christian conscience.

"It is so in the confines of folly," Jeremy Taylor writes, "that as soon as it is out of doors it is in the regions of sin."[15] During the poem's second half the satirist enters this very region, accompanying the Humorist through the London streets, attempting all the while to keep his friend by his side. Asking the Humorist to take him "for better or worse" (25), he attempts to wed himself to his friend—and to officiate, ironically, over his own marriage ceremony. And yet the poet is well aware that he cannot meet the dowry demands of one who would "consort none . . . / As though all thy companions should make thee / Jointures, and marry thy deare company" (33, 35–36). Of course the poet fails: the Humorist leaves him temporarily for more gaudy companions, abandoning him altogether for a mistress. And this failure points up the loss of constancy in a world that courts power and wealth to the point of prostitution, the instruments of courtship being fashionable behavior and affected speech. For the Humorist, like the "cheape whore" (53) and "prostitute boy" (40) he is compared to, sells his favors for personal gain. And as in Horace, what the Humorist sells—though to

13. *The Garden of Eloquence,* p. 35.

14. The phrase is Dryden's, who *does* try to separate Horatian folly (that is, "the pecadilos of life") from "the tragicall vices, to which men are hurried by their unruly passions and exorbitant desires" (*A Discourse Concerning the Original and Progress of Satire,* 2:83). Dryden here repeats critical judgments first formulated in Isaac Casaubon's influential *De Satyra Graecorum Poesi et Romanorum Satira.*

15. Sermon 23, "The Good and Evil Tongue," quoted in Raymond A. Anselment, *"Betwixt Jest and Earnest": Marprelate, Milton, Marvell, Swift, and the Decorum of Religious Ridicule,* p. 167.

others, not the satirist—is the language of flattering conversation. In
"Satyre I," then, where marriage and fidelity in social relations have
a metalinguistic reference (that is, where language becomes the primary vehicle of these relations), the breakdown of marriage signals
the breakdown of communication, the divorce between one's words
and intentions. The Humorist's adulterous relationship with the poet
thus speaks of a more perilous adulteration of discourse itself.

Yielding to the courtier's own "clothed" and hypocritical language, Donne's speaker, like Horace, now attempts to beat the
Humorist at his own game of ironizing and wordplay:

> wee went, till one (which did excell
> Th'Indians, in drinking his Tobacco well)
> Met us; they talk'd; I whisper'd, 'Let us goe,
> 'T may be you smell him not, truely I doe.'
> He hears not mee, but, on the other side
> A many-colour'd Peacock having spide,
> Leaves him and mee; I for my lost sheep stay;
> He followes, overtakes, goes on the way,
> Saying, 'Him whom I last left, all repute
> For his device, in hansoming a sute,
> To judge of lace, pinke, panes, print, cut, and plight,
> Of all the Court, to have the best conceit.'
> 'Our dull Comedians want him, let him goe;
> But Oh, God strengthen thee, why stoop'st thou so?'
> 'Why? he hath travail'd.' 'Long?' 'No, but to me'
> (which understand none,) 'he doth seeme to be
> Perfect French, and Italian.' I reply'd,
> 'So is the Poxe.' He answer'd not, but spy'd
> More men of sort, of parts, and qualities.
> (87–105)

The poet's words have become offensive weapons, bristling with
punning sarcasm. Significantly, though, they have no effect on the
Humorist, who "heares not" (91), "answer[s] not" (104) and, indeed, "understand[s] none" (103); this very lack of communication,
the futility of the satirist's language, will now prevail through the
poem's second half. How can we help but recall the opening monologue, wondering if the Humorist ever heard a word of the speaker's sermon on constancy, confession, and penance? "Satyre I,"
then, writes of the lack of reformative power in such "charitable
warnings." Much like a Catholic addressing a Protestant readership,
the poet's words have lost power to a competing language- and
value-system, here one of social compliment and "courtship." And

the poet further debilitates his satire by fighting fire with fire, countering the Humorist's affectations with a language equally affected and hypocritical.

But both theme and action come full circle when the Humorist, having lost a quarrel over his mistress, comes limping back to his impatient friend:

> At last his Love he in a windowe spies,
> And like light dew exhal'd, he flings from mee
> Violently ravish'd to his lechery.
> Many were there, he could command no more;
> He quarrell'd, fought, bled; and turn'd out of dore
>   Directly came to mee hanging the head,
>   And constantly a while must keepe his bed.
>   (106–12)

Here the poet enacts his final reversal of the Horatian plot, resolution coming not by the boor's departure but by his return. Equally significant is the satirist's return to the theme of constancy. In accompanying his friend, the poet himself chose to leave the "constant company" of his books; now, in the wake of the satirist's own inconstant choice, it is the Humorist who must "constantly a while . . . keepe his bed." Again the speaker reminds us of his inability to "shepherd" his friend, for if there is a lesson here, it has not been learned by the Humorist: his constancy will last but "a while" (112). In many ways, then, as M. Thomas Hester suggests, "Satyre I" is "a comic study in failure, a witty dramatization of the radical and seemingly irremedial gap between the intentions of the satirist and the obduracy of his *adversarius*."[16] One might add that the ineffectiveness of the satirist's intentions is due, by implication, to other causes as well: to the limitations of the classical model and its unique rhetorical strategies and, more suggestively, to the poet's own loss of such Catholic rites as confession and penance—the loss, in other words, of a pastoral role. In itself, though, Horatian technique proves peculiarly ineffectual as an instrument of Christian morality.

□   □   □

Delivered in a sermon, the following describes for Donne's congregation what his own first satire had confronted decades before: the problem of writing classical satire in a Christian culture.

16. *Kinde Pitty and Brave Scorn: John Donne's "Satyres,"* p. 17.

> We make *Satyrs;* and we look that the world shall call that *wit;* when
> God knowes, that that is in great part, self-guiltinesse, and we do but
> reprehend those things which we our selves have done, we cry out
> upon the illness of the times, and we make the times ill; so the calum-
> niator whispers those things, which are true, no where, but in him-
> selfe. (*Sermons,* 6:408)

Satire, the preacher asserts, is vanity. More than reform, the satirist
seeks fame and the world's applause through his "wit," and in so
doing neglects St. Paul's admonitions against "jesting" and "foolish
talking" (1 Timothy 6.20: *O Timothee . . . devitas profanas vocum novi-
tates*). "For Christians," as Erasmus paraphrases Paul, "have con-
tinuall battayle with vyces, and so daungerous battayle, that they
can have no leasure to applye such tryfles and sportes, but rather
they have to wepe."[17] And weep he must over his own condition as
well as the world's, since his subject—the weakness not of one man
but of fallen humanity—reflects the satirist's own "self-guiltinesse."
Far from reforming society, his ridicule can only worsen it: "we cry
out upon the illness of the times, and we make the times ill." And
his outcries become indistinguishable in motive from the "whisper-
ings" of the calumniator, in fact the satirist becomes the calumniator
who speaks, shamefully, of his own vicious nature. Donne makes a
similar argument in *Biathanatos*:

> Wee may soone become as ill as any offendor, if we offend in a severe
> increpation of the fact. For, *Climachus* in his *Ladder of Paradise,* places
> these two steps very neere one another, when hee sayes, *Though in the
> world it were possible for thee, to escape all defiling by actuall sinne, yet by
> judging and condemning those who are defiled, thou art defiled.* In this thou
> art defiled, as *Basil* notes, *That in comparing others sinnes, thou canst not
> avoide excusing thine owne.* Especially this is done, if thy zeale be too
> fervent in the reprehension of others. (*Selected Prose,* p. 27)

Though Donne refers specifically to the bitter invective of the Reformation polemicists, the passage becomes a broader critique of "zealous" satire, whether the model be Juvenal (as in "Satyre II"), Jerome,
or Basil: *"in comparing others sinnes, thou canst not avoide excusing thine
owne."*

By Donne's own reckoning a *"Poema Satyricon,"* the mock-epic
Metempsychosis explicitly repudiates its satiric technique:

> But snatch mee heavenly Spirit from this vaine
> Reckoning their vanities, lesse is the gaine

---

17. *The Seconde Tome or volume of the Paraphrase of Erasmus upon the new testament* (1552), fol. cxxxvii; quoted in Anselment, *"Betwixt Jest and Earnest,"* p. 9.

> Then hazard still, to meditate on ill,
> Though with good minde.
>
> (111–14)

Might we similarly describe "Satyre I," indeed the entire collection of *Satyres,* as a self-conscious, self-critical exploration of this literary form? I believe so, since it does not suffice to claim that a poem *is* a specific genre or written within a particular form. The question posed by each Renaissance poem to its reader (and the imitative poet is himself a reader and critic of his models) is whether the poem validates the genre by performing it or enacting its aims. Like other poems based on classical imitation, Donne's *Satyres* are radically self-reflective works, self-conscious discourses upon the possibility of their own form. And when a traditional form like satire claims for itself the power to achieve certain goals—the power to make guilty and reform humankind—it necessarily makes a claim for the power of its language: the satirist's words must have the capacity to curse and cure, the kind of punitive, persuasive force that Archilochus, the Greek precursor of Roman satire, claimed for his own verse. We must ask whether the poet's imitation claims for its own language a similar power to punish, persuade, or reform. In the case of "Satyre I," I suggest that it does not. It would be an understatement, then, to observe that Donne's *Satyres* reveal an ambivalence toward language: the satirist condemns the words of others for their deception and abuse, at the same time noting the inability of his own words to cause reform. And accompanying this ambivalence toward language is a skepticism about the satirist's role, whether he is ever capable of accomplishing anything other than his own self-incrimination. The poet's skepticism toward the form and function of satire perhaps results from such an ambivalence, for if his words fail to reform, then the classical model and the genre itself have equally failed. And yet, if we are not surprised by this failure we shall ourselves fail to appreciate one of the poem's crucial effects. Modern readers may, after all, be too swift (perhaps too Swiftian) in denying any satire, certainly Donne's, an essentialist, sacramental, or magical power of language. Viewing Renaissance satire through the spectacles of a modern linguistic skepticism, we *expect* satire not to succeed in its moral suasion; we expect little more than a brooding upon vice and a psychological exploration of the satirist's own mood. This attitude ignores, however, the almost universal optimism of Renaissance critics and poets toward the form: Scaliger, Sidney, Puttenham, Lodge, Hall, Marston—all assert its power to curse and cure. Their optimism provides a necessary context for Donne's *Satyres*, making more startling, and more poignant, his own critical testing of the genre's ability to carry out its aims.

Before the Fall, as Thomas Wilson suggests, man was an "ever-livinge Creature, unto the likenes of God, endued with reason," but through sin "al thinges waxed sauage, the earth untilled, society neglected, Goddes wil not knowen, man against manne, one agynst another, and all agaynste order." After Babel, the fall of man's language, God in his mercy "stirred up the faithfull and elect, to perswade with reason, all men to societye. And gave his appoynted ministers knowledge bothe to se the natures of man, and also graunted them the gift of utteraunce, that they myghte wyth ease wynne folke at their will, and frame them by reason to all good order. . . . Such force hath the tongue, and such is the power of eloquence and reason, that most men are forced even to yelde in that which most standeth agaynst their will."[18] The reader might at first marvel at Wilson's curiously Protestant, indeed Calvinist interpretation of the origins of rhetoric, eloquence being from the beginning God's gift of grace to the "elect," by means of which His "appoynted ministers" might control an otherwise weak and willful majority. More suggestive, though, is the "force" Wilson finds in primitive eloquence, a force that literally compels men, even "agaynst their will," to conformity with law. Such persuasive force forms the basis of classical satire's (in fact, of all literature's) claim to perform its edifying, socializing function. Thus, when Joseph Hall entreats his "daring Muse" to go "on with thy thankless taske, / And do the ugly face of vice unmaske,"[19] or describes his satire as a porcupine "That shoots sharpe quils out in each angry line, / And wounds the blushing cheeke, and fiery eye, / Of him that heares, and readeth guiltily,"[20] he accepts unquestioningly both the curative aims of satire and its capacity to achieve this end. More remarkable still is the confident, unquestioned assertion of the power of its language. The satirist's words become themselves the "sharpe quils" capable of "wound[ing]" the vicious man, drawing out his guilt. Again, this power to curse and cure is a traditional assumption, one reaching back to the earliest Greek satiric or iambic poet. In *Biathanatos* Donne himself recalls this tradition, claiming that "Hipponias the Poet rimed Bubalus . . . to death with his Iambiques" (p. 53). And

18. *The Arte of Rhetorique*, pp. 9–10.
19. *Virgidemiae*, Book I, Prologue, in *The Collected Poems of Joseph Hall*, p. 11.
20. Ibid., Book V, Satire iii, p. 83.

while one might be tempted to ironize such a claim, in fact "the iambic verse of a major poet," Robert C. Elliott observes, "were believed to exert some kind of malefic power. The power seems to have resided, not in secret, esoteric spells or in the mechanics of sympathetic magic, but in the character of the poet himself—in his command over the word. The word could kill; and in popular belief it *did* kill." Such power of language encapsulates, as Elliott suggests, "the essence of Archilocus' story" (who, like Donne's "Hipponias" or Hipponax, was a master of iambic poetry), and such a story in turn is "crucial for an understanding of the image of the satirist as it develops over the centuries."[21] Granted, Renaissance theorists of satire would downplay the malefic nature of this power (though Donne's sermon, quoted earlier, describes its proximity to sin); certainly they would consider the "killing" of the guilty anathema. They would agree, nonetheless, that the power of satire rests in the persuasive, reformative power of its language.

But what happens when a poet denies his language, and thus the literary genre, this traditional power of reform? Donne's readers have often observed the self-critical nature of the *Satyres*, though they offer different interpretations of the problem of genre. To Thomas Hester and Frank Kerins, for example, the five satires describe progressive stages in a poet's search for moral authority; Donne's satirist must learn, through trial and error, the appropriate stance toward vice, toward his own very human condition, and toward the aims and effects of his genre. The result, for both critics, is a collection that enacts the reformation of classical satire, a literary form now accommodated to a Christian understanding of human nature and moral suasion. A contrary interpretation, one suggested by John R. Lauritsen and A. F. Bellette, is that Donne does not so much reform as repudiate the conventional aims of satire. The five satires demonstrate nothing but the poet's lack of authority and the impossibility of reform—and they end, as Bellette argues, by abandoning the satirist's role entirely.[22] But whether one chooses

---

21. *The Power of Satire: Magic, Ritual, Art*, pp. 14–15. In *The Cankered Muse: Satire of the English Renaissance*, Alvin B. Kernan makes a similar point: the Elizabethan poet claims, optimistically, a particular social function and power over his audience. Kernan explores the language of the Elizabethan satirists at length, but only insofar as their style reveals the personality of a conventionalized spokesman, the satyr-figure: for him, more perhaps than for Elliott, the efficacy of this genre lies in the character or personality of the satyr-satirist.

22. "The Originality of Donne's Satires," pp. 139–40. See also John R. Lauritsen, "Donne's *Satyres:* The Drama of Self-Discovery"; Frank Kerins, "The

to read these poems as revision or rejection of their classical models, one thing at least is certain. Donne's critique of the Roman satirists is subsumed within a broader critique: the problem of genre becomes a problem of rhetoric, particularly of the competing theologies of language. Donne was "the first poet in the World in some things," as Ben Jonson observed to his admirer, William Drummond.[23] In English, surely, he is the first to discover the rhetorical as well as moral limitations of this classical form. What allows this discovery is the poet's radical reflection on the powers of language, an exploration that will continue and, indeed, deepen in "Satyre II," Donne's critical reinterpretation of Juvenal. We turn now to this poem and to the relation it establishes with its classical model.

As Juste Lipse notes, Juvenal "takes hold of vice, scolds and rebukes, often mixing in bitter wit, though rarely jesting; in all this he is the opposite of Horace, who is gentle, calm, quiet, and admonishes more often than he punishes."[24] For these reasons, presumably, Juvenal excels as a reformer as well as stylist: "no one," Lipse asserts, "is more capable of correcting morals."[25] Continental criticism is far from universal, though, in its praise of Juvenal. Bartolommeo Ricci, for example, criticizes both his personality and his moral efficacy: "although there are two ways to amend vices (which is most important in this poetic genre)," Juvenal,

> induced either by unsound judgement or by a perversity of nature, chose for himself the more offensive method, which is to attempt to lead sinners back to sanity through constant reproaches and placing before them the fear of punishment. In this method of accusation he acts as so fierce a castigator and so severe an admonitor that he drives

---

'Businesse' of Satire: John Donne and the Reformation of the Satirist"; and Hester, *Kinde Pitty,* pp. 11–16.

23. William Drummond of Hawthornden, *Ben Jonson . . . Conversations with William Drummond of Hawthornden,* p. 6.

24. "Tangit vitia, objurgat, inclamat: raro jocos, saepius acerbos sales miscet. quae omnia in Horatio contra, qui placidus, lenis, quietus, monet saepius, quam castigat" (*Epistolae* 4.9, in *Opera Omnia,* p. 240). On Juvenal's Renaissance reputation and the nature of his satiric art see Selden, *English Verse Satire,* pp. 11–14; and Clayton D. Lein, "Theme and Structure in John Donne's *Satyre II,*" pp. 132–33.

25. "Nemo idoneor ad mores corrigendos Juvenali" (*Epistolae* 4.15). Phillipo Beroaldo also argues for the moral efficacy of Juvenal's *saeva indignatio:* "in insectandis vitiis eminentissimus et in objurgandis moribus vehemens dicendi genus habet elegans atque venustum" (*Oratio in Principio Lectionis Juvenalis,* p. 63), and so does Julius Caesar Scaliger, perhaps the most influential critic of the later sixteenth century (*Poetices Libri Septem,* p. 336).

offenders to greater delinquency and even to despair, when they
should grow ashamed of or repent their sins.[26]

In fact Ricci finds the famous opening of Juvenal's first satire (*Semper
ego auditor tantum*) "too haughty, if not insolent," as if he writes out
of insolence rather than an interest in reform.[27] Of course, Juvenal's
Renaissance reputation as the *vir iratus* derives primarily from this
first satire, where his outbursts of anger and indignation, that his
heart "burns dry with rage" (*quanta siccum iecur ardeat ira*) or that
"indignation prompts his verse" (*facit indignatio versum*),[28] would
suggest Donne's own expressions of "hate" and "offence"—words
that evoke the decorum of the Juvenalian satirist, "hate" occurring
four times in "Satyre II" and but once elsewhere ("Satyre III," 34).
And yet to "thanke God" ("Satyre II," 1) for one's hatred would
extend Juvenal's *saeva indignatio* beyond the bounds of righteous
anger. At least initially, then, the poet assumes the same "haughty,
if not insolent" sense of moral superiority that Ricci criticizes in
Juvenal's first satire (and that Donne, we have seen, criticizes in his
sermon). And though Donne's satirist claims that the *saeva indignatio*
is righteous—that his is a "just offence" (40) against his nemesis,
Coscus—we should keep in mind the ambivalence with which Renaissance critics read Juvenal, an ambivalence that subtly pervades
Donne's own critical reinterpretation of this model.[29]

26. "Nolim in hoc . . . quispiam mihi Juvenalem audeat objicere. . . . Nam
cum ad castigandum, quod in eo fit maxime versuum genere, duae viae sint om-
nino, is, aut judicio non sano aut natura prava ductus, odiosiorem sibi delegit,
quae est ut perpetuis jurgiis ac poenae metu proposito peccantem ad sanitatem
traducere conetur. In qua accusandi ratione ita saepius acrem castigatorem atque
asperum agit commonitorem, ut magis ad gravius delinquendum ac etiam ad
desperationem reum impellat, quam ut suorum scelerum quicquam aut pudeat
aut poenitat" (*De Imitatione* 1:447).
   27. "Elatum nimis, vel dicam insolens videri potuit unde exorditur: 'Semper
ego auditor tantum? Nunquamne reponam?' " (ibid., 1:447).
   28. *Satire* 1:45, 79 (in *Juvenal and Persius*, pp. 6, 8).
   29. In persona, in style, and especially in its concern for exposing "tragicall
vices," the second satire is distinctively Juvenalian; admittedly, though, the Juvenalian decorum is easily misinterpreted, since the poem avoids obvious verbal bor-
rowing. Clayton Lein for example, one of the poem's more sensitive readers, notes
that the speaker's "hatred toward the City . . . embodies a Juvenalian virulence."
Ultimately he agrees, however, with Herbert Grierson in seeing "Horace as the
chief model" ("Theme and Structure," p. 132). Hester also describes a Juvenalian
persona within a Horatian plot: though the structural model, he suggests, is *Sermo*
2.1, Donne's speaker "goes beyond assault against the Horatian personal follies
mocked in the first poem to a vituperative exposure of Juvenalian crimes" ("The
Bona Carmina of Donne and Horace," p. 24; he elaborates in *Kinde Pitty*, pp. 33–38).

Sir; though (I thanke God for it) I do hate
Perfectly all this towne, yet there's one state
In all ill things so excellently best
That hate, towards them, breeds pitty towards the rest.
Though Poetry indeed be such a sinne
As I thinke that brings dearths, and Spaniards in,
Though like the Pestilence and old fashion'd love,
Ridlingly it catch men; and doth remove
Never, till it be serv'd out; yet their state
Is poore, disarm'd, like Papists, not worth hate.

(1–10)

What sort of "sinne," then, is poetry? Through the next twenty lines the satirist describes such "poore" and "disarm'd" creatures: the dramatists and love poets, those who write for favors (or simply for the sake of writing) and, finally, the worst of poetasters, the plagiarists or "wit pyrats," as Donne writes elsewhere ("Upon Mr Thomas Coryats *Crudities*," 65), the sort who is "meere nothing of him selfe," who "neyther eates, nor drinkes, nor goes, nor lookes, nor spitts, but by imitation" ("Character of a Dunce," in *Paradoxes and Problems*, p. 60). But all these "punish themselves" (39), the satirist tells us; however "poor" their state might be, such poets are in fact "disarm'd" (10), incapable of wounding others—incapable, indeed, of little more than self-incrimination (or as the preacher says, "self-guiltinesse"). All these deserve pity rather than blame.

All, that is, except for Coscus, a "scarce Poet" (44) turned lawyer whose "insolence . . . breeds" the poet's "just offence" (39–40), a person who "throwes, / Like nets, or lime-twigs, wheresoere he goes, / His title'of Barrister, on every wench, / And wooes in language of the Pleas, and Bench" (45–48). Mimicking Coscus's affected speech to a would-be lover, the poet at first depicts him as a comic, Horatian figure: " 'A motion, Lady.' 'Speake Coscus.' 'I'have beene / In love, ever since *tricesmo*'of the Queene' " (49–50). But "Horace's fools," as Hester writes, "have become Juvenalian knaves in Donne's poem," [30] and the satirist soon turns from caricature to a thoroughly juvenalian invective:

words, words, which would teare
The tender labyrinth of a soft maids eare,
More, more, then ten Sclavonians scolding, more
Then when winds in our ruin'd Abbeyes rore.
When sicke with Poetrie,'and possest with muse

30. "*Bona Carmina*," p. 25.

> Thou wast, and mad, I hop't; but men which chuse
> Law practise for meere gaine, bold soule, repute
> Worse then imbrothel'd strumpets prostitute.
> (57–64)

As the enormity of his crime prevents Coscus from remaining a comic figure, so the tragic results of his actions demand a grander, tragic style, for, "Shortly ('as the sea) hee'will compasse all our land; / From Scots, to Wight; from Mount, to Dover strand" (77–78). Encompassing all of England in the compass points of these four lands, such elevated, expansive language contrasts with the scurrilous humor of previous lines, and yet this very contrast is a hallmark of Juvenalian satire, whose style mixes the serious and the ludicrous, the base and the high tragic.[31] While "Satyre II" does not always rise so high or sink so low as Juvenal's own mixed style, there are instances of both stylistic extremes.[32] But even as the poem invokes Juvenal's stylistic decorum or *prepon*, elements of *kairos*—of changed circumstances, to which the poet must respond if his words are to achieve their aims—insinuate themselves, testing

31. As Juvenal writes of Alexander, "one globe is all too little for the youth of Pella; he chafes uneasily within the narrow limits of the world, as though he were cooped up within the rocks of Gyara or the diminutive Seriphos" (*Satire* 10:168–70). As with Coscus's insatiable greed, the world itself is too small to encompass such tragic ambitions as this Macedonian king's or, in the following, as Hannibal's: "This is the man for whom Africa was all too small—a land beaten by the Moorish sea and stretching to the steaming Nile, and then, again, to the tribes of Aethiopoia and a new race of elephants! Spain is added to his dominions: he overleaps the Pyrenees; Nature throws in his way Alps and snow: he splits the rocks asunder, and breaks up the mountain-side with vinegar!" (*Satire* 10:148–53). The passage sinks—deliberately so—in this final phrase, for again Juvenal's satiric effects "are derived from the clash of styles and from the resulting incongruity," a juxtaposition "of an idiom of high-style epic declamation and a demeaning naturalism or harsh and vulgar materialism" (Selden, *English Verse Satire*, pp. 39–40).

32. In lines 57–60 alone the imagery ranges from the elevated (the "ruin'd Abbeyes"), to the outlandishly humorous (the "Sclavonians scolding"), to the trivial (the "softe maids eare"). Ultimately it turns obscene. But while the images are mixed in tone, the phrasing is vigorous and impassioned, the hammer-like effect of the figure epizeuxis, for example ("Words, words . . . More, more . . .") lending grandeur to the expression, though the grandiloquence deflates with the mixture of subjects and styles. Indeed, the opening criticism of hack poets reveals that strange union of bombast and excremental imagery that (judging from John Marston's practice as well) characterizes the Elizabethan imitation of Juvenal: "dildoes" and "pox," "bastardy" and "sodomy," "carted whores" and "embrothel'd strumpets" all evoke what Selden terms the "demeaning naturalism" of Juvenalian style.

the model's adequacy in this new cultural setting. The poet alludes to the recent enclosure of common land (which Coscus hastens) and to the dissolution of Catholic monasteries, those "ruin'd Abbeyes" through which Coscus's own empty words echo, presaging the nation's religious, moral, and economic decay. The growing power of the Established Church is also part of the poet's changed circumstances, and as he criticizes the Law, so he criticizes the Church for its own abuse of language, its willingness to misread and misapply the language of Scripture to increase its temporal authority. Apparently, the complexities of contemporary power structures, whether legal, political, or religious, place the Juvenalian satirist in an untenable rhetorical situation, speaking to a strange and unreceptive, indeed untouchable and irredeemable audience. For while Coscus provides an appropriate subject for the poet's *saeva indignatio*, his crimes remain unpunished. The initial criticism of contemporary literature reinforces this critical, kairotic recognition: the satirist, *himself a poet*, is in this new age "disarm'd," incapable of reforming or in any way influencing his world. Poetry, even the very poem that the speaker himself writes, has become powerless.

Yet another recognition of difference separates Donne's text from the Juvenalian model, pointing sadly and irrevocably to the changed circumstances under which Juvenal must now fail: the poet's recognition of the fall, not just of man but of language itself. The dramatist, as the speaker describes him, "gives ideot actors means / (Starving himselfe) to live by'his labor'd sceanes" (13–14). And as the mock-epic simile following these lines suggests ("As in some Organ, Puppits dance above / And bellows pant below, which them do move" [15–16]), the actors become puppets prompted by the dramatist's panting "wind." The speaker condemns them all, then, for having divorced the heart from the tongue: the playwright does not speak for himself, nor do his actors speak their own thoughts. Similarly, there is no truth in the love poet, who would "move Love by rimes" (17), the charm-like sound of his verses prevailing over their empty sense. And if the love poet elevates manner over meaning, there is no meaning at all in the language of those "who write, because all write," and "have still / That excuse for writing, and for writing ill" (23–24), the fourfold repetition of "writing" and "write" turning composition into a mindless moving of pen across paper. Yet the "worst" of poetasters is one who treats another's words as his own or, as the satirist puts it, "who (beggarly) doth chaw / Others wits fruits,"

and in his ravenous maw
Rankly digested, doth those things out-spue,
As his owne things; and they are his owne, 'tis true,
For if one eat my meate, though it be knowne
The meate was mine, th'excrement is his own.

(25–30)

Even as it condemns the servile imitator the passage itself parodies
Seneca's discussion of imitation, which observes that "the food we
have eaten, as long as it retains its original quality and floats in our
stomachs as an undiluted mass, is a burden; but it passes into tissue
and blood only when it has been changed from its original form. So
it is with the food which nourishes our higher nature,—we should
see to it that whatever we have absorbed should not be allowed to
remain unchanged, or it will be no part of us. We must digest it;
otherwise it will merely enter the memory and not the reasoning
power."[33] In Donne's version, the product of imitation becomes not
nourishment or "sinew" but excrement—a devastating if scurrilous
attack on the theft of another's words. Note the levels of irony: the
poet, imitating Juvenal, here imitates Seneca on the subject of imitation, in order to ridicule others who imitate the poet himself! Necessarily, this tour de force becomes an implicit criticism of the satirist's own writing. Can the satirist, himself an imitative poet, escape
the charge he has just levelled against others? If poetry is harmless,
meaningless, powerless in contemporary society, how can the satirist's own words—the very satire he composes—claim in any way to
be authentic or efficacious? By casting doubt on the powers of his
medium, the poet necessarily weakens his own words as instruments of reform.

And thus "Satyre II," as Hester suggests, "addresses the nature
and potential of the satirist's medium—language."[34] As a consequence of his linguistic skepticism, an attitude shared by many in
his age, the poet can no longer treat discourse as a stable, secure
medium of truth and persuasion. The hack poet, the self-serving
lawyer, and the religious zealot turn language into charm, or flattery, or deception. And for Coscus especially, who "throwes / Like
nets, or lime-twigs wheresoere he goes, / His title'of Barrister, on
every wench" (45–47), language provides a "net" or snare to entrap
the innocent. The satirist inveighs against him for expressing a will
to power rather than a desire to communicate; Coscus's words, like

33. *Ad Lucilium Epistulae Morales*, 2:279–81.
34. *Kinde Pitty*, p. 33.

the imitative poet's, become mere waste, an excrement in meaning and moral value, even as they gain him great personal wealth and power. But if his legal influence—Coscus's very name or title—can be described in similes so concrete as this, his own wooing ultimately, like that of the love poet, is empty of meaning; it, too, is but "words, words" (57), a sound and fury. Though a pagan author, Juvenal would himself have sympathized with the Christian notion of a fallen, depraved humanity. But again, language has fallen with man, something that Juvenalian satire could not fully anticipate. And thus, while noting the powers of Coscus's words to deceive and work evil, Donne's imitation of Juvenal points only to the futility of satiric language to do good. Donne extends the model's concerns, then, from bad poetry and bad lawyers to the abuse and weakness of language itself; linguistic skepticism, recognition of the weakened powers of a fallen language, becomes the *kairos* that undermines Juvenalian satire in Donne's literary culture. Indeed, the poet's anxiety over the effect of language (his own especially) continues throughout "Satyre II," only partially allayed in the final lines:

> But (oh) we'allow
> Good workes as good, but out of fashion now,
> Like old rich wardrops; but my words none draws
> Within the vast reach of th'huge statute lawes.
> (109–12)

Juvenalian invective, the satirist here concludes, cannot compel reform, no matter how self-righteous or indignant or zealous the speaker's pose; his harsh language may attempt to shame criminal individuals like Coscus, may attempt, in the manner of Juvenal, to "punish" them with words, yet it cannot bring them to justice. The poet's words, in short, are too weak.

And what if his words were effective? Had his invective succeeded, the satirist could anticipate no less than his own ruin at the hands of a legal system controlled by the likes of his nemesis. Ironically, only the weakness of his language exempts him from "th'huge statute laws" (112) against libel. Thus the poet introduces a significant theme of subsequent satires, the third and fourth especially: the personal danger of writing. Here the poet escapes the punishment of statutory law only by having "disarm'd" his language.[35] In

35. Indeed, Frank Kerins reads the ambiguous final lines as an "ignoble retreat" from the satirist's traditional role; since the poet "takes pains to disavow

fact the satirist's own safety demands that his words fail: should they be read as anything more than an exercise in imitation—as anything more than mere "poetry"—they would themselves be deemed "worth hate" by the likes of Coscus, imperiling, we would presume, the poet himself. Thus the final lines call attention to the danger, and weakness, and unpopularity of such satire, comparing the poet's words to those "Goode workes" that, like "old rich ward-rops," are "out of fashion" (109–10). As Kerins suggests, "beyond the witty play on the Thirty-Nine Articles, the equation of fashion-able attire with moral actions serves to underline the superficial nature of the satirist's world."[36] Indeed, as the eleventh of these articles states, "We are accounted righteous before God, only for the merit of our Lord and Saviour Jesus Christ by Faith, and not for our own works or deservings."[37] Good works alone, including those sought through the reforming words of the satirist, cannot save—either the satirist himself or his society. Again, like a Catholic in a Protestant court, the new satirist confronts only his own isola-tion from current political and legal structures of power and must come to terms, then, with his own lack of persuasive or compelling authority.

And here we might recall the plight of those who are "poore, disarm'd, like Papists, not worth hate" (10). Perhaps a serious argu-ment is woven as if into the underside of the poem, an argument that Papists are *not* worth hate, that there are people and practices and attitudes at court far more insidious and dangerous to the na-tion. "Satyre II" is not a defense of Catholicism by any means, though the reference to "ruin'd Abbeyes" introduces a poignant

---

any moral earnestness in his work" ("'Businesse' of Satire," p. 45). Hester, too, observes the "ambiguous reference to 'none' in Donne's line (as a reference to himself as well as to those malefactors who go unpunished in spite of his revela-tion of their misdeeds)." As he suggests, the satirist "adds the melancholic and ironic admission that his satire is ineffective" ("Bona Carmina," pp. 27, 28). Hester does not, however, read the poem as an expression either of linguistic skepticism or of the moral ambivalence of Juvenalian satire. As he argues in *Kinde Pitty,* "Ignoring the irony of these concluding lines could support the view that the poem discloses Donne's dissatisfaction with the genre altogether and his squeamish inability to convert it into an adequate expression of his sup-posed skepticism. Such views overlook the rich ambiguity of the satirist's con-clusion" (p. 50). Granted, ironies abound. But no amount of irony can "save" or assert the efficacy of a text that takes as its major premise the fallen nature of language.

36. "'Businesse' of Satire," p. 44.

37. Quoted in E. J. Bicknell, *A Theological Introduction to the Thirty-Nine Arti-cles of the Church of England,* p. 199.

elegiac tone. Of the poem's many allusions to Catholic beliefs and ritual, half at least are critical (such as the traditional, almost tired invective against "Symonie'and Sodomy in Churchmens lives" [75]), and all strive for humor or wit: the woman guards her modest dowry as a holy "Relique" (84), while some lovers, in an excess of both emotion and language "out-sweare the Letanie" (33)—while others still are

> with sinnes all kindes as familiar bee
> As Confessors, and for whose sinfull sake
> Schoolmen new tenements in hell must make:
> Whose strange sinnes, Canonists could hardly tell
> In which Commandments large receit they dwell.
>   (34–38)

In the spirit of *Ignatius his Conclave,* the poet here ridicules the Scholastic dogma that reformers sought to dismantle. And yet the poet is equally critical of Protestant abuses, and the Canonist's confusion over the application of theological law reflects on all the combatants in the Reformation controversy. "Satyre II" is not simply about the abuse of temporal law, nor is it simply about the in/efficacy of poetic language; it is, rather, a broader exploration of the relations between discourse and power, of the ways religious and legal authority both derive from the control of language.

Though a poet-turned-lawyer, Coscus is described as a "new benefic'd minister" (45). The comparison, seemingly innocent, points to the Elizabethan court's attempt to assume religious as well as temporal authority. Doubtless the two are never entirely separate; throughout history, each of these authorities has sought to subsume the other, and often, for a time, one or the other has succeeded in the attempt. But at what cost? And by what means does the court make such claims? In a letter to Henry Goodyer, Donne complains that "the divines of these times are become mere advocates, as though religion were a temporal inheritance; they plead for it with all sophistications, and illusions, and forgeries: and herein they are likest advocates, that though they be fed by the way with dignities and other recompenses, yet that for which they plead is none of theirs. They write religion without it" (*Life and Letters,* 1:221). The point is simple enough: Reformation theology is reduced to the wranglings of lawyers or "advocates," each acting on behalf of some temporal authority. No longer a crisis of personal faith, religious controversy becomes a political struggle to control the meaning and application of Scripture. Thus Donne recognizes the perilous ease with which scriptural meaning bends to personal motives, a fault that he prays, in *Essays in Divinity,* to avoid in his own life: "I do not (I hope) in undertaking the Meditation upon this verse, incur the fault of them, who for ostentation and magnifying their wits, excerpt and tear shapeless and unsignificant rags of a word or two, from whole sentences, and make them obey their purpose in discoursing" (p. 39). In contrast, Coscus willfully misreads legal documents and "impaires" (97) his own writing, exploiting the ambiguity for his own profit.

And though "Lawyers, more then others, have ever been Tyrants over words, and have made them accept other significations, then their nature enclined," yet "Schoolmen, which have invented new things, and found out, or added Suburbs to Hell, will not be exceeded in this boldness upon words" (*Essays in Divinity,* p. 27). Similarly, though Coscus's abuse of law remains the explicit subject, the poet's own broader target, I would argue, has become the abuses of such "Schoolmen" or, rather, of polemicists on either side of the Reformation controversy:

> In parchments then, large as his fields, hee drawes
> Assurances, bigge, as gloss'd civill lawes,
> So huge, that men (in our times forwardnesse)
> Are Fathers of the Church for writing lesse.
> These hee writes not; nor for these written payes,
> Therefore spares no length; as in those first dayes
> When Luther was profest, he did desire
> Short *Pater nosters,* saying as a Fryer
> Each day his beads, but having left those lawes,
> Addes to Christs prayer, the Power and glory clause.
> But when he sells or changes land, he'impaires
> His writings, and (unwatch'd) leaves out, *ses heires,*
> As slily'as any Commenter goes by,
> Hard words, or sense; or in Divinity
> As controverters, in vouch'd Texts, leave out
> Shrewd words, which might against them cleare the doubt.
> (87–102)

The advent of such controversy has, in this "times forwardness," opened a floodgate of theological language, exemplified by Luther's (initially Erasmus's) emendation of so sacred a text as the Lord's Prayer. And if Reformation theology changes the words one prays, how might it change the meaning and effect of those words? Who are the "Commenter[s]" and "controverters" the poet inveighs against (on both sides, one assumes)? One could argue that such a passage, superficially an invective against Coscus's abuse of secular law, charts the entire course of the Reformation controversy, evincing both the need, and the perils—and, perhaps, the impossibility— of achieving certitude in the meaning and application of Scripture. And what problems of interpretation does the passage itself reveal? What, even approximately, does the poet mean by "hard words or sense"? What, in contrast, is a "shrewd" word? What is the "doubt" surrounding a text, word, or meaning? And how can a shrewd word "cleare" this doubt? Perhaps the reader's own partial understanding of such a passage must itself rest in linguistic skepticism. For "our speech has its weaknesses and its defects," as Michel de Montaigne writes: "Most of the occasions for the troubles of the world are grammatical. Our lawsuits spring only from debate over the interpretation of the laws, and most of our wars from the inability to express clearly the conventions and treaties of agreement of princes. How many quarrels, and how important, have been produced in the world by doubt of the meaning of that syllable *Hoc*!"[38] Montaigne's own description of the "weaknesses" and "defects" of language serves as a commentary on Donne's own second satire, not only for its exploration of the political and legal consequences of misunderstanding, but also for its only half-veiled allusion to the controversies of linguistic theology, particularly concerning the nature (and number) of the sacraments. For Montaigne here refers to Christ's, and the Catholic priest's, words of Eucharistic consecration (*Hoc est corpus meum*), an issue Donne, too, explores in his sermon:

> There have been *Verball Heresies*, and *Heresies* that were but *Syllabicall;* little *Praepositions* made *Heresies;* not onely *State-Praepositions*, precedencies, and Prerogatives of *Church* above *Church*, occasioned great *Schismes*, but *Literall Praepositions, Praepositions* in *Grammar,* occasioned great *Heresies* . . . . And we all know, what differences have beene raised in the *Church*, in that one poynt of the Sacrament, by these three Prepositions, *Trans, Con*, and *Sub*. There have beene great *Heresies*, but *Verball*, but *Syllabicall;* and as great, but *Literall*. (*Sermons*, 6:247)[39]

Doubt over the meaning of one word, of one syllable—of one letter, even—makes the crisis of Reformation again a linguistic crisis, and

38. "Apology for Raymond Sebond," p. 392.
39. Donne makes similar points elsewhere: "Words, and lesse particles then words have busied the whole Church. In the Councell of *Epheseus* . . . the strife was but for a word. . . . In the Councell of *Chalcedon*, the difference was not so great, as for a word composed of syllables. It was but for a syllable. . . . In the Councell of *Nice*, it was not so much as a syllable made of letters. For it was but for one letter" (*Sermons*, 9:71).

it is within this context that Donne's *Satyres* ask to be read. For what can a mere satirist's words avail when the word of God can be cast into doubt? Or simply ignored?

Like the first satire's criticism of Horace, "Satyre II" thus invokes the stylistic decorum of its Juvenalian model. And here, as in the first satire, Donne rejects the model's method of rebuke, repudiating any claim to effect change in a world where both man and language have suffered a fall. The *kairos* of "Satyre II," then, the acknowledgment of cultural change that leads Juvenal to fail as an effective model for satire, suggests that two things must be redeemed by a satire before it can succeed in its aims: human nature, and human discourse. And "Satyre II" redeems neither—which is not quite to say that it accomplishes nothing. For while the third satire attempts to recover the persuasive power traditionally ascribed to the genre, this second prepares for such a recovery by revealing the extent of language's decay. In short, "Satyre II" surpasses its classical model by asserting that language and genre alike have fallen in need of redemption; to write classical satire in the poet's changed circumstances without this recognition would be a naive exercise in imitation, an exercise in decorum without *kairos*. Significantly, this dialectical interplay between decorum and *kairos* continues throughout Donne's collection of satires: a rhetoric of decorous imitation, one seeking to recreate the stylistic features (and thus invoke the linguistic presence or "speaking image" of the model) confronts a kairotic recognition of change, of critical difference borne of the poet's unique political and religious circumstances.

Some questions, however, remain. What are the poet's circumstances? How is it that the poet's own religious beliefs place him in so perilous a relation to political authority? Is it in fact the poet's own religious beliefs that cost him his persuasive or moral authority *as a satirist*? Readers have often noted the poem's many allusions to Roman Catholicism.[40] It remains to be considered whether the Catholic allusions render such a poem—indeed, render the collection as a whole—problematic as classical imitation. For if the poet attempts to reform through a rhetoric dependent upon Catholic traditions of spiritual renewal (traditions that his reading audience, presumably, have chosen—or been compelled—to repudiate), then his satire again fails in its aims or else becomes a darker allegory, a

40. See Hester, "Henry Donne, John Donne, and the Date of *Satyre II*"; and Ronald J. Corthell, " 'Coscus Only Breeds My Just Offence': A Note on Donne's 'Satyre II' and the Inns of Court."

carefully concealed polemic in the contemporary war of faith. And the above raises some final questions: Do the *Satyres* assume an adversarial role toward their readers at court? Or do they expect that their coterie readership, recently described by Arthur Marotti,[41] would be sympathetic to the plight of the loyalist Catholic? Surely Donne's circle of friends were well acquainted with the poet's Catholic background, a religious upbringing that many (Donne's employer, Thomas Egerton, for one) would have shared. But regardless of any reader's private belief, an open profession of adherence to the Old Faith would be tantamount to political suicide—at the very least, the murder of one's *reputation* at court, a fear Donne himself continuously expresses in his letters and prose. Neither the poet nor his audience could address the Catholic question directly without danger. It is for this reason that I would describe the Reformation theological controversy as an allusive and indirect (in a word, an allegorical) subject of the *Satyres*. But delaying for the moment our discussion of "Satyre III," the next chapter turns instead to the fourth satire, a poem that explores in even greater depth the effect Catholicism has on the rhetoric, and the efficacy, of this classical form.

41. *Coterie Poet*, pp. 25–151. See also Ronald J. Corthell, "Style and Self in Donne's *Satires*."

3

The Politics of Private Conscience

Written at about the same time as *Biathanatos*, one of Donne's letters to Henry Goodyer admonishes his friend against even the appearance of irresolution in religion, an appearance made more palpable by the controversial nature of Goodyer's reading and some acquaintances. The letter is suggestive of Donne's own experience, for he knew intimately the danger of popular judgment, the way reputations, like texts, suffer at the hands of mis-translators:

> I am angry, that any should think, you had in your Religion peccant humours, defective, or abundant, or that such a booke, (if I mistake it not) should be able to work upon you; my comfort is, that their judgment is too weak to endanger you, since by this it confesses, that it mistakes you, in thinking you irresolved or various: yet let me be bold to fear, that that sound true opinion, that in all Christian professions there is way to salvation (which I think you think) may have been so incommodiously or intempestively sometimes uttered by you; or else your having friends equally near you of all the impressions of Religion, may have testified such an indifferency, as hath occasioned some to further such inclina-tions, as they have mistaken to be in you. This I have feared, because hertofore the inobedient Puritans, and now the over-obedient Papists attempt you. It hath hurt very many, not in their conscience, nor ends, but in their reputation, and ways, that others have thought them fit to be wrought upon. As some bodies are as wholesomly nourished as ours, with Akornes, and endure nakednesse, both which would be dangerous to us, if we for them should leave our former habits, though theirs were the Primitive diet and custome: so are many souls well fed with such formes, and dressings of Religion, as would distemper and misbecome us, and make us corrupt towards God, if any humane circumstance moved it, and in the opinion of men, though none. You shall seldome see a Coyne, upon which the stamp were removed, though to imprint it better, but it looks awry and squint. And so, for the most part, do mindes which have received divers impressions. (*Letters*, pp. 100–102)

The term "Primitive" of course reverberates with its own polemic force: the primitive church, which Puritans especially believed to be their absolute model and goal, would be to one born and raised Catholic (or even Anglican, for that matter) as a diet of "akornes." What, then, is the effect of changing one's beliefs? Is it a reshaping, or misshaping, of one's character? Such a mind, like a coin re-stamped, "looks awry and squint"; such a soul, once "well fed" by its "former habits" of worship, becomes "distempered" by the "Primitive diet and custome" of another church. Far from a call to orthodoxy, the letter becomes an argument for religious tolerance. The truly Catholic Church or "Church Universal" is one that keeps Christ as its cornerstone, the externals of worship being largely indifferent to salvation.

The "sound true opinion, that in all Christian professions there is way to salvation," is an expressly fideist, perhaps even spiritualist, solution to the Reformation controversy.[1] And yet it is at best a personal solution, a separate peace, since outward conformity to one and one church only remains politically enforced. As Donne continues in this letter,

> I will not, nor need you, compare the Religions. The channels of Gods Mercies run through both fields; and they are sister teats of his graces, yet both diseased and infected, but not both alike. . . . the *Roman* profession seems to exhale, and refine our wills from earthly Drugs, and Lees, more then the Reformed, and so seems to bring us nearer heaven; but then that carries heaven farther from us, by making us pass so many Courts, and Offices of Saints in this life, in all our petitions. (*Letters*, p. 102)

Roman Catholicism is not without error. Intercession for example, explicitly criticized in "Satyre V," becomes an obstacle rather than a bridge to salvation. Still, the final position Donne urges upon his friend is not to repudiate or adopt any one belief so much as to keep one's faith a private affair, for "when you descend to satisfie all men in your own religion, or to excuse others to al; you prostitute your self and your understanding, though not a prey, yet a mark, and a hope, and a subject, for every sophister in Religion to work on" (*Letters*, p. 103). Thus an older, and to all appearances conformed, Donne advises the show of orthodoxy and avoidance of public con-

---

1. "The spiritualist," as Hans J. Hillerbrand describes him, "saw the essence of religion not in externals, not even in doctrine, but in man's inward communication with God. Such an attitude detached him from the religious strife of the day. Since the value of externals was disregarded, the spiritualist found it possible to go through the routine of external observance of whatever tradition" (*The Reformation: A Narrative History Related by Contemporary Observers and Participants*, p. 273).

troversy. How well, though, does the more youthful poet of "Satyre IV" follow such advice? How does he depict the plight of the Catholic, even the loyalist Catholic, at court? Though "Satyre III" openly attacks court policies, defending the rights of private conscience against coercive political authority, "Satyre IV" finds the satirist himself under siege, his personal beliefs placing him in immediate danger.

Listing the anti-Catholic legislation enacted from 1581 to 1606, the Ellesmere manuscripts suggest just how dangerous an open espousal of the Old Faith might be to a visitor at court:

A. Comming and being: treason.
B. Practicing and seducing: treason.
C. Knowing and not discovering a Jesuit or priest: forfaiture 200 *li*.
D. Receaving and mainteyning within the realm: felonye.
E. Releiving those that be beyonde seas: praemunire.
F. Preists submitting not to come within 10 myles of the Courte. Forfaiture: to loose the benefit of their submission to be voyde. . . .
K. Recusants convicted not to come to the Courte nor to abide within 10 myles of London. Forfaite: 100 *li*.
L. Recusants convicted confined departing etc. Forfait: all goods and chattels, proffites of landes during life. . . .
P. Having or pretending to have any authority to withdrawe, etc., or to move them to promise obedience to the Pope: treason. . . .
Q. For absolving and reconcyling, using any bull, writing, bulles, instruments or authority from Rome . . . : treason. Aydors and comforters: praemunire.
R. Oathe.[2]

"Satyre IV" makes continual reference to such legislation, observing the penalty for attending "Masse," a substantial one of a "hundred markes, which is the Statutes curse" (9–10), the xenophobia of justices for whom foreigners or "Strangers" (26) are immediately suspected as Jesuit missionaries (27–29), and the "Pursevant[s]" (216) or spies employed to enforce these anti-Catholic measures, people who "make men speake treason" (46)—one of whom the poet himself confronts. Such allusions become even more signifi-

---

2. Anthony G. Petti, ed., *Recusant Documents from the Ellesmere Manuscripts,* pp. 163–65. The Ellesmere Manuscripts, begun and owned by Donne's own employer the Baron Ellesmere, Thomas Egerton, are an extensive compilation of records pertaining to the enforcement of the Oath of Allegiance and the proceedings against recusants; it would be highly unlikely that Donne was unacquainted with them.

cant if, as I shall argue, the poet presents himself as one whose religion would keep him from court, under penalty of law; indeed, feeling himself "becomming Traytor" (131), the poet goes so far as to imagine himself literally swallowed up by "one of our Giant Statutes" (132). What sort of statute would this be, if not one directed against recusants? Of what would his treason consist, if not in practicing—and needing to conceal—his religious beliefs? What happens, in short, when a loyalist Catholic addresses a Protestant audience? Will he be heard? If so, will he be understood? (Dare he?) Will he be *seen* through his language? (Seen as a loyalist Catholic? Or seen as a traitor?) Does he dare be seen? "Satyre IV" reflects the age's crisis both of faith and of discourse: addressed to an audience that presumably denies authority, and thus the right of speech, to this implicitly espoused Catholicism, the poem becomes a self-critical exploration of its language and genre and, most poignantly, of its ability to compel reform.

Like "Satyre I," Donne's earlier immersion in the drama of Horatian satire, "Satyre IV" fails to enact the traditional aims of its genre when it discovers, in the process of its own composition, the weakness of its language. The poet's inability to defend himself from the incriminating interrogation of his adversarius, a courtier-spy, is but one symptom of this weakness, while another symptom is the satirist's own increased reliance upon a Romanist vocabulary for guilt, punishment, and reform—a feature that Donne's readers often note, though tend to downplay. To Howard Erskine-Hill, for example, Donne's fourth satire expresses, "if somewhat covertly, something of the viewpoint of a Roman Catholic." After noting the allusions to anti-Catholic legislation he concludes, however, that "the Catholic background is subsumed in the Christian poem."[3] Thomas Hester is less timorous in asserting the Catholic influence, calling the poem "Donne's boldest commentary on his own situation in the 1590's through its equivocal but consistent glances at the predicament of the Catholic in Elizabethan England." Yet he, too, concludes that the plight of Catholics "never becomes the major thesis" and that "one must be careful not to overemphasize the effects" of this Catholic allusion: "The satirist does not champion Catholic devotion *qua* Catholic devotion over Anglican devotion. His technique is to compare and contrast failures in Anglican morality with sincere Catholic morality. The difference may be slight, but it amounts to the difference between pro-Catholic polemics and Christian sat-

3. "Courtiers out of Horace," pp. 282, 302.

ire."[4] If the predicament of the Catholic in Elizabethan England is not, as Hester suggests, the poem's major thesis, it is a theme that asks whether satire is even possible for this particular poet, whose language relies so heavily on Catholic sacramentalism for whatever salutary effect it might claim. And if the satirist's powers of reformation depend on the linguistic theology of Romanism (and thus, implicitly, upon the validity and efficacy of the Catholic doctrines and sacraments), then the theological controversy becomes central.

Rather than subordinate the pro-Catholic polemics to the fashioning of a Christian satire, we might explore the ways they struggle against each other, the former complicating the latter. Donne's contemporary readers, after all, particularly those sympathetic to Elizabeth's policy, would most likely define "Christian" satire as the antithesis if not the outright repudiation of the Old Faith. Hester is right: "Satyre IV" is not simply pro-Catholic polemic. But the Catholic allusions serve to destabilize the value system and the language of the poem, calling into question its authority, and thus its efficacy, as satire. The Catholicism, I suggest, never fully integrates itself into the broader Christian themes; the allusions are so pervasive and so *flaunted* in the text that they can only weaken the poet's language before a Protestant audience. And this, I imagine, is one of their intended effects. For to speak like a Catholic at a Protestant court is necessarily to give up one's authority, in much the same way that the Catholic sacraments are denied efficacy in Elizabeth's Protestant Church. It is as if the poet-priest, having lost the sacraments of confession and absolution, has also lost the power of persuasive speech. "Satyre IV" thus turns Horatian satire into an exploration of the perilous status of the Catholic in court society. But let us first establish the poem's relation to *Sermo* 1.9, its Horatian model.[5]

4. *Kinde Pitty,* pp. 74, 95.

5. Donne's imitation of Horace in "Satyre IV" has been discussed briefly by Selden, *English Verse Satire,* pp. 63–64, and in greater depth by Erskine-Hill, "Courtiers out of Horace," pp. 273–93. Hester explores both the classical and Christian elements in *Kinde Pitty,* pp. 73–97. He writes that the fourth satire "offers a tacit criticism of the conversational method of the Horatian satiric stance" and that "Horace proves a precarious model for the Christian satirist at court. The reasons for and ramifications of the satirist's implicit rejection of this ancient type of satiric discourse are clarified by the changes Donne makes in the adversarius borrowed from his classical model" (p. 77). The reasons for this rejection are clarified by other changes as well: in the satirist's departure from court, to speak as an outsider; in his shifting of models, from Horace to the native English tradition of complaint; and particularly in his skeptical attitude toward the weakened powers of language. Also, Hester concludes that the

The poet begins by fashioning a witty, self-revelatory, and self-deprecating voice imitative of this Roman, his familiar, conversational tone counterbalanced by a sophisticated rhetoric of ironizing and wordplay ("to see, or to bee seene, / I had no suit there, nor no new suite to shew") characteristic of Horace's *sermo* style. Beneath the wit, however, lies a more serious self-consciousness and self-condemnation than can be found anywhere in the classical model:

> Well; I may now receive, and die; My sinne
> Indeed is great, but I have beene in
> A Purgatorie, such as fear'd hell is
> A recreation to,'and scant map of this.
> My minde, neither with prides itch, nor yet hath been
> Poyson'd with love to see, or to bee seene,
> I had no suit there, nor no new suite to shew,
> Yet went to Court; But as Glaze which did goe
> To'a Masse in jest, catch'd, was faine to disburse
> The hundred markes, which is the Statutes curse,
> Before he scapt, So'it pleas'd my destinie
> (Guilty'of my sin of going,) to thinke me
> As prone to'all ill, and of good as forget-
> full, as proud, as lustfull, and as much in debt,
> As vaine, as witlesse, and as false as they
> Which dwell at Court, for once going that way.
>
> (1–16)

In Horace, the boor's onslaught ironically fulfills the poet's "sad fate, which a Sabine dame, shaking her divining urn, sang for me in my boyhood."[6] Donne, too, confronts his *fatum triste*, "my destinie / (Guilty'of my sin of going)." But while Horace assumes no personal responsibility for this chance meeting, Donne's satirist bears the full burden of guilt, admitting that he "sin[s]" in attending court. And the attraction he feels toward it only proves that he shares in the

poem "satisfies both the rhetorical requirements of verse satire and the moral injunctions of Christian ethics by embodying the moral and esthetic principles it defends. As such, it shows Donne's fullest and most audacious transformation of the ancient satirical techniques into zealous Christian satire" (p. 75). I would suggest, rather, that the poem denies efficacy to the classical techniques even as it denies authority to its Christian (if not, in fact, Catholic) speaker; the poem fully satisfies neither the classical nor the Christian requirements of moral suasion, ultimately revealing only the difficulty of Christianizing this classical form.
    6. "Confice; namque instat fatum mihi triste, Sabella / quod puero cecinit divina mota anus urna" (Horace, *Sermo* 1.9.29–30).

courtier's weaknesses. "Satyre I," Donne's first foray into Horatian satire, leaves the poet standing in guilty recognition of his own sinfulness. Returning to this same point, "Satyre IV" turns the poet's personal guilt into an explicit and central theme: as preparation for receiving the final sacrament, the satirist begins his confession (in fact, the satire itself becomes an act of contrition). From the outset, then, he declares his cultural difference from the Horatian subtext; here is a Christian poet whose values necessarily conflict with the conventional strategies of his pagan model.

But though he identifies with the vices of court, he has yet to identify with its power structures, political or religious. The opening lines are thus further complicated by the fact that the poet chooses, ironically or no, to speak not merely as a Christian but as a Catholic, particularly in his allusion to the sacrament of extreme unction. He equates his recent experience at court with the penitence necessary to "receive" (1) the final sacrament and, indeed, equates the court with a (Catholic) purgatory worse than the tortures of a (Protestant) hell. This may seem, on the surface, little more than blasphemous wit; and beyond the blasphemy such lines suggest at least the possibility that the poet may himself be purged of his sin, that he, if not court society, may be reformed. Yet the satirist, as well as his contemporary readers, could not escape the knowledge that such Catholic mechanisms of spiritual renewal as auricular confession, purgatory, and the final sacrament have been denied by the Anglican Church, the church supported by the court's great temporal power. The poet's physical safety, if not his spiritual state, can only be imperiled by reliance on such politically unpopular (and thus "false") doctrines. Glaze's punishment for attending "Masse in jest" (9) shows that Catholicism is too dangerous even to raise in jest; the hint of even the slightest divergence from court-sanctioned beliefs earns swift punishment. In the same way, the satirist shows that his own "jesting" at court can only bring danger to himself, not reform to court society. "Disarm'd, like Papists" ("Satyre II," 10), he is denied any mechanism of reform by the present value- and power-structures at court. And this powerlessness guarantees that he must himself suffer the verbal onslaughts of his adversarius:

> Towards me did runne
> A thing more strange, then on Niles slime, the Sunne
> E'r bred; or all which into Noahs Arke came;
> A thing, which would have pos'd Adam to name;
> Stranger then seaven Antiquaries studies,

> Then Africks Monsters, Guianaes rarities.
> Stranger then strangers.
>
> (17–23)

"Towards me did run . . ." recapitulates the Horatian model's *accurrit quidam notus mihi nomine tantum* (3): "up there runs a man I knew only by name." Yet the hyperbole of Donne's lines stresses the boor's lack of a fixed identity altogether. He is "One, whom the watch at noone lets scarce goe by, / One, to'whom th'examining Justice sure would cry, / 'Sir, by your priesthood tell me what you are'" (27–29): as the lines suggest, so thoroughly un-English (or so "cosmopolitan" and "courtly") is the boor's appearance that he could be mistaken for anything from a thief to a priest (either of which, if proved, could cost him his life, as harboring a priest cost the life of Donne's brother). Of course, more than a mimicking of foreign fashion, the motley dress symbolizes the boor's, and the Elizabethan court's, attempt to deceive through appearance. And deception, in speech as well as dress, is among the poem's significant themes.

In *Essays in Divinity,* Donne meditates not only on the powers and properties of names but on the ways God Himself blesses, and curses, through acts of nomination: "How often doth God accurse with abolishing the Name? *Thou shalt destroy their Name, Deut. 7. 24.* And in the same phrase God doth expresse his blessings to *Abraham, Gen.* 12. 2, and often elsewhere, *I will make thy Name great.* Which, without God, those vain attempters of the Tower of *Babel* endeavored: for it is said, *Gen.* 11. 4. *They did it, to get themselves a Name.*" To be named, therefore, is to be blessed by God and numbered among the elect, for "*He calleth his own sheep by name*" (*Essays in Divinity,* p. 44). The boor's very lack of a name is thus most telling. While Horace knew his adversarius "only by name" (*nomine tantum*), not even Adam could name the chimera confronting Donne's satirist. This subtle divergence from Horace more than sharpens the humor of the description (or rather nondescription) of the boor's character: it reveals the weakness of language to penetrate beyond appearances to the falsehood and corruption within, to defend itself against the moral depravity that the boor's motley dress and behavior attempt to conceal. Rather than be fixed and controlled—that is, named—by language, the boor has language, and therefore all appearances and "truths," under his own control. And also under the boor's linguistic control, significantly, is the satirist himself: "he *names* mee,'and comes to mee" (49; my italics).

Like his dress, the boor's language is macaronic ("Makeron" [117], indeed, is one of the few words the satirist finds to name him). But an important textual variant compels us to examine whether the boor "speakes *one* language" (38), as Milgate's edition reads, or, following Grierson's edition, "speakes *no* language" at all—that is, no plain, truthful, meaningful language:[7]

> This thing hath travail'd, and saith, speakes all tongues,
> And only know'th what to all States belongs;
> Made of th'Accents, and best phrase of all these,
> He speakes one language; If strange meats displease,
> Art can deceive, or hunger force my tast,
> But Pedants motley tongue, souldiers bumbast,
> Mountebankes drugtongue, nor the termes of law
> Are strong enough preparatives, to draw
> Me to beare this: yet I must be content
> With his tongue, in his tongue, call'd complement:
> In which he can win widdowes, and pay scores,
> Make men speake treason, cosen subtlest whores,
> Out-flatter favorites, or outlie either
> Jovius, or Surius, or both together.
>
> (35–48)

While Grierson's reading is the more forceful, Milgate's (which I follow above) introduces a subtle allusion to Genesis, the boor speaking "one" language "as men did before the confusion of tongues."[8] This implied reference to the tower of Babel becomes explicit in line 65, making Genesis one of the poem's more crucial subtexts. For men began building the tower with the determination, "let us make a name," in the same manner that the boor, who is unnameable, fashions a sort of mask or social identity for himself through language. In his commentary on Genesis, Martin Luther writes that, originally, "all men had one language, which served not only to preserve peace but also the (true) religion." (It is interesting to speculate how far Luther, or Donne, would press such an argument, one that places the schism between Catholicism and Protestantism on a linguistic basis.) Yet their sin was "to build the tower in the glory of their own name."[9] And the result of such pride in a self-fashioned name and identity becomes confusion, division, xenophobia. For "the one language," Luther suggests, "tended to unite

7. Grierson, *Poems of John Donne*, 1:160 (italics added).
8. Milgate, Commentary, *Satires*, p. 151.
9. *Luther's Commentary on Genesis*, 1:190, 192.

and keep together the people, while the different tongues created mistrust and hatred, since one did not understand the other. By the confusion of tongues the minds of men were divided, their customs changed, and their thoughts and enterprises turned into different channels."[10] Perhaps, then, the reader should keep both variants in mind, reading "no" as a palimpsest beneath the word "one." For Donne radicalizes the biblical subtext, revealing how thoroughly, how perilously, and how irrecoverably our fallen language breeds confusion and mistrust.

Yet the boor "speaks all tongues." *Anaclasis* ("tongue" repeated with different shades of meaning) thus evaluates the language by concretizing its effects, tongue becoming at the same time the capacity of speech, a synecdoche for language itself, and a symbol of flattery and deception. The reception of language also transfers metonymically from the ear to the tongue, which is the seat of "tast" (39), and, as part of the mouth, is the means whereby a hungry man ingests "strange meats" (38) and a sick man "preparatives" (42); thus hearing becomes a mode of ingestion or consumption, the boor's language analogous to different kinds of food and medicine (and poison). As an artfully prepared feast, his words seek to awaken the poet's "tast," that is, his appetite and desire, though the term now also refers to his practical reason or judgment, which the boor's words would deceive.[11] The boor's tongue flatters and surfeits his victim's taste or judgment, then, in the same way that a feast of "strange meats" surfeits and threatens health. Like Donne the satirist, Donne the preacher often compares language to food: "We must . . . crack a shell, to tast the kernell, cleare the words, to gaine the Doctrine. I am ever willing to assist that observation, That the books of Scripture are the eloquentest books in the world, that every word in them hath his waight and value, his taste and verdure" (*Sermons*, 9:226). Even in sermon, though, the image is not without its ambiguities. While each word has its "taste and verdure" or vigor, yet a "shell" encases the meaning of Scripture, in-

10. Ibid., 1:194.

11. In a sermon Donne plays on the relation between the Latin *sapere*, to taste, and *sapientia*, or wisdom: "it is a good Rule that S. *Bernard* gives . . . *Cui quaeque res sapiunt prout sunt, is sapiens est*, saies he: He that tasts, and apprehends all things in their proper and naturall tast, he that takes all things aright as they are, *Is sapiens est*, . . . he is wise. If he take the riches of the world to be in their nature, indifferent, neither good, nor bad in themselves, but to receive their denomination in their use . . . he that takes things so, is morally wise" (*Sermons*, 7:338–39).

deed encases all thought. What, then, does it mean to "cleare" the word from the thought or thing? Does it mean to "clarify" thought, to make the word itself transparent, so that the world or reality can be seen *through* language? Does it mean to "clear it off," to banish the *verbum*, leaving thought or meaning as a sort of transcendent, transverbal residue? Does it mean to "clean" the word, to purify it of falsehood and wrong meaning? Whatever their "waight and value," it seems that words, like shells, become as much the concealment as expression of meaning and authorial intention. Surely this is the case with the boor's speech and often the satirist's own. The effects of language, concretized as food, may poison as well as nourish. And as food must be transformed into sinew, so language itself must be "tasted," ingested and transformed into meaning. The satirist here dramatizes the familiar Platonic argument against sophistic rhetoric, which Socrates names, in the *Gorgias*, as the "cookery" of the soul "because it aims at pleasure" while "ignoring the good" (that is, the audience's moral health).[12] In the same way "complement" (44), a mask of wit, politeness, and flattery hiding the boor's ulterior motives, poisons (even as it sweetens) his words. The boor's medicine, worse than "Mountebankes drugtongue" (41) and other forms of linguistic snake oil, can only undermine the hearer's moral health even as it enriches the speaker; language has become a dangerous drug. As well as affectations of dress and behavior, "Satyre IV" thus describes the verbal onslaughts of a man who can "win widdowes" and "pay scores" with his words, literally living off his tongue.

And a reflection upon language, therefore, the satirist's as well as the boor's, becomes part of the poem's habit of self-criticism. In fact the wit of the dialogue becomes symptomatic of a weakness, perhaps even illness, in the language-use of satirist and court society alike. For Horace's opponent begins his importunities with a mixture of servile ingratiation and self-flattery: "How d'ye do, my dearest fellow . . . you must know me; I'm a scholar."[13] The boor in Donne's poem, similarly, begins with a faint attempt at self-gratulating wit: "Sir: / I love your judgement; Whom do you prefer, / For the best linguist?" (51–53). Language (indeed *lingua*, tongue) remains the subject. And no matter how the satirist responds, the boor's own answer—"Nay, your Apostles were / Good pretty lin-

12. Plato, *Collected Dialogues*, p. 247.
13. " 'Quid agis, dulcissime rerum?' . . . / 'Noris nos,' inquit; 'docti sumus' " (Horace, *Sermo* 1.9.4, 7).

guists" (58–59)—gulls the satirist into a blasphemous joke, punning on the Holy Spirit's "gift of tongues." The allusion to Acts makes a dark commentary on the boor's own linguistic skill, since the Spirit had worked this miracle to convert unbelievers and spread God's Word. "There is first an open profession of the tongue required," Donne writes in a sermon, "and therefore the Holy Ghost descended in fiery tongues, *Et lingua propria Spiritui Sancto,* sayes S. *Gregory,* The tongue is the fittest Instrument for the Holy Ghost to worke upon, and to worke by" (*Sermons,* 6:122). Or as Donne writes elsewhere, "it is not onely the Preacher, that hath use of the tongue, for the edification of Gods people,"

> but in all our discourses, and conferences with one another, we should preach his glory, his goodnesse, his power, that every man might speak one anothers language. . . . This is not the use of having learnt divers tongues, to be able to talk of the wars with Dutch Captains, or of trade with a French Merchant, or of State with a Spanish Agent, or of pleasure with an Italian Epicure; It is not to entertaine discourse with strangers, but to bring strangers to a better knowledge of God. (*Sermons,* 5:50–51).

And yet, what does the poet of "Satyre IV" do if not precisely "to entertaine discourse with strangers," neglecting God's teachings in the process? *"This is not the use of having learnt divers tongues,"* a maturer Donne would perhaps say of this poem: both speakers, poet and adversarius alike, subvert Pentecost, the boor (who "speakes all tongues" but "no" language) using this gift to "pay scores" and "Make men speake treason," while the poet's own speech, though in self-defense, becomes equally hypocritical.

Hearing Maecenas praised so glowingly by Horace, the boor responds,

> "You add flame to my desire to get closer to him."
> "You have only to wish it; such is your valour, you will carry the fort. He's a man who can be won, and that is why he makes the first approaches so difficult."
> "I'll not fail myself. I'll bribe his slaves."[14]

Horace dissembles encouragement here and the boor, mistaking this as a sign of intimacy, further incriminates himself. In a sense Horace's own "tongue" makes the boor "speake treason"—not that

14. "'Accendis, quare cupiam magis illi / proximus esse.' 'Velis tantummodo: quae tua virtus, / expugnabis; et est qui vinci possit, eoque / difficilis aditus primos habet.' 'Haud mihi deero: / muneribus servos corrumpam'" (Horace, *Sermo* 1.9.53–57.

that is difficult to do. But Horace shows that he, too, can play the boor's polite and deceptive game of flattery. Donne's satirist plays a similar game, feigning agreement with his adversarius and wryly praising the boor's vaunted skill in language. Not to be outdone by the boor's witty allusion to Scripture, the satirist himself evokes an appropriate biblical passage, one on language . . . and human presumption:

> Then, as if he would have sold
> His tongue, he prais'd it, and such wonders told
> That I was faine to say, "If you'had liv'd, Sir,
> Time enough to have beene Interpreter
> To Babells bricklayers, sure the Tower had stood."
> He adds, "If of court life you knew the good,
> You would leave lonenesse."
>
> (60–67)

While the boor doubtless takes the job of "Interpreter / To Babells bricklayers" as a high compliment, the existence of separate languages (and the very need for "travaile") is no less than punishment for human ambition. And because of such polyglots and proud men as he, a new "citie and a tower" has been built, not on the plains of Shirah but in England. The boor speaks of the court immediately after, adding, "If of court life you knew the good, / You would leave lonenesse" (66–67): this apposition of "Tower" and "court" makes for an almost typological identification between two monuments to human pride. And here, as Erskine-Hill suggests, Donne's satirist stresses the court's corruption through his most significant reversal of the Horatian plot.[15] As I have mentioned, Horace turns his satire into praise of the Maecenas circle, which he describes flatteringly as an ideal society of literate, egalitarian, and virtuous men; in fact, Horace's poem is in some ways less a satire on the boor than a celebration of the patron and his "court." Significantly, then, the boor in Horace's satire is an outsider scheming for entrance into an elite group. In Donne's poem the boor, rather, belongs to the "elite" social group, while the satirist is the outsider, and ironies between the two texts multiply when Donne's adversarius encourages the satirist to join freely in court life and share in its "good."

By making the boor a spokesman for the court, Donne's speaker delivers his harshest criticism of court society. And yet the satirist's retort implies an equally harsh criticism of his own satiric techniques.

15. "Courtiers out of Horace," p. 279.

> I said, "Not alone
> My lonenesse is. But Spartanes fashion,
> To teach by painting drunkards, doth not tast
> Now; Aretines pictures have made few chast;
> No more can Princes courts, though there be few
> Better pictures of vice, teach me vertue."
>   (67–72)

In the satirist's present culture, examples of virtue no longer "tast" (or "go down," as Grierson glosses the word, be swallowed or accepted as fashionable).[16] In a letter to Henry Wotton, Donne again writes of Pietro Aretino and, indirectly, of the weakness of poetic/pictorial representation. Composed around 1600, its observations become very nearly kin to the fourth satire:

> I am sory you should (with any great ernestness) desyre any thing of P. Aretinus, not that he could infect; but that it seemes you are alredy infected with the common opinion of him: beleeve me he is much lesse than his fame and was too well payd by the Roman church in that coyne which he coveted most where his bookes were by the counsell of Trent forbidden which if they had beene permitted to have beene worne by all long ere this had beene worne out. (*Selected Prose*, p. 112)

The reading (or, as Donne puts it here, the "wearing") of books has little effect. Aretino will not "infect" or lead his readers astray by bad example, but neither will his pictures make one "chast" (70). Thus the character study and exemplum, both fundamental strategies of classical satire, are denied powers to "teach . . . vertue" (72). And how can the careful reader not ask at this point: Then why write satire? Why write at all?

The poet's adoption of Horace's cool, ironic civility fails to free him from the boor's importunities. Hoping, then, to drive the boor away by irritating or "chaff[ing]" (88) him, the satirist now engages in a full-blown battle of verbal wit, a "'polite' duello," as Hester aptly terms the dialogue, in which "the weapons of the match are tongues."[17] (But is this a match the poet can win? Is it one he should even fight? Surely the poem's self-critical reflections on language invite such questions.) To the boor's enthusiastic praise of courtly conversation, "O Sir, / 'Tis sweet to talke of Kings" (73–74), the satirist finds a humorously deflating counter in the keeper of the Abbey tombs, who "for his price doth with who ever comes, / Of all our Harries, and our Edwards talke" (76–77). The boor, it seems, is

16. *Poems of John Donne*, 2:122.
17. *Kinde Pitty*, p. 151.

not the only *vendor verborum*, one who uses his tongue for profit. And yet undaunted by (or perhaps unaware of) the sarcasm, the boor picks up the subject:

> He smack'd, and cry'd, 'He's base, Mechanique, coarse,
> So'are all your Englishmen in their discourse.
> Are not your Frenchmen neate?' 'Mine? as you see,
> I'have but one Frenchman, looke, he followes mee.'
> 'Certes they'are neatly cloth'd; I,'of this minde am,
> Your only wearing is your Grogaram.'
> 'Not so Sir, I have more.'
>
> (81–87)

Asteismus, a typically Horatian figure, provides a vehicle for the poet's wit: willfully misunderstanding the boor's words and equivocating upon them, the poet takes the pronoun "your" in a personal rather than general sense. But more than evoke Horace's witty *urbanitas*, such equivocations suggest that communication has by now totally broken down between the two speakers. Given their ulterior motives, the conversation is reduced to Babel; each is unwilling, perhaps even unable, to understand the other. The metaphoric connections here between speech and dress are also suggestive, Frenchman being "neate" in their discourse while Englishmen are "coarse": language becomes once again a covering-up of motives, in the same way that clothing hides one's "naked" thoughts.

More important, the satirist's verbal tactics have failed a second time to fend off the boor: "Under this pitch / He would not flie . . . So, I (foole) founde, / Crossing hurt mee" (87–88, 90–91). Ironically, his next strategy in this verbal battle is to say nothing at all, when the boor, "To fit my sullennesse . . . to another key, his stile doth addresse" (91–92), turning to the "triviall household trash" (98) of domestic gossip. And again the satirist compares the language to food, concretizing its spiritually unsettling effect:

> He with home-meats tries me; I belch, spue, spit,
> Looke pale, and sickly, like a Patient; Yet
> He thrusts me more . . .
> Like a bigge wife, at sight of loathed meat,
> Readie to travaile: so I sigh, and sweat
> To heare this Makeron talk: In vaine; for yet,
> Either my humour, or his owne to fit,
> He like a priviledg'd spie, whom nothing can
> Discredit, Libells now 'gainst each great man.
>
> (109–11, 115–20)

Already weakened, the satirist is unable to stomach this verbal meal or medicine.[18] And to emphasize his passivity to the boor's "thrust-[ings]," he likens himself to a pregnant wife in childbirth. The pun on "loathed meat" as both food and penis to an already burdened woman comments on the satirist's passive state as well as the boor's gossip—which is otherwise a nauseating surfeit to a person already overburdened, as it were, by a "full belly." Indeed, it is an attempt at verbal rape. In either case, one is struck by the barrenness and futility of the boor's words.

Yet up to this point the boor has been little more than a discomfort; only when he begins to libel "'gainst each great man" (120) and invite the satirist, at his peril, to "speake treason" does he raise a genuine fear. For "the effect of speech upon the condition of the soul," as Gorgias declares, is like "the power of drugs over the nature of bodies. . . . just as different drugs dispel different secretions from the body, and some bring an end to disease and others to life, so also in the case of speeches, some distress, others delight, some cause fear, others make the hearers bold, and some drug and bewitch the soul with a kind of evil persuasion."[19] Similarly the satirist, now "more amas'd than Circes prisoners" (129), finds himself drugged and bewitched, held spell-bound by a Circe whose "drugtongue" has begun to turn him into a "Traytor,"

> and mee thought I saw
> One of our Giant Statutes ope his jaw
> To sucke me in; for hearing him, I found
> That as burnt venom'd Leachers doe grow sound
> By giving others their soares, I might growe
> Guilty, and he free: Therefore I did shew
> All signes of loathing; But since I am in,
> I must pay mine, and my forefathers sinne
> To the last farthing; Therefore to my power
> Toughly'and stubbornly'I bear this crosse.
> (131–40)

18. Horace, we have seen, exaggerates his reaction to the boor's onslaught: "Dreadfully eager to get away I now walk fast, at times stop short, then whisper a word in my slave's ear, while the sweat trickled down to my very ankles" ("misere discedere quaerens / ire modo ocius, interdum consistere, in aurem / dicere nescio quid puero, cum sudor ad imos / maneret talos" [*Sermo* 1.9.8–11]). The restlessness of Donne's speaker, his "sigh[ing]" and "sweat[ing]" similarly exaggerate his reactions, to which he adds images of vomiting or violent physical rejection.
19. "Encomium of Helen," p. 53.

As diseases of the flesh infect otherwise healthy bodies, so the boor's language threatens here to infect the poet's with the diseases of hypocrisy and, more dire, of treason. And with his own words infected, it is the language of law that now threatens the satirist, a danger expressed in the oral imagery of the statute opening its "jaw / To sucke" the satirist into itself. Before he had only to "swallow" the boor's importunities; now he himself (a tasty morsel, as the boor's favorite description for him is "sweet") may be swallowed up and destroyed by complicity in the words of a court spy. And for what cause would the satirist be found "Traytor" and "growe / Guilty"? What, we might ask, is his own and his "forefathers sinne" if not recusancy, a sin of private conscience for which the court has become his purgatory? Though "Crossing" (91) hurt him earlier, the poet must now bear his own "crosse," typologically asserting the poet's share in Christ's own suffering. By now fully defeated in this verbal crossing or duel, he chooses for his own imperiled safety to say nothing.

This one-sided conversation comes to an abrupt end when the boor borrows money (as in Horace, only the boor's own penury saves the satirist). And for the last time, the poet is coaxed into conversation, though his answer, not surprisingly, mistakes the boor's words: " 'Sir, can you spare me?' I said, 'Willingly.' / Nay, Sir, can you spare me'a crowne?' Thankfully I / Gave it, as Ransome" (143–45). The satirist must now endure the boor's "long complemen-tall thankes" (148), after which his adversarius departs, richer by a crown. The more serious implications surface through the wit and equivocation: "polite" conversation merely disguises the bad faith of the speakers, and compliment has become the abuse of meaning and motive in language. At this point, though, Donne "takes his leave of Horace."[20] Actually, Donne has followed Horace's satire (a relatively slight piece of some seventy-eight hexameter lines) to its conclusion, while his own satire has just reached midpoint. And the verbal strategies have changed, turning the poem's second half into an implicit commentary on both the preceding dialogue and the classical model. To be sure, such vignettes as Macrine (197–218) and Glorius (219–28) continue to enliven the monologue. The satirist's verbal strategies have nonetheless changed. In imitation of Horace, the satirist was at first personally involved in the action and dialogue; now, with a cry of *vanitas vanitatis*, he distances himself from the court and its vices. In addition he broadens his ethical

20. Erskine-Hill, "Courtiers out of Horace," p. 288.

discussion to embrace the entire court, not just the actions of an individual. And above all, he chooses now to "mourne" rather than ridicule the "wretchednesse / Of suiters at court":

> At home in wholesome solitarinesse
> My precious soule began, the wretchednesse
> Of suiters at court to mourne, and a trance
> Like his, who dreamt he saw hell, did advance
> It selfe on mee; Such men as he saw there,
> I saw at court, and worse, and more; Low feare
> Becomes the guiltie, not th'accuser; Then,
> Shall I, nones slave, of high borne, or rais'd men
> Fear frownes? And my Mistresse Truth, betray thee
> To th'huffing braggart, puft Nobility?
>   . . . hast thou seene,
> O Sunne, in all thy journey, Vanitie,
> Such as swells the bladder of our court?
>
>   (155–68)

No longer does the poet implicate himself in guilt. "Lowe feare," he claims, "Becomes the guiltie, not th'accuser," and by assuming the role of accuser he asserts his own righteousness and moral superiority, at the same time rejecting "the satirical stance of Horace as an inadequate response to the resolute immorality and devious maliciousness of the court."[21] In fact the dream vision announces a new set of models; no longer of pagan Rome, the poet turns to the native homiletic tradition of Christian complaint, exemplified by *Piers Plowman*.

In the poet's homily, London's "waxen garden" (169) becomes a symbol of the city's love for artifice and decadence: "Just such gay painted things, which no sappe, nor / Tast have in them, ours are" (172–73). Such courtly products have neither "sappe" (that is, authenticity) nor "Tast"—in other words, no truth, which becomes the final meaning of this much-used term. Observing the "scarlet gownes" (192) bought and worn by women as well as the "wits" (193) men buy from others to "wear" as their own words, the poet again compares courtly language to ostentatious dress: each becomes a commodity (an object to be bought and sold at profit) and a covering (a means of deception and superficial self-display). The "mortall / Great staines" on the clothes of Macrine, stains that he "call[s] to shrift" (200–202) in a mockery of confession, thus turn physical appearance into dark spiritual commentary. Similarly, the

---

21. Hester, *Kinde Pitty*, p. 130.

facial expression of Glorius is "as ill / As theirs which in old hangings whip Christ, yet still / He strives to looke worse" (225–27). Indeed, the poet observes a set of these "old hangings" at court, "the great chamber" being "hung / With the seaven deadly sinnes" (231–32)—in a sense, its own self-portrait. Again, the repudiation of dialogue for direct statement, the criticism of a whole group or class, and the tendency toward homily and more abstract discussion of vices all suggest the influence of Christian complaint. But while Piers is a likely English model, the poet himself alludes to Dante, for "a trance / Like his, who dreamt he saw hell, did advance / It selfe on mee; Such men as he saw there, / I saw at court, and worse, and more" (157–60). The reference to the *Divina Commedia* is subtly ironic, however: in the poem's first half, the satirist recounts his visit to "Purgatorie" (3), while in the second half, in his dreamstate, he travels to "hell" (158). The poet's own spiritual progress leads him, then, to a vision of hell-on-earth, and yet no beatific vision follows, no *paradiso*, no promise of redemption. And Donne's speaker, unlike Dante's, has no sure guide through his hell, only a court spy to lead him on to treason. Beyond the anti-apocalyptic ending of Pope's *Dunciad*, few satires in English achieve so desperate a climax.

Which leads us to ask: Given this shift in models, what authority, what powers of reform might the poet now claim? In contrast to Thomas Wilson's optimistic joining of the orator and preacher, an author like Andreas Hyperius speaks only of their divorce, claiming authority and the right of speech for the preacher who alone "chargeth, commaundeth, sharply rebuketh, threateneth, pronounceth, as one in place of authoritie, and as a Judge," while "the Rhetoritian," in contrast, "supposeth none of these things to bee lawfull unto him, but rather he is compelled nowe and then sowly to flatter and fawne upon the Judges."[22] Only the preacher or prophet can claim the power justly to "rebuke"; the rhetorician (like the satirist, it seems) can effect change only by "flatter[ing]" those actually in power—"Judges" in the passage above, Egerton, we shall find, in "Satyre IV." For "it is not a timorous prophecy" that claims authority, as an older Donne writes in a sermon on Micah; such discourse, rather, is "principally bent upon rulers and Magistrates, and great persons," such that "no Man [can] say, we need not heed him, for

22. Andreas Hyperius, *The Practice of Preaching, Otherwise Called the Pathway to the Pulpet* (1577), trans. John Ludham, folio 42v; quoted in Anselment, *"Betwixt Jest and Earnest,"* p. 175.

he is an upstart, a singular person, and all these his threatenings are rather *Satyricall,* then *Propheticall,* or *Theologicall"* (*Sermons,* 5:192). Here Donne explicitly separates preaching from the satirist's "threatenings," at the same time questioning the latter's *ethos* and intentions. Donne the poet makes a similar assertion, concluding that preachers, not satirists, are the only effective reformers:

> Preachers which are
> Seas of Wit and Arts, you can, then dare,
> Drowne the sinnes of this place, for, for mee
> Which am but a scarse brooke, it enough shall bee
> To washe the staines away; though I yet
> With *Macchabees* modestie, the knowne merit
> Of my worke lessen: yet some wise man shall,
> I hope, esteeme my writs Canonicall.
>
> (237–44)

The poet finds it task enough "to wash the staines away," to find his own path of penance and spiritual renewal, cleansing his own soul of the effects of this court visit. And thus the speaker implicitly raises the question, can Horatian satire ever be "Canonicall"? Can the contemporary satirist ever claim to write an authoritative text, one capable of asserting its own "waight and value" and of affirming the Christian virtues (particularly that of charity)? The answer "Satyre IV" provides, with its abrupt and deliberate shift from classical to Christian models of moral suasion, is no.

Surprisingly perhaps, the Horatian model offers little authority and small moral weight to the satirist writing in Renaissance culture. "In Greece or Rome," writes Pierre de Larivey, "the people used different languages, different dress, different laws and, most important, a religion completely opposite to our own."[23] Thus he exemplifies the age's growing awareness of cultural difference, particularly in religious belief, a difference that renders imitation of any classical model problematic. Similarly, when Erasmus's spokesman in the *Ciceronianus,* Bulephorus, surveys the distance between Christian Renaissance culture and classical antiquity he, too, could see only change, rupture, discontinuity: "Wherever I turn I see everything changed, I stand on another stage, I see another theater, yes,

---

23. "En Grece ou Rome on usoit d'un autre langage, d'autre façon de vivre, d'autres coustumes, d'autres loix, et—ce qui importe le plus—d'une religion toute contraire à la nostre Chrestienne et Catholique." Pierre de Larivey, Prologue to *La Constance* (1611), in Weinberg, *Critical Prefaces of the French Renaissance,* p. 277.

another world."[24] The Roman Horace does not provide a timeless model for moral reform: the historical and cultural and religious discontinuity between the *Sermones* and the Renaissance poem was too great to be naively laid aside. But only Donne—at least among Elizabethan satirists—seems fully aware of the implications of this cultural gap, aware that imitation proceeds through a kairotic, critical revision as well as decorous recreation of the classical model. By making Christian values the subject of his imitation Donne exploits this discontinuity, casting into doubt the efficacy of his pagan model and revealing its lack of authority in this new cultural setting.

And "Satyre IV," I would add, is less a critical revision than a repudiation of the classical form itself. For while *genera mista* inform many Renaissance poems, certainly many of Donne's, the satirist raises a real question here as to whether this particular classical genre can incorporate the traditions of Christian homily and complaint without becoming, to use the currently fashionable phrase, a self-consuming artifact. In his influential study of the native English tradition of complaint, John Peter emphasizes the tensions between the techniques and values of classical satire and "the Christian principle of sufferance and restraint."[25] As soon as the Elizabethans began imitating classical models, "the dilemma of Jerome was back to trouble the satirist, and once again he had to wrestle with the essential contradiction that arose when a Christian was found writing as only a pagan should have done."[26] And yet an argument like Peter's rests on the assumption that, among the Elizabethan satirists, "a temporary dependence upon the classical norms of satire displaces Christian ethics."[27] The tensions between classical and Christian elements of Elizabethan satire are unquestionable; that the classical ever fully displace the Christian norms remains doubtful, though, particularly in Donne's case. Indeed, the fact that Chris-

---

24. Desiderius Erasmus, *Ciceronianus: Or a Dialogue on the Best Style of Speaking* (1528), p. 62. As Thomas Greene writes of this dialogue, the awareness of cultural discontinuity highlights "the comedy, if not the moral shame, of classicizing in a Christian society" (*Light in Troy*, p. 182).

25. *Complaint and Satire in Early English Literature*, p. 20.

26. Ibid., p. 156. The letters of St. Jerome are Peter's model for exploring the problem of Christian satire. To Peter, the shifting in these letters between attack and apology illustrates "the immiscibility of Satura and Christianity" (p. 22). The Elizabethan satirists faced the same difficulty: "There were so many differences between the two modes, and so many downright incompatibilities, that they continued to be quite as imiscible as they had ever been in the writings of Jerome" (p. 121).

27. Anselment, *"Betwixt Jest and Earnest,"* p. 163.

tian values are never absent makes his *Satyres* problematic as classical imitations. Donne does not naively blend medieval with classical elements, as Thomas Lodge and Joseph Hall do, but rather resorts to complaint as a conscious alternative to Roman satire. Far from a classical, Horatian attitude, to "mourne" (157) the spiritual state of courtiers is to repudiate the sportful but thin and ultimately unsustainable humor of the poem's own first half. As "Satyre IV" suggests, the Christian must find in his own cultural tradition the techniques and attitudes that will not subvert charity (though they will, of necessity, repudiate the classical methods of ridicule and *ad hominem* attack). In composing "Satyre IV," Donne criticizes the classical model from which his own derives; as a result, the poem becomes equally self-critical, denying the premises of its own composition and asserting only skepticism toward the efficacy of its genre.

□   □   □

This analysis could end here were it simply a matter of asserting one model over another, as if the poet could claim or fashion his own authority by rejecting pagan satire for Christian homily. But even this remains problematic, since the poet remains skeptical of his own powers. "With *Macchabees* modestie" the satirist claims to "lessen" the "knowne merit / Of [his] worke" (242–43), thus repudiating Horace's modesty for a biblical model. But even with this change in model, and even with his concluding flattery of Egerton, of "some wise man" among the many at court who could grant authority to the speaker, the satirist still leaves the efficacy of his words in doubt: he has only the "hope" that someone will "esteeme [his] writs Canonicall." And in having to ask or hope that his satire be granted such authority he again admits its immediate powerlessness. Like the biblical prophet's, the satirist's words must be "proven" (that is, tested and enacted) at some future time, and someone else must "speak" or read them. Since the effect of this satire is thus made contingent upon its reception by a specific audience, the poet must turn outside of himself—pass the baton, as it were—to "preachers" or "some wise man" like Egerton, who holds power at court and could enact the changes the satirist himself is incapable of effecting. But until this wise man steps forward there is no one to grant the poem moral authority or the poet temporal power to initiate reform. And is it reform such preachers would achieve? They are to "Drowne the sinnes of this place" (239): a deluge of accusation and rebuke, their words shall lead not to reform but to punishment, in the manner of the biblical flood.

Finally, the Christian satirist may assume the zeal of Old Testament prophets, but why, we might ask, does the poet identify himself with Maccabees, whose "worke" is *denied* authority by Protestants (though Catholics deem it "Canonicall")? The very choice emphasizes that the authority, and therefore the efficacy, of his satire remains in doubt. And if the tensions between classical and Christian values appear unresolvable in this satire, the tensions between Protestant and Catholic seem impossibly so; in fact the second half of the poem, like the first, becomes a tissue of allusion to the Reformation controversy. Macrine, for instance, "arrests" a lady whom he attempts to love,

> And unto her protests protests protests
> So much as at Rome would serve to have throwne
> Ten Cardinalls into th'Inquisition;
> And whisperd 'by Jesu', so'often, that a
> Pursevant would have ravish'd him away
> For saying of our Ladies psalter.
>
> (212–17)

The very vocabulary of traditional Catholicism comes automatically under suspicion, as if the words themselves fall guilty of misdevotion. And yet "it is a miserable impotency," an older Donne writes, "to be afraid of *words;* That from a former holy and just determination of reall errors,"

> we should come to an uncharitable detestation of *persons,* and to a contentious detestation of *words.* We dare not name *Merit,* nor *Penance,* nor *Sacrifice,* nor *Altar,* because they have been abused. How should we be disappointed, and disfurnished of many words in our ordinary conversation, if we should be bound from all words, which blasphemous men have prophaned, or uncleane men have defiled with their ill use . . . ? (*Sermons,* 7:429)

Observe, nonetheless, how both theologies would condemn Macrine's language: his "protests" (thrice-repeated, suggesting the ease if not the idleness of "protesting"—of Protestantism?) endanger his life before the Catholic Inquisition, while his repetitions of "Jesu" implicate him in the litanies of Catholicism, whose liturgical excesses were forbidden by English law. In addition, Erskine-Hill notes an early manuscript variant of line 216: "Topcliff would have ravish'd him away / For saying our Ladies psalter." Richard Topcliff, he adds, was "the notorious priest-hunter, whose chief colleague had been responsible for the arrest of Henry Donne and his priest."[28]

28. "Courtiers out of Horace," p. 283.

Is it at all surprising that Donne should inveigh against the man responsible for his Catholic brother's death? In a later revision, it seems that Donne moderated his polemic, substituting "Pursevant" for "Topcliff." This, by the way, would not be the only instance where the pro-Catholic rhetoric is eventually softened: Grierson notes, for example, that the "Surius" criticized in line 48 is "Sleydan" in early manuscripts, Sleydan being a Protestant historian, Surius Catholic.[29] Thus the text itself falls prey to both theological controversy and political expediency; within the poem's own fiction, Glaze and Macrine both demonstrate the danger. And the poet himself, though in a trance, leaves the chamber shaking like a "spyed Spie" (237)—like a Jesuit whose disguise has been penetrated. Once again the Catholicism alienates and imperils the poet. Who, therefore, is the "spy" at court? The adversarius, or the satirist himself? Significantly, the term is used of both. Given the laws against his religion, the Catholic must himself resort to disguise and deception, in a word, to "spying," when at court; his dominant emotions, like the poet's here, are inevitably fear and mistrust.

How shall the reader react to a satirist who denies his satire authority? As the first part of "Satyre IV" demonstrates, court society demands that visitors and would-be courtiers play its games and assume its values, thus becoming part of the viciousness his satire criticizes. And even if the speaker maintains his own beliefs and values he must nonetheless hide them, for it is the satirist himself who will be punished in a world in which his Catholicism, his conservatism in dress and behavior, and his hatred of pretension, deception, and injustice run so strongly against the stream of contemporary court policies and practices. For his own safety the satirist must resort to deliberate obfuscation and indirection in his speech, actions that again leave him open to charges of hypocrisy, the same charges he makes against the court. Ronald Corthell rightly notes that Donne's *Satyres* "address directly the problem of relations between the self and religious and political authority" and that they are "informed by Donne's perception of the public consequences of a private religious commitment."[30] Let me add that Donne has failed to find in his Horatian model the literary authority that would grant his words a corresponding religious and political authority.

29. "It is quite possible," Grierson writes, "that Donne's first sneer was at the Protestant historian and that he thought it safer later to substitute the Catholic Surius" (*Poems of John Donne,* 2:120).
30. "Style and Self," p. 156.

The consequences of this "private religious commitment" therefore extend beyond his public image or self-fashioning to affect the poet's relationship with his literary genre, his classical model, and his linguistic medium—as well as with political authority.

We are left, finally, to consider Donne's third satire and its relation to the third Roman satirist, Persius. Whether this new poem finds or fashions an adequate rhetoric of reform, and whether the problem of satire remains a problem of faith, are subjects we shall continue to explore.

4

The Reformation, and Retraction, of Satire

As Thomas O. Sloane observes, "by an act of supremacy Elizabeth had been given the same authority over the church as was assumed by her father."

> Like her father, she recognized the political advantage of this authority and sought to strengthen it by enforcing allegiance to the English Church throughout her realm, regarding all recusants as potential traitors, refusing university degrees to young students (Donne among them) who would not swear allegiance to the Queen's supreme ecclesiastical authority, punishing Romanists (like Donne's younger brother, who died of "gaol fever") and Puritans who refused to submit. . . .
>
> "Laws" were the weapons the Anglicans used against Catholics and Puritans as the nineties began. In 1593 "The Act Against Popish Recusants" considerably increased the efficiency of the surveillance and punishment of those Catholics who steadfastly refused to attend Protestant services. In the same year, Anglican defense of the English Church began reaching a culmination with the publication of the first four books of Hooker's *Laws of Ecclesiastical Polity,* followed in 1597 by publication of the fifth book.
>
> . . . It is in this scene—soon after 1593—a scene of religious and political turmoil controlled into tense order by the magnificent though tyrannical Queen through "lawes / Still new like fashions," that the speaker of *Satyre III* delivers his exhortations to young men close to the Queen.[1]

But what, we might ask, is the nature of these "exhortations"? "To my satyrs there belongs some feare," Donne writes to Henry Wotton (*Selected Prose,* p. 111), and among other readers, Hester notes the political dangers risked in the fourth satire.[2] Yet it is to the third satire, with its outright rejection of Royal Supremacy, that such "feare" might especially belong. Corthell describes the argument

1. "The Persona as Rhetor: An Interpretation of Donne's *Satyre III,* " pp. 23–24.
2. *Kinde Pitty,* p. 73.

underlying "Satyre III," the poet's dilemma being "his proper relation to power, not his commitment to religious truth."[3] True enough.
Though it exhorts readers to "Seeke true religion" (43), devoting
some of its most memorable imagery to the search, the poem is
hardly a guide for such a quest; one learns little more than the ardor
of the journey. But even as the poem exhorts readers to seek religion
it inveighs against the political enforcement of conscience—and by
arguing, however obliquely, for religious tolerance, "Satyre III"
comes close to an act of treason. Our task, then, is to explore the
ways the poet's politically subversive intentions test and strain the
resources of his classical, specifically Persian model.

Such a reading, I believe, should help resolve questions of genre
that critics recently have raised. Clearly "Satyre III" avoids both the
raging, Juvenalian invective and the self-deprecating humor of
Horace; in what sense, then, many of its better readers ask, can it
even be called a formal satire? Nancy Andreason terms it "a solilo-
quy conducted in meditative isolation" and a number of critics,
Hester most notably, suggest the direct influence of meditative techniques on the structure and argument.[4] To describe the poet's thoroughly public, thoroughly political intentions—as Sloane and Corthell do—surely denies the role of meditation, and yet neither critic
resolves the problem of genre. By terming it a deliberative oration
explicitly addressed "to young men close to the Queen," Sloane
assumes a sympathetic relationship between the poet and his contemporary audience, when it is the nature of this relationship that is
precisely at issue: How can the poet write of religious tolerance
without implicating himself and the readers he seeks to persuade?
Political exigencies render his actual aim and subject literally unspeakable. Incapable of announcing what it wishes to persuade, the
poem becomes an essay, rather, in skepticism and negative argument. Similarly the poet's "status as a railer," which Corthell emphasizes, becomes precisely what the poem itself questions: "Can
railing," the poet asks, "cure these worn maladies" (4)? Why should
the speaker question the efficacy of "railing" if not to turn the poem
into a test of its own adequacy as satire?

Readers often describe "Satyre III" as the most forceful and most

3. "Style and Self," p. 181.
4. Andreason, "Theme and Structure," p. 69. Arguing for the poem's "union
of private and public discourse, its concomitant meditative and satirical stance"
(*Kinde Pitty*, p. 71), Hester compares the structure of "Satyre III" to the stages of
devotion outlined in Johan Gansfort's *scala meditatoria*, which Joseph Hall translates in his *Arte of Divine Meditation*.

confident of the collection. Yet its opening lines, asserting only the problem of discovering an efficacious rhetoric, reveal the poet's continued anxiety over the form and function of satire:

> Kinde Pitty chokes my spleene; brave scorn forbids
> Those teares to issue which swell my eye-lids;
> I must not laugh, nor weepe sinnes, and be wise,
> Can railing then cure these worne maladies?
>
> (1–4)

In contrast to Hall's or Marston's confident programmatic assertions of the power of their literary form, we note the very tentativeness of such language. The satirist begins by denying the splenetic outbursts of hate and "just offence" (40) that characterize the Juvenalian persona of "Satyre II." Pity now "chokes" his spleen. At the same time he "must not laugh" at sin in the manner of Horace, the ostensive model of "Satyre I" and "Satyre IV." Either attitude, though conventionally associated with the classical satirists, would conflict with his "kindness," "bravery," or "wisdom," so it is not surprising that his first question ("Can railing . . . cure these worne maladies?") is left unanswered.[5] The reference to "cure" may nonetheless surprise. For the first time in the collection, Donne's speaker suggests even the possibility of reform through this literary genre, a suggestion that gains greater significance when one recalls the cynicism that ends "Satyre I" and the sense of pessimism, in fact the admission of futility, that ends "Satyre II." In its search for an efficacious rhetoric of reform, "Satyre III" distinguishes itself from other of Donne's satires; whether it succeeds in this search remains our present focus.

Like Sloane, I read "Satyre III" as a poem stressing persuasion over meditative self-reflection, one in which the poet speaks as "rhetor." But he is, I would add, no less a satirist for seeking to persuade and for obscuring his politically dangerous persuasions behind a cloak of difficult, allusive language and a thoroughgoing

5. And if by "railing" the satirist means a Juvenalian invective, the reader of "Satyre III" would have even greater reason to doubt the likelihood of serious "cure" or reform. Norman Knox observes the two contemporary meanings of the term "railing," the first referring "simply to the act of verbal attack or criticism, without limits as to the method employed," and the second referring "specifically to angry invective." In either case, "the connotation of the word was highly unfavorable. . . . People who liked the witty invective of, say, a particular satirist usually preferred not to call it railing; people who did not used the word as a device of adverse criticism" (*The Word Irony and Its Context, 1500–1755*, pp. 190–91).

skepticism. Abandoning Juvenal's *saeva indignatio* and Horace's *sermo* style, Donne adopts the protreptic zeal and the obscure, abstruse, extravagant diatribe style of Persius, whom he turns into a vehicle for contemporary religious and political argument. We might note, finally, that most readings of the poem downplay or moderate its assertions of systematic doubt.[6] But while "Satyre II" and "IV" introduce themes of linguistic skepticism, "Satyre III" goes beyond their critique of language to cast a Pyrrhonist's doubt upon human reason itself. Given its historical connections with the arguments of Catholic fideism, the skepticism should for once be given full reign in interpretation. It is a skepticism that does not fear the difficulty (if not impossibility) of making a certain, secure choice of religion so much as it criticizes those motives that make choice—any choice— indefensible: apathy, acquiescence, and above all fear of the political force that seeks to impose its ideologies upon free conscience. Thus Donne, we shall find, turns Persian diatribe into an expression of Catholic-Pyrrhonist skepticism even as he turns the model's penchant for obscurity into a deliberate strategy of masking and indirection, a politically expedient stratagem of verbal self-defense.

Again, Renaissance theory stresses literature's simultaneously social and rhetorical function: the poet assumes the classical rhetor's *officia* or duties that, in the Ciceronian formula, are to teach and persuade as well as delight. To the Renaissance poet, however, classical satire seems to illustrate only the problematic relationship between morality and aesthetics—particularly between Christian morality and a classical aesthetics based on blame, name-calling, and licentious language. Is it enough for the new poet to imitate or faithfully re-create the classical model? Is an experiment in voice and style sufficient cause for writing? Must the satirist's words aim, rather, at reform? And how, if at all, can his words reform morality while conforming aesthetically to the pagan models? Far from curing sin, the classical satirist (and, by extension, his Renaissance imitator) may well commit sin in the act of writing, driving "offenders to greater delinquency," as Bartolommeo Ricci warns,[7] or abandoning morality altogether to indulge hybristically in stylistic display. Of the Roman satirists, only the stoic Persius consistently conforms to a Christian ethic. "The Divine Jerome names him the most learned

6. Thomas V. Moore proves a notable exception. See his article "Donne's Use of Uncertainty as a Vital Force in *Satyre III.*"

7. "Magis ad gravius delinquendum ac etiam ad desperationem reum impellat" (*De Imitatione,* 1:447). The reader might refer to an earlier discussion of Ricci in Chapter 2 above.

satirist," Pietro Crinito observes, "and deservedly so, for he is surpassed by no one in the sanctity of his writing, the gravity of his
sententiae, the dignity of his words, and satiric wit."[8] Joachim Vadian
agrees: "among teachers of morals he is surpassed by no one in
gravity and elegance, and he, most of all, is in accord both with the
truth and with our religion."[9] Since Persius is a pagan author, such
praise may initially surprise. Yet "Saint *Paul*," as Donne himself
notes, "cites sometimes the word of *secular Poets*, and approves
them; and then the words of those Poets, become the word of *God*"
(*Sermons*, 4:163). Persius, we might add, was one such poet, a classical satirist to whom the Church Fathers, Augustine and Jerome especially, turn time and again for quotations and illustrative argument.

In the preface to his famous edition of Persius (1605), Isaac Casaubon describes him as "unswerving in his devotion to virtue, a
steadfast and constant enemy of vice, always consistent," one who
"enriched poetry by means of graver arts" and "never forgot his
Stoic profession."[10] Demonstrating this commitment to virtue, his

8. "A divo Hieronymo dissertissimus nuncupatur: nec immerito: nam et
sanctitate scribendi, et sententiarum gravitate, et verborum pondere, et sat-
yrica urbanitate nulli postponendus esse videtur" (*A. Persii Flacci Satyrae Sex*,
fol. H7r). In *Auli Flacci Persii Poetae Satirarum Opus*, Bartolommeo della Fonte
offers similar praise: "Verum enimvero siquis ex omni numero poetarum: qui
hoc sancte integreque praestaret legendus esset: quem Persio praeferemus:
non haberemus" (fol. Ar).

9. "Id ausim de Persio dicere: salubrium eum praeceptorum gravitate et con-
cinnitate a nullo superari, et cum veritati tum religioni nostrae cum primis esse
consonum" (*De Poetica et Carminis Ratione*, p. 263). Vadian adds that Persius's
moral seriousness more than compensates for the difficulty of his verse: "Carminis enim elegantia quanquam est magnus, Horatio tamen et Juvenali collatus
indubie inferior existit. Hujus me lectio plurimum oblectat, non quidem quod
adeo suavis, sed quod tam fidelis est et gravis" (p. 264).

10. Translated by Peter Medine, "Isaac Casaubon's *Prolegomena* to the *Satires*
of Persius: An Introduction, Text, and Translation," p. 290. In contrast Horace,
as Casaubon writes, "was too inconsistent, nor did he act as a sure teacher of
virtue. . . . Often [Horace] may speak as a Stoic, often as an Epicurean or an
Aristippean. . . . Just as frequently he derided and bitterly ridiculed the Stoics,
in the possession of whom alone in that age was the teaching of wisdom." He
adds that "we know nothing of the morality of Juvenal. In his satires he touched
on 'philosophical matters' in such a way that appears certain that he labored for
a longer time with the rhetor than the philosopher" (p. 289). Thus he disparages
the other two Romans. Fonte also alludes to Persius's protreptic or persuasive
zeal, as does Giovanni Britannico, who describes its stoic, Senecan origins: "ex
praecepto Senecae monet, consolatur, et protrepticus est" (cited in ibid.,
p. 274).

third satire delivers a diatribe against moral sloth, specifically against a young friend's (perhaps a student's) neglect of stoic doctrine. Though he has been taught the ways of virtue, the youth's lethargy and "whining evasions" are particular instances of the poem's general proposition: apathy perpetuates moral weakness. Virtue, however, can be maintained only by continuous study and struggle, symbolized by the "steep path" that Pythagoras inscribes in the Greek letter Upsilon: "But you have learnt how to distinguish the crooked from the straight; you have studied the doctrines of the learned Porch . . . and the letter which spreads out into Pythagorean branches has pointed out to you the steep path which rises on the right. And are you snoring still? . . . Have you any goal in life? Is there any target at which you aim?"[11] Both Isidore of Seville and Jerome Christianize this "emblem of human life, whose right path, though steep, yet tends toward a blessed life, while the left path, though easier, leads to ruin and death."[12] In a sermon Donne himself elaborates on "that Proverbial, that Hieroglyphical Letter, *Pythagoras* his Y: that hath first a stalk, a stem to fix itself, and then spreads into two Beams . . . one broader, but on the left hand, denoting the Treasures of this World; the other narrower, but on the right hand, Treasure laid up for the World to come. Be sure ye turn the right way: for, *where your Treasure is, there will your Heart be* also" (*Sermons*, 9:174).

In similarly homiletic fashion, Persius looks beyond this youthful friend to address his larger reading audience, exhorting them to "Come and learn, O miserable souls, and be instructed in the causes of things: learn what we are, and for what sort of lives we were born . . . what part God has ordered you to play, and at what point of the human commonwealth you have been stationed."[13] The stylistic

11. "Haut tibi inexpertum curvos deprendere mores, / quaeque docet sapiens bracatis inlita Medis / porticus . . . / et tibi, quae Samios diduxit littera ramos, / surgentem dextro monstravit limite callem; / stertis adhuc? . . . / est aliquid quo tendis, et in quod derigis arcum?" (Persius, *Satire*, 3:52–60).

12. "Y litteram Samius ad exemplum vitae humanae primus formavit . . . cuius dextra pars ardua est, sed ad beatam vitam tendens; sinistra facilior, sed ad labem interitumque deducens. De qua sic Persius ait [et cit. *Sat*. 3.56]" (Isidore, Bp. of Seville, *Isidori Hispalensis Episcopi Etymologiarum sive Originum Libri XX*, 1.3.7). G. G. Ramsay notes that the letter was originally written with a sloping left and straight right stem (*Juvenal and Persius*, p. 349), thus yielding the two paths—one steep and difficult of access, the other easier (though "primrose," as it were).

13. "Discite et, o miseri, causas cognoscite rerum: / quid sumus et quidnam victuri gignimur . . . quem te deus esse / iussit et humana qua parte locatus es in re" (*Satire*, 3:66–72).

techniques again derive largely from the stoic-cynic diatribe, the polemical method of the popular moralists of Greek antiquity.[14] Its typical figures of language and argument (which Persius himself uses in his third satire) include paradox, hyperbole, and catachresis; *prosopopoeia* and an impassioned, second-person address; rhetorical questions and such schemes as *subjectio* and *ante occupatio;* and, above all, monologistic dialogue, with its abrupt transitions in both speaker and argument. Such figures recur in Donne's own third satire and help establish its stylistic decorum: Persius's third satire, I would argue, provides the stylistic and structural model of Donne's own satire on the politics of religious choice.[15] Like Persius, Donne's speaker exhorts his audience to quit its apathy and question its adherence to any dogma not sanctioned by the individual conscience. In so doing he turns to a favorite device of the diatribist, *percontatio* or a series of rhetorical questions:

> Is not our Mistresse faire Religion,
> As worthy'of all our Soules devotion,
> As vertue was to the first blinded age?
> Are not heavens joyes as valiant to asswage
> Lusts, as earths honour was to them? Alas,
> As wee do them in meanes, shall they surpasse
> Us in the end, and shall thy fathers spirit
> Meete blinde Philosophers in heaven, whose merit
> Of strict life may be'imputed faith, and heare
> Thee, whom he taught so easie ways and neare
> To follow, damn'd? O if thou dars't, feare this;
> This feare great courage, and high valour is.
> Dar'st thou ayd mutinous Dutch, and dars't thou lay
> Thee in ships woodden Sepulchers, a prey
> To leaders rage, to stormes, to shot, to dearth?
> Dars't thou dive seas, and dungeons of the earth?
> (5–20)

14. The seminal text on Persius's use of the diatribe style is François Villeneuve, *Essai sur Perse,* pp. 119–40, though see also Charles Witke, *Latin Satire: The Structure of Persuasion,* pp. 110–11; Edwin S. Ramage, David R. Sigsbee, and Sigmund C. Fredericks, *Roman Satirists and Their Satire: The Fine Art of Criticism in Ancient Rome,* pp. 118–19, 121–25; and Michael Coffey, *Roman Satire,* pp. 100–103.

15. Decades ago, George Williamson traced Donne's penchant for "strong lines" and the development of his later, "metaphysical" style to an early poetic apprenticeship under this Roman (*The Donne Tradition: A Study in English Poetry from Donne to the Death of Cowley,* p. 43). In Persius, it seems, Donne discovers the Silver Latin stylist with greatest affinity to his own maturing craftsmanship.

"We do ask because we would chide, and set forth our grief with the more vehemency."[16] Thus Thomas Wilson describes *percontatio*, and the above passage—like Persius's address to his slothful friend—asks just such "chiding" questions, seeking to intensify the reader's emotional involvement. Similarly, the shifts from pronouns "I" and "my" (1–3) to "we" and "our" (or, more often still, to "thou" and "thy") are a common feature of diatribe, occurring throughout Persius's third satire; such second-person address announces the poet's public, deliberative aims.

The imperatives also heighten the sense of urgency: "feare this" (15), "Know thy foes" (33), "aske thy father" (71), "Be busie to seeke her" (74), "doubt wisely" (77), "keepe the truth which thou'hast found" (89), and, most famously, "Seeke true religion" (43). Yet Donne's satirist, almost in defiance of this last exhortation, asks "O where?"

> Mirreus
> Thinking her unhous'd here, and fled from us,
> Seekes her at Rome, there, because hee doth know
> That shee was there a thousand yeares agoe,
> He loves her ragges so, as wee here obey
> The statecloth where the Prince sate yesterday.
> Crants to such brave Loves will not be inthrall'd,
> But loves her onely, who'at Geneva'is call'd
> Religion, plaine, simple, sullen, yong,
> Contemptuous, yet unhansome; As among
> Lecherous humors, there is one that judges
> No wenches wholsome, but course country drudges.
> Graius stays still at home here, and because
> Some Preachers, vile ambitious bauds, and lawes
> Still new like fashions, bid him thinke that shee
> Which dwels with us, is onely perfect, hee
> Imbraceth her, whom his Godfathers will
> Tender to him, being tender, as Wards still
> Take such wives as their Guardians offer, or
> Pay valewes. Careless Phrygius doth abhorre
> All, because all cannot be good, as one
> Knowing some women whores dares marry none.
> Graccus loves all as one, and thinkes that so
> As women do in divers countries goe
> In divers habits, yet are still one kinde,
> So doth, so is Religion; and this blind-
> nesse too much light breeds.
>   (43–69)

16. Thomas Wilson, *Arte of Rhetorique*, p. 184.

When Thomas Parnell, a minor Augustan poet and friend of Alexander Pope "versified" Donne's third satire, his expansion of line 43 ("Seek thou religion primitively sound— / Well, gentle friend, but where may she be found?") assumes a change in the speaker's role as well as in tone, a change from proponent to his own objector or adversarius.[17] Monologistic dialogue or this exchange between speaker and imaginary objector occurs in each of Persius's five satires, and Donne's poet makes use of the device throughout his criticism of the various churches.[18] Embedded dialogue preserves for him an air of innocence, keeping "his own mouth clean" when his words turn irreverent (as well as politically dangerous, given that the English Church is among his subjects). But by pointing to the failures of others in their search for religious truth, the imagined objector offers a cogent rebuttal to the satirist's own argument. How can he expect his readers to succeed where no one else has? For who among those described can prove he has found the true religion? The poet compares the fanatical adherent of each religion to a suitor of some "wench," thus reducing the differences between contemporary forms of religion to domestic comedy.

For "anyone," the spiritualist Sebastian Franck states, "can be pious all by himself, wherever he may be. He is not to run hither and yonder, seeking to establish a special sect, baptism, church or to look at a group of followers."[19] The poet of "Satyre III," apparently, would agree: no one practice of worship is infallible. Alluding to Rome's historical abuse of ceremonial authority, Mirreus loves the Roman Church's "ragges so, as wee here obey / The statecloth where the Prince sate yesterday" (47–48). Thus an ostensibly religious attack turns against the English Crown, the abuse of ceremony simply shifting from Pope to prince. Monarchy has created its

17. *The Poetical Works of Thomas Parnell*, p. 119. In his *Institutio Oratoria*, Quintilian writes that "we display the inner thoughts of our adversaries as though they were talking with ourselves"; thus he describes *prosopopoeia*, one of the diatribe style's most characteristic figures (9.2.29). The Ramist rhetorician Omar Talon connects this with yet another figure, *subjectio*, "when we discuss the objections which may be made against our case and reply to these ourselves . . . often using the form of *prosopopoeia* . . . to present the opposing argument as the direct speech of the opponent" (*Rhetorica*, quoted in Lee Ann Sonnino, *A Handbook of Sixteenth Century Rhetoric*, p. 174).

18. As Arnold Stein observes, "rapidly shifting dialogues with undesignated speakers" mark the tradition of satire that the Elizabethans inherit from Persius ("Donne's Obscurity and the Elizabethan Tradition," p. 105).

19. Sebastian Franck, *Paradoxa* (1534), in Hillerbrand, *The Reformation*, p. 293.

own cult and its own idols, the King (or Queen) becoming a second Pope. And Mirreus is not the only character to turn religious satire into political commentary. Graius, after all, embraces Anglicanism "because / Some Preachers, vile ambitious bauds, and lawes / Still new like fashions, bid him thinke that shee / Which dwels with us, is onely perfect" (55–58). Ambition spurs on such preachers, and the laws that enforce conscience are "new like fashions," subject to the whim of princes. In place of one's father (who would, presumably, speak the truth of religion), "Godfathers" impose the Anglican service upon Graius, thus usurping the place of rightful parental authority, for "Wards" must "Take such wives as their Guardians offer, or / Pay valewes" (60–62). John Shawcross identifies the double entendre: "wards who refused to marry their guardian's choices paid a sum equal to the value of such a marriage; recusants likewise paid for not attending the church established in their parish."[20] Compared to the choices of the other suitors, which are at least made in freedom, Graius's is a shotgun wedding. The threat of persecution, of prosecution, of legal and economic pressure compels his choice. Clearly this is the most critical of the vignettes; is it then likely, as many readers suggest, that the criticisms are somehow democratic (that is, equally harsh)? I read the lines on Graccus, for example, who "loves all as one, and thinkes that so / As women do in divers countries goe / In divers habits, yet are still one kinde" (65–68) and outside, perhaps, of the tentativeness in the word "thinkes," I cannot find the criticism. In fact Graccus embodies a maturer Donne's more tolerant, more Latitudinarian view, as expressed in *Essays in Divinity*:

> God in his eternall and ever-present omniscience, foreseeing . . . that this his dearly beloved Spouse, and Sister, and Daughter, the Church, should in her latter Age suffer many convulsions, distractions, rents, schisms, and wounds, by the severe and unrectified Zeal of many, who should impose necessity upon indifferent things, and oblige all the World to one precise forme of exterior worship, and Ecclesiastick policie; averring that every degree, and minute and scruple of all circumstances which may be admitted in either belief or practice, is certainly, constantly, expressly, and obligatorily exhibited in the Scriptures; and that Grace, and Salvation is in this unity and no where else; his Wisdome was mercifully pleas'd, that those particular Churches, devout parts of the Universall, which, in our Age, keeping still the foundation and corner stone Christ Jesus, should piously abandon the spacious and specious super-edifications which the Church of *Rome* had built therupon, should from this variety of Names in the Bible it

20. Shawcross, *Complete Poetry,* p. 397.

selfe, be provided of an argument, *That an unity and consonance in things
not essentiall, is not so necessarily requisite as is imagined. (Essays in
Divinity,* pp. 48–49)

It is a "severe and unrectified Zeal" that would "oblige all the World
to one precise forme of exterior worship, and Ecclesiastick policie."
Belief in Christ, the cornerstone of the Universal Church, is alone
essential for salvation; in comparison to this necessary act of faith
all other tenets and observances become largely "indifferent." But
while Donne the preacher makes Christ the cornerstone of belief,
the poet speaks of salvation even for "blind philosophers," those
virtuous pre-Christians "whose merit / Of strict life may be'imputed
faith" (12–13). "In heaven" shall "thy fathers spirit" meet them,
though there he shall "heare / Thee, whom hee taught so easie
wayes and neare / To follow, damn'd" (11, 13–15). Of course, the
pagan's "merit" (a thin disguise, perhaps, for the Catholic "good
works"?) is anathema to the Protestant, who asserts "justification
by faith" alone; but more important, the poet has from the beginning made all argument for one religion moot. Salvation belongs to
the virtuous and faithful, while a member of the "right" church,
when espoused for the wrong reasons, remains spiritually endangered. Such lines cast their shadow over later passages, and their
implication should not be ignored: the ways to salvation are many,
while acquiescence in a "forc'd" choice imperils the soul.

   In answer to this tirade, the satirist returns to an impassioned,
second-person address, reminding his imagined objector that

> unmoved thou
> Of force must one, and forc'd but one allow;
> And the right; aske thy father which is shee,
> Let him aske his; though truth and falshood bee
> Neare twins, yet truth a little elder is;
> Be busie to seeke her, beleeve mee this,
> Hee's not of none, nor worst, that seekes the best.
> To'adore, or scorne an image, or protest,
> May all be bad; doubt wisely; in strange way
> To stand inquiring right, is not to stray;
> To sleepe, or runne wrong, is. On a huge hill,
> Cragged, and steep, Truth stands, and hee that will
> Reach her, about must, and about must goe;
> And what the'hills suddennes resists, winne so;
> Yet strive so, that before age, deaths twilight,
> Thy Soule rest, for none can worke in that night.
> To will, implyes delay, therefore now doe.
>   (69–85)

The "huge hill, / Cragged, and steep" makes religious truth a difficult intellectual as well as spiritual enterprise, for "hee that will /
Reach her, about must, and about must goe." The repetitions imitate
verbally the indirections of the ascent, while the determination necessary for this search is expressed, once more almost mimetically, in
the balanced phrasing and repetition: "And what the'hills sud-
dennes resists, winne so; / Yet strive so."[21] The passage is not easy
to grasp, with its curt, Senecan phrasing, its zeugmatic clauses, and
its hyperbaton or divergence from natural word order; Donne
writes, it seems, with a seriousness and complexity of sense that
invokes his Persian model. He also writes with Persius's symbolism.
While the Hill of Truth has any number of sources,[22] it makes an
obvious parallel to Persius's own "steep path." I would argue that
Donne's "huge hill, / Cragged and steep" both echoes and amplifies
the Pythagorean emblem.

And since the poem's more controversial arguments are concealed within such tortuously complex syntax and ambiguous,
equivocal language, perhaps the satirist has other reasons as well
for imitating Persius; perhaps the rhetorical complexities of "Satyre
III" are attempts at deliberate obscurity.[23] Donne may simply be
responding to the stylistic decorum of his Persian model, with its
reputation for difficulty. More likely, the poet finds in obscurity a
political safeguard—and political expediency is assumed to be a
cause of Persius's own stylistic obscurity, as Isaac Casaubon notes:

> I shall not deny that there are certain very obscure parts in the fourth
> and also in the first satires. But I easily forgive the poet when I reflect
> that he poured in some ink of cuttlefish on purpose, out of fear of that
> most cruel and bloodthirsty of tyrants against whom they [his satires]
> were [written]; nor do I doubt that that very wise preceptor Cornutus
> supported such writings, who as an old man repeatedly whispered to
> him the words 'be obscure.' Although Probus, or whoever is the writer
> of the life, does not say this explicitly, he nevertheless reports matters
> from which we ought to infer this much.[24]

21. In his article, "Donne's 'Hill of Truth' " (pp. 100–101), Hester has pointed
out how syntax imitates the spiralling ascent.
22. Milgate gathers them in an appendix to his edition of the *Satyres*, pp. 290–
92.
23. J. B. Leishman, for example, suggests that the harshness and obscurity
of Donne's *Satyres* is "deliberately cultivated." See his *The Monarch of Wit: An
Analytical and Comparative Study of the Poetry of John Donne*, p. 108. See also
George Williamson, "Strong Lines," in *Seventeenth Century Contexts*, pp. 120–
23; and Arnold Stein, "Donne's Obscurity."
24. *Prolegomena*, in *De Satyra Graecorum Poesi et Romanorum Satira*, p. 296.

Casaubon alludes to the tradition, developed by the early biographers and scholiasts, that the dangers of satirizing in an age of censorship and political repression drove Persius to deliberate obscurity; as John Dryden puts it later in the century, "the fear of his safety under Nero compelled him to this darkness in some places."[25] No one under the emperors could enjoy complete freedom of speech. While contemporary vices and even specific individuals became their targets, neither Horace nor Juvenal could write without care for the political consequences. In fact both poets, Horace particularly, tended to court imperial power in their satires, claiming to be spokesmen, as it were, for their patron's or emperor's own moral and political authority. Granted, their flatteries are rarely more than a politically expedient pose; nonetheless Persius is thought to have openly attacked his emperor so blatantly, tradition has it, that his mentor and first editor, Cornutus, emended lines to obscure the criticism.[26] It is interesting to speculate whether Persius's problematic relations with Nero might have awakened Donne to his own need for indirection (the need, in short, for a Persian style) when his subject turned to the Queen's actions against recusants.

☐   ☐   ☐

The above might suggest that Donne imitates Persius faithfully, invoking his voice and manner in the new text. Stylistically this is the case; yet the poet's espousal of Pyrrhonist skepticism marks a radical divergence from the stoic model. True to its hyphenated name, the stoic-cynic diatribe splits historically into two styles of homiletic. Ethically, both the cynics and stoics preach virtue as the only good and self-control as the essence of that virtue; to this particular belief we can compare Donne's own praise of the pagan philosophers' "vertue" (7). But while the stoics preach adherence to tradition the cynics attack traditional morality, preaching only the arbitrariness of custom—different emphases born of radically dif-

25. *Original and Progress of Satire*, 2:70.
26. Ramsay recounts the early biography that interpreted (though he would say misinterpreted) the first satire "as an attack upon Nero and his poetical efforts. The original text of i.121, we are told, ran thus: *Auriculas asini Mida rex habet;* but alarmed by the boldness of these lines, which seemed to point too plainly to Nero, Cornutus emended the line, making it read (as in the now received text) *Auriculas asini quis non habet?*" This reading, Ramsay adds, "was soon developed by the commentators, and became parent of the idea that Persius was obscure" (Persius, *Juvenal and Persius*, pp. xxxi-xxxii).

ferent epistemologies. For the stoics assert the existence and accessibility of knowledge while the cynics, deprecating our human capacities, assert only the problem of knowledge. Persius uses diatribe in the stoic manner, as a vehicle for cognitive (and hence moral) certitude; Donne however, acting more the role of cynic or skeptic, turns diatribe into a vehicle for doubt. The intrusion of skepticism in Donne's own satire thus denies one of the most prominent features of Persian satire: its confidence in a singular, consistent ethical foundation. Ultimately, though, the poem asserts the danger of *any* doctrine, stoic or skeptic, Protestant or Catholic, that attempts to tyrannize over other choices and beliefs, denying them their right of speech. In style, then, it invokes the decorum of Persian satire; in direction of argument, however, and particularly in its reliance upon Pyrrhonist skepticism, "Satyre III" diverges thoroughly from its model. With this in mind, we may begin our second reading of the poem.

In his *Essays in Divinity* Donne characterizes "*Sextus Empiricus* the *Pyrrhonian*" of having "invented a way by which a man should determine nothing of everything" (p. 28), a way of systematic doubt that Donne explores in his funeral sermon to Sir William Cokayne:

> And how imperfect is all our knowledge? What one thing doe we know perfectly? Whether wee consider Arts, or Sciences, the servant knows but according to the proportion of his Masters knowledge in that Art, and the Scholar knows but according to the proportion of his Masters knowledge in that Science; Young men mend not their sight by using old mens Spectacles; and yet we look upon Nature, but with *Aristotles* Spectacles, and upon the body of man, but with *Galens*, and upon the frame of the world, but with *Ptolomies* Spectacles. Almost all knowledge is rather like a child that is embalmed to make Mummy, than that it is nursed to make a Man; rather conserved in the stature of the first age, than growne to be greater; And if there be any addition to knowledge, it is rather a new knowledge, than a greater knowledge; rather a singularity in a desire of proposing something that was not knowne at all before, than an emproving, an advancing, a multiplying of former inceptions; and by that meanes, no knowledge comes to be perfect. One philosopher thinks he is dived to the bottome, when he says, he knows nothing but this, That he knows nothing; and yet another thinks, that he hath expressed more knowledge then he, in saying, That he knows not so much as that, That he knows nothing. (*Sermons*, 7:260)

With this last assertion Donne himself distinguishes between the two modes of classical skepticism, the Academic and the Pyrrhonist—Pyrrhonism being the complete suspension of judgment concerning truth and knowledge, the philosophy of a man who "knows not so much as that, that he knows nothing."[27] Thus the Pyrrhonist suggests that one ought always to suspend judgment on questions concerning truth: that which typically passes as knowledge never rises above opinion. The propositions of such skepticism become an intimate part of European intellectual culture. We should ask *why* this is so. Why does it find such famous spokesmen as Erasmus, Montaigne, Donne?

Of course, the humanists' rediscovery of Pyrrhonist skepticism coincides with the Reformation controversy itself, making Pyrrhonism part of the intellectual crisis of the Renaissance. It is not a cause, surely, of this crisis, as contemporary critics were wont to argue. Far from instruments of atheism, nihilism, or libertinism (effects its opponents commonly ascribe to systematic doubt) the Pyrrhonist arguments become powerful weapons within the very polemics of religious controversy. For the "intellectual core of this battle of the Reformation," as R. H. Popkin suggests, "lay in the search for justification of infallible truth in religion by some sort of self-validating or self-evident criterion." Each side, however, by means of Pyrrhonist argument, "was able to show that the other had no 'rule of faith' that could guarantee its religious principles with absolute certainty."[28] The danger, inevitably, is that the skepticism becomes too powerful, bringing polemicists on both sides to discover logic's inherent weakness in the defense of their own beliefs: "no human knowledge," in a phrase, "can resist the arguments that can be opposed to it."[29] Thus the arguments first introduced by Catholic Pyrrhonists turn ultimately against them; its most famous adherents, nonetheless, turn to skepticism in support of Roman

27. Jerrold E. Seigel describes the skeptical epistemology of the New Academy, whose criticism of knowledge "was based on the criterion for truth set forth by the Stoic Zeno, namely that true perceptions 'were of such a sort that there could not be a false one of the same sort.' Arcesilas, the founder of the 'New Academy,' accepted this criterion, but he denied that men could ever attain such perceptions. None of our notions convince us of their truth by their character of being utterly different from false or misleading ones. Therefore nothing can be perceived—no knowledge is possible" (*Rhetoric and Philosophy in Renaissance Humanism: The Union of Eloquence and Wisdom, Petrarch to Valla*, pp. 16–17). See Cicero, *Academica* (2.25.113). The more radical Pyrrhonist sees even in this proposition the false claim of knowledge, holding that there is insufficient evidence (and inadequate human capacity) to determine if *any* assertion could be proven true and attain certitude.

28. *History of Scepticism*, p. 14.

29. Ibid., p. 35.

Catholic tradition. "So great is my dislike of assertions," Erasmus writes, "that I prefer the views of the sceptics wherever the inviolable authority of Scripture and the decision of the Church permit—a Church to which at all times I willingly submit my own views, whether I attain what she prescribes or not."[30] The fideism thus described by Erasmus counters all "assertions"—all, that is, which contradict his own Catholic faith—with skepticism, while it seeks refuge in custom and the traditional authority of the Roman Church. Montaigne, similarly, found in Pyrrhonism "the best defense against the Reformation," as Popkin observes:

> Since the complete sceptic had *no* positive views, he could not have the wrong views. And since the Pyrrhonist accepted the laws and customs of his community, he would accept Catholicism. Finally, the complete sceptic was in the ideal state for receiving the Revelation, if God so willed. The marriage of the Cross of Christ and the doubts of Pyrrho was the perfect combination to provide the ideology of the French Counter-Reformation.[31]

Again, such arguments never justify the Catholicism of their adherents, any more than they justify any theological position: Pyrrhonism remains, after all, the avowed enemy of dogma per se. Yet the suspension of judgment recommended by Pyrrhonists does not absolve the individual from living within his particular culture, with its unique laws and customs, and from making choices both of action and belief. The solution to uncertainty, rather, becomes fideism: an expression of one's will to believe without need of reason (*Credo quia absurdum est*, one is taught), and an acceptance of the traditions in which one was raised, the traditions of one's "father" (71)—which, in the poet's case, are Roman Catholic. How, then, does Pyrrhonism inform the arguments of "Satyre III"? How should such a rhetoric direct our interpretation?

Omar Talon's *Academia* (1548), a Pyrrhonist defense of his mentor Peter Ramus, seeks to "deliver opinionated men, enslaved by fixed philosophical beliefs, and . . . make them understand that true philosophy approaches things freely and openly and is not enchained to one opinion or to one author."[32] "Satyre III," similarly, aims not

---

30. *Diatribe de libero arbitrio* (1524), in *Erasmus-Luther Discourse on Free Will*, trans. Ernst F. Winter (New York: Frederick Ungar, 1961), p. 6; quoted in Sloane, *End of Humanist Rhetoric*, p. 77.

31. *History of Scepticism*, p. 49.

32. George Buckley, *Atheism in the English Renaissance* (Chicago: University of Chicago Press, 1932), p. 118; quoted in Margaret L. Wiley, *The Subtle Knot: Creative Scepticism in Seventeenth-Century England*, pp. 47–48.

so much to create or establish knowledge as to create doubt, to unsettle those beliefs that typically pass as knowledge. As the "artificer of persuasion," rhetoric is typically viewed as a means to inculcate belief; a rhetoric of skepticism, however, becomes an instrument of disbelief, aiming to disturb the reader's relation to received and unexamined "truths." And yet this is precisely where all persuasive argument must begin. For new belief, as Donne himself writes, requires first the destruction of the old, a deconstruction accomplished by means of language:

> The way of Rhetorique in working upon weake men, is first to trouble the understanding, to displace, and discompose, and disorder the judgment, to smother and to bury in it, or to empty it of former apprehensions and opinions, and to shake that beliefe, with which it had possessed it selfe before, and then when it is thus melted, to powre it into new molds, when it is thus mollified, to stamp and imprint new forms, new images, new opinions in it. (*Sermons*, 2:282)

As the sermon continues, this all-too-human rhetoric is contrasted with Christ's words to the Apostles, in which "there was none of this fire, none of this practise, none of this battery of eloquence, none of this verbal violence, onely a bare *Sequere me*, Follow me, and they followed. No eloquence enclined them, no terrors declined them" (*Sermons*, 2:282–83). For human rhetoric must work its persuasions "on weake men," a Pyrrhonist affirmation, once more, of the limitations of reason and the human susceptibility to error. A "verbal violence" and "battery of eloquence" shake the foundations of one's prior beliefs, seeking to "discompose, and disorder the judgment" in order to "empty it of former apprehensions and opinions." Only then will the speaker be able to instill new belief, pouring the old judgment "into new molds." There can be no persuasion, no change of mind, without the presence of a prior doubt, a skepticism that enables new belief even as it disables or, to use Donne's own word, "discomposes" the old. Mutually enabling and parasitic, skepticism and credence together allow for the possibility of persuasion: all appeal to belief must first be argued against a ground of doubt.

And religion is not immune to this same passage through doubt to inquiry and, finally, to conviction. "To come to a doubt, and to a debatement in any religious matter, is the voyce of God in our conscience: Would you know the truth? Doubt and then you will inquire. . . . As no one resolves of anything wisely, firmly, safely, of which he never doubted, never debated, so neither doth God withdraw a resolution from any man, that doubts with a humble purpose to settle his owne faith, and not with a wrangling purpose to shake another mans" (*Sermons*, 5:38). Of course, one might question whether Donne's skepticism is thoroughgoing, either here in sermon or in "Satyre III." Is reason itself cast into doubt? Or, as in Descartes's *Meditations* and *Discourse on Method* (both critiques of and attempts to revise Pyrrhonist philosophy), is the capacity of reason and the possibility of its purified use somehow exempt? As Mike Marlies has recently described the Cartesian position, reason is "a faculty of which all men are possessed," although

> to be possessed of a faculty and to make proper use of it are two different things, and until a man is loosed from the grip of prejudice, he is bound by habit to [false] reasoning and is devoid of the use, and even any notion, of Reason. The ability to use reason—"The Natural Light which is in our souls"—is what characterizes enlightenment. Once a man can use his reason unencumbered, confusion is dispelled, and truly clear and distinct ideas—ideas of and about purely intelligible things—can be brought to mind. Then and only then, Descartes believes, does a man achieve genuine knowledge.[33]

One might suggest that Donne, too, seeks to salvage human reason, that "Satyre III" escapes doubt through its reliance upon Christian faith—and this would still allow a role for skepticism in *purifying* reason. Read thus, "Satyre III" would anticipate Cartesian method, that therapeutic process of initial doubt that seeks to remove errors of habitual, prejudiced thought, in this way preparing the mind to receive truth and use reason correctly. For "Cartesian therapy," Marlies suggests, "must actually have a twofold thrust":

> In the first place, it must break down and remove the habitual attachment of thought to corporeal matters in which prejudice consists. This part of the therapy, though vital, is purely negative; the therapy cannot rest there, or its result would be skepticism. It must, in the second place, force the exercise of uncorrupted reason, and set the mind on its way down the path of truth.[34]

For Donne, however, one does not walk *down* such a path; the path, rather, is a steep, circuitous ascent. It may be enough to observe that doubt *can* be therapeutic, that Donne turns to it as to an antidote for false belief; yet the question is whether "Satyre III" ever moves beyond doubt, ever offers more than the *via negativa* of skepticism. Does "Satyre III" propose some method or foundation other than Pyrrhonism? I would argue that it does not. For the poem makes no

33. "Doubt, Reason, and Cartesian Therapy," p. 96.
34. Ibid., p. 97.

claim to knowledge. "Truth" stands "on a high hill," but rational argument—at least the poet's—fails to reach it. Paradoxically, the most confident and seemingly efficacious of the *Satyres* offers nothing to persuade, denying to have found what it asks its readers to seek.

Of course, all is *not* doubt and denial. There are implicit assertions lurking in this otherwise antidogmatic poem, arguments for religious tolerance and, deeply hidden, for Catholic fideism. But the poet's major target is once again more political than theological: "true religion," whatever that might be, shall never be found so long as temporal authority prevents the free search. And thus, over against the seemingly dogmatic exhortation to "Seeke true religion," we must explore the implications of a second, Pyrrhonist command to "doubt wisely," one suggesting the weakness of human understanding in matters of doctrine. The poet refers to pagan antiquity as the "first blinded age" (7); is his not a second? Is not blindness the radical condition of all humanity in relation to God? "Mysteries," the poet suggests, are "like the Sunne, dazling, yet plaine to'all eyes" (87–88); even the Christian, though, is blinded— by "too much light" (69), paradoxically, which becomes a kind of darkness. And what problems of interpretation lurk in such oxymora? Shedding its light on the world (and thereby enabling human sight), the sun itself nonetheless "dazzles" when observed directly, mesmerizing and confounding the sense—shrouding itself in the very light that makes all else "plaine to'all eyes." Similarly religious controversy, the very existence of different sects, arises from human weakness. "In all Philosophy there is not so darke a thing as *light*," Donne suggests in a sermon:

> as the sunne, which is *fons lucis naturalis*, the beginning of naturall light, is the most evident thing to be seen, and yet the hardest to be looked upon, so is naturall light to our reason and our understanding. Nothing clearer, for it is *clearnesse* it selfe, nothing darker, it is enwrapped in so many scruples. Nothing nearer, for it is round about us, nothing more remote, for wee know neither entrance, nor limits of it. Nothing more *easie*, for a child discerns it, nothing more *hard*, for no man understands it. It is apprehensible by *sense*, and not comprehensible by reason. (*Sermons*, 3:356)[35]

35. Both the satire and sermon allude to Paul's first letter to Timothy (6.15–16): "Rex regum . . . qui solus habet immortalitatem, et lucem inhabitat inaccessibilem: quem nullus hominum vidit, sed nec videre potest." Aristotle, though, is the *locus classicus*, and Aquinas a likely intermediary. The theme is of course double—our in/ability to understand. Human knowledge is forever only

God's light, God's truth, is "not comprehensible by reason." Rational argument fails before His presence. In fact, what "Satyre III" obscures by its deliberately convoluted syntax "A Litanie" puts plainly: "Let not my minde be blinder by more light / Nor Faith by Reason added, lose her sight" (62–63). As a result of this Pyrrhonist proposition, theological controversy is itself rendered moot: blinded, we are incapable of comprehending, let alone communicating, the mysteries of faith and God's grace.

"Though our naturall reason," Donne elsewhere observes, "and humane arts, serve to carry us to the hill, to the entrance of the mysteries of Religion, yet to possesse us of the hill it selfe, and to come to such a Knowledge of the mysteries of Religion, as must save us, *we must leave our naturall reason,* and humane Arts *at the bottome of the hill,* and climb up only by the light, and strength of faith" (*Sermons,* 8:54; italics added). Is this not the preacher's own gloss on the poet's earlier image? Certainly the case against reason in religious matters is here made explicit and unequivocal. What, then, is implied in the satirist's call to "doubt wisely"? Is it a call for or against the application of logic to faith? The lines may be read either way:

> doubt wisely; in strange way
> To stand inquiring right, is not to stray;
> To sleepe, or runne wrong, is. On a huge hill,
> Cragged, and steep, Truth stands, and hee that will
> Reach her, about must, and about must goe;
> And what the'hills suddennes resists, winne so;
> Yet strive so, that before age, deaths twilight,
> Thy Soule rest, for none can worke in that night.
> To will, implyes delay, therefore now doe.
>
> (77–85)

Doubt, from the Latin *dubitare,* suggests a state of critical reflection that wavers between alternatives. Yet the passage as a whole, speaking of the "way" and the path toward truth, invites a second meaning of *dubitare* into the play of signification: that is, to hesitate, delay, "stand still." Indeed, "To stand, inquiring right" reinforces this

---

partial. To know God's creation perfectly, as Colish observes, "would be to know God perfectly, and this is possible only to God himself. In this sense, a world created by God and endowed with its nature and purpose by God always retains some of God's own inscrutability, which is not so much a darkness as a brightness that makes it too dazzling to be seen" (*Mirror of Language,* p. 124). See also Joseph Pieper, *Silence of St. Thomas: Three Essays,* pp. 57–71.

sense of physical as well as cognitive hesitation, of the *refusal* to act
(and in acting "runne wrong"). Where in this "strange way" are we
left, therefore, if not in a state of suspended judgment regarding
both choice and action? The passage recognizes the delay and ends
by urging the reader to "do" something. But do what? Attempt the
ascent and risk error? Or stand still, "inquiring right" (which the
poet states "is not to stray")? Is one *doing* something when standing, inquiring? The passage enacts in this syntactic and semantic
ambiguity the very problem it addresses: the problem of choosing
and acting in the midst of cognitive uncertainty. And if one is to
"inquire right," of what or whom shall one make the inquiry? Perhaps we should recognize the simultaneous presence of *two* paths
one might take, two paths of belief and conduct: like the Pythagorean symbol, one is steep, on which one goes "about . . . and
about" (81), while the other offers "easie wayes and neare / To follow" (14–15), ways introduced earlier in the poem and taught by
one's father. These same "wayes" of tradition carried one's father to
"heaven" (12), though the poet fears that the father will see his son
"damn'd" (15) for leaving them. Might these "easie wayes" not
offer an implicit alternative to the "strange way" encountered in
ascending, by means of fallible reason, the perilous Hill?[36] As the
poet suggests, "To'adore, or scorne an image, or protest, / May all
be bad" (76–77): fideism, in that case, is the only viable choice, and
it is one born of "wise doubt."

The poet exhorts his audience, simply, to "aske thy father" which
is the true church, and "Let him aske his; though truth and falshood
bee / Neare twins, yet truth a little elder is" (71–73). As Milgate
suggests in his annotations, truth's being a "little elder" privileges
tradition as a solution (a Catholic-Pyrrhonist solution, one might
add) to religious doubt.[37] But fathers have lost the ability to oversee

36. Some years after the composition of "Satyre III"—and at a time,
obviously, when he felt confirmed in the Anglican communion—Donne wrote a
conciliatory letter to an otherwise unidentified Catholic friend: "I have a great
desire, not without some hope, to see you this Summer . . . and I have abun-
dantly more of both, that, at least, we shall meet in Heaven. That we differ in
our wayes, I hope we pardon one another. Men go to *China*, both by the
Straights, and by the *Cape*. I never mis-interpreted your way; nor suffered it to
be so, whensoever I found it in discourse. For I was sure, you took not up your
Religion upon trust, but paid ready money for it, and at a high Rate. And this
taste of mine towards you, makes me hope for, and claim the same disposition
in you towards me" (*Selected Prose*, p. 141). The relation of such language to
"Satyre III" is telling: once again, the "wayes" are many.
37. Commentary, *Satires*, p. 145.

and control their sons' actions and beliefs. (Is this not the poem's opening argument?) And what, at least to Catholic opponents, is the Protestant but a prodigal son who has abandoned the ways of elder generations, an upstart fashioning a religion without his father's blessing? The allusions throughout to father-figures, to those with the wisdom and authority to save their sons, become further arguments for maintaining Roman practices of worship. And thus the final command in this passage, with its curious shift in tense, is to "Keepe the truth which thou'hast found" (89), implying that some portion of truth *has* already been found and is to be protected rather than tossed aside. Tradition once again, the refuge of Catholic fideism, urges the free acceptance of the Old Church's teachings, an acceptance prepared for by Pyrrhonist doubts over man's ability to discover for himself a sufficient and infallible rule of faith. One can try, relying on one's own weakened powers, to discover truth by means of rational argument, taking the risk of "runn[ing] wrong." Or one can "aske" one's "father" (71) which is the true Church, falling back upon an implicitly Catholic tradition that had for centuries supplied an adequate rule of faith.

It is, in fact, temporal authority that ushers in intolerance. "Unmoved" (69), as the satirist states, one must through force of reason choose a way of faith; when "forc'd," as one is by the Crown, one must choose "*but* one" (70), which is of course the "middle way" or *via media* of Anglicanism. Yet the word "forc'd" alerts readers to the real obstacle, which is the arbitrary violence of "mans lawes":

> Foole and wretch, wilt thou let thy Soule be ty'd
> To mans lawes, by which she shall not be try'd
> At the last day? Will it then boot thee
> To say a Philip, or a Gregory,
> A Harry, or a Martin taught thee this?
> Is not this excuse for mere contraries,
> Equally strong? cannot both sides say so?
> (93–99)

The theological debate between Pope Gregory and Martin Luther yields "mere contraries, / Equally strong." Neither side proves fully victorious, adducing a self-validating authority; in fact, recognition of the disagreement among authorities provides yet another ground of Pyrrhonist argument. The contrast between a Roman and a Protestant king (Philip of Spain and Henry VIII) is equally poignant, pointing once again to the problem of authority. Kings who would force one's conscience are not "Vicars, but hangmen to Fate" (92). In usurping the religious authority of Popes, the traditional "Vicars" of Christ, kings become little better than "hangmen"—hardly a timorous accusation.

"That thou may'st rightly'obey power," the satirist continues, one must know "her bounds." But "Those past, her nature and name's chang'd; to be / Then humble to her is idolatrie," for "As streames are, Power is":

> those blest flowers that dwell
> At the rough streames calme head, thrive and prove well,
> But having left their roots, and themselves given
> To the streames tyrannous rage, alas, are driven
> Through mills, and rockes, and woods,'and at last, almost
> Consum'd in going, in the sea are lost.
>
> (100–108)

The English Crown has overstepped the bounds of its authority, much as a swollen river breaks out of its banks, sweeping all away with it; indeed the Crown has become this river, refusing to respect the "bounds" (100) between temporal authority and the individual conscience. At first, the flowers are "blest" (103); only after they have "left their roots" (105)—is the Old Religion their roots, the source of their initial blessing?—and have "themselves given" (105) to "the streames tyrannous rage" (106) are they "lost" (108). And they are "lost" spiritually as well as physically, for "So perish Soules," the poet concludes, "which chuse mens unjust / Power from God claym'd, then God himselfe to trust" (109–10). How close to treason, then, has the poet come in describing the court's "tyrannous rage" (106)?

◻   ◻   ◻

Suggestively, "Satyre V" echoes this last image, seemingly taking up where "Satyre III" leaves off. "Man is a world," the poet asserts in this final poem, "in which, Officers / Are the vast ravishing seas; and Suiters, / Springs; now full, now shallow, now drye; which, to / That which drownes them, run" (11–16). He elaborates:

> If Law be in the Judges heart, and hee
> Have no heart to resist letter, or fee,
> Where wilt thou'appeale? Powre of the Courts below
> Flow from the first maine head, and these can throw
> Thee, if they sucke thee in, to misery,
> To fetters, halters; But if th'injury

> Steele thee to dare complaine, Alas, thou go'st
> Against the stream, when upwards: when thou'art most
> Heavy'and most faint; and in these labours they,
> 'Gainst whom thou should'st complaine, will in the way
> Become great seas, o'r which, when thou shalt bee
> Forc'd to make golden bridges, thou shalt see
> That all thy gold was drown'd in them before;
> All things follow their like, only who have may'have more.
>
> (43–56)

Once again the poet inveighs against those who abuse power (which, like a stream, engulfs and drowns those who court its favors). Does "Satyre V" thus continue the third satire's attack on the English Crown? What is its relationship to Donne's earlier, recusant satire?

We might note, first of all, that the sincerity of "Satyre V" is often questioned, that it is often read as little more than a piece of self-serving flattery, a patronizing of the poet's new employer.[38] In fact its commitment to self-interested expediency extends even further, for "Satyre V" revises the language and imagery of "Satyre III" in order to distance the poet from its attacks against the monarch and her claim of Royal Supremacy. It is, I think, easy to see why the poet of "Satyre V," recently employed by the Lord Keeper of the Seal (and now sharing, in some small measure, in the Crown's authority) should feel the need to rewrite so dangerous a document. Much, evidently, had occurred between the composition of "Satyre III" and "Satyre V." No longer is the poet fearful or overtly resentful of the burdens his Catholic background had placed upon his advancement at court. His apostasy was apparently complete by the time of "Satyre V," an apostasy spurred on, perhaps, by his repulsion at his own brother's death through dealings with Jesuits; or else the poet had by now simply reconciled himself to the fact that in all outward show, perhaps even in his heart, he would conform to the Anglican articles of faith. In short, the laws against recusancy no longer loom so threateningly. In contrast to the fourth satire, court spies and "Giant Statutes" no longer seem as huge "jaw[s]" to "sucke" the poet in ("Satyre IV," 132–33); no longer, especially, is he an outsider at court, a stranger or "foreigner" with no influence, no voice, no place. No longer speaking as an alien at or indeed enemy of the court, Donne found, in his newly won post as secretary to

---

38. Leishman, for one, feels that "the particular abuse Donne professes to be satirizing is merely a topic for the display of his wit" (*Monarch of Wit*, p. 117). Milgate goes further, terming it the "weakest of the five satires," a "rather hastily-put-together occasional piece" (Commentary, *Satires*, p. 165).

Thomas Egerton, both an immediate audience and authority for his words. He had to sacrifice for this authority, though, and if any allegiance to the Old Faith remained then what he sacrificed was surely his conscience. And yet, if his sacrifice was only of conscience, perhaps "Satyre V" would pose fewer problems than it does. For the poem, universally regarded as the least of Donne's *Satyres*, demands nothing less than a revision of those preceding it and an outright sacrifice of its model—which is not Persius, though it, too, makes use of the diatribe style. The model, rather, is Donne's own third satire.[39] Weighing the evidence of manuscript tradition, Wesley Milgate suggests that Donne may have revised the collection as a whole, and that the occasion for such revision "might have arisen when Donne addressed to his patron and employer, Lord Keeper Egerton, the fifth Satire, written not many months after he entered Egerton's service in late 1597 or 1598. It is possible that Donne was then asked for a copy of his other four Satires."[40] Whether such a request might have followed, or preceded, the composition and presentation of "Satyre V" hardly matters; the point is that Donne's employment may well have occasioned the rewriting of earlier satires as well as his writing of the fifth.

For it seems that in achieving this privileged position as Egerton's secretary, the satirist's earlier political attacks had become suddenly embarrassing as well as potentially dangerous. The fourth satire, as we have seen, could be saved by softening its polemic, turning the attack against the Protestant "Topcliffe" (who, like Egerton, enforced the laws against recusants) to the less combative "Pursevant" (216) and Sleyden, a Protestant historian, to the Catholic "Surius" (48), revisions that would ameliorate, if not entirely remove, its criticism of the court's anti-Catholic policy. By changing a few names, Donne could save this poem from accusation; in addition, the reference to "some wise man" ("Satyre IV," 243), if this is indeed intended as a flattering allusion to Egerton, would smooth somewhat the tensions between the poet's disclaimer of authority and his critique of court. "Satyre III," however, by far the most

39. The poet's public address to his patron, Egerton, may deliberately invoke Persius's fifth satire, which was addressed to his own mentor, Cornutus, and devoted to the *vera libertas* of stoic virtue. But though Persian in style and structure, its crucial subtext, as I have suggested elsewhere, is "Satyre III." See James S. Baumlin, "Donne's Christian Diatribes: Persius and the Rhetorical Persona of *Satyre III* and *Satyre V*," pp. 100–105. The present chapter, however, revises its argument in significant ways.

40. Textual introduction, *Satires*, p. lviii.

critical and potentially treasonous of the poet's attacks upon Elizabethan religious politics, could not be saved by a change or two.
The entire spirit and thesis of the poem demanded revision, which
"Satyre V" offers by excusing the Queen, exhorting Egerton and,
above all, exempting English law.

Thus, while "Satyre III" speaks of "those blest flowers that dwell
/ At the rough streames calme head" (103-4), "Satyre V" explicitly
identifies this "calme heade" with Elizabeth, the head of Church
and State: "Greatest and fairest Empresse, know you this? / Alas,
no more then Thames calme heade doth know / Whose meades her
armes drowne, or whose corne o'rflow" (28-30). At a stroke the poet
exculpates the Queen, distancing her from the third satire's accusa-
tions of "tyrannous rage" and idolatry. This is not to say that the
satirist has become an apologist for Elizabeth's religious policies;
concern over the plight of Catholics remains, although, as in the
previous satires, the allusions to Reformation controversy refuse to
espouse one side explicitly. The poet ridicules Catholic theology
indirectly, for example, by comparing political bribery to the intercession of angels and saints: "Judges are Gods; he who made and
said them so, / Meant not that men should be forc'd to them to goe, /
By meanes of Angels" (57-59). Though such a practice may be mis-
guided, surely it is neither malicious nor sinful in itself. Yet the
"Pursivant's" actions in persecuting—actually, robbing—suspected
Catholics is condemned outright:

> Would it not anger
> A Stoicke, a coward, yea a Martyr,
> To see a Pursivant come in, and call
> All his cloathes, Copes; Books, Primers; and all
> His Plate, Challices; and mistake them away,
> And aske a fee for comming? Oh, ne'r may
> Faire lawes white reverend name be strumpeted,
> To warrant thefts.
>
> (63-70)

Theirs is an outrage against language as well as charity: to take
another's clothes, books, and plate, one need simply rename them—
the very vocabulary of Catholicism comes under assault. Thus the
poet restates his support, if not for the Catholics' faith, then at least
for their rights and economic welfare; certainly the poet maintains
his early stance against religious persecution. What has changed,
though, is the satirist's attitude toward law. "Fool and wretch," he
exclaims in the third satire (93-95), "wilt thou let thy Soule be ty'd /

To mans lawes, by which she shall not by try'd / At the last day?" Indeed the fourth satire reveals not the poet's hatred but, worse, his fear of the "Giant Statutes," laws that threaten one's personal freedom, one's property and, ultimately, one's life. How ennobled, in contrast, how clean and innocent law appears in the fifth, where the poet writes of "Faire lawes white reverend name" (69). Self-serving officers and lawyers (Coscus, for example, of "Satyre II") may pervert the legal system, but English law is itself made blameless.

Here then, as Thomas Hester notes, the poet "expands the possibilities and scope of his Christian satire by examining the role of satire *within* the legal machinery of the established state," speaking as an insider "who has the means, the opportunity, and the place to activate reform."[41] And implicitly, the poem claims to transcend its limitations as literature by becoming a proclamation against political and legal corruption, a proclamation addressed directly to Egerton and one that might claim the status, in fact the compelling force, of law. For "Many duties, in many great places consist in speaking," Donne suggests in a sermon: "Ours doe so. And therefore,"

> when Vices abound in matter of Manners, and Schismes abound in matter of Opinions, *Antequam dixerimus hoc,* till wee have said this, that is, that that belongeth to that duty, wee cannot sleepe *Stephen's* sleepe, wee cannot die in peace. The Judges duty lies much in this too, for hee is bound not only to give a hearing to a Cause, but to give an End, a Judgment in the Cause too . . . and when we ascend to the consideration of higher Persons, they and wee speake not one language, for our speaking is but speaking, but with great Persons, *Acta Apothegmata,* their Apothegms are their Actions, and wee heare their words in their deeds. (*Sermons,* 8:179)

Such a passage serves as a gloss on the fifth satire, especially in its distinctions between the speech-acts of lower and "higher persons." The preacher, and the satirist, we presume, finds his duty in speaking; yet "they" (judges, for instance) "and wee speake not one language, for our speaking is but speaking." And this precisely is the problem faced in each of the five satires, the problem of enacting change *by means of words.* For "great Persons" like Egerton, words and deeds coalesce, "their Apothegms are their Actions." It is this same task, to turn literature into social action, that the poet for once optimistically assumes. "Satyre V" attempts, in a phrase, to become something other than rebuke—something other than satire.

But does the poem succeed in so ambitious a transformation? In

41. *Kinde Pitty,* p. 98.

opposition to Hester's reading, Corthell suggests that the poet's relationship to authority remains ambivalent, the poet refusing to espouse or defend power wholeheartedly and continuing, if indirectly, to criticize court policy. "Donne's new position," Corthell concludes, "is not one of identification with power."[42] Yet Donne, I would argue, is ambivalent in spite of himself, incapable of complete identification with the powers he here courts and tries to assume for his own poetic voice. The attempt to praise and exhort Egerton, to exculpate Elizabeth, and to apologize for English law falls short, and this should not really surprise. Even here, even as he seeks to identify with the established authority, his relationship with that authority could never be without its uneasiness, without its ambivalences, without its recognition of the deep compromises that brought him to this position of influence as the apostate secretary to an apostate official of Elizabeth's Protestant and religiously intolerant court.

"Satyre V" does not fail entirely, however; its solution to the problem of political authority (a thoroughly Christian solution, one might add) is not so much to claim power for its own proclamations as to assert the importance of charity in all words and actions. As Donne writes in *Biathanatos*, "Contemplative and bookish men, must of necessitie be more quarrelsome than others, because they contend not about matter of fact, nor can determine their controversies by any certaine witnesses, nor judges. But as long as they go towards peace, that is Truth, it is no matter which way" (*Selected Prose*, p. 28). Commenting on this passage, Sloane interprets "peace" rightly, I think, as charity: all readings of Scripture, as Augustine argues in *De Doctrina Christiana*, are acceptable so long as their source and consequence is charity.[43] But perhaps more important, we might ask what Donne means by "Truth." Is it to be equated as well with the peace of God, a peace the faithful are sure to arrive at, "no matter which way"? Written so close in time to the composition of the satires, such a passage resonates with the language of these poems. The "way" to truth, to the peace of God, is in each case multiple: there is neither law nor "rule of faith" beyond charity, a theme to which "Satyre V" returns. The poet begins,

> He which did lay
> Rules to make Courtiers, (hee being understood
> May make good Courtiers, but who Courtiers good?)

42. "Style and Self," p. 177.
43. *End of Humanist Rhetoric*, p. 167.

> Frees from the sting of jests all who'in extreme
> Are wrech'd or wicked: of these two a theame
> Charity and liberty give me.
>
> (2–7)

"What is hee," the poet then asks, "Who Officers rage, and Suiters misery / Can write, and jest?" (7–9). He may be a classical satirist, faithful to the decorum of this vituperative genre, but he shall certainly not be faithful to his Christian values, which would temper "liberty" of speech with "Charity" toward fellow men. The third satire's rejection of spleen and laughter, "Kinde Pitty chokes my spleene; brave scorn forbids / Those teares to issue which swell my eye-lids; / I must not laugh, nor weepe sinnes" (1–3), thus inspires the fifth satire's equally somber, though more elaborate denial: turning a new leaf, as it were—"Thou shalt not laugh in this leafe, Muse" (1)—he explicitly renounces the ridicule of classical satire. For charity, the preeminently Christian virtue (and the very antithesis, it would seem, of ridicule and invective), now guides the poet, replacing zeal and "righteous indignation" as well with humility and an attitude of toleration. Of course, Donne is not the first to repudiate this *saeva indignatio*; such reformers of poetry as Lorenzo Gambara had already advised that satire be written "without bitterness" and "with the greatest sincerity, though without violating charity."[44] How might this Christian virtue serve to reinterpret the classical satirist's role?

We might note, first of all, that Donne the preacher returns often to the twin themes of "Charity and liberty," treating them as necessary attributes whenever competing authorities differ in opinion; in the following, then, though Augustine's interpretation of Genesis (*Confessions*, 12:30–31) is Donne's subject, the observations hold for all Christian discourse, satire included. "Lord," Donne writes, "thou hast writ nothing to no purpose; thou wouldst be understood in all: But not in all, by all men, at all times." One's understanding and ability to interpret are forever only partial, unfolding through time and subject both to the polysemy of language and the weakness of individual human capacity. And therefore,

> since divers senses, arise out of these words, and all true. . . What hurt followes, though I follow another sense, then some other man takes to

44. "Satyrae sine amarulentia, dum in haeresim, vitiaque Poete sincerissimi salva charitate invehuntur" (*Tractatio de perfectae poeseos ratione* [1576], p. 27; quoted in Bernard Weinberg, *A History of Literary Criticism in the Italian Renaissance*, 1:308).

be *Moses* sense? . . . Where divers senses arise, and all true (that is, that none of them oppose the truth) let truth agree them. But what is truth? God; And what is God? Charity; Therefore let Charity reconcile such differences. *Legitimè lege utamur,* says he, let us use the Law lawfully; Let us use our liberty of reading Scriptures according to the Law of liberty; that is, charitably to leave others to their liberty, if they but differ from us, and not differ from Fundamentall truths. (*Sermons,* 9:94–95)

Even as charity protects liberty, liberty promotes charity; they become the twin supports of law, simultaneously its defenders and its desired effects. To read and apply the Mosaic Law "lawfully," as Donne seeks above, is "charitably to leave others to their liberty." It is, in fact, to safeguard their freedom of belief and conscience, thereby preserving the "divers senses" of Scripture, each with its rightful application and claim to truth. Thus Donne states in a more explicitly theological context the political aim of "Satyre V," which is to assert the role Christian charity and liberty should play in English secular law as well. For "CHRISTIAN LIBERTY," as John Milton would later define it, "means that CHRIST OUR LIBERATOR FREES US FROM THE SLAVERY OF SIN AND THUS FROM THE RULE OF THE LAW AND OF MEN, AS IF WE WERE EMANCIPATED SLAVES. HE DOES THIS SO THAT . . . WE MAY SERVE GOD IN CHARITY THROUGH THE GUIDANCE OF THE SPIRIT OF TRUTH."[45] Doubtless we must observe the distinctions between such uncompromising Puritanism and Donne's more moderate stance. Asserting the absolute authority of grace and one's inner guide, Milton places the Christian conscience above human law; Donne, in contrast, seeks a more generous, just, and charitable *use* of law. Both men, nonetheless, follow Augustine in wedding *libertas* to *caritas,* and both (again, following Augustine) seek thus to resolve the conflict among competing authorities. So, when he asserts that "Charity and liberty" provide the "theame" of his fifth satire, we might keep in mind the full resonance of these terms: more than *satirica libertas* (that is, more than the satirist's traditional license to rail and rebuke), Donne claims a liberty of Christian conscience that law—when used "lawfully"—should preserve rather than deny.[46]

45. *Christian Doctrine,* in *Complete Prose Works of John Milton,* 6:537. See James Egan, *The Inward Teacher: Milton's Rhetoric of Christian Liberty;* and Mary T. Clark, *Augustine: Philosopher of Freedom.*
46. It should hardly surprise that Donne, in implicit sympathy with Catholic recusants, resorts to an argument otherwise associated with radical Protestantism; the *via media,* after all, excludes Puritan and Papist alike. We might also note that Donne's *Satyres,* as a collection, take charity as a central theme. "The five poems," Emory Elliott writes, "present a probing examination of the ideal

Of course, the enforcement of law does not occur in a rhetorical or interpretive vacuum; its workings, whether God's law or man's, describe a fundamentally discursive activity, the "texts" it interprets being human actions—though its pronouncements, unlike the discourse of poetry, are socially binding. As the poet describes it, the law "is established / Recorder to Destiny, on earth." Speaking no less than "Fates words," it declares "who must bee / Rich, who poore, who in chaires, who in jayles" (70–73). And yet we know that "Fates words," like the Delphic oracle, are ambiguous at best. "Satyre V," then, explores the relations among discursive language, religious liberty, and "lawful" action, between "charitable reading" and the reform of contemporary legal practices. Dealing ostensibly with the abuses of English courts of law, the poem's metalinguistic subject is in fact the charitable interpretation of law itself, of what constitutes crime, of what truly merits prosecution and punishment, of what deserves pity instead—of what distinguishes actions and beliefs that "but differ from us, and not differ from Fundamentall truths." As the preacher exhorts his congregation, "let us use the Law lawfully," applying charity and preserving liberty in reading and belief; this same exhortation lies at the heart of "Satyre V," a poem that seeks to reappraise (in a sense, to reread) the actions of "Officers" and "Suiters" (8) in order to free the innocent of blame, to look beyond the folly to the wretchedness of victims, and to give "charitable warning" to those who, for their own profit, abuse "Faire lawes white reverend name" (69). And this abuse, we might again note, is not limited to officers' actions in legal suits; the same accusation is leveled against the "Pursivant" (65) whose anti-Catholic activities, performed under the aegis of statutory law, threaten to institutionalize prejudice and the persecution of loyal Englishmen on the basis of their faith. "Satyre V" may publicly announce the poet's own apostasy and identification with Royal power; still his heart mourns for Catholics and their perilous political circumstances, and the poet seeks still to protect the rights of private conscience, placing charity above the blind and prejudicial enforcement of law.

---

of Christian charity as a fundamental principle for a life of social action and reform" ("The Narrative and Allusive Unity of Donne's *Satyres*," p. 105), a view that others have expressed (see Clarence H. Miller and Caryl L. Berrey, "The Structure of Integrity: The Cardinal Virtues in Donne's *Satyre III*"; and Bellette, "Originality of Donne's *Satires*"). But charity, as I have suggested, should be read in the context of Christian liberty (which should awaken us, in turn, to an even broader context: the Reformation controversy itself, which Donne's poems consistently, if subtly, address).

How shall we conclude this reading of the poem, indeed, of the collection as a whole? Where has this itinerary through Donne's *Satyres* taken us? Frank Kerins argues that "Satyre V" fashions an image of the self-reformed satirist, one who has "authenticated" his own public voice through a process of purification and soul-searching that was begun and, evidently, brought close to completion in the first four satires.[47] The premise of such an interpretation is one that I discussed in an earlier chapter, where the collection is to be read as a thematic progression, a progress of the soul, as it were, in which the poet learns his strengths and limitations as a Christian satirist, authoring himself as he learns to authenticate and make efficacious his own words of reform. There is a certain seductiveness to such an interpretation, given a reader's natural tendency to turn lyric collections into thematic narratives. Interpretation moves reciprocally (in fact, dialectically) *between* and *within* these poems; as the reader proceeds through the collection, prior meanings and memories inevitably flood into the new poem, revising and revaluing each with respect to the rest. Inevitably, though, problems arise. For the collection and the poet's own progress would thus culminate in the least artful and the least satisfactory of the five poems. In what way, then, does "Satyre V" represent the successful reformation of the genre as an instrument of social reform? In Kerins's own words, John R. Lauritsen "argues persuasively for a psychological development in Donne's satiric persona, but this process, as Lauritsen depicts it, seems to progress from a total moral aloofness to a final awareness of human corruption so profound that the satirist is left with no objective moral authority at all."[48] Arguably, the patent weaknesses of "Satyre V" would make the collection more an anti-sequence than a progressive development of the satirist's role. In contrast, Hester writes that "the appointment to Egerton's staff provided Donne the arena in which he could have his satire transformed into legal reform."[49]

Transformation, in fact, is the crucial issue. We have observed the poet's failure to "shepherd" a wayward friend in "Satyre I" and his failure to "punish" a criminal in "Satyre II"; but as "Satyre III" turns to diatribe, and "Satyre IV" to homily, so "Satyre V" attempts to transform itself into something other than classical imitation—to transform itself, in a word, into proclamation and law, which might

47. "'Businesse' of Satire," p. 55.
48. Ibid., p. 59. See Lauritsen, "Drama of Self-Discovery," p. 129.
49. *Kinde Pitty*, p. 116.

account for the "anti-satiric sentiment" Lauritsen finds in the poem, or for Emory Elliott's more extreme suggestion that "the speaker has abandoned the role of the satirist."[50] Perhaps there is, therefore, a progression in these poems, a progressive reach beyond the realm of literary form in order to validate and enact the author's aims, with diatribe, homily, and law taking the place of spleen and satiric laughter.

Still, why should Donne's *Satyres* seek so radical a transformation of their genre? As Sir Philip Sidney suggests, literature "affirmeth nothing," is but fiction and the show of truth. What persuasiveness, then, can there be in literary language? And what power, what efficacy, what self-generating, self-validating, self-sustaining force can there be in literary form? In contrast, the moral philosopher's diatribe, the preacher's homily, and the politician's law become socially, spiritually, and legally binding; each claims the power to determine and sustain truth, the power to compel belief, to have weight in the world, to be *Acta Apothegmata*—to be more than words. As I have suggested, Donne's poetry continually confronts an anxiety of validation; the *Satyres*, evidently, attempt to resolve this anxiety by becoming something more (or other) than satire, for diatribe, homily, and law again allow them to make claims upon social reality, to be as persuasive and efficacious, as socially binding, as other transactional or "nonliterary" modes of discourse. In this the *Satyres* anticipate many of the *Songs and Sonets*, where the transactional genres (and enabling vocabularies) of the theologian, the philosopher, the lawyer, the merchant, the scientist, and the mystic are appropriated in order to claim, *for poetry*, the authoritativeness and persuasiveness of a legal or historical document. Of course, not all documents, not all ideologies, not all "authorities" were declared socially binding within Donne's culture; the *Satyres* demonstrate this all too well. I refer, as the reader by now might expect, to the ways Catholic themes intrude time and again into this collection, undermining its authority as "Christian" (that is, Protestant) satire.

But whether the author of the *Satyres* was Catholic or Anglican is finally moot. What matters is that his writing never resolves the conflict satisfactorily, that even the latest poetic works, the Holy Sonnets and hymns, reveal a continuous struggle against an anxiety of faith. Donne's poems may attempt to argue such anxieties away; some may claim a temporary victory; some may fall in defeat before them; yet the anxieties are themselves part of the fabric of his

50. Elliott, "Narrative and Allusive Unity," p. 115.

writing, never allayed or fully removed. Once again, Donne's skepticism toward language and literary form, his many literary poses and his critical rewriting of models all have their origins in a mind and personality shaped by religious controversy, a controversy whose participants could cast all in doubt—particularly the stability of meaning in language, at the same time looking to language as an instrument of belief and persuasion. Far from convincing him of the force and efficacy of rational argument, his readings in the Reformation controversy would demonstrate time and again only its insufficiency, the speed and ease with which logic is overthrown. But when all had crumbled into disputation and been shot through with doubt, Donne the man still had to work out his own salvation; Donne the poet still needed a language.

And though the exigency of Donne's lyrics is in each case some crisis of love or interpersonal relation, their arguments continue to reflect the social, economic, and religious conflicts of their time. Indeed, in exploring the value of love, the poet is brought to explore cultural value in general. Whatever love is, whether an event, experience, state, or relation, it is never revealed in itself: love, like religion, becomes a radically mediated enterprise, perilously dependent upon language for its expression and shape. More perilously, though (and more surprising, given its popularity among poets) love is curiously lacking in its own vocabulary. While hearts, flowers, and the divine machinery of cupids provide a partial repertoire of conceits, the poet's search for an adequate rhetoric leads beyond Petrarchism to other cultural institutions. The vocabulary of mercantilism, for example, turns love into a mode of purchase, private ownership, and consumption; the vocabulary of law reinforces these property- and consumer-relations, at the same time revealing love's contractual bases. Thus "Communitie" speaks as much about the poverty of consumer-relations as of the hedonist's love relations, while "The Canonization" is as much a repudiation of the various worldly professions as of Petrarchism. Similarly, the search for faithful love appropriates the vocabulary of religious faith—often, specifically, the language of Roman Catholicism, of saint-worship, relics, and good works.

But as Article XXII of the Anglican Church states, "the Romish doctrine concerning purgatory, pardons, worshipping and adoration, as well of images as of reliques, and also invocation of saints, is a fond thing vainly invented, and grounded upon no warranty of Scripture, but rather repugnant to the word of God."[51] Like the

51. Cited in Bicknell, *Thirty-Nine Articles*, p. 276.

Satyres, then, the love lyrics continuously invoke modes of worship outlawed by the dominant political culture. A modern reader might consider these vocabularies as somehow culturally or ideologically neutral, reducing the poet's attempt to fashion a "religion of love" to an exercise of wit, removed from the theological conflicts that pulse through the discourse of Donne's own age. And perhaps, as Marius Bewley suggests, the more "libertine" of the *Songs and Sonets* were written, not simply "as a celebration of sexual experience, but as a subconscious strategy to assist Donne in prying himself free of Rome," their iconoclastic, paradoxical arguments becoming "a protracted exercise in how to blunt the precision of a philosophically exact language and make it unfit for its original purpose."[52] Perhaps. And yet such lyrics as "The Canonization," "A Nocturnall upon S. Lucies Day," and "Twicknam Garden" cling stubbornly, if naively, to the old theology. We might ask whether such a poem as, say, "The Relique" is critical of its implicitly Roman mode of worship (and therefore self-ironizing, self-defeating), or whether the criticism is directed elsewhere, at a culture that would bury such practices. Even if such a poem tolls the passing of Catholic devotion,[53] other of Donne's lyrics seek an imaginative withdrawal from public life (and, arguably, from politically sanctioned modes of worship) to practice a private faith, a priesthood of the poet-lover. In "The Canonization," for example, the poem itself creates a sacred space or scene where the language of an older faith and liturgy can be reenacted, restored to its place in one's private life and devotion. Thus, while aspects of Catholic sacramentalism have been denied by Protestant theology, they might still be claimed—nostalgically, naively, stubbornly, fleetingly—by the poet who invokes and celebrates his love as a divine Presence within the poetic space.

Practiced in the verse epistles as well as the *Songs and Sonets,* the worship of divinity in the lady seeks no less than to relocate religious experience in poetry. The question then becomes, *in what way is she to be worshipped?* Lewalski has explored many of the theological implications of Donne's verse letters to patronesses, where the lady is praised as an image or idea of the regenerate soul.[54] We need to recognize, though, the pervasiveness of a distinctively

52. "Mask of John Donne," pp. 24, 25.
53. In fact elsewhere, in "Religious Cynicism in Donne's Poetry" (pp. 625–28), Bewley argues that *The First Anniversary* tolls the passing of English Catholicism, personified by Elizabeth Drury.
54. See Lewalski, "Donne's Poetry of Compliment," in *Donne's Anniversaries and the Poetry of Praise: The Creation of a Symbolic Mode,* pp. 42–70.

Romanist vocabulary in these poems, and consider its implications. Do the Catholic allusions undercut their praise and worship? If the praise is ironic, then the poems themselves become little more than evaporations, "Tast[ing] of Poetique rage, or flattery," as the poet writes to the Countess of Bedford ("You Have Refin'd Mee," 63), and lacking in sincerity. But what if they are serious? Would their mode of compliment not seem more the product of a Counter-Reformation aesthetic than a Protestant poetic? "Reason is our Soules left hand," Donne writes elsewhere to the countess, and "Faith her right," two often complementary, often competing instruments of understanding, by means of which "wee reach divinity, that's you" (1–2)—that is, the lady herself. "But soone" in his theological studies the poet discovers that "the reasons" she is

> lov'd by all,
> Grow infinite, and so passe reasons reach,
> Then backe againe to'implicite faith I fall,
> And rest on what the Catholique voice doth teach;
>
> That you are good: and not one Heretique
> Denies it: if he did, yet you are so;
> For, rockes, which high top'd and deep rooted sticke,
> Waves wash, not undermine, nor overthrow.
>
> (13–20)

Though playful in tone, the poet's words draw continuously upon the arguments of Catholic fideism, claiming to "fall" "backe againe," to "rest on what the Catholique voice doth teach"—a teaching that, like a rock "deep rooted," no "Heretique" can "undermine" or "overthrowe." Indeed the lady provides the "Balme" (24) and "methridate" (27) or cure for any poisons that may infect "learning and religion" (25). Does the poet not reappropriate specifically Catholic modes of adoration in the guise, perhaps, of Petrarchan praise?

In yet another epistle to the countess ("You have refin'd mee") the poet's desire to behold the lady's physical beauty leads him on an imaginative pilgrimage to Rome, that he might "survay the edifice" of her body-temple, for

> In all Religions as much care hath bin
> Of Temples frames, and beauty,'as Rites within.
>
> As all which goe to Rome, doe not thereby
> Esteeme religions, and hold fast the best,
> But serve discourse, and curiosity,
> With that which doth religion but invest,

> And shunne th'entangling laborinths of Schooles,
> And make it wit, to thinke the wiser fooles:
>
> So in this pilgrimage I would behold
>   You as you'are vertues temple, not as shee,
> What walls of tender christall her enfold,
>   What eyes, hands, bosome, her pure Altars bee;
>   And after this survay, oppose to all
>   Bablers of Chappels, you th'Escuriall.
>
>   (35–48)

Whether the countess would appreciate the comparison of her bodily temple to a Catholic king's palace (Philip II's "Escuriall") is
doubtful; more to the point is his advice that the pilgrim "shunne
the'entangling laborinths of Schooles," choosing to emphasize,
instead, the appropriate use of her "pure Altars"—suggesting support for the active role of the senses in worship, for the "care" that
the Counter-Reformation Church has taken for "Temples frames,
and beauty" as well as for "Rites within." To worship the countess
correctly (that is, to "behold" "vertues temple" in a manner that
avoids idolatry while maintaining the sensuous, incarnate experience of worship) is, apparently, to conform in practice to the Coun-
cil of Trent. Indeed, the countess comes to personify a rectified or
reformed Catholic Church, in which "good and lovely" are "one"
(55) and "all hearts one truth professe" (64).

Taken seriously, the language easily sustains such a reading, but I
have no means (no "rule of faith," as it were) to demonstrate that we
should read the poems this way. I wish I could say, with certainty,
that the Catholic allusion is either serious or ironic. I cannot. The
problem, as I read these poems, is that they are committed to neither perspective, that they would like to be, and refuse to be, the
explicit sentiments of a Catholic poet. And thus the religion of the
poet-lover involves the reader in his or her own crisis of faith—that
is, a crisis of interpretation and sympathetic response. We may
doubt; at times, we may be *asked* to doubt. But we may also be called
to participate in the experiences recounted in such poems. The
poetic space itself may be sacred or ironic (or empty, a place where
language points merely to absence and lack, a place of nostalgia); in
reading we may ourselves perform acts of faith or sacrilege, finding
ourselves persuaded (and willing to be persuaded) or resistant to
the poet's world and words. How, then, shall we read Donne's lyrics? Which rhetorics—of doubt or of belief, of celebration or of de-

nial—shall we privilege? What theologies of language underlie—or undermine—Donne's poetry of love? Though subtly transformed, the Reformation controversy remains a subject of the *Songs and Sonets;* with this in mind, let us turn to the multiple rhetorical bases of these poems.

PART II

✳✳✳✳

The Rhetorics of
the *Songs and Sonets*

5

Sacramental Theology and the Poetics of Absence

"All that the soule does," Donne writes, "it does in, and with, and by the body. And therefore . . . The body is washed in baptisme, but it is that the soul might be made cleane . . . And againe, . . . My body received the body of Christ that my soule might partake of his merits. . . . These two, Body and Soule, can not be separated for ever, which, whilst they are together concurre in all that either of them doe" (*Sermons*, 4:358). Does this hold for reading and hearing, writing and speaking? Is interpretation, the mind's or soul's interiorization of discourse, done "in, and with, and by the body"? Perhaps words are "extensions of the body," as the theologian Arthur A. Vogel suggests, a sort of "meaning in matter, a location of presence"—literally an *embodied* presence. For meaning is in words, Vogel argues, "as we are in our bodies, and it is only because we are our bodies that we can 'be' our words—or, as it is usually put, mean what we say. We can stand behind our words because our presence overflows them and is more than they can contain, but we choose to stand behind them with our infinite presence because we are also in them."[1] Such is the existential foundation of an incarnationist theology of language, one that would claim the power to substantiate meaning, raising the poetic text above the status of imitation to an icon that, as Alla Bozarth-Campbell observes, "does not represent" merely but, rather, "evokes presence."

1. *Body Theology: God's Presence in Man's World*, p. 92. Earlier he writes, "it is not that man is a being who uses words merely as something outside of him and external to him. The statement that man is linguistic means that his most immediate and intimate existence has the nature of a verbal utterance. Man's being needs interpretation, as Paul Ricoeur has pointed out, for it is deep, not all on the surface. There is a sense in which man is a word; he does not just use words. In fact, man is able to use words only because his being has the nature of a word" (p. 92).

And the poem-as-icon, she adds, is "sacramental in this sense": "On a symbolic level the icon is a material body that moves on to a spiritual form, to unite the percipient with its prototype through the invocation of being and the evocation of presence. It is a meeting place, filled with the indwelling energy of its archetypal reality. Its energy is not that of *mimesis*, but of *logos*."[2] The poetic text becomes a "meeting place" for the reader and the reality to which it gives presence, initiating a dynamic confrontation between two substantive presences: the reader and the subject evoked within the text's (sacred-)space. The poem, then, is far from the passive instrument of a writer's (or reader's) will; itself an active presence, the incarnationist text claims the power to transform the interpreter, who does not read so much as listen, though internally, to the discourse, "receiving the word of the text into one's own being."[3] Jacques Derrida is right, it seems. An incarnationist theology of language is inherently phonocentric, the poem realized as an aural presence "immediately united to the voice and to breath," a writing whose nature "is not grammatological but pneumatological. It is hieratic, very close to the interior voice . . . the voice one hears upon retreating into oneself: full and truthful presence of the divine voice to our inner sense."[4]

Implicitly theological in character, this phonocentrism lies at the foundation of Western metaphysics; as Derrida argues, "the system of 'hearing (understanding)-oneself-speak' through the phonic substance—which *presents itself* as the nonexterior, nonmundane, therefore nonempirical or noncontingent signifier—has necessarily dominated the history of the world during an entire epoch," emphasizing the difference "between the worldly and the nonworldly, the outside and the inside," the "transcendental and empirical." Phonocentrism thus provides the basis (or illusion, Derrida would suggest) of "the self-presence of the cogito" and of intersubjectivity in general, "the co-presence of the other and the self."[5] Of course, poststructuralist theory makes this observation precisely to set writing *against* the rhetoric of presence, denying the interiority of phonocentrism and radically separating the signifier from its tran-

---

2. *The Word's Body: An Incarnational Aesthetic of Interpretation*, p. 104.
3. Ibid., p. 39. And "with the interpreter's bodily presence placed at its disposal," the poem thus "receives a human voice and achieves its entelechy, while at the same time it gives its potential speech over to a human subject" (p. 14).
4. Derrida, *Of Grammatology*, p. 17.
5. Ibid., pp. 7–8, 12.

scendental signified. In so doing, it would seem to question the very possibility of an incarnationism that asserts the unity of speech, meaning, and subjective consciousness—in terms of Christian theology, of the Word made Flesh. Now unlike the naive essentialism of, say, English Romantic poetry (still the most common prey of deconstructive readings), Donne's writing proceeds from an explicit and largely systematic theology of language, one the poet himself simultaneously exploits and questions; the problem his writing poses, therefore, is not simply its assumption of phonocentrism, but its ability to work out an adequate *theological* solution to the problem of presence, sacramentalizing language in such a way that each poem becomes a sacred space evoking the Real Presence of its subject. Incarnationist rhetoric is always subject to deconstruction (that is, to linguistic and epistemological skepticism); through the following analysis of Donne's letters I shall demonstrate as much, though we must also seek to understand this rhetoric on its own terms and explore its resources of argument.

In an epistle to the Countess of Montgomery, Donne admits "what dead carkasses things written are, in respect of things spoken." In religious and devotional writing, however,

> that soule that inanimates them, receives debts from them: The spirit of God that dictates them in the speaker or writer, and is present in his tongue or hand, meets himself again (as we meet our selves in a glass) in the eies and eares and hearts of the hearers and readers: and that Spirit, which is ever the same to an equall devotion, makes a writing and a speaking equall means to edification. (*Letters*, p. 25)

Vox and *verbum*, voice and word, form a theological unity; meaning, self-presence, and self-identity remain properties of the *spoken* word. Such a text, nonetheless, is "inanimated" by the living trinity of writer, reader, and "the spirit of God" that "dictates" and "is present" *in the writing*. Here Donne himself describes reading as a dialogic encounter, a "dictation" or conversation between two subjects mediated by the living, breathing word. Speech is produced and received by means of bodily organs; its habitus is the flesh—speech, literally, *is* the word made flesh, for the soul that "inanimates" such discourse "meets himself again . . . in the eies and eares and hearts of the hearers and readers," those who literally incarnate the discourse.

As a simultaneously theological and rhetorical perspective, then, incarnationism asserts the unity of dual worlds, observing that souls dwell in bodies and that souls or spirits can cohabit, meeting in the same sacred space: the body consecrated as God's Temple. As Donne prays, "Though this soul of mine, by which I partake thee, begin not now, yet let this minute, O God, this happy minute of thy visitation, be the beginning of her conversion, and shaking away confusion, darknesse, and barrenesse; and let her now produce Creatures, thoughts, words, and deeds agreeable to thee" (*Essays in Divinity,* p. 37). The speaker's own "Creatures," therefore, his living creations, are "thoughts, words, and deeds," born in response to God's "visitation," His indwelling presence in the speaker's soul. And though Donne complains elsewhere that words, "which are our subtillest and delicatest outward creatures, being composed of thoughts and breath, are so muddie, so thick, that our thoughts themselves are so," yet human discourse is at least partially re-stored by "that advantage of nearer familiarity with God, which the act of incarnation gave us" (*Letters,* pp. 110–11). Life and language thus intersect, words "being composed of thoughts and breath," providing the material that incarnates spirit; even God, he notes in prayer, "hast contracted thine immensity and shut thyself within Syllables" (*Essays in Divinity,* p. 37). In an early sermon, Donne elaborates upon this incarnationist rhetoric:

> The Son of God, is *Logos, verbum, The word;* God made us with his word, and with our words we make God so farre, as that we make up the mysticall body of Christ Jesus with our prayers, with our whole liturgie, and we make the naturall body of Christ Jesus appliable to our soules, by the words of Consecration in the Sacrament, and our soules apprehensive, and capable of that body, by the word Preached. (*Sermons,* 3:259–60)

While public prayer and liturgy turn the congregation itself into "the mysticall body" of Christ, "the word Preached" works upon the individual soul, making it "apprehensive, and capable" (from the Latin *capax,* "roomy" or "spacious"), clearing and cleansing the soul, as if it were a room or receptacle for Christ's indwelling Presence.

What power, however, is expressed in "the words of Consecration"? If they make "the naturall body of Christ Jesus *appliable* to our soules," do they also somehow "make" this body—that is, literally create it? Surely this would imply a belief in transubstantiation and, on the strength of such a passage, we might assume that the Anglican preacher's theology of language is in essence Catholic-sacramental; such, however, would be a dangerous assumption. Time and again an older Donne explicitly rejects the linguistic theology of Romanists who "bring the body of God, that body which the God the Sonne hath assumed, the body of Christ, too neare in their Transubstantiation. . . . We must necessarily complain, that they make Religion too bodily a thing" (*Sermons*, 9:77). We are posed with a question, then: Does Donne the poet claim a power for language that Donne the preacher, as a spokesman for the Anglican Church, either cannot or dare not claim? Or does his poetry explore the *loss* of this sacramentalism and the subsequent undermining of incarnationist rhetoric? If Catholics "make Religion too bodily a thing," one wonders what Donne the preacher would say of Donne the love poet?

One other question arises, one that points, paradoxically, to the very dualism that incarnation would overcome: In seeking to wed soul and body, does such a rhetoric not also admit their radical differentiation and, ultimately, separateness? Regardless of God's active intervention in the world by means of Christ's coming, the spirit has never learned to trust the flesh, nor does the flesh even believe in the spirit; life is itself countered by death, presence by absence. . . . In short, a rhetoric of incarnationism implicates language in epistemological problems that have plagued both Christianity and Western Philosophy from their inception. Even as it struggles to assert and maintain unity, a rhetoric of incarnationism faces continuously the prospects of divorce, separation, dissolution, absence—effects of its own dualistic epistemology, which are themselves inscribed in the nature of writing. Perhaps "an Epistle is *collocutio scripta*," a "written conversation" (*Sermons*, 1:285); perhaps, indeed, "*Scriptor manu praedicat*," as Donne asserts in *Essays in Divinity* (p. 41), the writer's hand speaking or preaching metonymically, in place of the living, breathing voice. Like so many of his comments on language, though, the terms struggle against each other. Is epistolography a mode of conversation or of writing? Are the terms equivalent? If not, which shall prevail? Is writing simply a transcription of living speech, or is it the death of speech and the loss of authorial presence, as postmodern theory suggests? While speech seems to unite two subjects in a dialogic encounter, writing offers but the *simulacrum* of a living presence within the words of the text. Incarnationism, in other words, and the very theology of Catholic sacramentalism come to rest perilously upon an argument for the performative—as opposed to the figurative—nature and effects of poetic/priestly language.

As an exploration of these issues, Donne's sonnet-letter to Thomas Woodward becomes a self-conscious writing upon writing. Ostensibly addressed to the poet's friend, the poem in fact speaks to itself, reflecting critically upon its own aims and the power of its rhetoric:

Hast thee harsh verse, as fast as thy lame measure
Will give thee leave, to him, my pain and pleasure.
I'have given thee, and yet thou art too weake,
Feete, and a reasoning soule and tongue to speake.
Plead for me,'and so by thine and my labour
I'am thy Creator, thou my Saviour.

                                                            (1–6)

In Petrarchan manner, the sonnet-letter is asked to "plead" or inter-cede for the poet during his physical absence from the friend, be-coming "Saviour," paradoxically, to its own creator. It is to save him from at least two conditions: his friend's absence, which makes the poet's city dwelling a hell (9–10), and "infections" (12) of a plague that has emptied the streets of London, threatening the poet him-self with death. But to these the poet adds a third "absence" or emptiness that the letter is commanded to overcome, the poet's own physical absence from a text that must substitute, therefore, for his speaking presence. It is an inadequate substitute, one might add, since the language is at once "too weake" to figure forth "a reason-ing soule and tongue."[6] The ending couplet thus describes two pos-sible functions for this sonnet-letter: "Live I or die, by you my love is sent, / And you'are my pawnes, or else my Testament" (13–14). In either case the writing seeks to become something other than lyric, transforming itself into a more powerful performative or socially binding text. More than polite compliment or fiction, it claims the status of a legal document. As his "pawnes" it would become the author's IOU, a collateral or record of debt; or, should the poet die of the plague, it would become his "Testament," a Last Will bequeath-ing his love.

For "letters have truly the same office as oaths," Donne writes, optimistically, to Henry Goodyer: "As these amongst light and empty men, are but fillings, and pauses, and interjections; but with weightier, they are sad attestations: So are Letters to some Comple-ment, and obligation to others." Anticipating the speech-act theo-ries of J. L. Austin and J. R. Searle, Donne here describes letter-writing as a symbolic action or social *trans*action, a complex unity of "deeds and words."[7] Yet the poem to Woodward ("Hast thee harsh

6. Alexander Sackton notes the problematic nature of these lines, where "the poem is made at once able and unable to speak" ("Donne and the Privacy of Verse," p. 77). His remains a useful survey of Donne's early sonnet-letters, though see also Marotti, *Coterie Poet*, pp. 34–43.

7. As Donne notes, "in the History or style of friendship, which is best writ-ten both in deeds and words, a Letter . . . is of a mixed nature, and hath some-

verse") raises a second issue, one confronted, if implicitly, by each
Renaissance poet: the capacity of writing to validate literary genre
and to perform (in fact, to become) what a poem formally claims.
And in this particular case the performance fails—consciously so,
one might argue, for by dwelling on the proximity of death and offering itself as the document that legally records the poet's death and
debt, the poem admits its failure to re-present, and thus preserve,
the poet through language. The poem fails, in short, to substantiate
him as a living, speaking presence. The sonnet-letter provides little
preservative against either plague-death or poetic absence. And yet
such preservative, presencing power is precisely what the episto-
lary form traditionally claims: "Sir," the poet writes in the verse
epistle "To Henry Wotton," "more then Kisses, letters mingle Soules;
/ For, thus friends absent speake" (1–2). Donne elaborates wittily
upon these propositions in a prose letter to George Garrard, only to
deny their possibility:

> Sir, I should not only send you an account by my servant, but bring you
> an account often my self, (for our Letters are our selves, and in them
> absent friends meet) how I do, but that two things make me forbear
> that writing: first, because it is not for my gravity, to write of feathers,
> and strawes, and in good faith, I am no more, considered in my body,
> or fortune. And then because whensoever I tell you how I doe, by a
> Letter, before that Letter comes to you, I shall be otherwise, than when
> it left me. (*Letters*, p. 240)

Thus the writer writes to declare what makes him "forbear . . .
writing." Writing provides no antidote for change: the speaker
whom it seeks to represent is "already otherwise." The "Song: Goe,
and catche a falling starre" reaches the same conclusion. The poet
would refuse to go to his friend should he find a faithful lover, for,

> Though shee were true, when you met her,
> And last, till you write your letter,
>   Yet shee
>   Will bee
> False, ere I come, to two, or three.
>   (23–27)

Not the lady simply but the letter would prove false. Writing fails to
fix either the world or the human personality.

Continually, then, if implicitly, Donne raises the question: Can

---

thing of both" (*Letters*, p. 114). See J. L. Austin, *How to Do Things with Words*,
and J. R. Searle, *Speech Acts: An Essay in the Philosophy of Language*.

the letter, as a written text, ever overcome its orphanage from the author's speaking presence? "No other kinde of conveyance," Donne writes to Henry Goodyer, "is better for knowledge, or love." Yet the physical and temporal distance of texts from their authors imperils all "conveyance," all writing—all meaning and value, especially of epistolography:

> though all knowledge be in those Authors [of letters] already, yet, as some poisons, and some medicines, hurt not, nor profit, except the creature in which they reside, contribute their lively activitie, and vigor; so, much of the knowledge buried in Books perisheth, and becomes ineffectuall, if it be not applied, and refreshed by a companion, or friend. Much of their goodnesse, hath the same period, which some Physicians of *Italy* have observed to be in the biting of their *Tarentola*, that it affects no longer, than the flie lives. For with how much desire we read the papers of any living now, (especially friends) which we would scarce allow a boxe in our cabinet, or shelf in our Library, if they were dead? And we do justly in it, for the writings and words of men present, we may examine, controll, and expostulate, and receive satisfaction from the authors; but the other we must beleeve, or discredit; they present no mean. (*Letters*, pp. 105–7)

The ambivalence here expressed toward writing echoes the Platonic dialogue *Phaedrus*, where writing is termed a *pharmakon*, simultaneously "medicine" and "poison" to memory—which are Donne's terms precisely. If writing could establish a living presence, could speak in dialogue on behalf of its author, a reader could "examine, control, and expostulate, and receive satisfaction" from the text as from the author himself. Text and author would speak with one voice; the text, literally, would *be* his voice. But radically separated from their writer's living presence, texts "present no mean" for testing their assertions and arriving at a meaning sharable by both reader and author. For writing is a dead thing, devoid of (though imitating the form of) human consciousness, in the same way that the representations of painting produce little more than death masks: "the painter's products," Socrates observes to Phaedrus,

> stand before us as though they were alive, but if you question them, they maintain a most majestic silence. It is the same with written words. They seem to talk to you as though they were intelligent, but if you ask them anything about what they say, from a desire to be instructed, they go on telling you just the same thing forever. And once a thing is put into writing [it] drifts all over the place, getting into the hands not only of those who understand it, but equally of those who have no business with it; it doesn't know how to address the right people, and not address the wrong. And when it is ill-treated and

unfairly abused it always needs its parent to come to help, being unable to defend or help itself.[8]

Donne could as easily write these words, as he shares Plato's fear of misinterpretation, his recognition of a text's stubborn silence before readers, and the need to discover "right readers." More importantly, Donne shares with Plato a mistrust of writing itself, a sense of its inadequacy, its potential for abuse, and its failure to represent an author's meanings fully or faithfully (or, rather, to re-present the author within its space).

With this ambivalence toward writing in mind we might turn back, if briefly, to the sonnet-letters, particularly one to Thomas Woodward, which dwells on the problems of authorial presence and the performance or validation of genre. The poet begins by admitting his physical separation from the writing: "At once, from hence, my lines and I depart, / I to my soft still walks, they to my Heart" (1–2). He then raises the possibility that his verse,

> The strict Map of my misery,
> Shall live to see that, for whose want I dye.
> Therefore I envie them, and doe repent,
> That from unhappy mee, things happy'are sent;
> Yet as a Picture, or bare Sacrament,
>   Accept these lines, and if in them there be
>   Merit of love, bestow that love on mee.
>
> (8–14)

The act of composing becomes an act of love that seeks to "merit" love in return. The reader should take the theological, indeed Catholic, implications of the term seriously, for the poem, in the final lines especially, invokes a theology of language upon whose workings the success or failure of the genre itself hangs. The letter is itself offered as a "Sacrament" (12), which Wesley Milgate glosses as a legal term, "a pledge which each of the parties deposited or became bound for before beginning a suit."[9] In this sense of the word, the poem would again become a pawn or pledge and, once again, the poet could claim to validate the literary text by making it something other than literary (that is, a legal or socially binding document). But "Sacrament," surely, has religious connotations as well. From the standpoint of Catholic theology, the poem-as-sacrament might claim, if even blasphemously, the capacity to substantiate the poet

8. Plato, *Collected Dialogues*, p. 521.
9. Commentary, *Satires*, p. 214.

through its own words of (self-)invocation. Need we remind our-selves, though, that the various Reformation theologies differ most crucially in their interpretation of the sacraments? Each theology's understanding of their nature, number, and efficacy would have profound implications for the poet as well as priest (or indeed, the poet as secular priest). *Can* the poem-as-sacrament be transubstan-tiative in a Catholic sense, asserting the power to re-present or incorporate the poet in the flesh of language? Or, following the more extreme Calvinist and Zwinglian interpretations of Eucharis-tic theology, is the poem reduced to a commemorative event, a rep-resentation or "Picture" (10), to use the poet's own word? What could a "*bare* Sacrament" suggest if not this latter, more radically Protestant interpretation, one that empties the priest's—and poet's—language of being, restricting the words of Eucharistic celebration to a figural representation rather than a re-presenting or presencing of its transcendental subject? And as a "bare Sacrament," what can the poem hope to achieve? The problem of validation, the ability of a literary form to enact an author's aims, has once again become a problem not simply of performative language but of the warring linguistic theologies of the Reformation.

A final letter to Thomas Woodward ("Pregnant again with th'old twins Hope, and Feare") describes reading itself as a sacramental event: "And now thine Almes is given, thy letter'is read, / The body risen againe, the which was dead, / And thy poore starveling boun-tifully fed" (7–9). Reading has become a mode of consumption. But mixed in with the grosser language of gormandizing is a more rev-erential language of sacramental communion, turning Woodward's "Almes," the charitable offering of his letter, into a spiritual "ban-quet" for which the poet's "Soule doth say grace,"

> And praise thee for'it, and zealously imbrace
> Thy love; though I think thy love in this case
> To be as gluttons, which say 'midst their meat,
> They love that best of which they do most eat.
> (11–14)

The "body risen" suggests that the reader's own flesh has become a receptacle of the risen Christ, that an infusion of grace, by means of communion, has renewed the reader, both body and soul. Thus the allusions to prayer, to praise, to the reader's "zealous embrace" of the alms-giver's love all mark the poem as a communicant's reverent thanksgiving for having received the sacrament. But whether mate-rial, literary, or spiritual, *what sort of feast* would the poet of this sonnet-letter love "best" and, therefore, eat "most"? Explicitly he pleads for more letters; indirectly, perhaps, he alludes to the rarity of Eucharistic celebration in the contemporary Anglican Church. Either way he makes claims for the *nature* of this language-feast, suggesting the possibility that writing re-presents the poet to a reader-communicant in the same way that the sacrament expresses Christ's Real Presence.

What tone is present in such sonnet-letters, though? How might the extravagant compliment ironize the sacramental theology here invoked as a theory of reading? Does Donne's poetry, the love lyrics especially, ever achieve this sacramental power? Before we even hazard an answer to these questions we must once again consider the poet's place in the Reformation controversy. For Protestantism seeks no less than to deconstruct the linguistic theology of Roman Catholicism, reducing the sacrament of Eucharist from a presencing or transubstantiative to a consubstantiative (and, in its extreme Zwinglian interpretation, a commemorative) event, at the same time reducing the language of sacrament to "figurative speeches and Metonymies." Thus William Perkins, one of the more influential English Calvinists, describes a thoroughly figurative Eucharist in which the bread becomes a "signe" of Christ, its signified:

> There is a certaine agreement and proportion of the externall things with the internall, and of the actions of one with the actions of the other: wherby it commeth to passe, that the signes, as it were certaine visible words incurring into the externall senses, do by a certaine proportionable resemblance draw a Christian minde to the consideration of the things signified, and to be applyed.[10]

By such an account the Lord's Supper does not embody so much as "resemble" its transcendental signified, becoming a representation of that which exists nowhere but in the mind or memory of its participants and is thus physically absent. Calvin himself defines sacrament as "an outward sign by which the Lord seals on our consciences the promises of his good will toward us in order to sustain the weakness of our faith,"[11] and the Thirty-Nine Articles of the Anglican Church is largely in agreement:

> Transubstantiation (or the change of the substance of Bread and Wine) in the Supper of the Lord cannot be proved by Holy Writ; but is repug-

---

10. *The Golden Chain*, in *Workes* (1612), 1:72. Quoted in Lewalski, *Protestant Poetics*, p. 80.
11. Jean Calvin, *Institutes of the Christian Religion*, 21:1277.

nant to the plain words of Scripture, overthroweth the nature of a
Sacrament, and hath given occasions to many superstitions.
   The Body of Christ is given, taken, and eaten, in the Supper, only
after an heavenly and spiritual manner. And the means whereby the
Body of Christ is received and eaten in the Supper is Faith.[12]

And what of Donne? Though his youthful verse letters and much
of the love poetry invoke a Catholic-sacramental theology of language, his later religious writings explicitly repudiate that "heresie
of Rome, That the body of Christ may be in divers places at once, by
the way of Transubstantiation" (Sermons, 9:201), the doctrine of
which is an "hereticall Riddle of the Roman Church, and Satan's
sophistry, to dishonour miracles, by the assiduity and frequency,
and multiplicity of them" (Sermons, 7:294).[13] The implication is poignant: miracles (of language, certainly) have ceased—for the poet,
one might presume, as well as the priest—since "the word of consecration alter[s] the bread, not to another thing, but to another use
. . . the enunciation of those words doth not infuse nor imprint this
grace, which we speak of, into that bread" (Sermons, 2:258). Adopt-
ing an explicitly Calvinistic view, then, Donne inveighs against
those who "attribute too much, or too little to Christs presence in
his Sacraments," who would "imprison Christ in Opere operato." For
"it is enough," the preacher concludes, "that thy Sacrament be a
signe" (Sermons, 7:267), a sign that awakens hope and memory
rather than invoke Presence, working its changes in consciousness
(that is, in the participants' "consciences") instead of the bread and
wine. Directing attention to the past (or future, as Calvin's "external
sign . . . seals on our consciences the promises of his good will")
rather than the present Eucharistic celebration, such language
speaks only of the deferral of the signified, the absence of the Person from the language. Indeed, though Donne is generally thought
to have repudiated Zwinglian interpretations,[14] he often describes
the Eucharistic celebration as a fundamentally significative and thus
commemorative event:

   12. Article XXVIII, Of the Lord's Supper. Quoted in Bicknell, Thirty-Nine
Articles, p. 382. The next article elaborates on the nature of a sacrament as that of
a "sign" (Article XXIX).
   13. He rejects, similarly, "that dream of the Ubiquitaries, That the body of
Christ must necessarily be in all places at once, by communication of the divine
Nature. . . . he cannot be here, here in the Sacrament, so, as you may break or
eat that body" (Sermons, 9:201–2). Thus an older Donne denies the sacramental
theology of Lutherans (that is, the "Ubiquitaries") and Catholics alike.
   14. See Itrat Husain, The Dogmatic and Mystical Theology of John Donne, p. 29.

God in giving the law, works upon no other faculty but this, *I am the Lord thy God which brought thee out of the land of Egypt;* He only presents to their memory what he had done for them. And so in delivering the Gospell in one principal seal thereof, the sacrament of his body, he recommended it only to their memory, *Do this in remembrance of me.* This is the faculty that God desires to work upon. (*Sermons,* 2:237)

Elsewhere again Donne suggests that the priest "*offers up* to God the Father (that is, to the *remembrance,* to the contemplation of God the Father) the *whole body* of the *merits of Christ Jesus*" (*Sermons,* 7:429). Thus *corpus* becomes *opus* or "merits," a figurative body: Christ's Real Presence, the theological ground of the Catholic priest's essentialist language, retreats into memory and promise as it shrinks to metonymy, becoming (like the poetic voice of Donne's youthful verse letters) a merely figurative presence that heralds absence. Only language remains.

Yet we might note, in passing, that this devaluation of Catholic sacramentalism reflects an age's broader revaluation of its cultural past, a rediscovery of history that displaces the "eternal present" of medieval consciousness. It is ironic that Petrarch, among the first to devote his life to the recovery of the past—one who writes epistles to the great authors of antiquity—is also first to sense the irrecoverableness of their voices as a living presence. Virgil has fled into the imperfect record of written language; no longer, as for Dante, is he a living voice and guide through the world. Promise and commemoration assert only future and past referents. Yet the individual must still discover in his or her own life the present assurance of a salvation that has at once been made uncertain. Predestination, through the inscrutable workings of providential history, reduces the future to a divine factandum; original sin, the genetic encoding of sin into the human organism, projects itself through time, limiting the freedom and powers of the individual living in the present moment. What certitude does one find in a theology of language that defaces the present before the tyrannous hold of past and future event, reducing religious rituals of language to commemoration and promise?

Where are we left? It may suffice to observe that Donne's verse letters explore the problems of authorial presence and literary form, that they undercut their own claim to express a priestly, presencing language and repudiate poetic form by turning into so many death notices and documents that record debt. Yet such observations bring us, more importantly, to a consideration of the *Songs and*

Sonets, works occupying a middle position between the implicitly Catholic sacramentalism of the early verse letters and the figuralist reduction of the sacraments in Donne's sermons. Surely such theological distinctions as transubstantiation, consubstantiation, and commemoration bring changes to one's understanding of the powers of poetic language. We might ask, therefore, whether the poetry of Donne's middle years admits, or laments, the loss of sacramentalism. Or does Donne attempt to compensate for this loss by relocating Catholic modes of worship—of idolatry, some might say, and superstition—within the poetry of love? Donne the preacher condemns the Roman Church for ascribing an "effective," that is, a performative power to ceremonies originally intended to be "significative":

> To those ceremonies, which were received as *signa commonefacientia,* helps to excite, and awaken devotion, was attributed an operation, and an effectual power, even to the ceremony it selfe; and they were not practised, as they should, *significativè,* but *effectivè,* not as things which should signifie to the people higher mysteries, but as things as powerfull, and effectuall in themselves. (*Sermons,* 10:90–91)

Would Donne the preacher equally accuse the more youthful poet, who makes similar claims for his rituals of language? The "bracelet of bright haire" described in "The Relique" has elicited responses ranging from wonder to repulsion; what, indeed, is the poet's attitude toward an image at once sacramental and necromantic?

> When my grave is broke up againe
> Some second ghest to entertaine,
> (For graves have learn'd that women-head
> To be to more then one a Bed)
> And he that digs it, spies
> A bracelet of bright haire about the bone,
> Will he not let'us alone,
> And thinke that there a loving couple lies,
> Who thought that this device might be some way
> To make their soules, at the last busie day,
> Meet at this grave, and make a little stay?
>
> If this fall in a time, or land,
> Where mis-devotion doth command,
> Then, he that digges us up, will bring
> Us, to the Bishop, and the King,
> To make us Reliques; then
> Thou shalt be'a Mary Magdalen, and I
> A something else thereby.
>
> (1–18)

The opening puns (ghest/ghost, entertain/inter) and the reduction of graves to adulterous beds are simultaneously witty and blasphemous, though not so outrageous as the poet's own implicit apotheosis, his claim to become "a something else"—that is, a resurrected Christ to the lady's Mary Magdalen. Most readers have emphasized the poem's ambivalent attitudes toward love and death; what, we might ask, are its attitudes toward contemporary practices of faith?

Does "mis-devotion" reign *because* of an age's superstitious belief in relics and miracles? Or might this relic and the "miracles" (22) of love be curative to an age's mis-devotion? Might the poet's own be such "a time, or land, / Where mis-devotion doth command"? The gravedigger who finds this bracelet is hardly likely to gain favor before a Protestant "Bishop" or "King," who would more likely burn their bones than "make [them] reliques." But if this mis-devotion is no more than superstitious relic-worship, then the lyric itself is at once disabled along with the Catholicism. In fact the poem would admit a double failure: "These miracles wee did; but now alas, / All measure, and all language, I should passe, / Should I tell what a miracle shee was" (31–33). The failure of words (and the refusal, finally, to write of transcendent experience) is only the second of the poem's disablements; first and most significant is the loss of the *world* here described, a world of miracles and relics and "Guardian Angells" (25) as well as of faithful love. For miracles have ceased, many Protestants would assert. And unless the poet's present age can learn from "this paper" (21)—that is, from the poem itself, particularly the third stanza, designed to have "taught / What miracles wee harmlesse lovers wrought" (21–22)—then more shall have died than the two lovers: true love and true piety, true devotion shall have died along with miracles, along with this poetry.

The Reformation controversy, therefore, remains a subject of Donne's love lyrics. And though the crisis is largely displaced, focused now on the words and deeds of private lovers, his writing continues to dwell in a crisis of faith, which itself remains a crisis of sacramental, performative language. Perhaps the poet becomes his own priest? Does he not claim (though nostalgically, naively perhaps) to create an imaginative realm in which the transforming powers of sacrament remain possibilities of poetic language? (And yet, who but a believer, a reader who participates in its sacramental reality, could ever know?) Or is the language but a nostalgic glance backward, empty of mystery, an elegiac commemoration that admits its own weakness? Or is it, simply, an exercise in wit, a verbal play that denies its truth-function at each turn, denying love-poetry in the process? It is, perhaps, all of these at once, though the reader must make his or her own choice; Donne, I believe, knew this as well, that his invocations of sacramental theology would challenge their readers' faith as well as their readers' powers of interpretation. In "Twicknam Garden," for example, the poet visits the Bedford ancestral estate not simply as an abject suitor but as a Romish priest, a "selfe traytor" (5) who brings with him the "spider love, which transubstantiates all" (6)—turning his "Manna," an Old Testament type of the Eucharist, to "gall" (7), thereby denying its powers to "cure" (4) or heal the love-sick poet. His tears, in addition, become "loves wine," invoking Christ's blood in the sacrament. But again, with what effect?

> Hither with crystal vyals, lovers come,
>   And take my teares, which are loves wine,
>   And try your mistresse Teares at home,
> For all are false, that taste not just like mine.
>   (19–22)

Though Gardner glosses "crystal vyals" as lachrymatories, tear-bottles left as funereal tribute to the dead, the passage is easily read as an elaborate parody of the Roman Mass, the poet's tears miraculously transformed into wine that others are to bear, in chalices, to their own lovers as both a communion sacrifice and a test of their faith. The poet-priest's communion, then, becomes a communion in bitterness and sorrow; though it can confirm a communicant-lover's faith its saving power, apparently, is denied.

While this and other lyrics ("The Canonization," say, and "A Nocturnall upon S. Lucies Day") invoke the language and liturgical practices of Romanism, my point is not that the mature Donne remains Catholic—though, of course, the influence of his religious upbringing would remain, regardless of later choices. Nor am I any longer interested in the Reformation controversy per se, though even the most secular of Donne's writings often take this as a theme, at times indirectly, at times explicitly. I am interested, rather, in the *consequences* of this controversy, in the ways it affects the poet's attitudes toward the powers and possible functions of language. Naively, many of the *Songs and Sonets* cling to belief in a powerful, performative language; naively, they hold fast to the hope of poetic presence, even as they admit the loss of Catholic sacramentalism. Others, however, attempt to compensate for this loss by appropriating alternative belief systems, alchemy especially, to prop up their essentialist theory of language. There is, after all, an implicit identification between Hermeticism and "such Catholic sacramental rites" as transubstantiation, where "the words uttered by the priest are considered to give effect to the miraculous change that occurs, the transformation of bread and wine into the body and blood of Christ."[15] Paracelsus, for one, describes the *opus alchymicum* as a saving sacrament, turning the alchemist's art into a private priesthood, one that retains belief in the miraculous power of words.[16] Of course, this displacement of sacramental theology from the priest to the alchemist is hardly a solution acceptable to Protestants, who treat Hermeticism with much the same skepticism. "There is a great difference," Luther writes, between such a sacrament as baptism and "all others invented by men," including the rites of "magicians" who "employ a sign or creature, such as a root or herb, and speak over it the Lord's prayer or some other holy word and the name of God," whereby it should "possess power and accomplish what it is used for." But "it is nothing and counts for nothing," Luther adds, "no matter what sign or word is used." Indeed, "even baptism would not be a sacrament without [God's] command."[17] The alchemist's invocations, like the priest's (like the poet's?), lack power in themselves. Divine grace, not human language, is the effectual force in the sacraments; baptism itself would fail to save, were it not for God's intervention.

Thus the alchemical allusions in Donne's love lyrics raise the same interpretive problems as the allusions to Catholic sacramentalism. Both invoke a theory of performative language whose workings are claimed for the poem itself but whose validation remains outside the poem, in the reader's response. Like religious ritual, the

15. John G. Burke, "Hermeticism as a Renaissance World View," p. 102. In many respects, Burke adds, Hermeticism arises in response to the Reformation controversy, seeking "to promote toleration between Catholics and Protestants" and thus "to reconcile and reunite Christianity" (p. 114). See also Frances A. Yates, "Religious Hermeticism in the Sixteenth Century," in *Giordano Bruno and the Hermetic Tradition*, pp. 169–89; and Keith Thomas, *Religion and the Decline of Magic*, pp. 3–173.

16. See Carl Jung, *Alchemical Studies*, p. 186.

17. *Werke* (Weimar: H. Boehlau, 1913), 44:128–29; quoted in Burke, "Hermeticism," pp. 102–3. Both Calvin and, in the following passage, Bishop Hooper argue similarly: the Roman Mass is "nothing better to be esteemed than the verses of the sorcerer or enchanter . . . —holy words murmured and spoken in secret" (quoted in Thomas, *Religion and the Decline of Magic*, p. 53). And "surely," Perkins writes, "if a man but take a view of all Popery, he shall easily see that a great part of it is mere magic" (*Golden Chain*, 1:40).

poem's performative rites are fundamentally appeals to a reader's faith, an invitation to worship within the poetic space, to join in communion with the magus or poet-priest. Whether writing provides this sacred space, whether the text becomes the scene of presence, remains an issue as well. Through the remainder of this chapter, then, I shall explore the ways Donne's incarnational rhetoric is questioned and undermined by the nature of writing itself, by the written text's loss of authorial presence. I turn specifically to two poems of departure and absence, "A Valediction: of my Name in the Window" and "A Valediction: of the Booke." For, more ambitiously than the verse letters, the valedictions search for a rhetoric to perform or enact the aims of their genre, a rhetoric (that is, a theology of language) that would enable the spiritual union of lovers—or rather, the continued *communion* of lovers—in spite of physical absence. One must still ask, of course, whether they succeed in this task, since they call self-critical attention to the problem of their own discursive procedures. How powerful, after all, how *presencing* is a rhetoric of icons (of *homunculi* drifting in tears and reflected on the surfaces of eyes)? Or of emblems (of compasses and beaten gold)? Or of signatures? And yet, is there ever a stronger charm than one's name? Scratched in a window, cannot the poet's name express, as in Plato's *Cratylus*, the full powers of its object? Or is the inscription always too weak, always a *figurative* presence—always, as the Calvinist Perkins would say, a "sacramental *metonymy*"?

□　　　□　　　□

"A Valediction: of my Name in the Window" oscillates between anxiety over absence and an extravagance of wit designed, it would seem, to defend against this anxiety, allaying it by rationalizing it away. But to such precarious swings of mood and argument the poet adds an attitude of linguistic skepticism. Early stanzas, admittedly, invoke an essentialist theory of language similar to that of the "*Cabalists*," those "Anatomists of words" who "have a theologicall Alchimy to draw soveraigne tinctures and spirits from plain and gross literall matter." By means of this verbal alchemy the Cabalist is able to discover the "mystick signification" and properties found "almost in every Hebrew name and word" (*Essays in Divinity*, p. 48), properties that the poet's own English name might share.[18] The

18. *The Divine Names* of Pseudo-Dionysius and Cornelius Agrippa's *Philosophy of Natural Magic* (1531) may be cited among many possible sources for

poet seeks to become just such an "Anatomist of words," conjuring
the lady's fidelity by means of his signature. And the signature
becomes coextensive with the living personality; to keep the name
"alive," to keep it in memory by means of a written text or monument, is to preserve the man himself. For a man is otherwise "but
oblivion," as Donne writes elsewhere, "his fame, his name shall be
forgotten" (*Sermons*, 9:62). It is as a charm against "oblivion," then,
a charm against his own loss of "fame" and identity—in short, his
loss of a "name"—that the poet inscribes his signature in the lady's
window. And yet the argument ultimately turns in upon itself, ironically questioning the power of such a charm, indeed questioning
the poem's own capacity, as writing, to persuade and sustain love in
absence.

I
My name engrav'd herein,
Doth contribute my firmnesse to this glasse,
Whiche, ever since that charme, hath beene
As hard, as that which grav'd it, was;
Thine eyes will give it price enough, to mock
The diamonds of either rock.

II
'Tis much that Glasse should bee
As all confessing, and through-shine as I,
'Tis more, that it shewes thee to thee,
And cleare reflects thee to thine eye.
But all such rules, loves magique can undoe,
Here you see mee, and I am you.

III
As no one point, nor dash,
Which are but accesarie to this name,
The showers and tempests can outwash,
So shall all times finde mee the same;
You this intirenesse better may fulfill,
Who have the patterne with you still.

(1–18)

Donne's "theologicall Alchimy." For discussions of his use of the occult sciences
see Joseph A. Mazzeo, "Notes on John Donne's Alchemical Imagery," in *Renaissance and Seventeenth Century Studies*, pp. 60–89, and Eluned Crashaw, "Hermetic Elements in Donne's Poetic Vision." Some useful general studies are
Jacqueline de Romilly, *Magic and Rhetoric in Ancient Greece*; and Brian Vickers,
"Analogy versus Identity: The Rejection of Occult Symbolism, 1580–1680,"
pp. 95–163.

His praise of the lady's eyes is of course a well-worn Petrarchan compliment, her gaze imparting to the engraved name a value greater than diamonds. More importantly, the compliment serves to draw her eyes to the text of his inscribed name, a text which, as she reads, he shall interpret—and by interpreting, by drawing "sov-eraigne tinctures and spirits from plain and gross literall matter," the poet shall "charme" (3) the lady's understanding. Thus the poet begins by asserting an absolute identity between *res* and *verbum*, the name sharing in the powers of the person. The name becomes, in Donne's own Cabalistic language, a "soveraigne spirit" that sub-stitutes for the poet's living personality, becoming a spiritual double that allows him literally to be in two places at once, expressing his "firmness," his fidelity, his "through-shine" (8) or innocent nature. Like the deep-drawn lines of his etched signature, neither "show-ers" nor "tempests can outwash" (15) the poet's fidelity.

The glass, however, the otherwise frail "body" that this name-spirit now inhabits, is itself multivalent. On the one hand, its trans-parency reveals the poet's selfless and pure devotion; on the other, it acts as the lady's mirror, reflecting her beauty (and, perhaps, her vanity). And the poet's own interpretation of this fragile text (this vitreous union of opposites, of transparency and opaque reflection) discovers yet another "mystic signification": with her reflected im-age superimposed upon his engraved name, the glass asserts, or rather inscribes, their essential unity—"Here you see mee, and I am you." The poet's own name thus claims the lady's reflection or visual representation as its signified, declaring its right and power to name her, in fact to possess her in the way that each mystic *verbum* invokes and unites with its *res*. "Loves magique," therefore, which here can "undoe" the "rules" or laws of separate physical identities, proceeds by an act of nomination.[19] But even as the poet seeks to control the interpretation, it is the lady who must "fulfill" this text, completing and actualizing it in her own life. She alone can ensure its "intirenesse," its unity of signifier and signified (that is, of the poet's name and the lady's self-image) by remaining in its physical presence; she must herself "read" it and adopt it as a "patterne" or Platonic ideal to emulate. The word "patterne" does enjoy this mys-tic sense, one that emphasizes the divine reality of archetypal love

19. Thomas Docherty, similarly, reads the valediction as an ironic explora-tion of the powers of naming, though he offers biblical rather than alchemical parallels (*John Donne, Undone*, pp. 174–85). A suggestive general discussion of the problem of nomination is Geoffrey H. Hartman's "Words and Wounds," in *Saving the Text: Literature/Derrida/Philosophy,* pp. 118–57.

("The Canonization" [45] provides a more famous example of such usage); yet it can also refer to the art of pattern-cutting or engraving, a meaning that emphasizes the sheerly material, even decorative rather than spiritual reality of this signature. Upon careful scrutiny, then, the language of this third stanza, even as it argues for the text's "firmnesse" and "entirenesse," becomes progressively unsettled. Though "no one point, nor dash" of this signature can be "outwash[ed]," nonetheless the engraving, the written inscription, has become "but *accessarie* to this name," but an *accidens* or supplement. A wedge is at once driven between the material sign and the breathed utterance, the living name and the dead letter.

To work "Loves magique," the name must be conjured, that is, *spoken*, rehearsed and invoked into the audience's (or speaker's own) mental presence, drawing its life-blood from the speaker's spirit-breath. And from this point on the poem asks, metadiscursively, Does the material inscription express the same powers as living speech? Does writing, and reading, imperil the workings of a word's magic? Is it unity and presence, or the poet's very absence, that his written name asserts? The Cabalistic "charme" of his name would unite the poet and lady, body and soul, signifier and signified in a *mysterium conjunctionis* of spoken language; but from this point on, almost with each succeeding stanza, the name loses more and more of this power, shattering the unity of the sign, of the lovers' souls, of the poet's own living relation with his discourse. For, so long as the poet serves as her tutor, interpreting its meaning in her physical presence, her fidelity is apparently secure; in his absence, though, how shall the lady herself choose to read it? By its very nature esoteric, does not the Cabalistic text prove inaccessible—senseless, worthless even—to all but the adept? In the poet's presence, the name is "hard" (4), firm and constant; in his absence it becomes, of a sudden, "*too* hard and deepe" (19), its "learning" (20) lost. Thus the poet casts the efficacy of his signature in doubt, questioning the capacity of writing to "teach" fidelity:

IIII
Or if too hard and deepe
This learning be, for a scratch'd name to teach,
   It, as a given deaths head keepe,
   Lovers mortalitie to preach,
Or thinke this ragged bony name to bee
   My ruinous Anatomie.
(19–24)

The lady has not learned this Cabalistic power of names, a power that would preserve the poet's living presence. As his "bone" (28) or skeleton, the etched lines become but fragments of the poet's "scatter'd body" (32); like a "deaths head," then, the engraved name will "preach" of "Lovers mortalitie"—more, in fact, than a *memento mori*, the inscription commemorates the author's own death and dismemberment in writing, his "ruinous Anatomie." For it is in the very nature of writing that it inscribes "absence, darknesse, death; things which are not" ("A Nocturnall upon S. Lucies Day," 18). Though it attests to an author's desire for presence, the poem itself becomes a sign or Zwinglian record of absence, the written trace of a (once-)living consciousness. Lacking the power to sustain life, the name leaves behind but a death-mask made in promise of a resurrection and return.

Thus admitting the failure of Cabala, the poet turns suddenly to the Christian *Eschaton*, when "the same body, and the same soul, shall be recompact again, and be identically, numerically, and individually the same man."[20] Here Donne the preacher restates with absolute conviction the ultimate restoration of soul and body, a doctrine of theology that the poet appropriates for his own "scripture" or signature: though the poet and name alike suffer death-in-absence, his return, recapitulating Christ's resurrection, will "repaire / And recompact" his "scatter'd body" (31–32), restoring breath and life to his "bony name" (23). Still, the promise of a resurrection offers little control over the present situation, a loss that the poet attempts to redress by reclaiming some measure of the name's former power. Though its "soveraigne spirit" has fallen silent, the poet now en-

20. Donne, *Fifty Sermons,* 29; quoted in Husain, *Dogmatic and Mystical Theology,* p. 73. Noting the poem's continuous allusion to Scripture, Gary Stringer offers a typological interpretation, where Christ's death and resurrection, his departure and promised return to the disciples provides the theological basis for the poet's own promise of return ("Learning 'Hard and Deepe': Biblical Allusion in Donne's 'A Valediction: Of My Name, in the Window,'" pp. 228–29). While Stringer's analysis uncovers the incarnationist theology of language that underlies the poem, other readers have questioned and ironized the poem's rhetorical procedures. John Bernard, for example, suggests that the poem explores "the subliminal struggle of faith and doubt in the religion of poetry" ("Orthodoxia Epidemica: Donne's Poetics and 'A Valediction: Of My Name in the Window,'" p. 384); though it initially claims the power of magic, it admits, ultimately, that "not magic but rules govern our lives" (p. 388). I would add that Donne's skepticism is simultaneously linguistic and epistemological, an argument already partially outlined by D. H. Roberts, who suggests that the poem illustrates the "ultimate denial of identification" between signifier and signified ("'Just Such Disparitie': The Real and the Representation in Donne's Poetry," p. 101).

dows it with the "vertuous powers" of "love and grief," twin "starres
. . . in supremacie" whose "influence" flowed into the word's "characters" at its conception/inscription:

VI
Till my returne repaire
And recompact my scatter'd body so,
    As all the vertuous powers which are
    Fix'd in the starres, are said to flow
Into such characters, as graved bee
    When those starres have supremacie,

VII
So since this name was cut
When love and griefe their exaltation had,
    No door 'gainst this names influence shut;
    As much more loving, as more sad,
'Twill make thee; and thou shouldst, till I returne,
    Since I die daily, daily mourne.

(31–42)

The argument, though neat, is undercut by its own rhetoric. Stars
may, perhaps, influence earthly creations; what influence, though,
can "love and grief" exercise when theirs is but a figurative "exaltation," when astrology is itself reduced to metaphor? Paradoxically,
the poet's death-in-absence becomes his own best argument for her
continuing fidelity: if not love, then a widow's grief shall compel
some observance of chastity, making her "daily mourne."

While early stanzas are complimentary, the tone and attitude
thus darken with each subsequent stanza, modulating from praise,
to "teach[ing]," to "preach[ing]," to ironic rebuke. For as his name
weakens in its powers, the lady's potential for infidelity seems stead-
ily to increase, turning her from a Laura worthy of Petrarchan admi-
ration into a Catullan Lesbia. And what begins as elegant, if somewhat extravagant compliment degenerates into domestic comedy:

VIII
When thy'inconsiderate hand
Flings out this casement, with my trembling name,
    To looke on one, whose wit or land,
    New battry to thy heart may frame,
Then thinke this name alive, and that thou thus
    In it offendst my Genius.

IX
And when thy melted maid,
Corrupted by thy Lover's gold, and page,

His letter at thy pillow'hath laid,
Disputed it, and tam'd thy rage,
And thou begin'st to thaw towards him, for this,
May my name step in, and hide his.

X

And if this treason goe
To'an overt act, and that thou write againe;
In superscribing, this name flow
Into thy fancy, from the pane.
So, in forgetting thou remembrest right,
And unaware to mee shalt write.

(43–60)

Offering but the illusion that his name shall come alive, becoming its author's "Genius," the poet himself notes the patent unpersuasiveness of such spells and his comic inability to control either the language or the lady. And though the pane seems to "trembl[e]," in fear of its own violation, when her "inconsiderate hand" flings open the casement, yet the text-window remains a dead letter: the lady shall but "*thinke* this name alive" (italics added). In his physical absence, moreover, a maid will take the poet's place as her tutor, "Disput[ing]" with her the truth and worth of a competing text, a rival's letter. Suddenly incapable of preventing the lady's "treason" (her own letter-writing to the rival), the most powerful defense his name now offers is a temporary dyslexia, a misreading, and a miswriting, on the lady's part. "In superscribing" or addressing her letter his own name shall "flow" into her "fancy," and "unaware to mee shalt write." Far from sustaining her memory, the inscription is no longer faithful even to itself: reduced to forgery, to its own misappropriation of another's writing, the poet's signature can hope only to contaminate the lady's own text and interpretation, causing her to "forget" rather than "remember right."

In *Essays in Divinity* Donne meditates upon a similar theme, the weakness of engravings or "Medalls" to sustain memory:

Amongst men, all Depositaries of our Memories, all means which we have trusted with the preserving of our Names, putrifie and perish. Of the infinite numbers of the Medals of the Emperors, some one happy Antiquary, with much pain, travell, cost, and most faith, beleeves he hath recovered some one rusty piece, which deformity makes reverend to him, and yet is indeed the fresh work of an Impostor.
    The very places of the *Obeliscs*, and *Pyramides* are forgotten, and the purpose why they were erected. Books themselves are subject to the mercy of the Magistrate: and as though the ignorant had not been

enemie enough for them, the Learned unnaturally and treacherously contribute to their destruction, by rasure and misinterpretation. (*Essays in Divinity,* pp. 43–44)

In what sense can poetry do better? Tied to the problem of preserving one's name and memory is the problem of forgery, of substitution-in-absence, which mocks the "faith" of those deluded by such fiction. Texts, like "Medals," become the "fresh work of an Impostor." Later in this essay Donne compares the book composed by human hands to the "*Book of Life*," an originary or arch-writing of which God is the author, and "Names honour'd with a place in this book, cannot perish, because the Book cannot" (*Essays in Divinity,* p. 44). Yet man's own writings, the "means which we have trusted with the preserving of our Names, putrifie and perish." In a similar vein, "A Valediction: of my Name in the Window" describes the poet's loss of the power of naming (or rather of self-presencing and self-preservation *through* naming). Far from sustaining his own living voice, the engraved name becomes the poet's grave—a gruesome pun that has echoed throughout the poem from the beginning stanza.

Writing, then, both the name and the poem itself, cannot guarantee the lady's faith. And thus the poem ends by denying its own arguments, explicitly rejecting the claim that writing sustains love:

XI

But glasse, and lines must bee,
No meanes our firme substantiall love to keepe;
Neere death inflicts this lethargie,
And this I murmure in my sleepe;
Impute this idle talke, to that I goe,
For dying men talke often so.

(61–66)

Their "firme substantiall love" is a love in and of the flesh (unashamedly so, given the suddenly sexual overtones of the poet's language). As a "dying" man, upon whom "Neere death inflicts" a "lethargie," one might imagine that the poem's climax becomes the poet's own, each spent in an act of verbal/sexual eroticism (as if the final stanzas had been spoken not from the window but from the bed). It seems, indeed, that only their continued physical presence can keep the (male) poet's (fleshly) love "firme" and "substantiall"—unless, of course, the whole poem has been but an elaborate fantasy of power, jealousy, infidelity, and sexual possession all played out in space of writing. It seems that the poetry of incarna-

tionism, of sacramental, bodily presence, is suddenly reduced to
carnal fantasy. All, even the dramatic situation, has been played out
in the imagination; all is in fact already absent, all is wish-fulfill-
ment—all is writing. A letter may "be written far off," yet acts of
writing and reading become a "Conference, and *seperatos copulat*
. . . we overcome distances, we deceive absences, and wee are together even then when wee are asunder" (*Sermons*, 1:285). Donne
cites St. Ambrose as his authority; one wonders, though, if the ambiguities and implications of the language here exceed the preacher's intentions, questioning the possibility, even, of an incarnationist rhetoric. For the letter does not "overcome" so much as
"deceive" absences, its feeling of intimacy and of dialogue reduced
to an effect of language, to a sophist's deception. Indeed the phrase,
seperatos copulat, suggests the sort of fantasy-union that Derrida,
interpreting Jean Jacques Rousseau, terms a "dangerous supplement," a transformation of written discourse into an act of auto-
eroticism[21]—surely a blasphemous thought, given Donne's divine
subject, and yet it is only within a genuinely sacramental theology
of language that such union-in-absence is ever more than a poet's,
or reader's, narcissistic fantasy. And the poet of "A Valediction: of
my Name in the Window" is unable to claim for his language the
power either of Hermetic or of sacramental presence.

  The subject of this final stanza is thus simultaneously sexual and
textual, a (written) fantasy of speech and physical presence. Observe the dual reference in "lines" (61), for example, suggesting
both the etched lines of the engraved signature and the poet's verses
about them (in a word, the present poem, which ends by ironizing
the whole enterprise of valediction, turning itself into "idle talk").
And beyond its possible sexual overtones, what is this "lethargie"
that "Neare death inflicts" if not the poem itself? As Derrida reminds us, writing is "the becoming-absent and the becoming-un-
conscious of the subject," the subject's "relationship with its own
death," for "on all levels of life's organization, that is to say, of *the
economy of death*, all graphemes are of a testamentary essence."[22]
Certainly "A Valediction: of my Name in the Window" discovers
such a grapheme in this name, the poem itself preaching the death
of living speech, the death of the transcendental subject, the death
of the author, in writing. Is there then no antidote for absence? Do
Donne's other valedictions end on so pessimistic a note?

  21. *Of Grammatology,* pp. 141–64.
  22. Ibid., p. 69.

"Amongst men, all Depositaries of our Memories, all means which we have trusted with the preserving of our Names, putrifie and perish" (*Essays in Divinity,* p. 43); thus Donne describes the humanist problem of history and cultural loss. In apparent contradiction, "A Valediction: of the Booke" turns to writing—the "booke" especially, that so thoroughly humanist symbol—as an antidote and preservative against time, absence, loss, ignorance, schism:

> I'll tell thee now (deare Love) what thou shalt doe
> > To anger destiny, as she doth us,
> > How I shall stay, though she esloygne me thus,
> And how posterity shall know it too;
> > > How thine may out-endure
> > > Sybills glory, and obscure
> > > Her who from *Pindar* could allure,
> > And her, through whose helpe *Lucan* is not lame,
> And her, whose booke (they say) *Homer* did finde, and name.
>
> > Study our manuscripts, those Myriades
> > Of letters, which have past twixt thee and mee,
> > Thence write our Annals, and in them will bee,
> To all whom loves subliming fire invades,
> > > Rule and example found;
> > > There, the faith of any ground
> > > No schismatique will dare to wound,
> > That sees, how Love this grace to us affords,
> To make, to keep, to use, to be these his Records.
>
> > > > > > > > > > (1–18)

"Destiny," so dreaded a divinity in the song, "Sweetest love, I do not goe," is here reduced to a court decree, "esloyn[ing]" (that is, eloigning or banishing) the poet from the realm and his lady alike. And in this banishment lurks a double crisis. The preservation of their love depends on the preservation both of their "learning" and their "faith" (15), each of which, in turn, shall depend on the lady's acts of reading and writing.[23] She is urged to "Study" their "manuscripts, those Myriades / Of letters" and, in an apparent exercise of humanist philology, to rewrite them, rendering them into a book of "Annals."

Such an act, such a *text*, would seek no less than to resolve the

23. Suggestively, Anne Ferry describes "A Valediction: of the Booke" as Donne's deliberate divergence from the classical conventions of "eternizing verse" (*All in War with Time: Love Poetry of Shakespeare, Donne, Jonson, Marvell,* pp. 67–125). In contrast, Raman Selden analyzes the poem as an expression of the poet's "incarnational conviction." See his article, "John Donne's 'Incarnational Conviction,'" pp. 64–65.

intellectual crises of Donne's age, completing the humanist recovery of ancient wisdom, the confirmation of modern science, and the Reformation defense of "faith" from schism. Recovered and reinterpreted as history, their letters would become no less than the repository of all recorded wisdom, of all cultural accomplishments and value, a veritable "universe" (26) of knowledge. The lady herself would become polymath, wisdom's protector and polemicist—a *defensor fidei* whose own fame, enrolled in the writing, shall "outendure / Sybills glory" (5-6) and all the great women of legend and literary history. Indeed the lady is to wage a pamphlet war, as it were, against love's "Vandals" (25) and "schismatique[s]" (16), "anger[ing]" the very forces that banish the poet from his homeland and his love. But more than legend, more than intellectual history (and more, certainly, than pamphleteering or religious polemic), her writing would be divinely inspired, for she has been chosen as Love's Exegete—a type of St. Paul whose words are granted the status and authority of Holy Writ. The lady and poet together are thus "to make, to keep, to use, to be these his Records." Of course such language is either profoundly naive or blasphemously arrogant in its implications: not only "mak[ing] but "be[ing]" these "Records," the lovers become simultaneously the living witnesses and written testaments to a god of love who has chosen them, called them to his priesthood, and inspired their "Booke" or bible.

Then again this, precisely, is the aim of valediction, to admit no divorce between lady and letter, name and numen, poet and poem. By becoming love's priests, by invoking a theology of language that preserves presence in writing, the poem unites (or confuses?) *ethos* and *bios*, writing and life. Her book would become the means by which the poet "shall stay" with her, the means by which "posterity" shall know their love, and the means by which the lady shall herself remain faithful. Thus the permanence and security of their love rests thoroughly, and perilously, in writing:

> This Booke, as long-liv'd as the elements,
>   Or as the worlds forme, this all-graved tome,
>   In cypher write, or new made Idiome;
> Wee for loves clergie only'are instruments.
>   When this booke is made thus,
>   Should again the ravenous
>   Vandals and Goths inundate us,
>   Learning were safe; in this our Universe
> Schooles might learne Sciences, Spheares Musick, Angels Verse.
>   (19–27)

"Long-liv'd as the elements," a *monumentum aere perennius,* the book would preserve learning from violence and loss, offering "rule and example" to its readers. Indeed the next three stanzas catalog the kinds of learning, secular as well as religious, this book would offer. Here "Loves Divines" (28) may study the more "abstract spiritual love" (30) whose meaning lies beyond the physical act of sex, or, if "loth so to amuze / Faiths infirmitie," such students of their love might instead "chuse / Something which they may see and use" (32–34): their love-making, rendered as a text or symbolic action, would offer a sensuous "type" (36) of spiritual union, their bodies becoming material signifiers that "figure" (36) or represent the spirit, enabling it to be "see[n] and use[d]." Lawyers, too, may learn here "More then in their books" (38), while "Statesmen, (or of them, they which can reade,) / May of their occupation finde the groundes" (46–47).

But how should writing accomplish this? The present poem does not itself claim to preserve love, either by enacting, sustaining or commemorating it; rather, it *urges the lady to write* this saving, preserving text. The poem also records a tension present in all Donne's valedictory poetry, that between writing and speaking: the poet will "tell" (1) the lady what she herself should write and what the effect of the writing should be, all the while ignoring (concealing?) the written nature of his own discourse, the fact that he asserts for her "Booke" or text a preservative power he does not claim for his own. Thus the security and continuance of love lies forever outside the present poem in a future writing, a new book that, alone, would be "long-liv'd as the elements." It would be, that is, *if* it were written; and even if written, in what way would it be interpreted? Since it is composed "in cypher . . . or new made Idiome," who other than the two lovers will be able to read it? The poet has already questioned whether many "Statesmen," the poet-priest's secular counterpart, "can reade" (46) such a text, and indeed, while none whom they now govern "dares tell" the "weaknesse" (52) of such rulers, those who can read would find that it "deadly wounds" their "art" (48) of governance—becoming itself "subject," one might presume, "to the mercy of the Magistrate . . . as though the ignorant had not been enemie enough" (*Essays in Divinity,* p. 44). Their "learning," therefore, the very text she is supposed to write, would be endangered by its subversive doctrine on the one hand, and on the other by its occult idiom, its hieroglyphics or grammatology. Like Scripture or a newly recovered ancient text, her book becomes not the preservation of learning but itself an object of "Study" (10), in need of translation (and capable, it would seem, of mistranslation and misuse).

"In this thy booke," the poet adds, "such will their nothing see, / As in the Bible some can finde out Alchimy" (53–54). What is this final knowledge, then, this "nothing"? Is the hidden wisdom of "Alchimy" actually recoverable from the Bible, or do they search the book in vain for a knowledge that is nonexistent, truly nothing at all? "As though the ignorant had not been enemie enough" for such a book, "the Learned unnaturally and treacherously contribute to [its] destruction, by rasure and misinterpretation" (*Essays in Divinity*, p. 44); in fact the book is put "under erasure" (*sous rature*, in Derrida's formula) even before it is written. For if Holy Writ cannot escape misreading, how should the lady's? Though "the word of God is an infalible guide," Donne the preacher observes, "God hath provided thee also visible, and manifest assistants, the Pillar his Church, and the Angels his Ministers in the Church. The Scripture is thine onely *Ephod*, but *applica Ephod*, apply it to thee by his Church, and by his visible Angels, and not by thine own private interpretation" (*Sermons*, 1:283). The word is itself "an infalible guide," and yet it remains in need of a professional priesthood, a professional critic or interpreter. The lay reader, lacking a spiritual guide or Inner Teacher, will inevitably find "nothing" (53), or simply read wrong. Of course, the two lovers are to be its "clergie" (22), a priestly caste in control of its interpretation; their own tradition, therefore, and not the individual reader's weakened powers, should regulate the meaning. And so long as they live to serve as its ministers, the book can be sustained in its singular and determinate, though mystic meaning. With their death, however, the book would lose its priesthood—and that which is to preserve culture shall fall silent, its learning forever inaccessible to the world. Though "long-liv'd as the elements" (19), in what way can this book claim, therefore, to live? Is its claim to life and permanence not undercut by its very status as an "all-graved tome" (20)? Once again the writing heralds absence: the "all-graved tome," an obviously punning phrase, becomes grave and tomb for the lovers, their faith, their private experience and knowledge. One is brought to remember that the "well-wrought urn" of Donne's "Canonization"—that seemingly firm and eternal monument to love—is a *funeral* urn, a literary monument that commemorates, and in commemorating proclaims but the absence, and the death, of the author in writing. For "it is this life of the memory," Derrida observes, "that the *phar-*

makon of writing would come to hypnotize: fascinating it, taking it out of itself by putting it to sleep in a monument."[24]

"Thus vent thy thoughts," the poet advises, reducing her writing to a purgation or exhalation (a dissemination?):

> abroad I'll study thee,
> As he removes farre off, that great heights takes;
> How great love is, presence best tryall makes,
> But absence tryes how long this love will bee;
> To take a latitude
> Sun, or starres, are fitliest view'd
> At their brightest, but to conclude
> Of longitudes, what other way have wee,
> But to marke when, and where the darke eclipses bee?
> (55–63)

One must "take" or survey loves, like "great heights," from a distance. No longer an involuntary banishment, the poet's departure becomes an attempt to gain perspective, to distance himself from his own subject of "Study," the lady's love and continued fidelity. Just as eclipses are used to measure longitude, the poet's absence now "tryes how long this love will bee." Departure has thus turned into a test, while the lady has herself turned into a text, the subject of reading and interpretation. Her writings, her actions, her fidelity in his absence will be carefully observed and evaluated ("graded," the academician might say) by the poet. Far from overcoming or lamenting his absence, the poem ends by rationalizing it, justifying it, as it were, in the interests of "knowledge."

On the surface, then, "A Valediction: of the Booke" expresses confidence in the lady's devotion and in the strength of their relationship; beneath the surface, however, and beneath the extravagant, Petrarchan praise lies a challenge to the lady, that she not slacken in her love. It is a challenge that the poem offers, but one whose outcome the poem cannot guarantee; thus the phrase "darke eclipses" casts its pall over preceding stanzas, reminding lovers and readers alike of what is actually at stake. Occasioned by the poet's departure, the valediction turns self-consciously to an exploration of poetry itself, of its in/capacity to sustain life and ensure the fidelity, not simply of the woman but of writing. For it is not just the physical separation of lovers, and not just the separation of spirit

24. Derrida, *Dissemination*, p. 105.

from flesh, that such a poem seeks to overcome: it must seek, ultimately, to overcome the separation of *verba* from their *res*, enabling the poet and lady, as two of the poem's crucial signifiers, to be incarnate in the flesh of language, literally to be in, indeed, *to be* those "Records" inscribed in the text. And if this incarnationism is denied? What happens when sacramental presence, the alchemy of poetic language, is reduced to a mere trace of memory? Then writing provides but a weak compensation and surely no antidote for absence, becoming a *pharmakon* or drug—or, more precisely, a compulsive action that seeks to allay (though it can never cure) the anxiety of separation.

6

Incarnationism and Transcendence

We have explored the crisis of presence and absence that Donne's valedictions continually confront, one that lies at the center of Western metaphysics. But even as they assert a realm of spirit above the sheerly physical (and assert, thereby, the paradox of united souls and separate bodies) these lyrics attempt, through language, to defeat the separation that their own dualistic epistemology assumes as a premise. Thus the problem of metaphysics, of spiritual presences asserted over against physical absence, becomes a problem of language in general and of writing in particular. And we might pause, if briefly, to question the impact of this crisis on the genre of valediction. Like the *Satyres*, it seems, Donne's valedictions are far from naive reproductions of a traditional form. They are, rather, self-reflexive discourses about their own possibility, explorations of the problems inherent in the relations between language, belief, and literary genre. They seek to convince the addressee (and often poet himself) about the possibility of consolation, the possibility of spiritual union and identity. They persuade that this union has occurred, or, at more pessimistic moments, that it should occur, for such alone provides a guarantee against absence and loss.

This is but the first task facing the poet. Having asserted an epistemology in which spiritual union seems possible, he must find a language capable of affirming this union and enabling consolation—that is, of enabling the poem itself to be written, and the form itself to be performed or enacted. And we are compelled to ask: Do the valedictions (or other of Donne's lyric genres, for that matter: the aubades, *reverdes*, anniversaries, emblems, meditations, and seduction poems, to name a few) ever find or fashion an efficacious language? Different speakers, different addressees, different attitudes toward experience and the powers of language bring each of these lyrics to confront the crises of love, poetic discourse, and poetic absence in strikingly disparate ways, some more or less triumphal than others. The previous chapter explored the frailty of incarnationism in "A Valediction: of my Name in the Window" and "A Valediction: of the Booke." In either case, a language of sacramental unity is continuously if subtly undermined by a competing rhetoric of skepticism. "A Valediction: of Weeping" similarly falls from incarnationism to skepticism, but we shall find that a fourth poem, Donne's "Valediction: forbidding Mourning," evinces a different movement in argument, seeking rest in a self-effacing language of silent meditation. The present chapter, then, continues our examination of the valedictory poetry, after which it turns, in some detail, to the theological interrelations between incarnationism and this second rhetoric, the rhetoric of transcendence. For here, once again, the problem of genre has become a problem of rhetoric, specifically of these two competing theologies of language.[1]

We might note, first of all, that poems of departure abound in classical literature, and that ancient theory observes their great variety.[2] Attempting to revive the classical forms, Scaliger focuses somewhat narrowly, however, on the *propempticum*, a *laudandi occasio* or occasion for praise and prayers that might accompany a traveler on his journey. A common subject of such prayer is deliverance from the hazards of travel (*adversus pericula*), a constant source of anxiety in Donne's own poetry of departure. More significant for Donne, though, is Scaliger's discussion of the *amatorium propempticum*, a poem on the parting of lovers in which praise and prayer turn to complaint:

> If you wish to console your beloved in a speech of farewell, what means do you have to move or express emotions? Both history and fable shall

---

1. Discussions of the valedictions as a collection or genre are surprisingly few, though Donald L. Guss examines their Petrarchan conventions (*John Donne, Petrarchist: Italianate Conceits and Love Theory in the Songs and Sonets*, pp. 69–75, 139–41). See also Nancy J. C. Andreason, *John Donne: Conservative Revolutionary*, pp. 223–29, and Marotti, *Coterie Poet*, pp. 97–102, 167–83.

2. Perhaps the fullest discussion in ancient theory, Menander's *Peri Epideiktikon* describes the *syntaktikos logos*, in which a traveler "laments the necessary parting, praises the people left and that to which one is going" (Theodore Burgess, "Epideictic Literature," p. 112). There are, in addition, three kinds of *propemptikos* logos, depending on the addressee: "if between equals, it is of a lover-like character; if to a superior, laudatory; a superior may address an inferior, then advice is prominent; when addressed to a ruler it resembles the *basilikos logos*," that is, an elevated speech of formal praise (ibid., p. 111). See also Francis Cairns, *Generic Composition in Greek and Roman Poetry*, pp. 284–86, who cites a remarkable number of ancient examples, and Kenneth Quinn, *Latin Explorations: Critical Studies in Roman Literature*, pp. 239–73.

provide you with materials, and what ornaments (*flores*) shall be gathered from Nature herself, taken from animals, plants, the very elements? For all things in Nature strive toward unity. "Why did Fate give him to you, only to take him away? What hope is there now? How shall I live, if I am to be without you?" Let these themes be part of the love poem.[3]

Although *Alloquium* or consolation remains the ostensive aim of the genre, it is placed beyond the poet's reach; a sense of loss, rather, pervades all, a sense of hopelessness, of helplessness before the tyranny of fate. Suggestively, the form as Scaliger describes it seeks to elicit rather than to allay grief.

The search for models, then, and for possible influences must take us beyond the classical to Provençal traditions and, ultimately, to Petrarchism, perhaps the most pervasive generic and stylistic influence on the *Songs and Sonets*. Absence and departure are recurrent themes of Petrarch's *Rime*, numerous sonnets recounting the poet's forced absences (Sonnet XV: "Io mi rivolgo in dietro a ciascun passo," for instance) as well as Laura's departures, both temporary (as in Sonnet XVII: "Pióvommi amare lagrime dal viso") and permanently from this world, with her death (Sonnet CCCXXVIII: "L'ultimo lasso! de' miei giorni allegri," and Sonnet CCCXIX: "O giorno, o ora, o ultimo momento"). Of this last sort most poignant is Sonnet CCCXIV ("Mente mia, che presaga de' tuoi danni"), in which the poet laments his failure to bid his deceased love farewell—though he writes, in a typically mixed, Petrarchan metaphor, of having left both "his dear thoughts and heart" with her eyes ("Come ardavanno in quel punto ch'i'vidi, / Gli occhi, i quai non devea riveder mai, / Quando a lor, come a' duo amici piú fidi, / Partendo, in guardia la piú nobil salma, / I miei cari penseri e'l cor lasciai!").[4] Typically elegiac in tone, the tradition of valedictory poetry thus describes departure and absence as a kind of death, for which it offers such ritual consolations as the memories that remain, the affections that continue in the loved one's absence, and the mutual fidelity symbolized, though often tritely so, by a figur-

---

3. "Si amicam propemptico alloquere: quales tibi affectus vel movendi, vel declarandi? Quas attinges tum fabulas, tum historias. Qui flores ex intima rerum natura delibandi? Ab animalibus, a plantis, ab elementis ipsis: quorum conditio universa spectat ad unionem. Quare tibi illum dederit Fatum, ut auferret? Quid amplius tibi sperandum: quo vivendum modo, qui sine teipso sis futurus? Esto hoc igitur *erotikon*" (Scaliger, *Poetices*, p. 157).

4. Quotations from Petrarch are taken from Anna Maria Armi's edition of the *Sonnets and Songs*, p. 436 et passim.

ative exchange of hearts. Donne's own valedictions make use of such well-worn topoi, but, unlike predecessors in the form, who seem satisfied with metaphoric assertions of spiritual union, Donne turns his valedictions into an exploration of the metaphysics of unity and separation, identity and difference, presence and absence.

"A Valediction: of Weeping" offers ample proof. Rather than lessen the grief of parting, the poet "powre[s] forth" (1) his own sorrow (much as Scaliger advises), his tears becoming the "Fruits" (7) or offspring of this grief:

> Let me powre forth
> My teares before thy face, whil'st I stay here,
> For thy face coins them, and thy stampe they beare,
> And by this mintage they are something worth,
>   For thus they bee
>   Pregnant of thee;
> Fruits of much griefe they are, emblemes of more,
> When a teare falls, that thou falls which it bore,
> So thou and I are nothing then, when on a divers shore.
>
>   (1–9)

Suddenly "pregnant" (6) of the lady's reflected image, his tears are transformed into living material bodies that incarnate the lady's *imago* or soul (8). Initially, then, the poet asserts the identity of lovers by means of an incarnational symbol uniting body-tear and soul-image, one that animates or inseminates the body-tear with her visual presence. And yet the foundations of such a rhetoric, the mutual presence and material, bodily communication of its participants, are utterly destroyed by absence; when "on a divers shore," the two lovers become "nothing," unspirited bodies and disembodied souls. Interpreted in this way, absence again points to the crisis of incarnational rhetoric. And a second crisis, in many ways more perilous, arises with the poet's implicit recognition of the rhetorical, indeed written nature of his arguments, of the fact that the incarnational symbolism threatens throughout to be reduced to mere sign, a dead letter or inscription. Can his tears, in other words, be both "Fruits" or inspirited offspring and "emblemes" (7) as well (that is, external representations or signs)? The terms seem mutually supportive, but the rhetorics they invoke remain radically opposed, each suggesting a different relation between the poet's tears and the lady's *imago*. As "Fruits," the tears literally "bore" (8) her soul, as if her image animated them, transforming them into *homunculi*. As "emblemes," though, the tears are denied life, reducing the lady's presence to a surface-image, turning the tears themselves into "coins" that repre-

sent rather than incarnate the poet's love. Even before his departure, then, the lady is reduced to a series of signifiers, heralding her
physical absence from the textual space.

The remaining stanzas continue to explore this disjunction between fruits and emblems, the real and the representation:

> On a round ball
> A workeman that hath copies by, can lay
> An Europe, Afrique, and an Asia,
> And quickly make that, which was nothing, *All*,
> So doth each teare,
> Which thee doth weare,
> A globe, yea world by that impression grow,
> Till thy teares mixt with mine doe overflow
> This world, by waters sent from thee, my heaven dissolved so.
>
> O more then Moone,
> Draw not up seas to drowne me in thy spheare,
> Weepe me not dead, in thine arms, but forbeare
> To teach the sea, what it may doe too soone;
> Let not the winde
> Example finde,
> To doe me more harme, then it purposeth;
> Since thou and I sigh one anothers breath,
> Who e'r sighes most, is cruellest, and hasts the others death.
>
> (10–27)

More than *homunculi*, the poet's tears are now said to incarnate
worlds (which the lady's tears, those "waters sent from thee," threat-
en to drown and dissolve). The lady thus assumes godlike powers,
but her effect on nature (on the poet's nature, surely) is hardly
beneficent. Is she then responsible for "drowning" the very worlds
she has herself created? What sort of god would annihilate her own
creation by such a flood? What sort of world, what sort of life is so
easily threatened? In fact the second stanza ends by dissolving
something that, from the beginning, was never more than a world-
in-appearance, the lifeless products of a mapmaker or "workeman"
(11)—a series of "copies" (11) or artistic reproductions pasted on
the surface of "a round ball" (10). No longer claiming to bear the
lady's living presence, his tears no more than "weare" (15) her,
much as a globe wears or displays its cartographic representations.

But while this penultimate stanza subtly questions its own rhetoric, the last stanza seems thoroughly persuaded (indeed, fearfully
so) of its incarnational symbolism. As "more then Moone" (19), her
physical presence again exercises the same power over the poet that

the moon wields over seas and tides. Of course her "spheare" (20), in which the poet might himself drown, is either a tear of her own or perhaps her eye, a second globe reflecting the poet's image. But in this mirror he discovers an unsettling, if superstitious omen: his own self-image drowned, literally dissolved in a tear-flood. There lurks a danger in her power to "teach the sea" (which the poet shall himself soon navigate), for his continued presence before her, para-doxically, now ensures his "drowning." And thus, beneath this stale Petrarchan conceit (the departing lover's death in a sea of tears) lies his own deeper fear of death. From the poet's own incarna-tionist perspective, each lover's sigh "hasts" (27) the other's demise; yet it is the poet who imperils his life at sea—and it is the poet, finally, who hastes from his love. Seeking to overcome his own grief, he can find no means (at least no verbal means) to safeguard their continued union or even allay fears while in her presence. Departure, not poetry, becomes grief's antidote.

The poem proves unable to preserve the lady (or the poet, for that matter) as a living, speaking presence within its space; though it turns the lovers both to "nothing . . . when on a divers shore" (9), in fact the poet and lady are always already "nothing," reduced to the traces or effects of language—to emblems, mirror-images, coins, "copies," and maps. Far from overcoming departure, absence, and death, the poem *inscribes* absence, inscribes a *poetics* of absence that undoes the poet's own naive incarnationism. A similar anxiety over representation and presence occurs in "Witchcraft by a Picture." Seeing his image "burning" in his lady's eye and "drowning" in her tears, the poet leaves her physical presence to counteract this im-plicitly murderous "art" or witchcraft:

> I fixe mine eye on thine, and there
> Pitty my picture burning in thine eye,
> My picture drown'd in a transparent teare,
> When I look lower I espie;
> Hadst thou the wicked skill
> By pictures made and mard, to kill,
> How many wayes mightst thou performe thy will?
>
> But now I'have drunke thy sweet salt teares,
> And though thou poure more I'll depart;
> My picture vanish'd, vanish feares,
> That I can be endamag'd by that art;
> Though thou retaine of mee
> One picture more, yet that will bee,
> Being in thine own heart, from all malice free.

One would think that such pictures are charm-like guarantors of the poet's continued presence, if not in the language or textual space, then at least in the lady's memory and imagination. And yet the poet discovers nothing but the frailty of such self-representations, images that survive (and thus sustain both the lady's memory and fidelity) only so long as he generates them by means of his own bodily presence. Representation becomes itself a kind of death that the poet "feares" (10) and attempts to avoid by means of departure. The supreme irony, then, is that "Witchcraft by a Picture" does not grant the poet the power of witchcraft, a power to conjure the exchange of hearts and thus to remain either within the beloved or within the language of his text. For the exchange of hearts is shown to be little more than Petrarchan conceit, a verbal formula that offers small consolation and, certainly, no victory over absence.

Thus far we have explored the failure of Donne's incarnationist rhetoric to overcome absence; this should not surprise, given that incarnationism inscribes a rhetoric of bodily presences and that the genre of valediction entails separation and departure. We have still, however, to consider "A Valediction: forbidding Mourning." Here, as in "A Valediction: of the Booke," the poet and lady are called to be love's clergy. But there the poet seeks to preserve their love in a literary monument, while the poet of "A Valediction: forbidding Mourning" repudiates public display, in fact repudiates public discourse. Theirs is now a private love, a private religion, and "To tell the layetie" (8)—that is, the lay reader (of this very poem?)—becomes "prophanation" (7), a vulgarization of their love that violates its sanctity. Their spirituality, then, distinguishes their love from the multitude; this same spirituality also distinguishes the rhetoric of the poem, which wavers between incarnationist paradox and a rhetoric of transcendence.

> As virtuous men passe mildly'away,
>   And whisper to their soules, to goe,
> Whilst some of their sad friends doe say,
>   The breath goes now, and some say, no:
>
> So let us melt, and make no noise,
>   No teare-floods, nor sigh-tempests move,
>   'Twere prophanation of our joyes
>   To tell the layetie our love.
> . . . .
> Dull sublunary lovers love
>   (Whose soul is sense) cannot admit

> Absence, because it doth remove
> Those things which elemented it.
>
> But we by'a love, so much refin'd,
> That our selves know not what it is,
> Inter-assured of the mind,
> Care lesse, eyes, lips, and hands to misse.
>   (1–8, 13–20)

In such poems as "The Expiration" and "A Valediction: of Weeping" the poet pleads against the lady's sighs and tears (for these, as exhalations of "spirit" and "life-blood," threaten to "hast" their mutual death). Here, in contrast, the speaker does not fear dissolution or death but freely invokes it. In fact the third and fourth stanzas make an ironic commentary upon the genre itself, suggesting why the loves (and the rhetorics) of Donne's other valedictions inevitably fail. Since absence removes, and thus destroys, the physical basis of "dull sublunary" love (13), the poet chooses to give up the body's claims, centering instead upon the soul. And though the lovers cannot have direct knowledge of the soul—they cannot even say what it is they love—their essential unity is not threatened by absence. For theirs is a marriage of true minds, minds "inter-assured" (19) of each other's strength and faithful devotion, an assurance that allows them to "Care lesse, eyes, lips, and hands to misse" (26). And thus, while the opening stanzas return to the most tired of Petrarchan tropes, departure-as-death, the poet attempts to transvalue the image, translating it into the language of religious mystery.

Were the body's death the end of all, and were their love not "virtuous," the lovers could not look upon absence with such equanimity. For only "virtuous men" (1) willingly leave this world, "whisper[ing] to their soules, to goe" (2), thus "pass[ing] mildly'away" (1). In the same manner these saintly lovers, asserting the immortality of the soul (and of soulful love), willingly dissolve or "melt" (5) their physical union, seeking out a holy death—from which, given their steadfast faith, they are assured a resurrection. Departure remains the body's "death," the loss of physical relation and bodily pleasure; in this respect "A Valediction: forbidding Mourning" agrees with Donne's other poems of absence. Yet in forbidding mourning, in forbidding the conventional lamentation accompanying death-in-absence, the poem denies the finality of this absence—the finality even of physical death. The souls live on, and they live on as one, resting in the promise of their resurrection when "the same body, and the same soul, shall be recompact again," with "the same integrity of body and soul, and the same integrity in the organs . . . and in the faculties of the soul too."[5] While "Dull sublunary love" (13) is "elemented" (16) by the material body, their own love is already "refin'd" (17), cleansed of physical imperfection and raised—in the alchemist's language, sublimated—to a higher spiritual state. The lovers die a holy death, therefore, ensured of a physical reunion, the effect of which will be a further cleansing of their love, a purification (of the body especially) by means of a spiritual alchemy. As J. D. Jahn describes it, "the eschatological conflagration which clears away corrupted substance involves a mysterious alchemy" in which, "in that last fire, flesh will be transmuted into eternal material."[6] More than a tissue of Petrarchan wit, and more than a show of quasi-logic, "A Valediction: forbidding Mourning" claims a theo-logic basis for its eschatological argument, one stronger (in theory, at least) than the failed astrology and hermeticism of, say, Donne's "Valediction: of my Name in the Window."

Here too, however, a problem arises. Having asserted their spiritual union, the poet must still find words to express "a love, so much refin'd, / That our selves know not what it is" (17–18), a soul-love that eludes naming even as it eludes direct knowledge. Is there a language equally "refin'd"? The language of the spirit, after all, performs acts of violence upon nature, wresting words from their physical referents; the language of the spirit, in short, is thoroughly and unashamedly metaphor, and this separation of the literal from the metaphoric points yet again to the dualistic epistemology of Western culture. For the philosopher of physical nature and the mystic inhabit radically different realms, speaking radically different languages, each denying the efficacy, the reality, of the other's world and words. The alchemist, in contrast, engenders an epistemology, and a theory of language, that seeks to overcome dual

5. Donne, *Fifty Sermons,* 29; quoted in Husain, *Dogmatic and Mystical Theology,* p. 73.
6. "The Eschatological Scene in Donne's 'A Valediction: Forbidding Mourning,'" p. 38. Among the Church Fathers, Gregory of Nyssa describes this purification as an alchemical process: "Not in hatred or revenge for a wicked life . . . does God bring upon sinners those painful dispensations; He is only claiming and drawing to Himself whatever, to please Him, came into existence . . . Just as those who refine gold from the dross which it contains not only get this base alloy to melt in the fire, but are obliged to melt the pure gold along with the alloy" ("On the Soul and the Resurrection," trans. H. A. Wilson, in *A Select Library of Nicene and Post-Nicene Fathers of the Christian Church,* 5:451; quoted in ibid., p. 39). As Jahn adds, "rarifying a corruptible body into immortal material is God's alchemy at the general resurrection" (p. 39).

ism. Of course the philosopher and mystic alike look with suspicion upon the alchemist's verbal performances; totally committed neither to the spirit nor to the material, his language seeks to confound these realms, literalizing the metaphoric, asserting the material aspect of spirit, the spiritual aspect of matter, moving freely, fluidly, between both states. Thus it is to that mysterious intersection or conjunction of mind and matter, the *mysterium conjunctionis*, that the language of alchemy directs us. More compelling, perhaps, than the arguments of Donne's other valedictions, this union of spiritual alchemy and Christian eschatology seeks to empower and sustain the poet's incarnationist rhetoric, providing a theological basis for his private eschatological claims. In what are among Donne's most memorable conceits, then, the final stanzas of this poem seek, however paradoxically, to express spiritual union as a rarified and extended physical relation, the unity of the lovers' souls (and the "expansion" of this greater soul through physical space) expressing the mysterious properties of beaten gold:

> Our two soules therefore, which are one,
>   Though I must goe, endure not yet
> A breach, but an expansion,
>   Like gold to ayery thinnesse beate.
>   (21–24)

The word-magic of such lines lies in their resolute refusal to admit dualism, separation, or absence. In theory, gold can be beaten so thin that it becomes invisible while remaining entire; so the lovers are but drawn-out, expanded in their essential unity, rather than drawn apart. And as the perfection of matter, gold becomes the hypostasis or substance of soul itself—lover and beloved are made one substance, joined and kept entire by the *poesis* of alchemy, the alchemy of poetic language.[7]

Curiously, though, having conjured their continued union by means of a golden language, the poet refuses to end, offering a

---

7. In "Donne's 'Valediction: Forbidding Mourning' and the Golden Compasses of Alchemical Creation," Eugene R. Cunnar argues that "a unified alchemical analogy control[s] the poem" (p. 96) and that the poet's "ability to project himself into the role of the spiritual alchemist . . . suggests his success in reconciling the disparate aspects of his life" (p. 110). Of course, the poem's "success" in such reconciliation must still depend on two things at least: the actual power of alchemy as a theology of language and the reader's (for that matter, the poet's) *belief* in such alchemy. Here, as in all Donne's valedictions, the crisis of argument remains a crisis of faith.

second, more elaborate, and more problematic analogy, that of the
"stiffe twin compasses":

> If they be two, they are two so
>   As stiffe twin compasses are two,
> Thy soule the fixt foot, makes no show
>   To move, but doth, if the'other doe.
>
> And though it in the center sit,
>   Yet when the other far doth rome,
> It leanes, and hearkens after it,
>   And growes erect, as it comes home.
>
> Such wilt thou be to mee, who must
>   Like th'other foot, obliquely runne;
> Thy firmnes make my circle just,
>   And makes me end, where I begunne.
>   (25–36)

The poet promises return and is confident in this promise, confident as well in the lady's good influence, whose "fixt foot" (27) and
"firmnes" (35) ensure his own end. In fact the circle itself provides a
symbol of integrity, unity, closure: if one imagines the center point
as a period or mark around which a circle is drawn, the alchemical
symbol for gold results.[8] Thus the alchemy of language seems still
to sustain the lovers' union, joining them within the poem's sacred
space. Nonetheless we must ask, do these final stanzas assert the
poet's continued presence and the lovers' unity? Or are they but a
promise (that is, of the poet's return) and a plea, therefore, for the
lady's continued faith? Though the poem seems to have come full
circle, guaranteeing the lover's swift return, the compass figure at
once casts doubt upon the miracle of unity. Unlike the integrity of
beaten gold, the integrity or unity of compass points remains problematic. What does this second foot do if not circle endlessly about
the first, never finally touching, never joining to become the same
point? And if its motion should be that of a spiral, of an elliptical
departure and return, as John Freccero suggests, then their golden
unity and the integrity of the circle itself are destroyed.[9] It seems
that the compass figure serves less to reinforce than to qualify this
golden reality, admitting the possibility that the lovers' souls might
still "be two" (25), their lives still marked by duality and division.

8. Peter L. Rudnytsky has made this point ("'The Sight of God': Donne's
Poetics of Transcendence," p. 193).
9. See "Donne's 'A Valediction: Forbidding Mourning.'"

And thus "A Valediction: forbidding Mourning" suggests that absence remains, on one level at least, a linguistic problem. Where shall one discover words that assert identity over difference, or at least demonstrate the ways language fails to express, faithfully or even adequately, the spiritual reality of transcendent, transverbal love? Though the conceit of beaten gold asserts, with confident naiveté, the power of language to conjure such a reality, the final conceit, with its "if," "as," and "like," more self-consciously observes the problem of argument by analogy, the fact that it is words the poet inscribes, not the realities themselves. Indeed, if the poem is itself circular, "end[ing]" where it had "begunne," then we are invited back to the opening stanzas—which may now, in a second, meta-textual reading, suggest *why* such a poem undoes its own incarnationist rhetoric. In departure the poet and lady are to "make no noise" (5), which becomes the very denial of their human linguistic nature. For man is himself "but a voice, but a sound, but a noise," as Donne writes in a sermon:

> he begins the noise himselfe, when he comes crying into the world; and when he goes out, perchance friends celebrate, perchance enemies calumniate him, with a diverse voice, a diverse noise. A melancholique man, is but a groaning; a sportfull man, but a song; an active man, but a Trumpet; a mighty man, but a thunderclap: Every man but *Ish*, but a sound, but a noyse. (*Sermons*, 9:61–62)

To "make no noise," then, as the opening stanzas advise, is to give up the very essence of one's being; to die, after all, is to give up one's breath-spirit. And yet the lovers are to "whisper to their soules, to goe" (2) in such a way that friends could not say whether "the breath" (their life, their love, his speech, *the present poem*) "goes now" or "no" (4). It would, in addition, be "prophanation . . . / To *tell*" (7–8) of their love: not "teare-floods," not "sigh-tempests" (6), but the very inadequacy of language, of "tell[ing]," would cause such profanation. Subsequent stanzas, even the boldest of Donne's incarnationist paradoxes, thus call the lover and reader alike to meditative silence; the poem is itself an effacement of poetry.

□   □   □

We shall find that this movement from incarnationism to transcendence is common in the *Songs and Sonets*. The diversity of human experience and the limited powers of language demand at the very least these two rhetorics, and many of Donne's lyrics (some of his finest, in fact: "The Canonization" and "The Exstasie") arise out of their subtle interplay. Indeed, exploring the problematic unity of soul and body, of that "subtle knot, which makes us man" (64), "The Exstasie" is no less than a poetic disputation on these competing theologies of language, for which reason we might turn now to this remarkable poem. St. Augustine provides the theological context: "the condition of man," he writes, "would be lowered if God had not wished to have men supply His word to men. How would there be truth in what is said—'For the temple of God is holy, which you are'—if God did not give responses from a human temple . . . ? For charity itself, which holds men together in a knot of unity, would not have a means of infusing souls and almost mixing them together if men could teach nothing to men."[10] Though separate in the flesh, Christians partake of one spirit, that of charity, which provides a divine exemplar for the physical love that seeks, similarly, to mingle souls. And the means of this infusing or mingling (in fact the rhetorical foundation of this linguistic theology) has at once become dialogue in-the-flesh. For communication is a mode of communion, God (and man) speaking to man through the material human body; the preacher—and the lover, we might add—is thus entrusted with the task of carrying on the Incarnation, bringing charity to all, knitting men together in a "knot of unity." Is the sharing of words any less an act of love than the more physical sharing of "blood," say, or semen? It is, perhaps, a greater sharing in that words are the lifeblood of the spirit; indeed, their reality *is* spirit. By means of its paradoxical "dialogue of one" (74), "The Exstasie" thus seeks to defeat physical separation, raising participants to a level of consubstantiality, *psyche, eros,* and *logos* meeting in the space of the love poem.

The first six stanzas, one third of this relatively long lyric, describe a scene of erotic play and rhetorical as well as physical posturing between the lovers. But though joined physically by hands and eyebeams, they seem otherwise far from united, their only "propagation" being "pictures on our eyes" (11–12), an image that

10. *On Christian Doctrine,* pp. 5–6. More than a ritual of language, similarly, Paul Tillich describes worship as a bodily action: "the body participates, because genuine faith is a passionate act. The way in which it participates is manifold. The body can participate both in vital ecstasy and in asceticism leading to spiritual ecstasy. But whether in vital fulfillment or vital restriction, the body participates in the life of faith" (*Dynamics of Faith,* pp. 106–7). Donne's "Exstasie," we shall find, both anticipates and questions such an incarnationist theology.

at once subtly questions the poet's incarnationist argument, pointing again to the disjunction between the real and the representation: while acts of love beget breathing human offspring, the love poet here, as in "A Valediction: of Weeping," begets but "pictures." Thus the early stanzas prepare for the lovers' physical union by the paradox of *extasis*, the very disembodiment of their souls (and a suspension, it would seem, not only of the souls but of incarnationism itself):

> As 'twixt two equal Armies, Fate
>   Suspends uncertaine victorie,
> Our soules, (which to advance their state,
>   Were gone out,) hung 'twixt her, and mee.
>
> And whil'st our soules negotiate there,
>   Wee like sepulchrall statues lay;
> All day, the same our postures were,
>   And wee said nothing, all the day.
>
> If any, so by love refin'd,
>   That he soules language understood,
> And by good love were grown all minde,
>   Within convenient distance stood,
>
> He (though he knew not which soule spake,
>   Because both meant, both spake the same)
> Might thence a new concoction take,
>   And part farre purer then he came.
>   (13–28)

Disembodied, the lovers "said nothing, all the day" (20), an apparent denial of physical speech. At the same time, however, the poet asserts the reality of "soules language," which only someone "so by love refin'd" would have "understood" (21–22)—or would simply be able to hear and, in hearing, bear witness to their love. The following lines, presumably, form the discourse such a lover would overhear:

> This Extasie doth unperplex
>   (We said) and tell us what we love,
> Wee see by this, it was not sexe,
>   Wee see, we saw not what did move:
> . . . .
> When love, with one another so
>   Interinanimates two soules,
> That abler soule, which thence doth flow,
>   Defects of lonelinesse controules.

> Wee then, who are this new soule, know,
> Of what we are compos'd, and made,
> For, th'Atomies of which we grow,
> Are soules, whom no change can invade.
> (29–32, 41–48)

Though souls are "Th'intelligences" and bodies "the spheare" (52), nonetheless the body and soul form a complex unity, an inspirited material substance or "allay" (56). Human nature is itself inherently mixed, after all, the soul necessarily dwelling in the body, coming to know and love other souls through the body's senses. Love "interinanimates" the souls, then, creating an intersubjectivity or "dialogue of one." And the body becomes the meeting place of these souls, the means through which "soule into soule may flow" (59).

Then again, if human nature is mixed, so writing, too—at least from an incarnationist perspective—claims this mixed status, providing a material substance (that is, the written text) that embodies and conveys spirit. Once more Donne's letters provide a model: "I make account that this writing of letters, when it is with any seriousness, is a kind of extasie, and a departure and a secession and suspension of the soul, which doth then communicate it self to two bodies: . . . I would every day provide for my souls last convoy, though I know not when I shall die, and perchance I shall never die; so for these extasies in letters, I oftentimes deliver my self over in writing" (*Letters*, p. 11). Paradoxically, one of the "two bodies" in which the soul must "communicate it self" is the letter-text itself; writing, then, becomes a kind of *extasis* that relocates the soul, enabling it *to speak from within* the writing, literally *to be* the writing. If we follow this logic to its conclusion, the lovers of "The Exstasie" become themselves ghostly inhabitants and speakers within the body-text: they *are* their words, in the same way that we live our bodies. At the same time, however, this relocation of the lovers' souls causes a dislocation or confusion in the language. Who writes? Who speaks? Presumably the poet writes what "we"—that is, the disembodied (or rather, the textualized) souls—"said" (30) in dialogue. Perhaps; but let us not forget the poet's earlier assertion that "wee said nothing, all the day" (20). Apparently, the lovers' physical bodies no longer provide the material organs of this speech. Shall we then ascribe that first "we" to the ecstatic souls, this second "wee" to the lovers in-the-flesh? Again, perhaps; but it seems that the poem simultaneously invites and defies the reader to locate the "speaker" of/in any stanza. For a pronoun that would seem to speak of unity, of the very possibility of "we," suddenly speaks of separation and the slippage of reference, of a "we" that is and is not the lovers, that does and does not speak.

Far from asserting their unity, the pronoun divides the lovers against themselves and, indeed, against the poet. For again, who speaks? Do the combined souls? If so, which words do they utter, and which remain the poet's? Another question: Has this higher soul *spoken* the "dialogue of one" (74)? Or must we remind ourselves that the words are the poet's, who has *written*? And if the poet writes (as most assuredly he does), would a full and faithful transcription of the souls' dialogue serve still to (trans-)substantiate them in the "flesh" of poetic language? However we respond to this last troublesome question, we must once again decide whether representation (of another's words) is the same as invocation and enactment. Does "The Exstasie" write out, or write *about*, the souls' dialogue? If the latter obtains, then the souls fail, in fact, to incarnate themselves in the "flesh" of poetic language, never achieving aural presence. The reader, therefore, can never be sure he or she has read, let alone understood, the souls' actual discourse. For their words remain either inaudible—insensible—or senseless to all but that fit audience, "so by love refin'd, / That he soules language understood" (21–22), and even this person's ability to understand depends on a previous knowledge of "refin'd" love. And who, finally, among mortals has "grown all minde" (23), as the souls claim such a reader must do? The combined souls do not claim to teach or fashion their audience into "some lover, such as wee" (73), and the poem's search for this fit audience may well prove vain.

Recognizing the inaccessibility, the incomprehensibility, the very *inaudibility* of their communion, the souls must seek a different means to interpret, one that inverts (and perhaps subverts) the incarnationist rhetoric of body-texts. No longer is the poem a *simulacrum* of the material human body; rather, the human body becomes itself a poem whose motions are a chain of signifiers, whose very gestures inscribe a text in time and space. As a performative language, physical love thus becomes a mode of symbolic action, an incarnationist text *par excellence*. The poet exhorts his lady,

> To' our bodies turne wee then, that so
>   Weake men on love reveal'd may looke
> Loves mysteries in soules doe grow,
>   But yet the body is his booke.
>
> And if some lover, such as wee,
>   Have heard this dialogue of one,

> Let him still marke us, he shall see
> Small change, when we'are to bodies gone.
> (69–76)

The disembodied souls may not have achieved aural presence, revealing "Loves mysteries" in spoken language. And yet "the body," the poet suggests, has become love's "booke" (72), a written text revealed to the spectator-turned-reader. And though the adept or fit audience (again, "some lover, such as wee," who has "heard this dialogue") will "*see* / Small change" when spiritual love is inscribed in a bodily text, it will be otherwise for "weake men," the majority of mankind, who will "look" (70) upon this love and see only the surface or "dead letter"—only the sexual act, in the same way that the hidden meaning of mystic texts eludes the uninitiated (though the words rest before them in their materiality, just as the lovers' bodies rest in plain sight). In this sense, "The Exstasie" is a poem about the perils of interpretation as well as a persuasion to love, turning acts of love into radically textual events. And here, as in other lyrics, the poet explicitly questions whether or not his audience (either the actual reader or, within the interior fiction, the addressee) will be able to read aright—that is, will already share in an experience that, like *extasis,* is itself transcendent—and thus participate in the poet's world and words.

We might pause here to consider an ancient controversy similar to *extasis,* which is speaking in tongues. Common among the early churches, it "manifests itself in an ecstasy" that, as Jim W. Corder observes, "realizes itself in a torrent of sound typically untranslatable by a hearer."[11] In his first letter to the Corinthians, St. Paul addresses this controversy directly; distinguishing tongues from "prophecy" or teaching, he criticizes those who overly value any private, transcendent language (by implication, the poet's included). Though such language "speaketh mysteries," as Paul writes, engendering a dialogue-of-one with God (or, in the poet's case, with the lady's own soul), yet its consequences are spiritual pride—the possessor may boast of divine favor—and a neglect of the proper use of language, which is to instruct fellow Christians:

> For he that speaketh in an *unknown* tongue speaketh not unto men, but unto God: for no man understandeth him; howbeit in the spirit he speaketh mysteries.

11. "Varieties of Ethical Argument, With Some Account of the Significance of *Ethos* in the Teaching of Composition," p. 21.

But he that prophesieth speaketh unto men *to* edification, and exhortation, and comfort. . . .

So likewise ye, except ye utter by the tongue words easy to be understood, how shall it be known what is spoken? For ye shall speak into the air.

There are, it may be, so many kinds of voices in the world, and none of them *is* without signification.

Therefore if I know not the meaning of the voice, I shall be unto him that speaketh a barbarian, and he that speaketh *shall be* a barbarian unto me.

Even so ye, forasmuch as ye are zealous of spiritual *gifts*, seek that ye may excel to the edifying of the church.

Wherefore let him that speaketh in an *unknown* tongue pray that he may interpret. (1 Cor. 14.2–3, 9–13)

More useful than tongues, then, is "prophesying": teaching, preaching, appealing to one another's "understanding." And this teaching, significantly, must be realized *in speech*. Hence, no matter how valued by the lovers themselves, their *extasis* threatens to defeat the edifying intentions of language. "Thou verily givest thanks well," Paul adds, "but the other is not edified," and for this reason "I had rather speak five words with my understanding, that *by my voice* I might teach others also, than ten thousand words in an *unknown* tongue" (1 Cor. 14.17, 19). Again the Christian paradoxes appropriated by the love poet (the paradoxes of transcendent love, of dialogic union, of *extasis* itself) immerse readers in a crisis of interpretation. *"Let him that speaketh . . . pray that he may interpret"*: as Paul here advises, we might question whether the poet of "The Exstasie" edifies by adequately *interpreting* the lovers' dialogue. Or must the reader remain "unto him that speaketh a barbarian," unable, in a word, to understand?

Then again, the poet's failure to interpret and edify—to "tell the layetie," as it were, of their love ("A Valediction: forbidding Mourning," 8)—may be a deliberate necessity. As Augustine observes, the sacred authors themselves often write "with a useful and healthful obscurity for the purpose of exercising and sharpening, as it were, the minds of the readers," so that the impious "are either converted to piety or excluded from the mysteries of the faith."[12] Might the mystery of ecstatic love, like the opacity of Scripture, serve a similar purpose, at once exercising the capacities of the fit reader and test-

12. *On Christian Doctrine*, p. 132. In his article, "Donne's Obscurity," Arnold Stein traces Donne's difficulty of sense to his imitation of the Silver Latin poets, Persius especially. It seems that Augustine is a second important influence.

ing, in fact excluding, the unworthy? For while vocabulary can only partially enfold experience it is experience, nonetheless, that sustains and gives meaning to one's words, and the reader who lacks experience of transcendent love is rendered incapable of reading. He or she would inevitably apply the wrong rhetoric—a rhetoric, say, of the flesh (like the poet's own rhetoric in "The Indifferent"), of "business" (as in "The Sunne Rising"), or perhaps of sophistic persuasion (as in "The Flea"). Similarly, we might question whether such a poem as "The Exstasie" intends to include or initiate the lady herself into "Loves mysteries" (71). After all, any ritual act of initiation remains at the same time an act of exclusion: the full "mysteries" that the lady has experienced (or might experience—it is not clear that they have yet made love) are open, once more, only to "some lover, such as wee" (73). And we are led from here to one final question. Given its rhetorical complexities, is such a poem intended to celebrate the "mysteries" of love, to meditate upon its mixed nature, or to persuade, perhaps even seduce, a reticent lady?[13] Thus far we have assumed that the lady is a willing participant (or novitiate) in this love, that she shares the poet's experience, vocabulary, and values. Perhaps she does, and yet it is equally likely that she must be persuaded; perhaps the poet's enjoyment of her love is part even of the "negotiat[ion]" (17) to be worked out between their souls. Read this way, "The Exstasie" becomes an erotic comedy similar in spirit to the elegy, "To his Mistris Going to Bed," where love-making becomes an activity simultaneously erotic and hermeneutic, the lady transformed into a "mystique book" whose "fit" reader claims the inspiration of "imputed grace":

> Like pictures, or like bookes gay coverings made
> For lay men, are all women thus arraid;
> Themselves are mystique bookes, which only wee
> Whom their imputed grace will dignify
> Must see reveal'd. Then since I may knowe,
> As liberally as to a midwife showe
> Thy selfe.
>
>   (39–45)

As its inspired priesthood, the poet alone claims the right to open this body-text, removing the lady's "gay coverings" (39) or clothing

13. Pierre Legouis reads "The Exstasie" as just such a seduction (*Donne the Craftsman: An Essay upon the Structure of the Songs and Sonets*, pp. 68–69). But see also Helen Gardner, "The Argument about 'The Ecstasy,' " for a survey of the controversy and reactions to Legouis.

to penetrate to the holy mysteries or divine "sense." Of course, the poet has only asserted rather than proved his inspiration. His own reading, in fact, lacks a genuinely spiritual sense—the body-text, in other words, may itself be uncovered, yet his object of study remains the flesh alone (or rather the "dead letter," not the spirit). Thus the elegy undercuts the private religion of the priest-lover, even as it claims, though ironically, to preserve love's mysteries from the misunderstanding and abuse of "lay men" (40).

While "The Exstasie" would thus solve the problem of the souls' communion by their physical, sexual union in bodies, the problem of communication remains: though it is love's "booke" (72), the body may still be read wrong, read as an instrument solely of pleasure than of religious mystery. "Weake men" (70), after all, will privilege the surface or "fleshly" meaning of the lovers' body-text, even though the soul, like Augustine's inner teacher in *De magistro*, speaks its mysteries from within (that is, speaks a transcendent language that eludes material inscription even as it lies beyond the perception of fleshly ears). As the Renaissance spiritualist Sebastian Franck writes, "the letter refers to the grammatical sense as does everything which the worldly wise through flesh and blood understand, tell and comprehend without spirit and grace." Of itself, therefore, "Scripture kills, for without the spirit it is never truly understood."

> The spirit makes that which is written alive and interprets it properly. The meaning of Christ and of the spirit is alone God's Word and makes alive when it livens, interprets and applies the letter in our heart. Otherwise it is of itself and by itself not only contradictory and discordant, but without such teacher, leader, guide, key, interpreter . . . it is also the bitter death, a closed book and a confused labyrinth.[14]

We are brought once again to the problem of the "fit" lover whom "The Exstasie" seeks to address, one who understands—in a word, who reads—the motions of love through "spirit and grace," not "flesh and blood." For the love expressed by the body is otherwise, as Franck suggests, a "closed book and a confused labyrinth." And since "the spirit makes that which is written alive and interprets it properly," a reader-witness will thus be shown fit only if he has "*heard* this dialogue of one" (73), attending to the wordless voice of "that inner light of truth," as Augustine describes it: "if the one who hears my words sees those things himself with that clear and

14. *Paradoxa*, in Hillerbrand, *Reformation*, p. 293.

inner eye of the soul, he knows the things whereof I speak by contemplating them himself, and not by my words. Therefore, even when what I say is true, and he sees what is true, it is not I who teach him. For he is being taught, not by my words, but by the realities themselves made manifest to him by the enlightening action of God from within."[15]

And thus, though an argument for the spiritual value and necessity of sexual love, "The Exstasie" fails to incarnate the souls' discourse, fails to render "Loves mysteries" in fleshly language. Paradoxically, Donne's boldest assertion of incarnationism retreats to an Augustinian rhetoric of transcendence, whose theology of language we turn now to describe. Though readers typically note its affinities to Platonism, Augustine's rhetorical theory is often compared to Ciceronian and sophistic rhetoric, the traditions in which he was himself schooled. In fact Augustine's writings, like Donne's after him, exhibit a range of attitudes toward the powers and effects of language. Language can speak truly, though only partially, about reality, and this "partial truth" yields two tendencies in discourse, emphases that ultimately draw apart from each other (yielding two complimentary though distinctive rhetorics, both of which Augustine exploits in his own practice).[16] Interpretations of Augustine's rhetorical theory have generally privileged one aspect of this partial truth over the other (though again, most readers stress the transcendent or Platonic elements in his rhetorical practice); nonetheless, Augustine is never simply an incarnationist or a transcendentalist. He is both. And in this way his writings anticipate Donne's.

Though the Platonic dialogues were among the first to teach Augustine a mistrust of rhetoric, it was the Bible that would teach him both the absolute power of Adamic language and its fall with Babel, human language having at once become inadequate to experience, the words never matching fully or faithfully a speaker's intentions and internal states. Nor could it ever fully recover its heuristic function, ever again become conducive to knowledge. For language now serves merely to suggest that we look for the underlying realities that the words themselves, as Augustine observes, inadequately represent: "It is perfectly logical and true to conclude

15. *The Teacher*, p. 54.
16. See Colish, *Mirror of Language*, and her later article, "St. Augustine's Rhetoric of Silence Revisited." Footnotes shall suggest my indebtedness, but see also Joseph A. Mazzeo, "St. Augustine's Rhetoric of Silence: Truth vs. Eloquence and Things vs. Signs," in *Renaissance and Seventeenth Century Studies*, pp. 1–28; and Sherwood, *Fulfilling the Circle*, pp. 35–44.

that whenever words are spoken, we either know what they mean or we do not. If we know, they recall rather than teach something to us; if we do not know, they cannot even recall something, though they may lead us to inquire."[17] Thus language serves a purely commemorative function; without a prior indwelling presence in the soul, words can do no more than "lead us to inquire," whereas knowledge itself lies beyond words. And if language is inadequate to the commonplaces of physical and mental experience, how can it express the highest mysteries of the spirit? Donne's own answer to such a question is distinctively Augustinian:

> Though the faithfullest heart is not ever directly, and constantly upon God, but that it sometimes descends also to Reason, yet it is not thereby so departed from him, but that it still looks toward him, though not fully to him. . . . By this faith, as by reason, I know, that God is all that which all man can say of all Good; I beleeve he is somewhat which no man can say nor know. . . . For all acquired knowledg is by degrees, and successive; but God is impartible, and only faith which can receive it all at once, can comprehend him. (*Essays in Divinity,* pp. 20–21)

God's mysteries remain uncomprehended by human language, inspiring a rhetoric aware of its own weakness.

Granted, the Christian finds adequate evidence of God's existence, for

> to see that there is a God, The frame of Nature, the whole World is our Theatre, the book of Creatures is our Medium, our glasse, and naturall reason is light enough. But then, for the other degree, the other notification of God, which is, The knowing of God, though that also be first to be considered in this world, the meanes is of a higher nature, then served for the sight of God: and yet, whilst we are in the World, it is but *In aenigmate,* in an obscure Riddle, a representation, *darkly,* and *in part,* as we translate it. (*Sermons,* 8:225)

Donne's translation of Paul (*videmus nunc per speculum in aenigmate;* 1 Cor. 13.12) suggests that knowledge of God, "whilst we are in the World," is forever mediated by signs. Rendering *speculum* (mirror or "glass," in the King James version) as "representation," Donne seems to imply that human language lacks the power to invoke Presence. For as a representation, image, or copy, language is again relegated to a mimetic or commemorative function, one which it can perform but "*darkly,* and *in part.*" In his *Expositions on the Psalms,* Augustine explores at length the same issues, citing the same Pau-

17. *The Teacher,* p. 49.

line text: "Before you perceived God, you thought that you could express God."

> Now you are beginning to perceive Him, and you think that you cannot express what you perceive. But, having found that you cannot express what you perceive, will you be silent, will you not praise God? . . . "How," you ask, "shall I praise Him?" I cannot now explain the small amount which I can perceive in part, through a glass darkly . . . . All other things may be expressed in some way; he alone is ineffable, Who spoke, and all things were made. He spoke, and we were made; but we are unable to speak of Him.

At this crucial point, confronting simultaneously God's majesty and ineffability, Augustine seeks in Christ the recovery of human speech: "His Word, by Whom we were spoken, is His Son. He was made weak, so that He might be spoken by us, despite our weakness."[18] In assuming our nature Christ restores humankind, empowering the faculty of speech to "carry on the work of Incarnation in expressing the Word to the world," a "redeemed speech" that, as Colish notes, "becomes a mirror through which men may know God in this life by faith. And Christian eloquence becomes, both literally and figuratively, a vessel of the Spirit, bearing the Word to mankind, incorporating men into the new covenant of Christ and preparing them through its mediation for the face-to-face knowledge of God in the beatific vision."[19] Yet we must emphasize even here that rhetoric, even redeemed rhetoric, remains a mediative enterprise, little more than a preparative to truth. Truth itself, only partially revealed in speech, awaits its full disclosure "in the beatific vision."

Here, then, Augustine's theory modulates from incarnationism to transcendence—that is, from a rhetoric of aural or dialogic presence to one of silent vision. In the *Confessions*, Augustine recounts that joyously mystical experience shared with his mother when they "were conversing together very sweetly," wondering "what the future eternal life of the saints would be like."

> And when speech had brought us to the point where no sensuous delight and no corporeal light whatever could compare with the joy of that life, . . . lifting ourselves with a more ardent yearning to that life, we traveled gradually through corporeal things and through heaven itself. . . . And we came to our own minds and transcended them, in

---

18. *Expositions on the Psalms*, 99.6; trans. in Colish, *Mirror of Language*, p. 26.
19. *Mirror of Language*, p. 26.

order to arrive at the place . . . where life is that Wisdom by Whom all these things were made.

Such an experience first requires, but must go beyond, "the noise of our mouth, where words both begin and end."[20] Language remains but an earthly medium; in Heaven, rather, all knowledge becomes immediate, revealed in face-to-face communication with God. And it is upon this transcendent experience especially that Augustine formulates his rhetoric of silence:

> If, for any man, the tumult of the flesh were silent; if the image of the earth, the waters, and the air were silent; if the poles were silent; if the soul itself were silent, and transcended itself by not thinking about itself; if dreams and imaginary revelations were silent—for to him who listens, they all say, "We did not make ourselves, but He Who abides in eternity made us"—if, having said this, they were silent and He spoke, raising our ears to himself Who made them, not by the voices of angels, nor by the noise of the thundercloud, nor by the riddles of a simile . . . but by Himself, Whom we love in these things; were we to hear Him without them . . . and if it continued like this . . . would it not be entering into the joy of the Lord?[21]

Through his own written words, paradoxically, Augustine pleads for silence, for the cessation of earthly words so that we might "raise our ears" to the Lord Himself, "to hear Him without them." The preacher's task is thus to prepare himself and his audience for that moment, fully realized in death, when human language itself can be abandoned for eternal vision. For Augustine, then, language begins as dialogue but effaces itself, finally, in silence. As a system of physical signs it does little more than point to those higher realities that it cannot fully encompass; its truths remain forever partial, enigmatic, and sustained by faith.

What happens, however, when Augustine's linguistic theology is appropriated by the Renaissance love poet? We have observed the poet's retreat from incarnationism to this rhetoric of meditative silence; does this latter rhetoric always, as in "The Exstasie," provide an apparently safe haven? Is the spiritual love celebrated by such a rhetoric always one that the poet himself chooses to espouse (or even recognize)? Is such discourse exempt from doubt? Donne's poetry tests the adequacy of incarnationism; does it not also put the

20. Augustine, *Confessions*, 9.10.23–24; trans. in Colish, *Mirror of Language*, p. 33.

21. Augustine, *Confessions*, 9.10.25; trans. in Colish, *Mirror of Language*, p. 34.

question to this Augustinian rhetoric? Initially, "Aire and Angels" seems to assert the reality and primacy of transcendent experience, the poet claiming to have loved "twice or thrice" before learning his lady's "face or name" (1–2). Yet his soul, "whose child love is, / Takes limmes of flesh" (7–8) and must, in fact, "take a body too" (10)—must, in a word, incarnate itself, if it is to find and express its love. The poet continues,

> And therefore, what thou wert, and who,
>   I bid Love aske, and now
> That it assume thy body, I allow,
> And fixe it selfe in thy lip, eye, and brow.
>   (11–14)

Before, the poet saw only "some lovely glorious nothing" (6), the spirit inaccessible to the material human organs of perception. Now though, having granted or "allow[ed]" that the spirit dwells in "limmes of flesh," the poet finds his experience of love "over-fraught" (18). Her body, like a Petrarchan ship-of-love, proves unsuited to its divine "freight":

> Whilst thus to ballast love, I thought,
>   And so more steddily to have gone,
> With wares which would sinke admiration,
> I was, I had loves pinnace overfraught,
>   Ev'ry thy haire for love to worke upon
> Is much too much, some fitter must be sought;
>   For, nor in nothing, nor in things
> Extreme, and scatt'ring bright, can love inhere;
>   Then as an Angell, face, and wings
> Of aire, not pure as it, but pure doth weare,
>   So thy love may be my loves spheare.
>   (15–25)

The "overfraught" "pinnace" (18), an obviously sexual pun, suggests that their love has become exclusively physical in expression, the penis or body bearing the entire burden.

Though incarnate, then, the "shapelesse flame" (3) of spiritual love remains hidden—in and by the flesh, paradoxically, thus remaining as "extreme" (22) and inaccessible as when disembodied. And though far from a flattering description of women's love, the enigmatic ending points less to the difference between the sexes than to the difference between spiritual and fleshly love (indeed, between spirit and flesh, for "Just such disparitie / As is twixt Aire and Angells puritie, / 'Twixt womens love, and mens will ever bee"

[26–28]). Even air, the rarest and lightest substance or "body," clothes the spirit with some impurity. And yet, is this act of clothing or "wear[ing]" (24) not absolutely necessary, if lovers are to be brought together? An angel or other spirit cannot otherwise be known, as Donne himself suggests in a sermon:

> Now when we would tell you, what those *Angels* of God in heaven, to which we are compared, are, we can come no nearer telling you that, then by telling you, we cannot tell. The Angels may be content with that *Negative* expressing, since we can express God himselfe in no clearer termes, nor in termes expressing more Dignity, then in saying we cannot expresse him. . . . we know they are *Spirits* in *Nature*, but what the nature of a spirit is, we know not: we know they are *Angels* in *office*, appointed to execute God's will upon us; but, *How* a spirit should execute those bodily actions, that *Angels* doe, in their owne motion, and in the transportation of other things, we know not. (*Sermons*, 8:105)

From "Aire and Angels," similarly, one would conclude that the necessity of incarnationism—of taking "limmes of flesh"—renders transcendent love impossible, at least on the human plane: souls cannot meet, much less love, without the mediation of bodies.

And yet other lyrics ("Negative Love," for example, and "The Undertaking") argue quite the opposite, though the problem they address shifts from experience to expression. As Sebastian Franck suggests, "we can neither tell anybody nor write nor read" of the spirit, even if "everyone will in himself experience it," for "the holy Spirit does not allow itself to be regulated, nor suffers truth to be put into letters nor speak God's Word. It is all only picture and shadow what one can speak, rule, write or read, conceived as from afar."[22] In "Negative Love" the poet makes a similar argument, retreating to a kind of "holy ignorance," seeking refuge in the irrationality and incommunicability of spiritual love:

> I never stooped so low, as they
> Which on an eye, cheeke, lip, can prey,
>   Seldome to them, which soar no higher
>   Then vertue or the minde to'admire,
> For sense, and understanding may
>   Know, what gives fuell to their fire:
> My love, though silly, is more brave,
> For may I misse, when ere I crave,
> If I know yet, what I would have.

22. *Paradoxa*, in Hillerbrand, *Reformation*, pp. 293–94.

If that be simply perfectest
Which can by no way be exprest
   But *Negatives,* my love is so.
   To All, which all love, I say no.
If any who deciphers best,
   What we know not, our selves, can know,
Let him teach mee that nothing; This
As yet my ease, and comfort is,
Though I speed not, I cannot misse.

Though "sense, and understanding may / Know, what gives fuell to their fire" (5–6), the transcendent subject lies beyond perception, beyond reason, and ultimately beyond language, for that which "can by no way be exprest / But *Negatives*" (11–12) is simply inexpressible. One can say only what such a love is not, and never what it is. Like God, its great exemplar, such a love dwells in its own ineffability, reducing the poet's language to the single word, "no" (13). Admitting "the leane dearth of words" ("The Anagram," 18) and denying both the mind and body as instruments of knowledge, "Negative Love" rejects an incarnationist theology of love—and of language alike, inscribing a negative, transcendent rhetoric in its place, one to match its Augustinian theology.

But "Negative Love" is not immune to a skeptical reading: "The Nothing" is a common title variant, as Marotti observes, one that casts an ironic perspective over the rhetoric and form simultaneously.[23] For a negative love, the skeptic would argue, remains no love at all. Itself a "nothing," the poem becomes an "evaporation" or self-consuming artifact. "Aire and Angels," we might add, invites the same linguistic skepticism: to love "some lovely glorious nothing" (6) is to love . . . what? Emptying itself of reference, the poem challenges our response, for it is the reader who must ultimately judge the truth-functions of such discourse—judge, that is, whether or not the poem ironizes its own discursive instruments, whether or not paradoxy is ever anything more than an expression of the impossible. "Negative Love" raises other issues as well, such as the problematic natures of reading or "decipher[ing]" and "teach[ing]." Who, precisely, is the reader that "deciphers best" (14)? How is one to read a poem that willfully closes itself to interpretation, that seeks to empty itself of objective meaning or communicable knowledge, choosing simply to "say no" (13)? Is such a poem at all designed to teach? Or does it become a test of its readers, a test of their own (self-)knowl-

23. *Coterie Poet,* p. 201.

edge and of their adequacy as (self-)teachers and interpreters? It is, after all, "our selves" that we "know not" (15). By dwelling upon the radically textual nature of selfhood and poetic expression alike, such a poem ties its own performance or self-enactment—its crisis of validation, as I have termed it—to a crisis of interpretation.

It is a commonplace that the *Songs and Sonets* engage both their reader and imagined interlocutor in dialogue; often the reader is invited to take on the interlocutor's role, to speak for the interlocutor, answering on his or her behalf. And when this occurs, interpretation itself proceeds within the dialogic interplay between the text's and each reader's perspectives, vocabularies, and opposing arguments. But more than teach or persuade, Donne's lyrics often specify, test, criticize, and even construct their readers. Like "The Exstasie," much of his poetry explores the in/ability of a particular audience (again, sometimes the beloved, sometimes a male interlocutor, sometimes the reader) to interpret and understand—in short, to incarnate—the symbolic action and argument. In "Natures Lay Ideot," for example, as in other of Donne's Ovidian elegies ("The Perfume," for example, and "Jealousie") the poet describes the variety of private languages fashioned by lovers and the ways their actions, as a system of signs, must be "read" or interpreted. The poet of "Natures Lay Ideot" claims, in fact, to have fashioned the lady into a lover by means of "sophistrie" (2)—an instruction, in other words, in the arts *of discourse*, in "the mystique language of the eye" and "hand" (4) and "the Alphabet / Of flowers, how they devisefully being set / And bound up, might with speechlesse secrecie / Deliver errands mutely,'and mutually" (9–12) as well as in the arts of interpretation, of "judg[ing] the difference of the aire, / Of sighes, [to] say, this lies, this sounds despair" (5–6). But finding himself unable to speak, write, read or "teach" effectively, the poet fails to control (or even correctly interpret) the lady's own words and actions.[24] Here, as elsewhere in the *Elegies* and *Songs and Sonets*, the poet reveals little more than the failure of his "sophistrie," describing the loss of love as a breakdown of discourse.

"A Jeat Ring Sent," similarly, meditates on the loss of meaning that a ring suffers when returned, in breach of faith, to the despondent lover. I have called it a meditation; it is, perhaps, more properly an *explication de texte*, though the text or object of semiotic analysis is not the ring per se so much as its return (or rather, the ring-text

24. Lois E. Bueler argues similarly in her article, "The Failure of Sophistry in Donne's 'Elegy VII.'"

as it is *rewritten* by the lady, denied its conventional meaning as a
symbol of faithful love).

> Thou art not so black, as my heart,
> Nor halfe so brittle, as her heart, thou art;
> What would'st thou say? shall both our properties by thee bee
>   spoke,
> Nothing more endlesse, nothing sooner broke?
>
> Marriage rings are not of this stuffe;
> Oh, why should ought lesse precious, or lesse tough
> Figure our loves? Except in thy name thou have bid it say,
> I'am cheap, and nought but fashion, fling me'away.
>   (1–8)

In asking the ring "What would'st thou say?" the poet admits his inability to control its meaning, at the same time lamenting love's instability as a semiotic system, the fact that it must be "figure[d]" (7)
or signified by a material text "lesse precious" and "lesse tough" (6)
than the poet's own devotion. No longer a visible sign or "figure"
that proclaims (and in a sense, seeks to guarantee) the lady's fidelity, the ring is reduced to mere "fashion," a bauble to fling away.
Thus the poet comments metadiscursively on the disjunction between the signs and intentions of lovers' discourse, much as he
does in "The Funerall," where the object of interpretation is a lady's
gift of her hair, braided and made into a bracelet. Typically, an emblem poem exploits the semiotic resources of its material text; but
while its companion piece, "The Relique," explicates this same
bracelet-emblem confidently and unequivocally, "The Funerall"
puzzles over the meaning, only to give up in the end. "What ere
shee meant by'it" (17), the bracelet in this latter poem is to be buried
with the poet who, as "Loves martyr," fears "it might breed idolatrie, / If into others hands these Reliques came" (19–20). That others
would misinterpret this emblem is in fact less significant than the
poet's own inability to read and interpret the lady's intentions; the
emblem's ambiguity thus reflects the opacity of language in general
and the "leane dearth of words."

Similarly, "The Undertaking" confronts the seemingly insur-
mountable task of communicating transcendent experience by
means of a material language, one that separates the world into
discrete entities and categories, denying the unity of lovers' souls—
denying the mystery of their union:

> I have done one braver thing
> Then all the *Worthies* did,

> Yet a braver thence doth spring,
>   Which is, to keepe that hid.
>
> It were madnes now t'impart
>   The skill of specular stone,
> When he which can have learn'd the art
>   To cut it, can finde none.
>
> So, if I now should utter this,
>   Others (because no more
> Such stuffe to worke upon, there is),
>   Would love as but before.
>
>   (1–12)

Communication of the poet's transcendent experience would require that he discover or fashion a renovated language, a language expressive of mystic unity rather than physical divisiveness. Though alchemy has traditionally supplied such a language or symbol-system, the poet's present age has lost this "skill," here symbolized by "specular stone" (6). In fact the stone itself is inaccessible to our human senses—simply lost to experience—and with this loss the vocabulary of alchemy, a language that might otherwise claim the power to communicate spiritual unities and essences, is denied its physical referent. For "it is said often in Philosophy, *Nihil in intellectu, quod non prius in sensu;* till some *sense* apprehend a thing, the *Judgment* cannot debate it, nor discourse it" (*Sermons*, 5:176).

Of course, language itself introduces a principle of difference into the human perception or construction of reality. Words so common, so small and seemingly innocent as "Hee" and "Shee" rend the unity of spirit into fragments of individuality and gender. Then again, language asserts the identity of phenomena precisely by means of difference: "Hee" is *not* "Shee," and vice versa. But to "forget" or repudiate the words whereby one speaks is necessarily to deny communicability to experience:

> If, as I have, you also doe
>   Vertue'attired in woman see,
> And dare love that, and say so too,
>   And forget the Hee and Shee;
>
> And if this love, though placed so,
>   From prophane men you hide,
> Which will no faith on this bestow,
>   Or, if they doe, deride:
>
> Then you'have done a braver thing
>   Then all the *Worthies* did,

And a braver thence will spring,
Which is, to keepe that hid.
                    (17–28)

As Augustine writes, "nothing is learned by means of its signs. For when I am shown a sign, it cannot teach me anything if it finds me ignorant of the reality for which the sign stands; but if it finds me acquainted with the reality, what do I learn from the sign?"[25] With a wedge thus driven between the poet's words and their referents, and with the language pointing to essences unlocatable in physical reality, the poem ends by denying itself; given the problem of communication, the likelihood that only ridicule and misunderstanding would follow upon his words, the poet writes a love lyric that refuses to speak about the nature of love, refuses, in a word, to speak. Greater than the accomplishments of Worthies, his sad task is to "keepe that hid" (28).

Traditionally the Nine Worthies are personages of communal celebration and fame; their very names, like charms, invoke reverence and public emulation. Similar to these Worthies, presumably, are the lovers whose history the poet celebrates in "The Canonization," a poem that claims, if naively, the power to fashion itself into just such a chronicle and hagiography. "The Undertaking," in contrast, makes no such claim for its language; though it refers to spiritual love, the poem writes only of the impossibility of communicating that love by means of language. Thus it repudiates fame and public celebration, turning instead to private meditation—and falling back, ultimately, upon a rhetoric of silence. For the alternative to silence, to "hid[ing]" one's love "from prophane men" (22) is an act of "madnes" (5), since "all the world will finde us both mad," as Donne the preacher writes, "for going about to expresse inexpressible things" (*Sermons*, 3:143). This sentiment is repeated in "The Broken Heart," where the very language of Petrarchism renders persuasion, praise, blame—even communication, even truth itself—problematic:

He is starke mad, who ever sayes,
That he hath beene in love an houre, . . .
   Who will beleeve mee, if I sweare
   That I have had the plague a yeare?
Who would not laugh at mee, if I should say,
I saw a flask of *powder burne a day*?
                    (1–2, 5–8)

25. *The Teacher,* p. 47.

Regardless of his sincerity, the lover's "say[ing]" and "swear[ing]" earn nothing but ridicule and disbelief. To what, however, shall we ascribe this disbelief? Is it an indictment of the poet's folly, of the weakness of language, or of the audience's own failure to share in the experience of transcendent love? While I have described the poet's admission of failure to interpret, teach, and persuade, does he not also explore the possibility of failed readers? "The Relique" takes this insight even further, questioning whether the lovers themselves are capable of comprehending the "miracles" of spiritual love:

> First, we lov'd well and faithfully,
> Yet knew not what wee lov'd, nor why,
> Difference of sex no more wee knew,
> Then our Guardian Angells doe;
> Comming and going, wee
> Perchance might kisse, but not between those meales;
> Our hands ne'r toucht the seales,
> Which nature, injur'd by late law, sets free:
> These miracles wee did; but now alas,
> All measure, and all language, I should passe,
> Should I tell what a miracle shee was.
>
> (23–33)

Dwelling in a private (in fact, an implicitly Catholic) world of guardian angels and "holy ignorance," the two have performed "miracles"—have themselves become miracles—that others, in the Established Church especially, would refuse to recognize. The poet must therefore "passe" (that is, both surpass and go beyond or repudiate) "all language" (32), since the words fail to persuade. The poem ends, then, by refusing to "tell" (33) of such a love. In truth, though, it is incapable of telling.

Once again love and faith meet in a crisis of language, a crisis repeated in "Farewell to Love." There, before he could claim direct knowledge or experience of "some Deitie in love," the poet "gave / Worship, as Atheists at their dying houre / Call, what they cannot name, an unknowne power" (2–5), thus claiming an implicit identification between knowing and naming: that which is unknown becomes unnameable, and vice versa. Is such a love then a problem of faith, of revelation, or of language? Or does the lack of a stable, verifiable referent devalue the language of poetry, of love, and of theology alike? Significantly, the poet claims to be himself an atheist or unbeliever who "Shall not desire what no man else can finde" (32) and "no more dote and runne / To pursue things which had,

indammage" him (33–34). Thus the poet renounces something he
and, he argues, "no man else" has ever known. We might add that
the same problem of language confronts the cynic as well as mystic;
it is the very in/capacity of language, its partial truth and partial
efficacy as an instrument of communication, that generates and
sustains both attitudes toward experience, shaping the character
and discourse of believers and doubters alike. And yet each stands
in his unique experience as on the other side of a chasm that language fails to bridge; perhaps the chasm *is* language, or at least its
differential structure, separating the signifier from its reference or
transcendental signified.

Of course "The Undertaking" warns the reader against "prophane men" (22) who would "deride" (24) talk of spiritual love and
"love but as before" (12), unchanged by such instruction. Evidently,
the libertine poet of "Loves Alchymie" is another such individual,
one who finds "imposture" (6) in the language of mystic experience
(once again, the language of alchemy):

> Some that have deeper digg'd loves Myne then I,
> Say, where his centrique happinesse doth lie:
>   I have lov'd, and got, and told,
> But should I love, get, tell, till I were old,
> I should not finde that hidden mysterie;
>   Oh, 'tis imposture all:
>
>   (1–6)

Ostensibly, the poet seeks the true nature of love; yet his challenge
to some lover to "say" where happiness lies suggests that language
itself and the problem (or, more to the point, the possibility) of
communication have become his subject. The poet has "told" (3) of
his loves, but always he has lacked knowledge of that "hidden mys-
terie" (5), a love of the mind or spirit. And without personal experience of this spiritual dimension, all vocabulary of such experience
has lost the power of reference. He adds, "no chymique yet th'Elixar
got, / But glorifies his pregnant pot" (7–8), inveighing against the
alchemists' very claim to have achieved something inaccessible to
his own experience—something thus inexpressible by its very nature, something untestable, *unknowable*, by means of language.
Lacking concrete physical referents, the alchemist's (and lover's)
words speak only of their lunacy, for

> That loving wretch that sweares,
> 'Tis not the bodies marry, but the mindes,
> . . . .

> Would sweare as justly, that he heares,
> In that dayes rude hoarse minstralsey, the spheares
> (18–22)

And though the poet attacks Platonic love in no uncertain terms, his allusion to the Platonic theory of celestial harmony is subtly ambiguous. Is there no music at all in the spheres, or is a man foolish for claiming he "heares" it? The former possibility denies altogether the reality of such otherworldly experience; the second asserts instead our human inability to perceive this higher reality, asserts the weakness of a faculty of hearing dulled by the "rude hoarse minstralsy" of material life (which again suggests the weakness of language as an instrument of the spirit). And how shall the reader of "Loves Alchymie" respond to such an argument? Are we to agree with the speaker's materialist interpretation or come to the defense of transcendent love? Or are we to admit, simply, that without underlying experience no vocabulary can rise above metaphor to claim full and faithful communicativeness? However we choose to read it, "Loves Alchymie" demonstrates once again that the problem of love remains a problem of language and belief.

And yet, wondrously, brashly, does "The Canonization" not attempt to fashion what such lyrics as "The Undertaking" and "Loves Alchymie" assert is impossible—that is, a language capable of communicating love's highest mysteries? The dramatic opening, "For Godsake hold your tongue" (1), seems at first to preclude argument, shutting down the dialogue between poet and addressee. But more than silence, he seeks to convert his friend's understanding of love from a foolish waste of time to one of religious mystery. And to accomplish this, he must refute those value-systems—those worldviews, in fact, each with its enabling vocabulary—that devalue or cast doubt upon his love:

> For Godsake hold your tongue, and let me love,
>   Or chide my palsie, or my gout,
> My five gray haires, or ruin'd fortune flout,
> With wealth your state, your minde with Artes improve,
>   Take you a course, get you a place,
>   Observe his honour, or his grace,
> And the Kings reall, or his stamped face
>   Contemplate; what you will, approve,
>   So you will let me love.
>
> Alas, alas, who's injur'd by my love?
>   What merchants ships have my sighs drown'd?

> Who saies my teares have overflow'd his ground?
> When did my colds a forward spring remove?
>   When did the heats which my veines fill
>   Adde one man to the plaguie Bill?
> Soldiers finde warres, and Lawyers finde out still
>   Litigious men, which quarrels move,
>   Though she and I do love.
>
> (1–18)

First to fall is the hyperbolic language of Petrarchism, which the addressee does, apparently, understand (though he, like the poet, both scorns and repudiates it); the languages of law, court, and commerce fall next, describing interests and activities no more defensible than love (and indeed, involving greater personal danger and risk). Yet the third stanza becomes suddenly ambiguous: are the language-systems of myth and mysticism here parodied or seriously, even liturgically invoked?

> Call us what you will, wee'are made such by love;
>   Call her one, mee another flye,
> We'are Tapers too, and at our owne cost die,
> And wee in us finde the'Eagle and the Dove;
>   The Phoenix ridle hath more wit
>   By us, we two being one, are it,
> So, to one neutrall thing both sexes fit.
>   We dye and rise the same, and prove
>   Mysterious by this love.
>
> (19–27)

How can such puzzlements be persuasive or even informative? Is this an argument or an impossibility? Perhaps then, even in the midst of such boldly incarnationist paradoxy, the poet strives for something other than communication, strives, rather, to prove that his addressee *does not know what love is,* that every conception his friend has held of the value and effects of love has proved faulty. For the poet does not teach or reveal love so much as unsettle his audience's previous understanding of this complex emotional experience. Though readers have often attempted to rationalize its extravagant images and paradoxes, yet it is not by logic that the poem succeeds in its aims. The addressee's imagined objections are not refuted so much as they are rendered irrelevant; in fact the poet defends his own love by demonstrating the extent to which his audience *cannot understand* the language. By its very nature the love exceeds if not refutes logical categories, seeking to be glimpsed, rather, through the unreason of the poet's divine paradoxes.

Tilottama Rajan reads "The Canonization" as a failed attempt to transvalue poetic argument, a failure, that is, to turn Petrarchan paradox into sacred paradox. From a theological perspective, sacred paradox is capable of transforming reality "because it fuses contradictories in a single unity," asserting "a higher and not simply a divergent reality." The paradoxy of Donne's "Canonization," however, remains "one of duality," where the poet constructs "a separate but illusory world existing only at the level of words." The speaker's claim to transvalue argument thus "turns out to be, on closer inspection, nothing but a piece of Petrarchan wit."[26] On one level this is true. Yet there are alternatives to such a reading: more than an instance of failed incarnationism, perhaps "The Canonization" inscribes a rhetoric whose very aim is to exclude the uninitiated, protecting the poet's experience by sealing it off from the critical, indeed wounding words of others. In this sense the poem invokes Augustine's practice of exegesis, one that reappears (albeit in more secular garb) in Bacon's "enigmatical" method, "the pretence whereof is, to remove the vulgar capacities from being admitted to the secrets of knowledges, and to reserve them to selected auditors, or wits of such sharpness as can pierce the veil."[27] Read this way, the poem becomes itself a "Phoenix ridle" (23), a series of "covert and darke speaches" presented "by way of riddle . . . of which the sense can hardly be picked out, but by the parties own assoile,"[28] a text that simultaneously asserts and preserves its mysteries by refusing to conform to conventional logical categories, pleading instead for a reader's faith. He or she is to "Beg from above" (44) that pattern of love that the poet and lady, as newly canonized saints, shall offer in answer to prayer; humbled, then, to an attitude of prayerful worship, the reader is invited not so much to understand as to adore—or rather, to believe *before* he or she will understand (*credo, ut intelligam*, Augustine teaches). If the reader is to prove worthy, he or she must yield to the unreason of its paradoxy, the very same paradoxy that underlies Christian mystery. To express doubt over the poet's paradoxes would be tantamount, then, to an act of atheism: how can one give the lie to his words without implicitly denying the Christian Phoenix, whose Incarnation and Resurrection provide the poem's typological model?

Of course "The Canonization" invites many different readings,

26. " 'Nothing Sooner Broke,' " pp. 810–11, 812.
27. *Advancement of Learning*, pp. 141–42.
28. George Puttenham, *The Arte of English Poesie*, p. 198.

for it is at once an incarnationist's celebration of love and a sophist's persuasion of an addressee as well as a mystic's expression of the inexpressible. Indeed, these three rhetorics together mobilize against the silent addressee's own rhetoric of skepticism, a rhetoric whose expression lies in some sense on the margin of the discourse even as it occasions and directs the poet's own response: "Call us what *you* will" (19), the poet cries, and "For Godsake hold *your* tongue" (1). Thus the poem's task is not just to fall silent in its devotion but to silence its opponents, those who would deny its transcendent experience by refuting or questioning its paradoxy. Again, the extent to which the addressee cannot penetrate the speaker's language is the extent to which this love can remain what it is in its essence: a mystery to the uninitiated. Only lovers of similar experience, after all, and sharing similar vocabularies are to invoke the poet and lady as their saints. The interlocutor's presence and projected words, by the poem's end, are no longer even felt as pressures upon the poet's own thoughts as he inscribes the chronicle and tomb of his love by means of this very poem.

The pivotal fourth stanza, then, becomes itself an exploration of the powers of language and literary form, describing sonnets as "pretty roomes" (32) and "urne[s]" (33)—as concrete, physical locations where, preserved in the space of writing, the lovers' memory might repose:

> And if unfit for tombes and hearse
> Our legend bee, it will be fit for verse;
> And if no peece of Chronicle wee prove,
> We'll build in sonnets pretty roomes;
> As well as well wrought urne becomes
> The greatest ashes, as halfe-acre tombes,
> And by these hymnes, all shall approve
> Us *Canoniz'd* for Love:
>
> And thus invoke us; You whom reverend love
> Made one anothers hermitage.
>   (29–38)

Like the final stanza of "The Indifferent," the fifth stanza of "The Canonization" transforms itself into a "hymne," a song of praise and prayer by which these sainted lovers shall be celebrated.[29] For

---

29. Frank Manley terms "The Canonization" a "*tenso* or *débat d'amour* placed in a dramatic context" ("Formal Wit in the *Songs and Sonets*," p. 9), and Clay Hunt agrees, finding in it "the logical structure, if not the dramatic character, of a debate . . . in which the speaker proceeds, by an ethical and metaphysical

"thus" (that is, by means of such a text) should the world "invoke" (37) them. And yet the poem seeks to turn reading into a silent encounter where, once again, one seeks not to understand so much as to experience or participate in the mystery of the love described, evoking within the textual space that which is unwritten but somehow spiritually present; as Bozarth-Campbell observes, in terms reminiscent of Augustine's *De magistro,* "what is ineffable to an extent—anything that contains elements of mystery not directly accessible by any means of analysis—cannot strictly speaking be taught but can only be evoked, awakened from within."[30]

Ever since Cleanth Brooks appropriated the phrase, this "well wrought urne" has come to symbolize the integrity, closure, and self-sufficiency of the verbal artifact. The urn image epitomizes the poem-as-generic-vessel, an iconic structure whose very substance is written language. But the urn is once more a funeral vessel that heralds absence and the poet's death in writing, themes we have traced throughout Donne's valedictions. And while the poet's language transforms love into a text or narrative of experience, the poem itself admits that no text lies beyond the necessity of interpretation. Like the sonnet and Catholic hagiographies to which the poem is compared, love (and love poetry) can be misread, misappropriated, abused; indeed "The Canonization" can be accused rather than read, accused of heresy, of idolatry, of modes of worship outlawed by the poet's own Established Church. For "we must not relie upon the prayers of Saints," an older Donne preaches to his congregation (*Sermons,* 9:218) while he writes elsewhere that "Our Adversaries"—that is, the Romanists—"will not say, that all Saints in Heaven heare all that is said on earth: I know not whether they be in Heaven or no," and "I know not whether those Saints were ever upon earth or no; our Adversaries will not say, that all their Legends were really, historically true, but that many of them, are holy, but yet symbolicall inventions, to figure out not what was truly done

---

justification of his love, to a final rebuttal of the opponent with whom he was contending at the beginning of the poem." But debate is no more than the beginning, as Hunt also notes: "After the first line of stanza 3 the speaker seems to work away from a direct concern with his opponent and, as his mind turns inward to an examination of his love, [it] takes on instead the character of an analytic private meditation" (*Donne's Poetry: Essays in Literary Analysis,* p. 75). More than a movement from argument to meditation, "The Canonization" is in fact a poem-within-a-poem, an exploration of the powers of poetic-priestly language.

30. *Word's Body,* p. 44.

before, but what we should endeavor to doe now" (*Sermons*, 4:311). The lovers of "The Canonization" might themselves, similarly, be declared "holy, but yet symbollical inventions" and the poem itself a fiction, however edifying, of spiritual love. One might choose to ironize the poem, then, reading it as a parody of Catholic saint-worship rather than an attempt to relocate in private love those modes of public worship that reformers had so recently denied. But were it serious in its assertions of mystic knowledge and of a "holy communion" between lovers, would such a poem not serve to re-value hagiography as well as love? The greatest irony lies in this sense outside the poem, in that Donne's contemporary readers are expressly forbidden to engage in such adoration. And in this sense a reader's loss of such love becomes again a loss of faith, or at least of an older mode of faith and religious worship.

To conclude, "The Canonization" begins by seeming to argue but becomes, ultimately, a repudiation of the procedures and instruments of conventional argument, a poem that retreats into enigma and paradoxy, refusing to persuade but asking instead for the reader's faith. This refusal to argue—a refusal, finally, to speak—marks Donne's rhetoric of transcendence, but it serves also to question the role of reasoning and argument in the *Songs and Sonets* as a whole. What, we are led to ask, is the nature of poetic argument and its relation to truth and experience? Under what conditions, and within what aims or modalities of rhetoric, is argument ever enabled, ever capable of persuasion? Such questions bring us to an analysis of argument per se and the interrelations between two other competing rhetorics, skepticism and sophism; these are the subjects of our next chapter.

7

Skepticism and Sophism

It seems that antithetical reasoning, the discursive play between dogma and doubt, is a central feature of the *Songs and Sonets*.[1] Describing a world of contradictory experience, the lyrics by their very nature generate contradictory arguments, the *dissoi logoi* of the sophists Gorgias and Protagoras. Of course, among classical rhetoricians, the sophists stand alone in *celebrating* this contradiction and relativism. In his aptly named treatise, *De sophisticis elenchis* ("On Sophistical Refutation"), Aristotle seeks rather to overturn opposition in order to preserve a singular, stable reality; though multiple arguments arise in any issue there is, nonetheless, one truth that argument is presumed adequate to discover and affirm. Such dogmatism argues for the possibility of refutation in argument—for the triumph of one *logos* over another—and logic, the grammar or morphology of a stable truth, becomes the instrument of this refutation. Within so optimistic a perspective, such poems as "The Canonization," "A Valediction: forbidding Mourning," "The Sunne Rising," and "A Lecture upon the Shadow" become attempts at self-validating argument, poems that search for a logic or system of analogy capable of sustaining their own worldview over and against the world of commerce and quotidian concerns, the commonplace world where absence and change threaten to undermine the poet's love; in such lyrics the lover's private experience defines a world that the poem itself offers to share. Yet we have seen how frail

1. Donne's readers have often made this observation. Arnold Stein's book, *John Donne's Lyrics: The Eloquence of Action*, is a seminal discussion, as is Earl Miner's "Wit: Definition and Dialectic," a chapter from his *Metaphysical Mode from Donne to Cowley*. In his *Dialectical Criticism and Renaissance Literature*, Michael McCanles situates Donne's lyrics within a dialectic of antinomies, while Sloane outlines Donne's habitual use of antithetical or, as he terms it, "controversial" thinking (*End of Humanist Rhetoric*, pp. 65-207), the sophist's *dissoi logoi* surviving in Roman and Renaissance rhetoric as the *argumentum in utramque partem*, the rhetorical exercise of arguing on both sides of an issue.

the poet's world-of-words appears once the reader (or, often, the poet himself) admits it to be a world *of words*; how weak and insufficient the arguments become. Denied the priestly power of invocation and sacramental communion, denied even the power to persuade, the poet then resorts to the unreason of paradoxy, thereby relying on a reader's faith—or else falls into skepticism, or retreats, finally, to silence. Even the most brilliant and apparently successful of Donne's lyrics thus pose the question: Can poetic argument ever discover a self-validating logic? Does any one argument ever really demonstrate its own absolute power while disabling its antitheses?

Consider, for example, the poet's own ironizing of argument in "Womans Constancy":

> Now thou hast lov'd me one whole day,
> To morrow when thou leav'st, what wilt thou say?
> Wilt thou then Antedate some new made vow?
>   Or say that now
> We are not just those persons, which we were?
> Or, that oathes made in reverentiall feare
> Of Love, and his wrath, any may forsweare?
> Or, as true deaths, true maryages untie,
> So lovers contracts, images of those,
> Binde but till sleep, deaths image, them unloose?
>   Or, your owne end to Justifie,
> For having purpos'd change, and falsehood; you
> Can have no way but falsehood to be true?
> Vaine lunatique, against these scapes I could
>   Dispute, and conquer, if I would,
>   Which I abstaine to doe,
> For by to morrow, I may thinke so too.

Though other interpretations are possible, let us for the moment assume a woman speaker, one who has heard, evidently, all the arguments against constancy before: the legalistic analogies that give preference to "Antedate[d]" vows (3) and would nullify "oathes" (6) made under fear of punishment; the perverse comparisons of sleep to death that, according to Canon law, "untie[s]" (8) marriage contracts; the Heraclitean arguments which assert that a man's love, like nature, is necessarily subject to change; and the play with moral terms (for example, a man shows he is "true" (13) not by being faithful, but by being true to his character—which is, of course, false and changeable). The speaker in fact runs through a large portion of the changeling, chauvinist arguments in other libertine poems of the *Songs and Sonets*. And in this sense, "Womans

Constancy" is a poem about libertine poetry, about the folly and
falsehood and triteness of its reasoning: the lover who resorts to
such arguments is a "vaine lunatique," the arguments themselves
mere "scapes" (14). They are indeed escapes—of both valid logic
and moral responsibility, "scape" meaning on the one hand flight
or avoidance, on the other mistake, transgression, sin. But now,
having asserted the libertine's folly and false reasoning, the woman
might be expected to refute these arguments of appetite and inconstancy. No such thing happens. The speaker *could* "dispute, and
conquer" (14–15), if she wanted, but "abstaine[s]" (16) from doing
so.

She does not abstain from appetite, though; "by to morrow"
(17) she, too, may change—and then so, too, will her arguments.
And in this reversal of position and refusal to argue lies the irony of
the title, "Womans Constancy." The poem, implicitly criticizing the
deliberate falsehoods of other lyrics in the *Songs and Sonets*, ultimately critiques itself. At the same time that it suggests the possibility of refuting appetite and false argument, it falls prey to its
own libertinism; it seems to conquer but is conquered in turn.
"Loves Infiniteness" is yet another poem that would turn writing
and loving alike into commodities, the means of investment, acqui-
sition, possession, and consumption. "Sighs, teares, and oathes,
and letters" (6) have become the "treasure" that the poet has "spent"
(6) in order "to purchase" (5) the lady's love. And yet the poet appears to have "spent" in every way except sexually as, self-consciously, he admits his inability to "bargaine" (8) for the lady's love;
the poem itself, as an "oath" or "letter," proves too weak. A similar
ironizing of argument occurs in "The Apparition" where the speaker, at the very moment he seems to have achieved verbal mastery
over his false mistress, refuses to curse her ("What I will say, I will
not tell thee now, / Lest that preserve thee" [14–15]). In fact the poet
ends by denying himself any motive for writing: since his "love is
spent" (15), all argument is disarmed.

Though I have just illustrated the self-refuting, self-disabling tendency of argument in Donne's libertine poems rather than poems of
mutual love, a skeptical reading of the collection as a whole would
suggest that victories of logic are forever illusory. For the *dissoi logoi*,
antithetical arguments that assert, as Yin and Yang, their simultaneous validity, describe a world marked not by singularity and
stability but by multiplicity, change, and contradiction. Within such
a worldview the antitheses of poetic argument engage in a continual, unresolvable struggle against each other, no one victorious

over the rest and yet all, in a very real sense, enabling each other as systole retreats from and in the act of differentiating itself enables diastole. Poems like "The Flea," then (or "Communitie," or "The Indifferent," in which arguments of libertinism and change confront counterarguments of constancy, fidelity, and mystical union) do not resolve the *dissoi logoi* but rather are caught within the grasp of these simultaneously conflicting and mutually sustaining viewpoints, incapable of yielding full victory to any one of their own arguments (or indeed, to any supplied from without, by the antithetical, dialogic, or refutative motions of a reader). Given that contradiction is inherent in the world, all argument about the nature of being becomes arbitrary, reason itself reduced to an insufficient measure (*ratio*) or method of truth; reason itself becomes irrational, as the sophist Gorgias suggests. From this perspective, Donne's love poems demonstrate precisely the irreconcilability and the irrefutability of their contrasting *logoi*. The more they argue, the less they prove. Taking conventional logic as far as it can go, such poems entrap themselves in antinomy, in the paralyzing epistemological and ultimately moral skepticism generated by these contradictory claims. Observe the poet's confusion in "The Prohibition," for example, when he cannot decide if the lady should "Take heed" (1) of loving or hating him. Almost schizophrenically, both *logoi* are simultaneously admissible in the morally (and epistemologically, and perhaps psychologically) uncertain world he describes: "Yet, love and hate mee too" (17), he concludes. Cut off from a stable ontology and value-system that would sustain mutual love, such lyrics demonstrate only the dearth of value—and the weakness of any logic that seeks to defend or sustain value—within a skeptical worldview. Such a world offers the speaker a choice, typically, between but two moral styles, cynicism and libertinism (though either attitude, let us note, is ultimately born of skepticism).

The more cynical of the *Songs and Sonets*, Marius Bewley suggests, are "a protracted exercise in how to blunt the precision of a philosophically exact language and make it unfit for its original purpose."[2] Perhaps. Yet this implies that language begins in a state of precision, clarity, and fitness. And we must ask: Do the more skeptical lyrics render language unfit for argument, deliberately "blunting" its precision? Or do they exploit its already-inherent weakness as an instrument of truth? And are there not alternatives to cynicism, even in a world of uncertainty and change? Consider

2. "Mask of John Donne," p. 25.

the poet's libertinism, expressed in such lyrics as "Loves Usury" and "Communitie." Given the relativity of custom and the arbitrariness of cultural values, the poet installs appetite as the center of value and selfish pleasure as the only sure criterion of action, choice, argument. Thus, while such cynical lyrics as "Breake of Day" and the "Song: Goe, and catche a falling starre" lament the weakness of language to fix human personality and defend traditional morality, the libertine lyrics exploit this weakness, for theirs is a nominalist, word-killing rhetoric in which such a notion as spiritual love is reduced to fiction while honor, continence, fidelity become words with merely conventional (and hence arbitrary) meanings, lacking the sanction and force of Nature.[3] In these poems sin, too, is but a word, in contrast to its powerful, controlling presence in such a lyric as "Twicknam Garden." To the libertine poet, appetite alone persuades. Cognitive skepticism, therefore, becomes the foundation of moral skepticism: the sophistic doctrine of *metron anthropos*, that "man is the measure of all things," reaches beyond epistemology to question conventional morality, turning discourse into a will-to-power.

Previous chapters have explored the problem of incarnationism and the poet's retreat into such alternative rhetorics as transcendence and skepticism, both in a sense "negative" rhetorics, the former a rhetoric of meditative silence, the latter a rhetoric of refutation, doubt, and denial. Do these three then encompass the whole of discourse? Or is there not a fourth term, a further devolution—this time, perhaps, from skepticism? Historically, skepticism is often linked to sophistic tradition, and Gorgias is in many ways a founder of both, his treatise "On Nature, or The Non-Existent" being among the first documents of radical skepticism, while his "Encomium of Helen" provides an early instance of sophistic display. But though related, each posits a distinctive worldview, which in turn gives shape to two unique rhetorics. What then separates sophistic rhetoric from pure skepticism? How does the sophist exploit, as it were, a world of uncertainty and change?

In the treatise "On Nature," Gorgias "proposes three successive headings: first and foremost, that nothing exists; second, that even if it exists it is inapprehensible to man; third, that even if it is apprehensible, still it is without a doubt incapable of being expressed or explained to the next man."[4] While this utter denial of being

3. See William Rockett, "Donne's Libertine Rhetoric."
4. Sextus, *Against the Schoolmasters*, p. 42. It is by means of Sextus's summary-analysis that Gorgias's philosophical position survives.

seems to carry doubt to the point of absurdity, his point is that we can know nothing *directly* and that language cannot actually convey experience, for Gorgias saw "not simply that man's view of reality was distorted through language, but that man's world was contradictory and antithetical when approached rationally."[5] In other words, any discussion of being immerses us in apparently insoluble contradictions. If there is being, then (as Sextus interprets the Gorgianic argument) there must be a *cause* of being, and this must be something that is *other than* being—that is, nonbeing, which necessitates that nonbeing or the nonexistent exists. And yet, he continues, it would be "entirely absurd for something to exist and at the same time not to exist. The nonexistent, therefore, does not exist. And to state another argument, if the nonexistent exists, the existent will not exist, for these are opposites to each other, and if existence is an attribute of the nonexistent, nonexistence will be an attribute of the existent."[6] Sextus continues to multiply proofs of this sort, not all of which entirely convince. But the point is clear enough: reason proves incapable of demonstrating the reality of phenomena. Things may exist, but they cannot be known in and of themselves, in the same way that thought presents itself to consciousness. For thought alone, presumably, achieves self-presence; all else is mediated—in a sense, *turned into* thought (or rather, into language). For words such as "white" or "bitter" do not constitute the color or the flavor; all they can claim is the capacity to evoke a mental image that may, perhaps, parallel the speaker's perception of an otherwise silent reality. So even if things do exist, and even if one could "know" them, a speaker can never communicate this knowledge directly; all a speaker can give are words that create images in an audience's mind, images that may (or again, may not) reflect his or her own mental experience. "For that by which we reveal is *logos*," as Sextus observes, "but *logos* which is something other than substances. Thus, just as the visible would not become audible, and vice versa, similarly, when external reality is involved, it would not become our *logos*, and not being *logos*, it would not have been revealed to another."[7] Discourse, mental experience, and physical reality are, at

5. Richard A. Engnell, "Implications for Communication of the Rhetorical Epistemology of Gorgias of Leontini," p. 177. See also Richard Leo Enos, "The Epistemology of Gorgias' Rhetoric: A Re-Examination"; and John Poulakos, "Toward a Sophistic Definition of Rhetoric."

6. *Against the Schoolmasters*, p. 43.

7. Ibid., p. 46. And "even if *logos* has substance," he remarks, "still it differs from all the other substances, and visible bodies are to the greatest degree dif-

best, parallel universes. Speech does not reveal the world so much as create a second world *in the mind,* the force of speech being thoroughly psychological, and never directly referential. Discourse, then, particularly persuasive discourse, creates new mental states; the sophist's words may not coincide with physical reality—the words are not the things—but they have the power to affect an audience's feeling and belief.

Again, the skeptic argues that it is impossible to know the truth, and the truth he assaults is that of the dogmatist: singular, objective, absolute. The sophist, like the skeptic, denies the possibility of objective, impersonal knowledge. But while the skeptic ends in commitment to no truth whatsoever, the sophist seeks refuge in the relativity and multiplicity of truth.[8] The skeptic, in this sense, is paradoxically as much an absolutist as his dogmatic opponents (Plato, for a famous example): it is a singular, universal truth that eludes him, and relative truths offer no consolation. In fact the very notion of relativity prompts his skepticism; to him, as to the dogmatist, a truth that changes with time and place is no truth at all. Not so to the sophist, who views truth under the aspect of *kairos* (that is, the Timely or Opportune) and as a product of language. The sophist thus embraces a truth that is relative and multiple, one that changes with persons, time, place, and circumstance. In his discussion of decorum George Puttenham, the Elizabethan courtier-critic, initially describes a stable, knowable world—quite the opposite of Gorgias's epistemology, which is at once unknowable and ineffable:

> This lovely conformitie, or proportion, or conveniencie betweene the sence and the sensible hath nature her selfe first most carefully observed in all her owne workes, then also by kinde graft it in the appetites of every creature working by intelligence to covet and desire: and in their actions to imitate and performe: and of man chiefly before any other creature aswell in his speaches as in every other part of his behaviour. And this in generalitie and by an usuall terme is that which the Latines call *decorum.*[9]

Presumably, discourse expresses the real harmony between "sence," or human powers of perception, and the "sensible," the decorum of

---

ferent from words. What is visible is comprehended by one organ, *logos* by another. *Logos* does not, therefore, manifest the multiplicity of substances, just as they do not manifest the nature of each other" (p. 43).

8. See Jack W. Meiland and Michael Krausz, eds., *Relativism: Cognitive and Moral,* pp. 2–3.

9. *Arte of English Poesie,* p. 269.

the writer becoming that of Nature itself, where beauty lies in a perception of the "congruencie" between language and being (while ugliness lies in a perception of disproportion and discord). Verisimilitude and organic unity become the double aim, then, of decorum, which becomes itself the reigning principle of literary production. And thus the demand for decorum, as Puttenham here describes it, fashions a poet whose craft is constrained on one hand by representation or *mimesis* and on the other by a conservative conception of genre—that is, of genre as a formal ideal, a timeless Platonic *ideon*. A recognition of time, however, and of changing circumstances shatters the timeless and ideal, for "by reason of the sundry circumstances, that mans affaires are as it were wrapt in, this *decencie* comes to be very much alterable and subject to varietie, insomuch as our speach asketh one maner of *decencie*, in respect of the person who speakes: another of his to whom it is spoken: another of whom we speake: another of what we speake, and in what place and time and to what purpose."[10] And "some things and speaches," therefore, "are decent or indecent in respect of the time."[11] But is there not a contradiction in Puttenham's discussion of decorum, an opposition between timelessness and timeliness, between logical form and the form-shattering exigencies of circumstance? Why should decorum imply two thoroughly antithetical operations? In fact the Latin *decorum* translates simultaneously the Greek philosophical terms *to prepon* and *to kairos*, the Fitting and the Timely. While *prepon* stresses the timeless ideal and the stability of logical form, *kairos* stresses "the contradictory multiplicity of the real world," a world subject to conflict among its elements and subject, above all, to change.[12] Through *kairos*, a writer or speaker asserts the mutability of the world and the power of language to shape and color, indeed constitute reality. Judgments even of ethics must bow to *kairos*, for "pleasant speeches and favoring some skurrility and unshamefastnes have now and then a certaine decencie, and well become both the speaker to say, and the hearer to abide, *but*

10. Ibid., p. 270.
11. Puttenham offers an example: "when a great clerk presented king Antiochus with a booke treating all of justice, the king that time lying at the siege of a towne, who lookt upon the title of the booke, and cast it to him againe: saying, what a divell tellest thou to me of justice, now thou seest me use force and do the best I can to bereeve mine enimie of his towne? every thing hath his season which is called Oportunitie, and the unfitnesse or undecency of the time is called Importunitie" (ibid., pp. 273–74).
12. Mario Untersteiner, *The Sophists*, p. 113.

that is by reason of some other circumstance."[13] Much the same can be written of Donne's libertine poetry, whose "skurrility and unshamefastnes" describe not a world of stable, timeless values and logical consistency but a world of change.

Donne's verse letter to the Countess of Salisbury makes just such an appeal to *kairos:* while "Some things are not together true," yet "to say so, doth not condemne a man, / If when he spoke them, they were both true than" (47–50). Changing times and circumstances uphold the claims of opposing arguments; *together* they contradict, each demanding the sacrifice of the other, and yet they are "both true." Donne's sophistic poems face the same conclusion: logic in itself fails to persuade, and yet the success of any argument rarely rests in logic alone. (Where, outside of the most confident—or naive—of Donne's incarnationist poems can such a logic even be described?) More often (and surely this holds for the sophistic poems), the possibility of success rests in the poet's fashioning of a new language or vocabulary for experience—or rests, rather, in a verbal transvaluation of human relations and a creation of community, of linguistic *communion*, between the speaker and his beloved, the poet and his reader. Thus, while the sophist admits the failure of logic to affirm truth, he also recognizes that logical form gives way to the creative powers of language, powers to charm and enthrall, affect and persuade. As Gorgias asserts, "sacred incantations sung with words" become "bearers of pleasure and banishers of pain, for, merging with opinion in the soul, the power of incantation is wont to beguile it and persuade it and alter it by witchcraft."[14]

In addition, sophistic rhetoric asserts the *bia* or violence of language, its capacity to ravish and enthrall: "through the agency of words," Gorgias writes, "the soul is wont to experience a suffering of its own." Indeed, his defense of Helen asserts that she was raped *by language*, that she had "come under the influence of speech, just as if ravished by the force of the mighty."[15] Though markedly ambivalent in his terms, the youthful Donne ascribes similar powers to "Eloquence":

> Let our life bee a sea, and then our reason, and even passions, are wind enough to carry us whither we should goe, but eloquence is a storme and tempest that miscarryes us. And who doubts that Elo-

13. Puttenham, *Arte of English Poesie*, p. 274; my italics. For a full discussion see James S. Baumlin, "Decorum, *Kairos*, and the 'New' Rhetoric."
14. "Encomium of Helen," p. 52.
15. Ibid., p. 52.

quence (which must perswade people to take a yoake of Soveraignty and then beg and make lawes to tye them faster, and then give monny to the Invention, repaire and strengthen it) needes more shadowes and colourings then to perswade any man or woman to that which is naturall. (*Paradoxes and Problems,* pp. 33–34)

Though "reason" and "passions" or appetite can move us to particular choices and actions, nonetheless "eloquence" is an irresistible force, capable of compelling one's belief—and eminently open, therefore, to abuse. A "storme and tempest that miscarryes," it misleads and manipulates its auditors, persuading them not just "to take a yoake of Soveraignty" but to collaborate in their own self-bondage. Moreover, its "shadowes and colourings" take the place of nature, substituting for reality itself. And thus he recognizes both the violent, tempestuous force of Gorgianic speech and its potential for misuse, an accusation Donne the preacher would repeat: "All sin is but fallacy and *Sophistry,*" he writes, while "*Religion* is *reason* and *Logique;* The devill hides, and deludes, Almighty God demonstrates and proves" (*Sermons,* 5:104). It is by deception that we are led to sin; poignantly, sin has become a consequence *of rhetoric,* or at least a particular kind of rhetoric. If God is the first and best logician, Satan is the sophist.

We might read Donne's libertine poetry, then, as exercises in Gorgianic argument rather than as expressions of pure skepticism or cynicism, as works that reveal both the irrational and the amoral side of this sophism, attempting continually to overturn the laws of conventional morality by asserting in their place the laws of "nature," that is, the speaker's appetite.[16] "Communitie" provides an example, entangling the reader in its initial show of logical argument. The opening lines appear disarmingly innocent, after all: who would deny that "Good wee must love, and must hate ill, / For ill is ill, and good good still" (1–2)? Though a trivialization of argu-

16. Of course, I do not argue for the direct influence of Gorgias, Sextus, or any other classical author on the *Songs and Sonets;* there is no need to do so, though the pre-Socratic texts, published both first- and secondhand, were part of the intellectual milieu of continental humanism and readily accessible to Donne. I argue no more, nor less, than that sophism is a potential within discourse itself. Thus Gorgias happens to have outlined a form of rhetoric that we all at times use, even if we have often lacked a name for it. We are all, similarly, skeptics when occasion calls, all incarnationists when situation makes such a demand on our discourse. Put simply, the *Songs and Sonets* demonstrate that the varieties of experience, perception, and need—the very reasons one speaks or writes—require contrasting rhetorics: no one rhetoric can serve a person in all places and all ways.

ment, is the tautology not also absolutely true? Is not "good" *necessarily* "good still"? The problem is that "good," while it seems stable and uncontroversial in its meaning, is never defined or fixed in its sense until, too late even for the wary, critical reader, its settled meaning becomes pleasure-in-use. Thus the poet violates the first principle of logically valid argument, at least as Plato describes it in the *Phaedrus:* the need to define, clarify, and regulate the meaning of one's value-terms. And even when the author explicitly defines such a term (as in Paradox VIII: "That good is more common then evill," p. 17), the definition is grounded sophistically in appearance, convention, and "use." Thus the youthful Donne proposes time and again the arbitrariness of custom, in sexual morality as well as discourse:

> For the fashions of habits, for our moving in gestures, for phrases in our speech, we say they weare good as long as they weare usd, that is as long as they weare common: and wee eate, wee walke, wee sleepe onely when it is, or seemes good to do so. . . . And of indifferent many things are become perfectly good by beeing common; as Customes by use are made binding Lawes. But I remember nothing that is therfore ill because it is common but women. (*Paradoxes and Problems*, pp. 18–19)

In such discourse, "good" is never an absolute quality, a timeless ideal or *prepon,* for a thing's goodness is determined solely by its desirability, its status as a commodity or consumable. "Confined Love" plays variations upon these same arguments, asking rhetorically whether the "Sunne, Moone, or Starres" are "by law forbidden, / To smile where they list, or lend away their light?" (8–9). Like "Communitie," such a poem seeks to repeal the "law" that one woman "should but one man know" (5–6). And here again the poet equivocates, arguing that "Good is not good, unlesse / A thousand it possesse" (19–20). Though the word is repeated, the meaning is in each case antithetical: the stoic's "good" versus the epicure's "good," or virtue versus pleasure-in-use. Perhaps paradoxically, there is a sort of logic operant in these works, a logic of appropriation and consumption, all grounded in the sophist's will-to-power.

To the sophist then, as to the cynic or skeptic, formal logic can neither persuade nor defend itself from refutation and the deceptions of rhetoric. Is persuasive argument therefore impossible? Or might it work by means other than logic? Consider "The Sunne Rising," a boldly paradoxical, in fact sophistic lyric that denies not only the value but the reality of the ordinary world. Tilottama Rajan criticizes the poem for basing its arguments on the deceptions of a figurative, hyperbolic language rather than on the firmer ground of valid logical form—for attempting, as in the following lines, to "create through rhetoric what cannot be affirmed through logic."[17]

> She'is all States, and all Princes, I,
>   Nothing else is.
> Princes doe but play us; compar'd to this,
> All honor's mimique; All wealth alchimie.
>   (21–24)

"The reader," Rajan adds, "must therefore be cautious about taking at face value the 'rhetoric of hyperbole' that critics such as Brian Vickers see as sustaining the truth of the affirmations reached in the poems of mutual love. . . . Such rhetoric is rhetoric only, not logic."[18] But perhaps the rhetoric does not stand on the shoulders or crutches of conventional logic. Perhaps the poem seeks to question this logic, asserting by means of paradox and hyperbole that reason itself is inadequate to experience—or as the poet boldly, egotistically asserts in his arguments against the morning's "beames" (11), "I could eclipse and cloud them with a winke, / But that I would not lose her sight so long" (13–14). Granted, "one cannot eclipse the sun by closing one's eyes," as R. T. Jones suggests, "one can only give oneself an illusion of its eclipse. Nor can one circumvent the power of time by asking rhetorical questions: one can only confuse one's awareness of it." And yet the poet "can sustain the illusion," Jones adds, "as long as he continues to argue."[19] Actually, the world-of-illusion lasts only so long as the poet *writes*, its habitus being the poem itself, beyond whose confines all remains subject to time and change. For the reader knows that the world *does not* literally go away, that the sun's orbit *does not* contract to the bedroom of the lovers; but as one reads, one observes how the beliefs, emotions, and values of the lovers themselves undergo a sea change. Hyperbole may lack the power to change the external physical world; still it changes the private world of the lovers, a world of emotion and experience that proves stubbornly resistant to logic, though marvelously—miraculously—open to language. If this is the case, then logic itself is given the lie, its assertion of a singular, stable truth falling before the sophist's multiple reality and play-

17. " 'Nothing Sooner Broke,' " pp. 809–10.
18. Ibid., p. 809. She refers to Vickers's essay, "The *Songs and Sonets* and the Rhetoric of Hyperbole." For other poststructuralist readings see Hartman, *Saving the Text*, pp. 148–54; Docherty, *John Donne Undone*; and Claudia Brodsky, "Donne: The Imaging of the Logical Conceit."
19. "John Donne's *Songs and Sonets*: The Poetic Value of Argument," p. 37.

fully creative language. And whether the poet's words create a *monde*, or a *folie, à deux* is finally moot, for the lovers do become the center and source of value, if for themselves only, and only within the textual space.

The sophist, then, seeks to reverse the skeptic's judgment concerning the dearth of language. Does "The Flea," for example, demonstrate the weakness of conventional logic or the resilience, the sheer resourcefulness of argument? The final stanza can be read either way, as self-confident sophistry or self-ironizing skepticism:

> Cruell and sodaine, hast thou since
> Purpled thy naile, in blood of innocence?
> In what could this flea guilty bee,
> Except in that drop which it suckt from thee?
> Yet thou triumph'st, and saist that thou
> Find'st not thy selfe, nor mee the weaker now;
> 'Tis true, then learne how false, feares bee;
> Just so much honor, when thou yeeld'st to mee,
> Will wast, as this flea's death tooke life from thee.
> (19–27)

Arrogantly assured of his own victory, the poet speaks of "when" (26) rather than "if" she yields. Yet the skeptic will observe that the lady (and reader) remains far from convinced, while the poet, to project beyond the poem's fiction, remains sexually unsatisfied. In this sense "The Flea" becomes an "evaporation" and its arguments so many "alarums to the truth," terms Donne uses elsewhere to describe his *Paradoxes and Problems:* the poem erects logically and morally specious arguments that the skeptical reader, taking the addressee's part, must seek to refute. Indeed, like the reader of Donne's prose paradoxes, the reader of "The Flea" is implicitly challenged to "overthrow" the persuasion, finding the "better reasons" against it (*Selected Prose*, p. 111).

But surely this is too facile an account of the reading experience. After all the poet, though not entirely persuasive, remains himself undefeated. The flea has been literally deconstructed—crushed between the lady's finger nails—and yet the speaker finds a verbal resource rising out of the corpse (or carapace) of his preceding argument; in fact the lady's own implicit response proves ultimately self-defeating, for when she resorts, in seeming triumph, to her own skeptical argument (that is, neither she nor the poet is "weaker" for having lost blood) she falls prey in turn to the speaker's word-killing nominalism—"'Tis true," he at once counters, and the lady will lose "Just so much honor" when she yields as she has lost blood to the flea. Blood it seems, whether lost through intercourse or an insect bite, has little to do with loss of honor. Of course the reader has no means to infer from the poem itself what the lady should now say, whether she can even find a retort, will yield herself to him, or simply leave the room. And asked implicitly to take up the lady's part, how shall the reader respond to this last sortie? One thing at least is certain: though the speaker may not win the object of his desire, he refuses to give up the verbal battle, defying refutation even as he invites it, resisting all counterargument at the same time that his own words confound the vocabulary of conventional morality.

Richard Lanham describes the personality of just such a speaker in his portrayal of "rhetorical man," one who is "an actor," whose "sense of identity, his self, depends on the reassurance of daily histrionic reenactment."

> He is thus centered in time and concrete local event. The lowest common denominator of his life is a social situation. And his motivations must be characteristically ludic, agonistic. He thinks first of winning, of mastering the rules the current game enforces. He assumes a natural agility in changing orientations. . . . he has dwelt not in a single value-structure but in several. He is thus committed to no single construction of the world; much rather, to prevailing in the game at hand.[20]

Refusing to be refuted, "The Flea" demonstrates, in miniature, the sophist's exploitation of the *dissoi logoi,* a rhetorical resilience that potentially extends argument ad infinitum. Surely such a poem illustrates the sophist's "ludic, agonistic" techniques of argument and his "natural agility in changing orientations"—that is, his "center[ing]" in *kairos,* "in time and concrete local event." The sophist's enemies, therefore, are permanence, the absolute, and above all eternity, since time alone allows for change, and change—of mind, certainly—is his aim. Time, indeed, has at least a twofold aspect in discourse, involving itself in the reading experience as well as the exigencies of a rhetorical situation. Argument establishes an itinerary, as it were, through a text, a linear (and thus necessarily temporal) unfolding; one line of thought confronts, transforms, refutes, consumes another, and is itself confronted and changed in turn. Unfolding sequentially, even causally, the previous steps of an argument enable new lines of reasoning that will then consume previous lines—even those that gave them being. Thus the final

---

20. *The Motives of Eloquence: Literary Rhetoric in the Renaissance,* p. 4.

stanza of "The Flea" demands the refutation of earlier, failed lines of thought, the argument itself adapting to internal changes within a dynamic, dramatically unfolding discourse. Though the poet cries out against its "cruel and sudden" death, the flea must, in fact, be sacrificed (and with the flea his own earlier arguments) if the poet is to find his last best resource. For when the flea dies so, presumably, dies the word "honor."

Unlike the Augustinian speaker of "The Undertaking" or "Negative Love," whose transcendent subject seeks to deny the exigencies of time, change, and circumstance, the sophistic speaker always faces a specific and unique occasion or a particular line of argument to which his own discourse responds. A rhetoric of dynamic becoming rather than of static, stable being, sophism thus reserves the right to change arguments, to change position entirely, depending upon the *kairos* of a speaker's own changing interests and circumstances. Let us then reconsider the ending of "Womans Constancy," where the speaker claims that "I could / Dispute, and conquer, if I would, / . . . For by tomorrow, I may thinke so too" (14–17). Does this remain, simply, a cynic's refusal to argue, or can it be read as a sophist's exercise of choice among times and circumstances—and lovers—as well as arguments, a relativizing not simply of morality but of discourse itself? Given the sophist's relativist epistemology, what is it that matters? The logical and moral consistency of an argument, or the efficacy?

A reader may still struggle against such a poem as "The Flea." Yet it cannot fully be defeated, for its arguments resist a reader's resistance, refusing to deconstruct. From this sophistic perspective it is the reader, not the rhetor, who is overthrown. And in this sense "The Flea" resembles Socrates' own sophistical refutation of Callicles in the *Gorgias,* where "what is produced is not belief but a sense of helplessness or defeat, a sense that one has been manipulated by a mind more clever than one's own but not more sound."[21] As Callicles responds to Socrates's paradoxical argument, "It seems to me, I know not how, that you are right, Socrates, but I feel as the many do. I am not quite convinced by you."[22] And thus the interlocutor "is left wishing he could respond" but "knowing that he cannot, and feeling frustrated and competitive. The effect of the 'proof' is not to persuade but to disorient him, to break down for the moment his

21. James Boyd White, *When Words Lose Their Meaning: Constitutions and Reconstitutions of Language, Character, and Community,* p. 105.
22. Plato, *Collected Dialogues,* p. 295.

sense of security and competence in the command of his language, to place him, as it were, nowhere, for he has nothing to say."[23] It is here, precisely, that reader and addressee are left in "The Flea": once "honor" has lost its conventional meaning, both are left unsettled with respect to language, unwilling to admit defeat but unable to find an answer. Ironically, the *elenchus* or "refutation" of Socratic dialogue works in ways surprisingly similar to sophistic argument: a proposition, initially accepted by both Socrates and his interlocutor, "is then shown,"

> by reasoning sometimes sound, sometimes fallacious, to lead to conclusions opposite to those previously asserted by the interlocutor. . . . The effect of all this is to disturb the relation between self and language, to break down the sense of natural connection and coherence between them. One comes suddenly to see both self and language as uncertain, as capable of being remade in relation to each other. The true aim of a dialogue that works this way, the *Gorgias* among others, is the reconstitution of self and language.[24]

We might here recall Lanham's model of human personality, which posits a number of dramatic, "rhetorical" selves arrayed around a serious, "central" self. One might argue (and I suspect Lanham might ultimately agree) that the central self, which we identify as the stable, unchanging core of our personality, is as much a "rhetorical" invention as the social roles/selves arrayed around it. The perceived stability and fixture of our central self becomes an act of will and not an expression of soul or essence; in other words, the apparent fixture and stability of human identity is dramatically enacted—invented and maintained through habits of language-use and behavior. As such the central self, our sense of a fixed identity, becomes susceptible to the movements of rhetoric and capable of change.

Significantly, Donne the preacher describes this same process. Though he defines persuasion as a means to "discompose and disorder the judgement," it is in fact language, the *vehicle* of belief and judgment, that is displaced, discomposed, and disordered:

> The way of Rhetorique in working upon weake men, is first to trouble the understanding, to displace, and to discompose, and disorder the judgement, to smother and bury in it, or to empty it of former apprehensions and opinions, and to shake that beliefe, with which it had possessed it self before, and then when it is thus melted, to powre it

23. White, *When Words Lose Their Meaning,* pp. 105–6.
24. Ibid., p. 95.

into new molds, when it is thus mollified, to stamp and imprint new
formes, new images, new opinions in it. (*Sermons*, 2:282)

The passage is remarkable for its deconstructive metaphors, describing the destabilizing effects of persuasive language upon psyche,
first troubling the mind, then emptying it "of former apprehensions
and opinions," then giving it new shape and content, pouring it
"into new molds." Donne terms this rhetorical process immediately
afterward a "fire," a "battery of eloquence," and a "verball violence" (*Sermons*, 2:282), all reminiscent of Gorgias's description of
the violence of persuasive language. To change an audience's mind,
therefore—which is to change its perception of the self and its relation to the world—a speaker must dislocate this audience from its
own language.

Of course, community itself rests upon communication, upon
words of shared value and experience. And each worldview must
seek adequate words: different words, different worlds. Thus such
poems as "The Sunne Rising" and "A Lecture upon the Shadow"
become scenes of conflict (and often, even, of collaboration) between a speaker's and an audience's perceptions, each with its
unique vocabulary and value-terms: pleasure and appetite versus
honor, for example, freedom of action versus the constraints of conscience. Again, to persuade a reticent lady to love, the sophist must
dislocate such words as "honor," "truth," "good," and perhaps
even "love" itself from their more conservative meanings, supply-
ing different value-terms in their place—"pleasure," for instance.
Among the libertine lyrics, "The Dampe" makes explicit this dis/
composing, word-killing, and world-building game of sophistic
seduction:

> But if you dare be brave,
> And pleasure in your conquest have,
> First kill th'enormous Gyant, your *Disdaine,*
> And let th'enchantress *Honor,* next be slaine
> (9–12)

The personifications should not hide from us the fact that the very
vocabulary of Petrarchan morality has come under assault. And as
"Twicknam Garden" demonstrates, the failure to control the meaning of words makes for the failure of persuasion. Consider its concluding lines, "O perverse sexe, where none is true but shee, /
Who's therefore true, because her truth kills mee" (26–27): though
they inveigh against the lady, the perversity is really the poet's own,
and is reflected in the idiosyncracy if not perversity of the language.

For what are the subtle semantic shifts in his thrice-repeated true/truth? How can a word like truth "kill"? Is it the poet who has been killed, or has his own *language* been killed or disabled? His inability to control the meaning of such words causes the poem itself to fall from persuasion into a plaintive meditation.

And finally, is it through verbal combat, as Lanham suggests, or through collaboration that victory is won? Indeed, is persuasion not an act of *collusion* between a speaker and his audience, foregrounding *lusus* or play? Combativeness may be adequate to self-defense, protecting one's own position (as the poet's in "The Flea"); yet it rarely, if ever, wins an audience over, as this same poem again suggests. For if the poem fails *as persuasion,* it fails because the lady (and the reader) remains outside its projected world, rejecting, even if she cannot refute, its redefinitions of value. Persuasion, then, need not be a moment of victory so much as a moment of healing, of identification and of reconciliation between participants. Since antiquity rhetoric has, at least ideally, aimed at the emotional as well as moral and political health of its audience. With little exaggeration, the first psychiatric practice begins not in nineteenth-century Vienna but in Corinth of the fifth century b.c. In the *Lives of the Ten Orators,* traditionally ascribed to Plutarch, the sophist Antiphon is said to have "set up a scheme for relieving spiritual distress, like the treatment of physical diseases by physicians. He built a kind of office in Corinth near the market-place and advertised that he was able to cure anguish in persons through words alone. He would inquire into the causes of his patients' distress and give them relief."[25] And healing words make cures of the body possible, as Plato's Gorgias observes: "I have often, along with my brother and with other physicians, visited one of their patients who refused to take their medicine or submit to the surgeon's knife or cautery, and when the doctor was unable to persuade them, I did so, by no other art but rhetoric."[26]

25. Quoted in Moses Hadas, *Ancilla to Classical Reading,* p. 265.
26. *Gorgias,* in *Collected Dialogues,* p. 239. Even Plato's criticism of Gorgias assumes the health and reconciliation of audience as its singular criterion: "right rhetoric," Socrates claims, is a medicine or physic for the soul, while discourse aimed at victory—indeed, at anything other than the audience's well-being—undermines health, flattering the audience and pandering to their pleasures "without consideration of what is best" (p. 249). See James S. Baumlin and Tita French Baumlin, "*Psyche/Logos:* Mapping the Terrains of Mind and Rhetoric." See also Tita French Baumlin, "Petruchio the Sophist and Language as Creation in *The Taming of the Shrew.*"

Granted, prior to speech, Lanham's rhetorical man "is committed to no single construction of the world." But is not the "game at hand," his reason for speaking, always precisely the attempt *to construct* the world, even if in his own image? Taken on its own terms, sophistic discourse is not so much the denial as it is the reconstitution of social reality. To neglect this is to neglect the very premise of sophism: seeing (or imagining) and saying are one. Thus sophistic rhetoric becomes the verbal activity of "playing man" or *homo ludens,* as Johan Huizinga describes the human species. "Play," Huizinga notes, "creates order, *is* order. Into an imperfect world and into the confusion of life it brings a temporary, a limited perfection."[27] Play is world-building, in other words, allowing for imaginative transport out of one's self "without, however, wholly losing consciousness of 'ordinary reality.' " Thus the playing child's (and one might add, the sophist's) representation of a game-world "is not so much a sham-reality as a realization in appearance: 'imagination' in the original sense of the word."[28] Most significant, though, Huizinga asserts that play fosters identification among participants, which in turn fosters community: "a play-community generally tends to become permanent even after the game is over. . . . the feeling of being 'apart together' in an exceptional situation, of sharing something important, of mutually withdrawing from the rest of the world and rejecting the usual norms, retains its magic beyond the dun of the individual game."[29] Is not this description of imaginative play—of voluntary imaginative activity taking place within a unique situation and time, apart from the world but genuinely affecting the spirit of the participants—a description of sophistic persuasion?

As Donne's lyrics demonstrate, the ludic element of sophism does not reduce its serious epistemic consequences, nor, for that matter, does it reduce the risk involved in choice: honor, fidelity, love itself are no small stakes. Paradoxically, then, the sophist's verbal play emphasizes the necessity of moral/interpretive choice even as it affirms its reader's freedom to choose among alternatives. The reader or audience, like a player, "still has the freedom to decide one way or the other, for one or the other possibility," as Hans-Georg Gadamer writes, but "this freedom is not without danger. Rather the game itself is a risk for the player. One can only play with

27. *Homo Ludens: A Study of the Play-Element in Culture,* p. 10.
28. Ibid., p. 14.
29. Ibid., p. 12.

serious possibilities. This means obviously that one may become so engrossed in them that they, as it were, outplay one and prevail over one. The attraction of the game, which it exercises on the player, lies in this risk."[30] In other words, the risk is that game can become actuality, that choices made in play can become choices of life. Textual play, the sophistic game of argument and counterargument, interpretation and response, can outplay us. In a sense we do not play the game: the game—in Donne's case poetic argument—plays us, taking over our consciousness, making its rules of interpretation, decision, and conduct our own. To participate in discourse, whether by reading, writing, or speaking, is to join in just such a serious, world-building game. For "the work of art," as Gadamer suggests, "has its true being in the fact that it becomes an experience changing the person experiencing it."[31]

Surely Gorgias and the sophists who follow him recognize the ludic nature of persuasion as well as the existence of a manifold reality. Speech, Gorgias asserts, "can stop fear and banish grief and create joy and nurture pity,"[32] and what gives speech such power is its ability to create mental images—to substitute images in the mind for palpable phenomena—and in this way give imaginative reality to that which remains as yet only possible. The play of language allows the potential and hypothetical to come to temporary imaginative life in the mind of a reader. That which is imagined *is* only potential; it is up to the reader to give life to a thought, to embody a belief or adopt a course of action, ultimately, as its own. The classical rhetorical concept of *enargeia*, which Chaim Perelman resuscitates in the notion of "presence," is thus instrumental in establish-

---

30. *Truth and Method*, p. 95.

31. Ibid., p. 92. And thus reading, as Marshall W. Alcorn, Jr., and Mark Bracher suggest, "can influence if not actually mold the structure of the reader's self," since "one's own identity is set aside and the text constitutes a new subjectivity within oneself" ("Literature, Psychoanalysis, and the Re-Formation of the Self: A New Direction for Reader-Response Theory," p. 342). Persuasion requires, therefore, a temporary negation or effacement of self: to be persuaded we must cease being only ourselves, cease reacting and thinking in ways we have become habituated to, and give ourselves over to an alien, often chaotic, inevitably unstable mixture of interests, values, desires. We mix another's values—we mix another's world—with our own. And out of the chaos we may see patterns of behavior and belief emerge that we can give fresh and perhaps full assent to. These beliefs were not originally our own; the self that emerges within these new patterns was not originally us. Rather, self invents itself anew in the free play of wor(l)ds.

32. "Encomium to Helen," p. 52.

ing belief: potentially new worlds, potentially new roles—potentially new selves—are given imaginative presence in the audience's mind, revealing for examination and choice a new realm of experience.[33] Again, the logic of discourse may or may not convince; yet the extent to which discourse invites such imaginative participation will determine its success or failure as persuasion. Reality, then, becomes the residue of one's speech-games, what is left *after* one has spoken and persuaded—at least from the sophist's perspective, whose goal is *to create* the very community, the communion, the consubstantiation between speakers that incarnationism celebrates as its firm, substantial truth (and that skepticism, we might add, thoroughly denies).

▢   ▢   ▢

This chapter began with a brief discussion of the problem of argument though, increasingly, it has turned to the problems of truth and conviction and reality itself, all complicated by the problem of language. As a context for Donne's lyrics, previous chapters explored competing theologies of language and their underlying epistemologies; the first part of this present chapter, in contrast, has examined the psychology of persuasion, outlining the effects of sophistic discourse upon the emotions and belief-structures of its readership. We might now turn, if briefly, to the interpersonal or sociological dimension of sophistic rhetoric, since much of an individual's language is socially, indeed institutionally determined. To speak and write as a Catholic or Protestant, a lawyer or merchant, a courtier or man of the country is necessarily to locate oneself within a specific semantic realm, one that shapes the intentions and forms,

---

33. *The Realm of Rhetoric*, pp. 35–36. Here we might observe that persuasion, like poetry in general, relies heavily on compelling images to draw the imagination into new worlds and new roles. It does not surprise, then, that the histories of rhetoric and poetry have been intertwined since antiquity. Gorgias, for example, looks upon his speeches as prose-poems, and both Isocrates and Cicero claim a close kinship between the orator and poet. Undoubtedly, that kinship tie is their mutual grounding in the imaginative play of language. For "*Poesis*," as Huizinga suggests, "is a play-function. It proceeds within the playground of the mind, in a world of its own which the mind creates for it. There things have a very different physiognomy from the one they wear in 'ordinary life', and are bound by ties other than those of logic and causality" (*Homo Ludens*, p. 119). Poetic imagery, therefore, is inherently sophistic in its effects, so much so that there are, quite possibly, elements of *poesis* (and certainly of *enargeia*) in all persuasive discourse. See James S. Baumlin, "Persuasion, Rogerian Rhetoric, and Imaginative Play."

the meanings and effects, of one's discourse. The individual both constitutes, and is constituted by, the objective sociology of language: class or community in general becomes in its essence a community *of discourse*, and one's self-identity will always be anchored within the verbal practices of some class, occupation, or ideology. Not surprisingly, though, the human personality—like human discourse—takes shape within a dialectic.[34] Even as the individual appropriates or incorporates the conceptual structures of culture, turning objective sociological phenomena into the content of subjective psyche, so the psyche works in turn upon objective phenomena, reshaping and distorting and supplementing their otherwise impersonal values and public meanings. Language is the means whereby the social is appropriated and turned into psyche; language is also the means whereby a social and external reality is reshaped or colored, given its unique private meaning within the mental life of the individual. As a simultaneously social code and subjective experience, love situates itself within this same dialectic. The speakers in Donne's lyrics inherit numerous public vocabularies (of literary traditions: Platonic, Petrarchan, Ovidian; of occupations: legal, mercantile, scholastic; of moral philosophies: libertine, skeptic, Platonic; of theologies: Catholic, Anglican, Calvinist). In varying degrees, each of these vocabularies represents a unique

---

34. See V. N. Vološinov, "Philosophy of Language and Objective Psychology," in *Marxism and the Philosophy of Language*, pp. 25–41. We might add in passing that Douglas Ehninger interprets the history of rhetoric as an evolution of distinct systems, a progression from the grammatical or technical rhetoric of Greek antiquity to the psychological rhetoric of the British eighteenth century to the sociological rhetoric of contemporary theory ("On Systems of Rhetoric," pp. 132–34). Perhaps Ehninger's systems describe the major emphases within each of these epochs; are we to believe, though, that such terms operate in exclusion? The sociological or social-constructionist model is certainly among the current reigning theories of rhetoric, and in its more extreme versions not just discourse but the individual subject becomes a socioideological construct. Thus the processes, Vološinov writes, that "define the content of the psyche occur not inside but outside the individual organism" (*Marxism and the Philosophy of Language*, p. 25). Consciousness itself becomes sociological rather than psychological in origin. And yet the individual consciousness cannot be banished altogether, for, between the psyche and ideology there exists, as Vološinov suggests, a continuous dialectical interplay: the ideological sign "must immerse itself in the element of inner, subjective signs" and "must ring with subjective tones in order to remain a living sign" (p. 39). Inhabiting all three realms simultaneously, discourse unites within itself the grammatical or technical, the sociological, and the psychological aspects of language (see Baumlin and Baumlin, "*Psyche/Logos*," pp. 245–46).

orientation or social/epistemological perspective; and each, as a conventional, *public* language, grants some measure of public, objective meaning (some measure, in a word, of communicability) to the poet's otherwise private and radically subjective experience. In fact the very conventionality of such vocabularies enables meaning to begin with. Typically, though, Donne's lyrics turn to such vocabularies not as proof of their communicative efficiency but precisely as a test of their adequacy, exploring the ways private experience eludes and even defeats conventional language. Donne's lyrics (or at least the most ambitious—and most celebrated) thus enact a search for the language-systems adequate to the love poet's task. We might call this task communication in the broadest sense, the attempt to give public language to private, subjective experience; yet the poet's task is far more complex even than this, for his words must fashion and sustain love as well as define its nature.

Like matters of faith, then, love relations initiate a crisis of language. The crisis arises from the fact that, in addition to the public vocabularies of cultural stations/institutions in which the individual is immersed, the mental life of each human being gives shape to a private vocabulary or idiolect, a set of unique experiences, insights, and beliefs to which words are idiosyncratically, often arbitrarily, assigned. The uniqueness of the individual is reflected not simply in the unrepeatability of each fleeting thought and action; it is reflected in the unique shape and range of each person's speech habits. Love relationships best thrive when lovers fashion their own community-of-two out of a common vocabulary, discovering adequate words for the world they attempt to share (or, arguably, construct). Within this community, conflicts inevitably arise between idiolects, just as they arise between two individuals' values and interests; indeed, tensions between the otherwise separate worlds of lovers, between apparently conflicting interests and desires and interpretations of experience, are resolvable only to the extent that one lover's discourse can transform the meanings—and in a real sense the being—of the other. To understand the other person, to share the same worldview by means of the same words: this is an aim of love. To allow the words—and thus the values, the feeling-tones, the realities—of another to penetrate and remake one's world, to open oneself to another's vocabulary: this, too, is an aim of love. Where such openness to the other's language is lacking, there one will find small space for love, community, or simple understanding.

For "rhetoric," as I. A. Richards astutely defines it, is "the study of misunderstanding and its remedies."[35] It seems that conflict itself has a linguistic basis, that it arises from the intersection of competing vocabularies and worldviews. Since conflicts in love arise from misunderstanding then love, too, becomes a persuasive, discursive, and, above all, interpretive activity; here, moreover, as in other areas of social reality, the creation of community (or resolution of conflict) becomes an essentially *rhetorical* activity. And in this creation of community, definition—the sharing and fixing, as it were, of meaning in public language—is perhaps the most powerful of strategies, for it is precisely in the meaning or definition of any word that rhetoric, ethics, and epistemology interact. Thus Plato's debate with the sophists becomes a struggle precisely over definitions, the sophist arguing any position he wishes by multiplying rather than controlling meaning; equivocating upon crucial value-terms, the sophist is capable of turning the vocabulary of conventional morality on its head—of making, in Plato's words, "the worse argument appear the better." Donne's own sophistries demonstrate this convincingly: the meaning of value-terms continuously shift in such poems as "Communitie" and "The Flea," and Plato would prevent this shifting through explicit, formal definition, a practice intended to remove ambiguity from argument and subordinate language to logic. Plato's entire canon, in fact, can be read as an attempt to discover adequate definitions of his Athenian culture's value-terms; always he asks, through the character of Socrates, What *is* Justice? Temperance? Courage? What is the Good? But is there not an element of sophism in Plato's own method? Is it the conventional or, rather, the transformational definition that he seeks?[36] In the dialogues, Justice and the Good become themselves paradoxical, tied to unpopular or uncommon meanings—meanings that the Athenian community, to Socrates's peril, does not share. Actually such destabilizing, transformational definitions lead to his death, as they pose too great a threat to the common language and conventional morality. To his accusers, Socrates subverts rather than af-

35. *The Philosophy of Rhetoric,* p. 12.
36. As Otis Walter observes, "Plato has usually been misunderstood as simply recommending that the rhetorician define terms using a genus and species, know the truth, and understand the 'soul' or persona of the audience. But the most important characteristic of Plato's rhetorical advice is that definitions, especially of terms designating values, must state the 'transforming' meaning of the value and that all communication involving the term should be based on this meaning" ("Plato's Idea of Rhetoric for Contemporary Students: Theory and Composition Assignments," p. 29).

firms and regulates the meanings of words; to them *he* is the sophist, making the worse argument appear the better, and vice versa.

The transvaluation of value-terms is not, therefore, immoral in
itself; of all philosophers, Plato is its greatest practitioner.[37] His
argument against the sophists, rather, is that they subordinate their
redefinitions to a conception of *kairos*—again, the Timely, Opportune, or Circumstantial—rather than the *prepon* of an absolute, timeless, transcendent reality. Once more, it is epistemology that distinguishes Platonic from sophistic theories of rhetoric, Platonic
absolutes warring against sophistic contingencies and relativism.
The sophistic rhetoricians of antiquity are famed for their paradoxical speeches, their praises of things conventionally considered un-
praiseworthy, their defenses of notorious people and seemingly
indefensible propositions. Yet their penchant for paradoxical argument is more than virtuoso display; rather, their subversion of conventional belief illustrates, in clearest possible relief, the world-
building potential they claim for discourse. Giving new meaning to
value-terms will initially tear into a community's web of beliefs, but
it will also allow for a reconstruction of values and a reconstitution
of community along new lines. To the dogmatic, absolutist Plato
this practice could lead only to falsehood and the subversion of
truth; to the ancient sophist, and Renaissance love poet, this practice becomes liberating. Argument can, of course, be abused, ma-
nipulating an audience by pandering to appetite; the libertine
poems demonstrate as much. And in such lyrics as "The Dampe"
and "The Flea," the lady's moral dilemma becomes an interpretive
problematic for the reader as well who, like the lady, must ask
whether he or she will *allow* such a word as "honor" to be so disabled or dislocated from its conventional meaning. Still, it seems
that our reading of the *Songs and Sonets* needs to distinguish between the arguments of the libertine skeptic, who places himself
beyond morality, and those of the sophist, who seeks to transform

37. As Plato's Gorgias suggests, the sophists who teach rhetoric "are not
guilty, and the craft is not for this reason evil or to blame, but rather, in my
opinion, those who make improper use of it." The rhetorician, he continues,
may be "competent to speak against anybody on any subject, and to prove
himself more convincing before a crowd on practically every topic he wishes,
but he should not any more rob the doctors—or any other craftsmen either—of
their reputation, merely because he has this power. One should make proper
use of rhetoric as of athletic gifts" (*Gorgias*, in *Collected Dialogues*, p. 240). Plato
may disagree with Gorgias concerning the nature of truth and reality; both,
nonetheless, agree on the highest aim of discourse and persuasion, which is the
health of the soul.

or redefine morality, valorizing freedom, health, harmony, community, pleasure. We need also to remind ourselves that not all of Donne's sophistic persuasions claim success. "Sapho to Philaenis," for one, expressly admits the failure of poetic language to charm and persuade, having lost its once "inchanting force":

> Where is that holy fire, which Verse is said
> To have, is that inchanting force decai'd?
> Verse that drawes Natures workes, from Natures law,
> Thee, her best worke, to her worke cannot draw.
> Have my teares quench'd my old Poetique fire;
> Why quench'd they not as well, that of desire?
>
> (1–6)

Like "Twicknam Garden," the poem falls into complaint, itself incapable of "quench[ing]" the speaker's suddenly destructive "desire." And we might add that, in contrast to the melancholy of this "heroicall epistle," many of the *Elegies* parody rather than repudiate sophistic argument. "On his Mistris" provides an example: a comedy of language, the poem self-consciously exaggerates its claims to express a "masculine perswasive force."

> By our first strange and fatall interview,
> By all desires which thereof did ensue,
> By our long sterving hopes, by that remorse
> Which my words masculine perswasive force
> Begot in thee, and by the memory
> Of hurts which spies and rivalls threatned me,
> I calmely beg; but by thy parents wrath,
> By all paines which want and divorcement hath,
> I conjure thee; and all those oathes which I
> And thou have sworne, to seal joint constancie,
> Here I unsweare, and over-sweare them thus:
> Thou shalt not love by meanes so dangerous.
>
> (1–12)

Initially the language builds a swelling, Ciceronian period, heaping up clauses through the charm-like, liturgical repetitions of *anaphora* ("By our . . . By all . . . By our . . ."), only to deflate in an anticlimactic "beg"—hardly persuasive in effect, though the poet proceeds to "conjure" the lady's obedience, asserting his right to "unsweare, and over-sweare" vows. But while the poet here naively claims an irresistible, god-like power of commandment ("Thou shalt not . . ."), the poet of "Natures Lay Ideot" finds his own "sophistrie" to have worked too well—indeed, to have backfired, having instructed the lady so efficiently that she is now, herself, the greater sophist.

When tied to sheerly libertine ends, it seems that Donne's sophism rarely, if ever, rises above a comic stubbornness of argument, fully aware (and half-willing even to admit) its deliberate obfuscations and verbal violence. More subtle, then, and perhaps more successful, is a group of sophistic persuasions that argue not for a release from morality so much as for the creation, and maintenance, of faithful, mutual love. Valuing love over business and personal ambition, such lyrics as "The Sunne Rising," "The Anniversarie," "The Autumnall," "Loves Growth," and "A Lecture upon the Shadow" seek to liberate the lovers from all obstacles the world places against their union; such poems openly solicit the reader's assent to their morality, inviting the audience, both reader and internal addressee, to share in their renovated vocabularies and worlds of experience. More than victory or pleasure-in-use, their goal is to create community among participants, and they seek to achieve this community, this communion of language and experience, by redefining (and thereby transvaluing) social value. "The Autumnall" provides a classic example. A paradoxical encomium (at least one manuscript entitles it "A Paradox of an ould woman"), it attempts to praise and empower that which is typically held in contempt—in this case, a lady's advanced age:

> Call not these wrinkles, graves; If graves they were,
> They were Loves graves; for else he is no where.
> Yet lies not Love dead here, but here doth sit
> Vow'd to the trench, like an Anachorit.
> And here, till hers, which must be his death, come,
> He doth not digge a Grave, but build a Tombe.
> Here dwells he, though he sojourne ev'ry where,
> In Progresse, yet his standing house is here.
> Here, where still Evening is; not noone, nor night;
> Where no voluptuousnesse, yet all delight.
> In all her words, unto all hearers fit,
> You may at Revels, you at Counsaile, sit.
>   (13–24)

The poem is no less than a series of transforming definitions. So unworthy a thing as a wrinkle need not make a woman unworthy of love, nor does it "kill" love so much as revalue it: love "lies not . . . dead" (15) in this grave, though it repudiates "voluptuousnesse" (22) or its sheerly physical nature for a spiritual devotion, seeking refuge in her face as would a hermit or "Anachorit" (16).

Thus the sophist can choose to defend rather than abuse chastity and a lady's honor, as Gorgias's own "Encomium of Helen" comes to the aid of an accused woman, commenting at the same time on the nature of persuasion itself. "Surely it is proper," Gorgias writes, "for a woman raped and robbed of her country and deprived of her friends to be pitied rather than pilloried."[38] Helen herself is not at fault, for she was violently ravished (though again, by the language of appetite and unlawful pleasure). "How then," he asks at the end of this paradoxical defense, "can one regard blame of Helen as just, since she is utterly acquitted of all charge?" And the means of this acquittal, he boldly claims, is the irresistible force of his own persuasive language: "I have by means of speech removed disgrace from a woman."[39] "But," the skeptical reader might observe, "such redefinitions and transvaluations remain figures of rhetoric—mere *impossibilia*. Surely the poet is either hopelessly naive or else a liar, a deliberate and self-conscious liar who expects his readers to catch him in the lie." Maybe so. Nonetheless the sophist turns truth and reality itself into properties of language and of psyche, rather than properties of a stable, though silent, external being. Far, then, from sharing the skeptic's pessimism or despair over the "lies" of literary language, the sophist deliberately seeks deception—the Gorgianic *apate*—as the foundation of persuasion, and he seeks this persuasion as a means to overcome the paralyzing effects of contradictory *logoi*.

As Gorgias suggests, "all who . . . persuade people of things do so by molding a false argument."[40] In fact the sophist seeks this deceptive persuasion in order to remove cognitive uncertainty and resolve the paralysis of will bred by competing worldviews. For "in all human decisions and actions," the humanist Francesco Guicciardini observes,

> there is always a reason for doing the opposite of what we do, for nothing is so perfect that it does not contain a defect. Nothing is so evil that it does not contain some good, just as nothing is so good that it does not contain some evil. This causes many men to remain inactive, because every tiny flaw disturbs them. . . . That is no way to be. Rather, having weighed the disadvantages of each side, we should decide for the one that weighs less, remembering that no choice is clear and perfect in every respect.[41]

38. Pp. 51–52.
39. Ibid., p. 54.
40. Ibid., p. 52.
41. *Recorde*, #213 (ca. 1530); quoted in Sloane, *End of Humanist Rhetoric*, p. 65.

Guicciardini does not follow the Greek sophist in prescribing *apate* or deception as the cure for indecision, concealing or suppressing one half of a contradictory truth; rather, he follows the Academic philosopher or Ciceronian who weighs both sides of a controversy, discovers which is the greater (and which the lesser) good, and then makes a choice. He confirms, nonetheless, the sophist's major premise. The grounds for all belief, all action, and therefore all argument are relative: "nothing is so evil that it does not contain some good, just as nothing is so good that it does not contain some evil." Thus the rhetorician's persuasions, like the love poet's, must seek to break the cycle of cognitive and moral paralysis that contradiction engenders in the human consciousness. "A Lecture upon the Shadow" makes just such an attempt, though the poem invites both sophistic and skeptical or deconstructive readings. "Explicitly about the impossibility of maintaining a perfect love within the temporal cycle," the poem is also, Rajan argues, "about the impossibility of communicating or arguing for this love in a discourse free of rhetorical dissimulation."[42] It is indeed about dissimulation and disguise, though such a reading ignores the sophistic insight that persuasion is by definition a mode of deception. Persuasion demands "rhetorical dissimulation" precisely because it seeks the deliberate suppression of contradiction—the denial, in brief, of half the world, the denial of *dissoi logoi* for the sake of some singular *logos.*

The fact that "A Lecture upon the Shadow" argues *against* dissimulation and disguise in love makes this recognition all the more poignant. The lyric begins, apparently, in the midst of an already-unfolding argument, the poet responding to the lady's reticence in revealing their love to the world:

> Stand still, and I will read to thee
> A Lecture, Love, in loves philosophy.
>   These three houres that we have spent,
>   Walking here, two shadowes went
> Along with us, which we our selves produc'd;
> But, now the Sunne is just above our head,
>   We doe those shadowes tread;
> And to brave clearnesse all things are reduc'd.
>   So whilst our infant loves did grow,
>   Disguises did, and shadowes, flow,
> From us, and our care; but, now 'tis not so.

42. "'Nothing Sooner Broke,'" p. 817.

That love hath not attain'd the high'st degree,
Which is still diligent lest others see.

(1–13)

The lovers', especially the lady's, initial concern for the secrecy of
their "infant" (9) love was itself a source of deception (though others were deceived: parents perhaps, and friends, not the lovers
themselves). Now, however, "to brave clearnesse all things are re-
duc'd" (8) . . . including their love, it seems. At this point the
speaker's argument translates moral values into the vocabulary of
physical nature, honesty and openness of action becoming the sunlight that reveals the lovers fully and candidly to the world as well as
to one another, while the disguises of social behavior become mere
shadows hiding selfish interests. The noontime sun thus provides
the *kairos*, the appropriate occasion and circumstance, for the poet's
argument against continued secrecy; it is time for the lovers to
"bring to light" or reveal their intentions. All this, once again, is in
implicit response to the lady's desire that they remain "still diligent
lest others see" (13):

Except our loves at this noone stay,
We shall new shadowes make the other way.
    As the first were made to blinde
    Others; these which come behinde
Will worke upon our selves, and blinde our eyes.
If our loves faint, and westwardly decline;
        To me thou, falsly, thine,
And I to thee mine actions shall disguise.
    The morning shadowes weare away,
    But these grow longer all the day,
But oh, loves day is short, if love decay.

Love is a growing, or full constant light;
And his first minute, after noone, is night.

(14–26)

Of course the "logic" of such an argument is easily countered: as
the sun itself must decline, so love, to press the analogy to its conclusion, cannot continually remain at noon. As a preacher Donne
himself deconstructs the argument, demonstrating its physical impossibility: "No man hath *veram lucem*, true light, thorough light;
no man hath *meridiem, Augem*, that high point that casts no shadow. . . . Slacker men have a declination even in their *mornings*; a
West even in their *East*; coolings, and faintnesses and after-noones,
as soon as they have any dawnings, any breake of day, any inchoa-

tion of any spiritual action or purpose" (*Sermons*, 3:355–56). Time
and the sun cannot stand still. Yet time, paradoxically, has enabled
the poet's argument, allowing him to exploit the sun's motion within, of all things, an argument for honesty and constancy. The poem
proceeds, then, precisely by suppressing counterargument. To admit or in any way address this other half of the *dissoi logoi* would lead
to paralysis—both of the lovers' will and of persuasion itself. For the
sophist's persuasion, as Mario Untersteiner observes, "becomes
will, decision, which [is] realized in a *kairos* endowed with the property of breaking up the cycle of the antitheses and creating something new, irrational: that epistemological process defined as 'deception', 'persuasion', the power of which lies in the imposition
of one of the two alternatives."[43] Read sophistically, such a poem
counters skepticism by privileging psychology over logic, by rendering the commonplace world irrelevant to emotional experience,
by substituting for referential language a language of paradox and
hyperbole that deliberately deceives, and in deceiving remakes, an
audience's language and understanding.

   Once again the sophist, like the speaker in Donne's lyrics of
mutual love, need not deceive for the sake of appetite or self-inter-
est. Though Plato accuses the sophists of self-serving flattery and
opportunism, such a speaker seeks "not to falsify truth in opposition to morality, but to impose by means of 'deception' that which is
possible."[44] And in the poems of mutual love is there anything more
noble, more highly *moral*, than the creation of community? For it
seems, finally, that sophism aims at nothing less than the actualization or incarnation of its possible worlds. "We do not will a situation," as Bozarth-Campbell suggests, "but being in a situation, we
assent to it and find that the existential circumstances we are in
make us be one kind of person instead of another and cause us to
will one way rather than another." And thus one's existential circumstances "arise . . . from the body":

> The body assures metamorphoses and is the means whereby ideas and
> images are transformed into realities and acts. The body converts ele-
> ments of a situation through its total gesture in response to it. Move-
> ment toward another is movement of and in the body, changing the
> situation by a true inclination. When the body opens itself to others, it
> finds its own voice in an active coexistence beyond itself. Intention
> toward another transforms one's bodily existence, which is itself

43. *Sophists*, p. 161.
44. Ibid., p. 198.

a perpetual incarnation. Even though we do not know how this transformation happens, it does happen.[45]

Thus we have come full circle: sophistic persuasion, as a mode of
communication, is grounded in intersubjectivity, turning its texts
into a scene of dialogue, of dual presences—and invoking, perhaps
surprisingly, the mystery of incarnation. And if persuasion leads
the two lovers to actualize what the poet asserts is possible, if they
in fact make a new world of value, fashioning a new language and a
new world of experience (in a word, if they incarnate their noble
hopes and desires, becoming the arguments they utter) then in
what way can such lyrics be held even to *apate*?

We now have before us the major rhetorics inhabiting Donne's
Songs and Sonets, the rhetorics of incarnationism, transcendence,
skepticism, and sophism. As a final note to this discussion, let me
add that the modes of interpretation fostered by these rhetorics seek
to establish particular relations with the reader, textual relations
that are in some sense comparable to human sexual relations. While
incarnationism unites the subjectivities of reader and text in an I-
Thou relation, the libertine skeptic's denial of meaning and authorial intentionality, expressing an almost narcissistic will-to-power,
reduces reading to a subject/object, I-it relation. And while transcendence seeks to negate the "I," emptying the reader before the
text's mystic presence (an act of self-effacement resembling the
Christian's *agape*), the sophist's exploitation of polysemy (his insem-
ination, as it were, of meaning) expresses a kind of *eros*—an erotics
of interpretation, seeking to fashion love or a sense of community
between the reader and the poem. Though these do not exhaust the
possible relations between reader and text, they do, nonetheless,
recall Paul Tillich's discussion of the theology of love, one that contrasts Greek *eros* with Christian *agape* only to unite them—incarnate
them, as it were—in a maturer vision. For while *eros* would define
love as "the desire for self-fulfillment by the other being" and *agape*
as "the will to self-surrender for the sake of the other being," neither
by itself is an adequate description. As Tillich observes, "no love is
real without a unity" of the two, for *eros* without *agape* is "chaotic
desire," while *agape* without *eros* is "obedience to a moral law without warmth, without longing, without reunion."[46] Let me beg the
reader's indulgence as I turn Tillich into an allegory on the nature of
interpretation. Implicitly, I have argued that meaning arises out of

45. *Word's Body*, pp. 118–19.
46. *Dynamics of Faith*, pp. 114–15.

the tension among competing rhetorics; no reading can approach completion without recognizing the equal claims of *eros* and *agape*, sophism and skepticism, incarnationism and transcendence. The theology of love, then, shares much with the theology of language. Like reading, love arises out of an interplay of attitudes, values, premises, perspectives. It is the very tension between perspectives that makes love possible, and reading possible as well. Again, the various rhetorics are inherently fragmented and angular visions; though they war against each other, each by itself remains incomplete, forever in need of supplement, qualification, and response. Such, at any rate, are the explicit arguments of the final chapter, to which we now turn.

8

The Four Shapes of Rhetoric

What shape will discourse assume and what powers will it claim in a world that acknowledges its origins in divine creation, a world where truth and being are eternal, singular, and knowable—a world that is rational and stable in its rationality? Such a world, created and sustained by God's Word, will yield its truth to humanity's powers of reasoning, powers that, however imperfectly, reflect God's own. What shape of discourse, on the other hand, will describe a world where truth is unknown—unknowable—where being becomes unstable and subject to change, where cognitive certainty yields to chance and truth is reduced to social convention (or, lower yet, to convenient fiction)? Such a world will prove irrational, refusing to yield its meanings to humankind. What shape will discourse assume when language itself is efficacious, capable of giving presence to phenomena? Such discourse will assert the congruence, indeed the perfect identity, between *res* and *verbum*, its utterance ranging in effect from a stable and faithful representation to a magical (as it were, a sacramental) incarnation of being—a performative *fiat lux*. What, in contrast, will be the shape of discourse when language is weak, incapable of claiming substantial presence? Reduced to a series of arbitrary signs, language will forfeit its identity with external phenomena and all claim to clarity and stability of reference; the saving power of sacrament will be denied to such language, which fails as well to affirm and sustain truth. As the preceding suggests, the dominant rhetoric of any discourse—that is, its privileged verbal epistemology—will tend to be either dogmatic or relativistic with regard to knowledge, essentialist or nominalist with regard to language. And significantly, the rhetorics rising out of these ratios conform, if roughly, to the four most influential theories of Western tradition. Incarnationism is grounded in the verbal epistemology of Aristotle and St. Thomas, in which truth is knowable and language capable of expressing it. Transcenden-

263

talism corresponds to the linguistic theology of Plato and St. Augustine, in which truth, though accessible, is radically separated from utterance, words being too weak to express it fully. Skepticism invokes the radical episteme of Pyrrho and Montaigne, in which language is too weak to discover or confirm a truth that is itself both unstable and ultimately unknowable. Sophism, finally, is the rhetoric of Gorgias and such word-magicians as Shakespeare, in which a language of demiurgic power compensates for the instability of being and truth by making truth, literally creating the world out of words.[1] No longer, then, should we consider the major texts of rhetorical tradition as offering exclusive definitions of a singular phenomenon. Plato does not refute Gorgias, Aristotle does not disprove Plato, Augustine does not triumph over Aristotle; these different theories of historical rhetoric simply isolate the most extreme and, in a sense, the purest manifestations of discourse. Each of them describes a portion of (and a potentiality within) language use; each of them has its own necessity; none of them comprehends discourse in its entirety.

And this, by the way, is true for the individual speaker or writer as well as for an age or tradition: no one rhetoric can serve at all times and in all ways. Regardless of an author's conscious espousal of a particular philosophy or belief-system (whether he is a relativist, positivist, dogmatist, agnostic, or what else) his text never ties itself slavishly to one rhetoric. We may thank God for this, since a singular rhetoric would otherwise become a disablement rather than facilitation or enablement of meanings. For each rhetoric is describable as much by what it cannot see and say as by what it

1. Note that these rhetorics largely confirm Aristotle's division of discourse (*Rhetorica*, 1358a–1359a). What I have termed sophistic rhetoric typically describes a rhetoric of persuasion and can be associated with Aristotle's deliberative mode. Skeptical rhetoric, with its emphasis on refutation, makes considerable use of accusation and defense, strategies of the judicial mode. Incarnational rhetoric tends toward celebration of some truth or experience and thus incorporates many of the traditional aims and techniques of *epideixis*. And while transcendental rhetoric is not a part of Aristotle's tripartite division, yet it conforms to a mode of discourse popular in the Renaissance (and one that Augustine surely anticipates): meditation, a rhetoric of silent self-scrutiny and prayer. Of course, we should not reduce the four rhetorics to these Aristotelian/Augustinian modes, and vice versa. The point I wish to make here, simply, is that the classical systems recognize a range of perspectives and that some of these systems, Aristotle's especially, are highly sensitive to the variety of aims, audiences, occasions, and styles. Structurally, at least, Aristotle observes the multeity of rhetorics, though he fails to appreciate their radically divergent epistemologies.

can—in a word, by what it denies a speaker's (and audience's) language and worldview. A person may, in theory, thoroughly deny essentialist properties of language but pray hard for just such a power when his or her own words become "I love you; please love me," or "I'm sorry; forgive me." Regardless of the conscious epistemology or language-attitude of that speaker, such words yearn for the sophistic power to charm and change an audience and, when uttered in good faith, turn this very desire into a premise of the discourse, giving shape to an essentially sophistic rhetoric. And we can use language to curse and wound as well as cure. As Geoffrey Hartman writes, we might assume

> that words are always armed and capable of wounding, either because, expecting so much of them . . . we are hurt by their equivocal nature; or because the ear, as a psychic organ, is at least as vulnerable as the eye. What is unclear . . . is why we should expect so much of words. This overestimation, which may of course turn into its opposite, into contempt of talk, can suggest that words themselves caused the hurt we still feel, as we look to them for restitution or comfort.

And "where there is a word cure," Hartman adds, "there must be a word-wound."[2] Though hyperbolic (and hence implicitly self-critical) in its claims, Donne's lyric "The Expiration" asserts the power of words not simply to wound but to kill, particularly words uttered by departing lovers:

> We ask'd none leave to love; nor will we owe
> Any, so cheape a death, as saying, Goe;
>
> Goe; and if that word have not quite kil'd thee,
>   Ease mee with death, by bidding mee goe too.
> Oh, if it have, let my word worke on mee,
>   And a just office on a murderer doe.
> Except it bee too late, to kill me so,
> Being double dead, going, and bidding, goe.
>   (5–12)

Within the poetic fiction, the word "Goe" becomes itself the instrument of murder and suicide. Obviously, however, such a lyric questions the performative power of language, as does yet another poem, "The Curse." Invoking the medieval formula for anathema, the poet-priest here performs a ritual act of excommunication, a

2. *Saving the Text*, p. 123. See also Thomas Szasz, *The Myth of Psychotherapy: Mental Healing as Religion, Rhetoric, and Repression*.

wounding charm meant to preserve the "holy mystery" of his love:[3] "Who ever guesses, thinks, or dreames he knowes / Who is my mistris, wither by this curse" (1–2). And yet "it is a miserable impotency," Donne the preacher writes, "to be afraid of *words*" (*Sermons*, 7:429). Indeed "increpation" or another's chiding, he suggests elsewhere, "may easily be suffered, because it is but *verbum*, but a word, a word and away. . . . they are but *Verba*, not *Verbera*, They are but words, and not blowes" (*Sermons*, 9:354). Here Donne invokes in order to deny the common etymological confusion of *verbum* with *verber* (that is, "beating" or "lashing"). Of course, we have all at some time felt threatened by another's words and worldview, needing to deny that person's language the power to curse or charm. And a nursery rhyme, in all likelihood, is our first lesson in the rhetoric of nominalist skepticism: "*Sticks and stones* may break my bones, but *names* (substitute 'words' or 'texts') will never hurt me." As Donne would say, "they are but *Verba*, not *Verbera*." But is it not ironic that the rhyme itself provides a countercharm against the power of another's language? The rhyme's very argument for nominalism proceeds by means of its own essentialist magic, claiming implicitly to do what it says: that is, disable another's language, denying it the power to hurt.

What a text says, therefore, about the nature of discourse and what it does as discourse itself is often at odds. Rhetorical theory demonstrates this as convincingly as poetic practice: the most influential texts in the history of rhetoric at times argue by means of a series of contrary rhetorics, attempting through their words quite the opposite of what their explicit definition of language allows. Consider the Socratic dialogue, which prepares its participants to receive transcendent knowledge by first cleansing them of opinion and error. Initially, the *elenchus* or refutation of error demands a rhetoric of questioning and doubt, while the vision of truth (the myth of the cave in the *Republic*, for example, or the charioteer in the *Phaedrus*) modulates to a mythopoetic mode or rhetoric of transcendence. Thus a systematic application of skepticism becomes preparative to transcendent vision—even though skepticism, paradoxically, is a position Socrates attacks in his opponents. Moreover, his attacks against sophistry succeed (unconsciously or deliberately?) precisely through Socrates's own rhetorical pyrotechnics, his own exploitation of sophism.[4] And, as circumstances often demand more

3. See Robert A. Bryan, "John Donne's Use of the Anathema," p. 310.
4. See, of all texts, Robert Pirsig, *Zen and the Art of Motorcycle Maintenance*, pp. 304–61; and Jasper Neel, *Plato, Derrida, and Writing*.

than the enablement or disablement of language's performative/ persuasive power, so we avail ourselves of other rhetorics besides sophism and skepticism. We have all at some time celebrated a truth through language, attempting to give it presence, to (trans-)sub-stantiate it in words written or read, spoken or heard. For some this truth rests fully and faithfully inscribed in the King James transla-tion of the Bible; for others it lies in the quasi-liturgical repetitions of a national anthem; for others still it resides in the confident pro-nouncements and seemingly precise technical vocabulary of a sci-entific treatise. All such discourse celebrates the firm truth that becomes both its premise and subject, a truth fixed in a stable, knowable world and fully, confidently expressible in language. Such discourse also, if implicitly, claims for itself the *authority* to pronounce upon truth and the nature of reality. Thus the urge toward logical certitude and a stability of values gives birth to an incarnational rhetoric, just as a desire to express what language cannot say—what it literally cannot *see* or make visible to us—gives birth to a negative rhetoric or transcendentalism. In such cases dis-course seeks out a language conscious not of its clarity and power but of its own inadequacy, which indeed assumes its inadequacy, its separation from experience, as a premise; paradoxically, such dis-course seeks to efface itself as language, struggling to turn from a "saying" into a "seeing" as it points toward some transverbal real-ity—a truth that lies not within but behind the words. While incar-national rhetoric thus attempts to sacralize experience, re-present-ing it in poetic/liturgical language, a transcendent rhetoric asserts the reality of that which is forever absent from the discourse, turn-ing itself into a talking about what cannot properly be spoken.

Finally, texts that consciously espouse and even champion a par-ticular rhetoric are not limited in use to that rhetoric; other shapes inevitably express themselves in one and the same discourse. Often these rhetorics are mutually enabling, as the verbal deceptions of sophistic persuasion seek literally to create or sustain the realities incarnationism would celebrate. But it is also equally likely that this intersection or multeity will destabilize each rhetoric's aims and meanings, as when a sudden admission of weakness in language reduces the incarnationist's reality to fiction and merely figurative speech. Thus the different rhetorics potentially resident in any text may complement and even require each other; they are also equally combative, warring against each other for hegemony. No longer, therefore, should we speak of *the* rhetoric of a text. And while we may speak of a dominant rhetoric (the incarnationism of "The

Exstasie," say, the libertine skepticism of "Womans Constancy," or the sophism of "A Lecture upon the Shadow"), speak even of the rhetoric consciously espoused and championed by an author, we must keep in mind that domination is never sole possession of the field; paradoxically again, any one rhetoric achieves domination through the cooperation of those very rhetorics it ultimately attempts to subjugate. (And tyrants also tend to fall, in reading as well as in life: the polysemy that arises from this intersection of competing rhetorics is as responsible for a text's loss of control—for its destabilization and deconstruction—as for its enablement.) Whatever the implications of all this to theory, the first point to make is simple enough: we are all, as discourse-makers, both sophists and skeptics when occasion demands, all nominalists and word-magicians when the need arises.

Incarnationism and transcendentalism, skepticism and sophism again form four extreme poles of discourse, none of them in any absolute sense superior to the rest, all in some sense necessary to create and maintain the complex sociolinguistic reality of Renaissance culture (and of Western culture generally). Where, then, does such an insight take theory? Traditionally, rhetoric has taught its students to reflect on the aims and effects of discourse, to ask such questions as, "What must I say in order to achieve my ends?" and "How shall I say it?" Yet the preceding points to a question more fundamental (though rarely conceived as the founding premise of discourse): "What must the world look like, and what must language itself be able to accomplish, if a speaker's need—one's reason for speaking or writing—is to be satisfied?" In short, the different rhetorics grow directly out of the diverse shapes of human desire. Desire expresses itself through each situation and each rhetorical act: medium, audience, occasion, and one's materials are rarely more than instrumental within this need to speak or write.[5] The aim of rhetorical theory might therefore be restated as a study of the motivational premises as well as the structures of discourse, an articulation of the linguistic, epistemological, and psychological assumptions whereby meaning is enabled and at least partially regu-

5. Kenneth Burke's *Rhetoric of Motives* is an early discussion of the intersection of rhetoric and motive (a position that Richard Lanham critiques, by the way, in his *Literacy and the Survival of Humanism*, pp. 15–23). More recently, Lacanian psychology has described in detail the unconscious forces that pulse through discourse, turning one's texts into symptoms of the speaker's or writer's hidden (and typically forbidden) desire; see Robert Con Davis, "Pedagogy, Lacan, and the Freudian Subject."

lated. And as such, rhetoric describes both the writer's creation and reader's interpretation or re-creation of discourse. This latter is not a novel suggestion: a system of rhetoric, as the Renaissance clearly recognized, becomes the prior condition of all meaning and therefore the necessary ground of interpretation as well as invention. And we might add that all interpretation (especially those modes of systematic interpretation referred to as literary criticism) is describable *as a rhetoric*, that is, a procedure to articulate the premises and potentialities of meaning in a text.

We might also add that all criticism manifests itself as a rhetorical system. Poststructuralist criticism, for example, records the impossibility (as well as a text's own naive assertion) of structural unity, logical coherence, clarity of reference and, ultimately, of cognitive certitude. Such a reading proceeds from the reigning linguistic epistemology of deconstruction, which is a radical skepticism.[6] Proving precisely what it takes for granted, each deconstructive reading is no less than a confirmation of its own premises concerning the nature of language, truth, and being. For if language is a system of differences with unstable, shifting meanings and no anchor or fix in silent reality, then discourse necessarily discloses the contradictions within and, inevitably, the breakdown of Western metaphysics; the conclusion, as it were, is contained in the premises. Like all modes of interpretation, then, deconstruction reduces a text to its own rhetorical perspective. One might speak of "friendly" and "hostile" readings of any text, and deconstruction is considered by many a hostile if not terrorist form of criticism. A hostile reading, I take it, is one that refuses to match its strategies of interpretation to the rhetoric dominant in a text, thus denying perhaps the most crucial aspects of an author's intentions in writing— that is, the epistemological/linguistic premises that enable and regulate the text's initial composition. In their place a hostile reading asserts alien premises, asserts, one might say, an alien rhetoric (though "alien" conceals the fact that alternative systems are already present, if *in potentia*). And poststructuralist critics are justifiably quick to observe that a text deconstructs of its own accord since it contains, repressed or hierarchized within itself, the contrasting rhetorics that rob it of a univocal and stable meaning. Texts

6. Suggestively, Terry Eagleton describes Anglo-American deconstruction as "the latest stage of a liberal scepticism familiar in the modern histories of both societies" (*Literary Theory: An Introduction*, p. 147), while Victoria Kahn compares Renaissance and "new" skepticism in some detail (*Rhetoric, Prudence, and Skepticism*, pp. 21–28).

do, in fact, conceal within themselves a multiplicity of rhetorics even when they argue explicitly for the presence and strength of one only, turning a blind eye (a scotoma unconsciously willed?) toward the rest. No utterance, in other words, no single word even, is limited in its operations *to* a particular rhetoric, though each utterance is limited in its meaning *by* any one rhetoric. This the vocabulary of Donne's libertine poetry demonstrates convincingly: "good," "honor," "truth," even "love" itself are terms that the rhetorics of skepticism and sophism struggle to appropriate and control. Any one rhetoric enables a range of meaning, but it is always a limited range; the intersection and multiplicity of rhetorics multiply the meanings of discourse.

But having mentioned the possibility of hostile interpretations, we might observe that deconstructive readings can bring some measure of healing to a text by restoring its excluded voices and unconscious premises, allowing the repressed desire to speak and repossess the discourse, however irrational, however arbitrary, however violent this reopening of the text might appear. The dialectic between *prepon* or decorum and *kairos* can be thus reinscribed as the play between formal restraint and the multivalent rhetorics of desire, the expression of which lie *behind* or beneath authorial intention. For even as *kairos* (or is it here *eros*?) motivates discourse, often it must conceal itself from/within the discourse. It falls to the reader, therefore, to observe an author's conscious rhetorical strategies, at the same time recovering the many contradictions and acts of exclusion that a literary text unconsciously performs. The texts of our own lives, by the way, are no different. We often accuse each other of hypocrisy, duplicity, contradiction, of saying one thing and doing (or again saying) its opposite, of changing positions with the regularity that we change clothes. Criticism, simply, has learned to make the same accusation of texts.

But does contradiction necessarily imply a willful, self-interested sort of double-dealing? Might it not be more accurate, at times, to place contradiction and hypocrisy beyond or beneath intentionality, and impute it to a text's susceptibility to shifting orientations and rhetorics? Like Heidegger's *Sprache*, we do not think these various orientations so much as they think (or speak) us, taking us over, temporarily filling our consciousness in such a way that they seem to become coterminous with consciousness itself. It is perhaps an author's (or a text's) unawareness of such shifts that makes for hypocrisy and contradiction: seeming to speak from one perspective and with one voice, the text discovers within itself a multivalence, a multitude of voices that imperil the author's intentions. Or perhaps we should say that the author surrenders his intentions and even identity to the text, allowing its arguments to speak through him, to articulate their own multivalent rhetorics of which the author is, at best, only partially aware. It falls, then, to the critical reader to articulate and make conscious what might otherwise remain unconscious from/within discourse: not simply the premises but the shifting itself, the very movement between orientations that is typically concealed from the speaker/author/text. The intersection of rhetorics enables such shifts, and I suspect that neither the intersection nor even the shifts can be entirely observed from within the act of composition. The rhetorical grounds shift from underneath us unawares, in the same way that our roles—our selves—shift with changing interests, audiences, and circumstances.

Of course modern literature, like its modes of criticism, has become increasingly aware of this shifting. "I was not one man only," writes Marcel Proust's narrator,

> but the steady advance hour after hour of an army in close formation, in which there appeared, according to the moment, impassioned men, indifferent men, jealous men. . . . In a composite mass, these elements may, one by one, *without our noticing it,* be replaced by others, which others again eliminate or reinforce, until in the end a change has been brought about which it would be impossible to conceive if we were a single person.[7]

Here Proust describes the intimate if unconscious relations between a speaker's orientations, desires, and *ethos* or rhetorical identity. And what of Donne? Are the various speakers of the *Songs and Sonets* not a similar series of "impassioned men, indifferent men, jealous men," some more (and some less) aware than others of their problematic multiplicities of language? At the same time, however, are these many voices not an author's conscious verbal creation? I would hesitate to suggest that Donne is himself unconscious of the rhetorical complexities of his own poetry; few English poets (of the Renaissance, surely) reflect so intensively on the problems of language and meaning. But I would go so far as to say that the interworkings of the various rhetorics are not always under the poet's control; often, rather, they exceed the poet's intentions, taking over the discourse and its potentialities of meaning. For again, the effi-

7. *The Sweet Cheat Gone,* trans. C. K. Scott Moncrieff (New York: Vintage Books, 1970), p. 54; quoted in Spivak, translator's preface to Derrida, *Of Grammatology,* p. xi (the italics are Spivak's).

cient cause of discourse is not conscious authorial intentionality per se but rather the underlying need, the exigency (in classical terms, the *kairos*) that turns writing into its own instrument. What lies prior to discourse is a lack that, ideally, is made present and "filled" by the discourse, seeking its own satisfaction by means of writing; in fact this lack is rarely if ever fulfilled, each text condemned, with every reading, to repeat and multiply its fears and aggressions, duplicities and desires.

Donne's lyric "The Triple Foole" playfully anticipates this Proustian-Lacanian-Derridean theme. "I am two fooles," the poet declares, "For loving, and for saying so / In whining Poetry" (1–3). Though literary form would seem to constrain emotion, such emotion is in fact released and dispersed through its performance:

> I thought, if I could draw my paines,
> Through Rimes vexation, I should them allay,
> Griefe brought to numbers cannot be so fierce,
> For he tames it, that fetters it in verse.
>
> (8–11)

Indeed the poem describes more than *le plaisir du texte*; it asserts, in miniature, the conflict between form and rhetoric, between structures that seek to "tame," "fetter," and "restraine" the poet's emotional subject and the words/notes that disseminate and multiply themselves in song. The more one writes, the more one gives up one's identity to the text and its performance:

> But when I have done so,
> Some man, his art and voice to show,
> Doth set and sing my paine,
> And by delighting many, frees againe
> Griefe, which verse did restraine.
> To Love, and Griefe tribute of Verse belongs,
> But not of such as pleases when 'tis read,
> Both are increased by such songs.
>
> (12–19)

"For both their triumphs so are published," the poet concludes, "And I, which was two fooles, do so grow three" (20–21)—and perhaps more still, with each reading. Literary form fails to regulate meaning and ensure the poet's intentions; in fact the poet is himself decentered, shattered, dispersed in the reading. Writing thus refracts the individual historical subject, reducing the poet to the verbal behaviors of a particular social role, reinscribing him as a libretto or text.

Critical theory, then, should be able to describe the underlying rhetorics in the discourse of a culture. It should also be able to describe the impact of varying epistemologies and language attitudes on the structural elements of discourse, particularly the elements of traditional, "technical" rhetoric as outlined, say, in Quintilian's *Institutio Oratoria* or Thomas Wilson's *Arte of Rhetorique*. If we are to believe such manuals, all discourse draws upon an apparently finite and codifiable set of verbal structures and strategies; the divisions of *inventio, dispositio,* and *elocutio,* the schemes and tropes, the three "duties" or *officia* and the three "proofs" or *pisteis* are applicable, if in varying degrees, to each text, regardless of its ideology or epistemological assumptions. Each text, surely each Renaissance text, yields to an analysis of its arrangement and style, its verbal structures and strategies; whether the subject be literature, law, religion, or any other aspect of text-based culture, the terms and concepts of technical rhetoric thoroughly pervade Renaissance theory. And here, perhaps, arises a confusion over the presumed unity or diversity of historical rhetoric: while the theories (and actual shapes or manifestations) of discourse are multiple, the presence of discernible structures (tropes, for example, the *exordium* or *narratio,* the deliberative oration) has often led theorists to identify the aggregate of such structures as *the* rhetoric of discourse. This confusion is understandable, since technical rhetoric is presumed to be universally applicable, a codification of the structuring principles to which all Western discourse, perhaps all cultural artifact, conforms. Gorgias's "Encomium of Helen," Augustine's *On Christian Doctrine,* and Bacon's *Advancement of Learning* posit radically different verbal epistemologies, yet each draws upon the resources outlined in contemporary handbooks. Christian culture readily assimilates the classical theories of discourse for this very reason: its polemicists, from Augustine and Bede to Erasmus and Calvin, find the elements of technical rhetoric fully exploited in Scripture, of which "there are not so *eloquent* books in the world," as Donne himself writes: "there is no secular Authour, *Qui jucundis vocum allusionibus, et figuris magis abundat,* which doth more abound with perswasive *figures* of Rhetorique, nor with musicall *cadences* and *allusions* . . . then some of the *Secretaries of the Holy Ghost*" (*Sermons,* 10:103). Is God then the first and best rhetorician? Such is a common Renaissance argument, language being God's own creation and gift to humankind. Or is it simply that the Bible, as discourse, must of necessity make use of the rhetorical structures first codified by classical theory? Though naive, such questions point to the fact that humanism itself—with its tense, often troubled synthesis of Judeo-Christian religion and Greco-Roman literary culture—is a thoroughly rhetorical creation, fully aware that pagan philosophy and Christian theology share language as their medium, that *logos* is borne of *Logos*.

And technical rhetoric reaches beyond verbal discourse, as I have suggested, lending its vocabulary to the study of culture itself. In the Renaissance particularly, when the terminology of technical rhetoric was on every schoolboy's lips (if not quite in his heart and mind), the fields of art, architecture, and music were both organized and taught by means of rhetorical models.[8] A typical textbook on painting would thus describe the artist's resources of invention, arrangement, and style; Renaissance art becomes subject to the same rhetorical and interpretive procedures as its literature, the Horatian *ut pictura poesis* describing their mutual relation—in fact the subject matter of Renaissance painting, typically scriptural, historical, or literary/mythological in origin, demands a systematic "reading," one that discloses a painting's thoroughly semiotic character. The musician, likewise, discovers figures of emphasis and repetition in notes as well as words: the schemes of rhetoric become the structural principles of musical as well as verbal composition, each yielding a similar range of effects. In this technical sense the Renaissance is a thoroughly and consciously rhetorical age, acutely aware of the discursiveness of its cultural performance or production and aware of its resources for creative structure—in short, an age continually analyzing its own invention, arrangement, and style. Modern theory has begun to rediscover what the Renaissance learned long before: culture itself, to the extent that its instruments, institutions, and artifacts are of human composition, yields to the structural analysis of technical rhetoric.

Perhaps, then, we should rename technical rhetoric as the *meta-rhetoric* of discourse, the systematic articulation of rhetorical structure per se. But what relationship might the pervasive, indeed all-encompassing vocabulary of technical rhetoric have to the manifested rhetorics of actual discourse? Must technical rhetoric (the codification, once again, of apparently universal structuring capacities) reduce discourse to its own generalized terms? Are texts an

---

8. See, for example, Paolo Pini's *Dialogo di Pittura* (1548) and the work of Joachim Burgermeister, whose *Musica Autoschediastike* (1601) "eulogizes music as a higher form of oratory" (Kennedy, *Classical Rhetoric and Its Christian and Secular Tradition*, p. 215). See also Claude Palisca, "*Ut Oratoria Musica:* The Rhetorical Basis of Musical Mannerism."

aggregate, simply, of so many tropes, proofs, and topoi? Though technical rhetoric describes the verbal patternings and strategies operant in all discourse, it remains forever indifferent to shifts in verbal epistemology; and these, we have seen, make for the fundamental differences among manifested rhetorics, not simply the presence or absence or combination of specific verbal structures. A theory that codifies only the verbal structures loses sight of the epistemic, the kairotic, and even the linguistic assumptions that distinguish Gorgianic modes of discourse from Platonic and Augustinian from Thomist. To observe that each uses "rhetoric" (that is, structural or technical rhetoric—that each draws upon the same resources of invention, arrangement, and style) is true enough. But they are in every case informed by other, more significant premises, and it is once again the powerful governing presence, in all discourse, of such assumptions that gives each rhetoric its distinctive shape or character.

I have suggested that technical rhetoric is itself blind to shifts in epistemology; let me add, however, that the local effects of any figure or rhetorical structure are conditioned by a text's verbal epistemology. Similar figures, for example, occur in radically different genres; yet these same structures will vary in function and effect, depending on the rhetoric dominant in a particular text. Brian Vickers, for one, argues that the figures of rhetoric "contain within themselves a whole series of emotional and psychological effects, almost prior to the presence of meaning or argument."[9] This is not quite true, though theorists from Quintilian to Peacham are equally optimistic in describing a range of a priori effects. I would argue, rather, that the different rhetorics manifest differing tropologies, and that one cannot adequately describe what a trope or scheme *does*, how it affects meaning and charts the relations between words and concepts, until one outlines the verbal epistemology in which that figure operates. Consider Donne's way with paradoxy. As readers from Dryden to Eliot have observed, paradox is perhaps his stylistic hallmark, his most characteristic figure. But does it assume one shape only? Donne's readers, even one and the same critic, have described the paradoxy in numerous ways. Need we choose among their definitions? Or might each describe the workings of paradoxy *within a particular rhetoric*? Dwight Cathcart, for example, suggests that paradox "denies wholeness and clarity of truth," that "it denies universality. The defense of the indefensible act empha-

9. *Classical Rhetoric in English Poetry,* p. 79.

sizes the heterogeneity of things. . . . It seems to deny the unitary nature of truth and the power of law to express that truth so that it is clearly applicable in the affairs of men."[10] Thus he outlines an explicitly skeptical mode of paradoxy, one painfully aware of the relativity of truth and argument. Indeed, the skeptical rhetoric dominant in many lyrics ("The Paradox," for example, "The Indifferent," and the song, "Goe, and catche a falling starre") as well as the *Paradoxes and Problems* turn the figure into an instrument of doubt, a means to question received truths and subvert conventional morality. Elsewhere in the same analysis, though, Cathcart describes both truth and paradoxy itself from an implicitly sophistic perspective:

> The ideas that Donne's speaker holds about truth—what it is, how it is perceived, the end to which it is put—illuminate what he says in the poems of the *Songs and Sonets*. One assumes that all poems attempt to embody some truth and that, as men differ among themselves and are different at different times in their lives, their needs for truth change and the truths they need change.[11]

This is no longer a skeptical paradoxy, one that denies the existence or accessibility of truth; rather, it claims for poetic argument the power to fashion truth, however relative, however fleeting, however private this truth might be. Elsewhere again, in contradiction of such observations, Cathcart suggests that for Donne "truth is single, sublime, perfect." That is, the multiplicity of the visible world is only apparent; in fact Donne "shows repeatedly throughout the *Songs and Sonets* that it is the contradiction between *words* that perplexes—or delights—and that the reality beyond the word is solid and single, often expressed in a drive toward unity between the 'you' and the 'I.' "[12] Perhaps unconsciously, Cathcart here shifts from a sophistic to a transcendent or Augustinian conception of paradoxy. For reality now lies beyond language: a firm, singular truth confronts the failure of words to express it adequately. It is all too easy to criticize such an analysis of Donne's paradoxy, accusing it of inconsistency or downright hypocrisy—of continually shifting its definitions and crucial terms. The fact is that Cathcart, though unaware, is very accurate in his inconsistency, describing the ways each rhetorical perspective appropriates the figure to its own distinctive ends.

Of course the recognition of dual worlds, of the Christian-Pla-

10. *Doubting Conscience: Donne and the Poetry of Moral Argument*, p. 39.
11. Ibid., p. 33.
12. Ibid., pp. 39, 40; my italics.

tonic opposition between a world of the flesh and a world of the spirit, typically entails such a transcendent paradoxy. The "Phoenix ridle" of "The Canonization" provides a secular example, while the "Annunciation" (from the sonnet sequence *La Corona*) illustrates this paradoxy among the divine poems. There, as Michael McCanles observes, the poet invites his reader "to transcend discursive thought and to wonder at the mystery of the Incarnation" by rendering this mystery overtly "in language which communicates precisely its incommunicability."[13] In fact the rhetoric of *La Corona* is more complex even than this, for it marks the intersection of two linguistic theologies, the rhetorics of transcendence and incarnationism. The paradox of the Incarnation is itself, after all, the Unspeakable made speakable, the transcendent Word made Flesh; *La Corona* inscribes a paradox precisely because the transcendent is for once made immanent with Christ's birth. Given its implicitly Catholic-sacramental theology of language, *La Corona* reveals the play between two distinct rhetorical perspectives, in the process demonstrating once more the "partial truth" of language: that one can, and cannot, speak. Of itself, neither incarnationism nor transcendence is adequate to experience. And yet Cathcart's suggestion that "unitary truth" might be "proven" in language asserts this final, incarnationist version of paradoxy: "Donne's speaker makes extraordinary use of the contradictions inherent in language, but this does not lead him finally to a perplexity about things. Ultimate truth, no matter how formulated, remains unitary, and the whole of the law is believed—if not proven—to express that unitary truth."[14] Belief in the "unitary," whether of truth, of love, of being, or of faith, becomes the central value and premise of incarnationism. And as celebrations of union, such Christian paradoxes as the Trinity and Incarnation become models for Donne's own incarnationist paradoxes. "The Exstasie," for example, attempts to fashion one spirit of the two lovers, expressing this unity through a thoroughly paradoxical "dialogue of one," its alchemical symbolism describing a state in which souls and bodies, like metals, are alloyed or made one substance; but underlying the verbal alchemy, once again, is an

13. "Mythos and Dianoia: A Dialectical Methodology of Literary Form," p. 36.

14. *Doubting Conscience*, p. 51. Let me add, in passing, that Rosalie L. Colie analyzes four modes of paradoxy: verbal, logical, epistemological, and ontological. In so doing she confirms, if implicitly, that its nature and effects change with the rhetoric of discourse. See her *Paradoxia Epidemica: The Renaissance Tradition of Paradox*.

incarnationist rhetoric that seeks to celebrate the union of spirit and flesh, the spirit *in* the flesh.

To be sure, the intersection of rhetorics in such a poem (that is, the rhetorics of celebration, persuasion, and self-effacing meditation) invites a dialectical, perspectivist reading. The following stanzas, nonetheless, boldly assert the essential, sacramental union of the two lovers, refusing to retreat from their incarnationist paradoxy:

> Wee then, who are this new soule, know,
>   Of what we are compos'd, and made,
> For, th'Atomies of which we grow,
>   Are soules, whom no change can invade.
>
> But O alas, so long, so farre
>   Our bodies why doe wee forbeare?
> They'are ours, though they'are not wee, Wee are
>   Th'intelligences, they the spheare.
>
> We owe them thankes, because they thus,
>   Did us, to us, at first convay,
> Yeelded their forces, sense, to us,
>   Nor are drosse to us, but allay.
>
>   (45–56)

The repetition of pronouns strives for more than a grammatical force, each repeated word asserting the (spiritual) union that overcomes the (physical) difference among "we," "us," "our," and "they." Indeed the language becomes liturgical in its repetitions, invoking in the secular realm those higher realities that religious communion makes accessible to worshippers. But at stake is more than the celebration or "thankes" (53) that the poet himself alludes to, more even than the invocation or incarnation of spirit: the very identity and nature of the lovers themselves hangs in the balance. So small a word as "us," repeated four times in the final lines, proceeds in affirmation of the very existence of such a thing as "us," repeatability here confirming the reality and perdurability of a union that the poet sacramentalizes in the act of utterance. The repetitions seek both to assert and to sustain the reality (or illusion?) of an enlarged soul, of two-made-one.

Or illusion? The question remains, it seems, whether "The Exstasie" empowers its language or immerses its reader in a crisis of iteration and repetition. "In speech," the Renaissance rhetorician John Hoskyns suggests, "there is no repetition without importance."[15] Perhaps. But do figures of repetition enjoy a predictable

15. *Directions for Speech and Style*, p. 12.

function and effect, regardless of the rhetorical shape or character of the discourse? Can one repeat the same word, with the same meaning, twice? Or do the different rhetorics once again manifest unique tropologies? When read as a poem incarnating experience, Donne's divine poem "The Crosse" discovers repetitions of this emblematic image throughout physical nature:

> Who can blot out the Crosse, which th'instrument
> Of God, dew'd on mee in the Sacrament?
> Who can deny mee power, and liberty
> To stretch mine armes, and mine owne Crosse to be?
> Swimme, and at every stroake, thou art thy Crosse,
> The Mast and yard make one, where seas do tosse.
> Looke downe, thou spiest out Crosses in small things;
> Looke up, thou seest birds rais'd on crossed wings;
> All the globes frame, and spheares, is nothing else
> But the Meridians crossing Parallels.
> Materiall Crosses then, good physicke bee,
> And yet spirituall have chief dignity.
>
>   (15–26)

Such manifestations of the cross may reveal differences in their materiality or physical makeup; yet as signs referring to Christ's cross they participate in a singular, stable, all-encompassing reality. The poet can claim the "power" (17) to reenact the Crucifixion precisely because the cross, the symbol of Christ's Incarnation and sacrifice, remakes the Christian's language. The poet's words claim a dialogic or participatory relation with the Word; thus the language of sacrament, of words that incorporate Christ into communal worship, implicitly underlies the poet's own symbolic action, enabling his own human speech to conserve the spiritual meaning of "Crosse" with each verbal repetition (and enabling him, therefore, to reenact Christ's sacrifice within the poet's daily experience).

Within a skeptical rhetoric, however, the repetition of words inevitably fails to repeat the same meanings. Audial and orthographic representations may recur in a text, yet the meaning slips and shifts from underneath; like Heraclitus questioning the identity of a flowing, changing stream, such a reader shall never read the same word, with the same sense, twice. "Loves Deitie" provides an example. I quote the final stanza, though the poem as a whole fails (or refuses) to fix and stabilize the meaning of the word "love":

> Rebell and Atheist too, why murmure I,
>   As though I felt the worst that love could doe?

> Love might make me leave loving, or might trie
> A deeper plague, to make her love mee too,
> Which, since she loves before, I'am loth to see;
> Falsehood is worse then hate; and that must bee,
> If shee whom I love, should love mee.
>
> (22–28)

The differences between myth, emotion, and concept (that is, between love-as-personification, love-as-experience, and love-as-abstraction) are the least sources of ambivalence; confusions arise in the poet's own understanding of the term, the entire lexicon of the word at once present in such a passage, "love" shifting in meaning from lust, to infatuation, to abject worship, to mutual respect— and, finally, to the highest fidelity that leads the lady, perhaps ironically, to deny him her love. For the lady, already pledged to another, would prove false to love should he enjoy her (in her vocabulary love *does* have a singular and stable meaning: faithfulness). Thus the poet repeats one word a score of times, places it even in the poem's title, and yet loses control over its sense. One might for this reason read the poem as an exercise in linguistic as well as moral skepticism, as a self-conscious, self-ironizing exploration of the poet's failed attempt to fix the meaning of a word. And we should read the word "fix" quite literally: the comedy of "Loves Deitie" lies in the lover's failures to make the word stand still.

"Image and Dream," similarly, provides a scene of conflict between the vocabularies of libertinism and faithful love.[16] Dwelling within his heart, the lady's dream-image leads the poet to glimpse love in its transcendent, transverbal reality; yet his inability to sustain (or, worse, to understand) this ideal leads him to reject it for a more palpable, physical love.

> Image of her whom I love, more then she,
> Whose faire impression in my faithfull heart,
> Makes mee her Medall, and makes her love mee,
> As Kings do coynes, to which their stamps impart
> The value: goe, and take my heart from hence,
> Which now is growne too great and good for me:
> Honours oppresse weake spirits, and our sense
> Strong objects dull; the more, the lesse wee see.
>
> (1–8)

16. The lyric's title, by the way, is Gardner's, who prints it among the *Songs and Sonets*, though Grierson prints it as "Elegie X." It is at home in either collection.

The "Image" becomes "more then she," more beautiful, more faith-ful, more *ideal* than the actual lady; indeed, the ideality of dream-representation points to a higher and greater reality. Her presence within his heart transforms him, then, making him "her Medall" and making "her love mee," though we should note the potential for ambiguity in this last phrase. Does her impression make her love him, or literally *make him into* her love, uniting the emblem or "Medall" and the love itself, just as a form or "stamp" and matter together become one? And we should also note that the poet repudi-ates this refined, ideal love. A "weake" spirit, suddenly oppressed by a love "growne too great and good," the poet here places himself among those "weake men" described in such poems as "The Ex-stasie" and "The Undertaking," men whose reliance on frail phys-ical "sense" prevent them from comprehending fully the mystery of transcendent love: "Honours oppresse weake spirits, and our sense / Strong objects dull; the more, the lesse wee see" (7–8).

Through following stanzas the poet continues to repudiate spir-itual love, choosing the "joyes" of "Fantasie," of an empty (if safe) figment of the mind over the actual, the all *too* real, pains and stress of a love based in "Honours":

> When you are gone, and Reason gone with you,
>   Then Fantasie is Queene and Soule, and all;
> She can present joyes meaner then you do;
>   Convenient, and more proportionall.
> So, if I dreame I have you, I have you,
>   For, all our joyes are but fantasticall.
> And so I scape the paine, for paine is true;
>   And sleep which locks up sense, doth lock out all.
>
> After a such fruition I shall wake,
>   And, but the waking, nothing shall repent;
> And shall to love more thankfull Sonnets make,
>   Then if more honour, teares, and paines were spent.
> But, dearest heart, and dearer image stay.
>   (9–21)

The skepticism of this second stanza reduces the world and human experience to sheerly physical phenomena: by locking out "sense," sleep "Lock[s] out all" (26). The proposition, "if I dreame I have you, I have you" (13) is of course far from an incarnationist's cele-bration of union (whether the union be of man and woman or of the representation, the "Image of her," and the reality); neither is it a sophist's conjuring of mental states. Rather, it casts a skeptic's doubt upon ideal love and the possibility of achieving permanent joy. With such words the poet denies the value, the very possibility, of transcendent experience, reducing all pleasures of love to the "fantasticall" (14) unreality of a dream-state. And yet the dream itself is a "fruition" (17) without fruit, a narcissistic love lacking an external object.

"Image and Dream" thus charts the tensions between rhetorics that would control the poet's understanding (as well as his valuation) of love by giving shape to his vocabulary. Love, heart, honor, sense, reason, fantasy, joy, pain, even dream itself: each term shifts in meaning, and value, depending on the rhetoric. Or rather, each assertion of a transcendent reality, of the possibility of ideal love, is at once falsified by the poet's own tendency to adopt physical over spiritual meanings. Within the transcendent rhetoric of the poem's first stanza, the lady's image is an ideal, a "more then she" (1). But given the speaker's "weake" (7) powers of understanding, a weakness that rationalizes his skepticism, her image (like her physical presence, perhaps?) soon reduces to an object of enjoyment, the loving of which is equivalent to "hav[ing]" (13). In fact so simple a word as "have" becomes a locus of struggle between the libertinism that would reduce "having" to the pleasures of sex, and the spirituality that denigrates physical "joyes" (11), terming them empty and fleeting. In fact the poet already "has" the lady (in his heart, that is, if we can give credence to such Petrarchan language). Apparently, though, he would choose to have her in a different way, limiting their relationship to one of sexual possession and pleasure. The skepticism dominant in this middle stanza thus reduces the lady's in-dwelling presence to mere "Fantasie" (10). The speaker shall "repent" "nothing" (18), therefore, because his dream, far from revealing the highest spiritual reality, is itself a nothing; without the lady's virtual presence in his heart all dream, all representation, and all poetry is reduced to fiction—a fantasy of possession and an "expense of spirit."

But even here, it seems that skepticism exacts a price too steep for the poet to pay. Life itself becomes but a dream whose passage is far too short, while "true joyes at best are dreame enough" (22). Thus the brevity and the poverty of the libertine's joy drive the poet back to the ideal as to a refuge. Of course the libertinism is not entirely defeated, since it remains as one of two choices, neither of which is wholly satisfactory:

> Though you stay here you passe too fast away:
> For even at first lifes Taper is a snuffe.

> Fill'd with her love, may I be rather grown
> Mad with much heart, then ideott with none.
>   (23–26)

The poet can either grow "Mad with much heart," losing his sense of reality through the overwhelming presence of an ideal love (one that causes pain and oppresses the "weake" spirit), or he can grow "ideott with none," which is an escape not just from pain but from feeling entirely. He chooses the former. But there remains a powerful ambivalence in the choice, since he never gains insight into the ennobling quality of spiritual love; rather than grow greater himself, the poet continues, simply, to find pain. Such makes for a remarkable counterpoint to other of Donne's transcendent lyrics: the poet has chosen a spiritual love despite the pain and confusion it creates in him, but neither understands it nor grows better because of it. Other speakers (of "Negative Love," for example) strive to lose themselves in this mystery, embracing through faith what they can neither see nor say; here, however, the poet would prefer "joyes meaner . . . / Convenient, and more proportionall" (11–12) to a love "growne too great and good" (6). His heart may be "faithfull" (2), as he claims. But unable to understand or interpret his own heart, and unable (unwilling?) to give up the desires (and we might add, the language) of the body, he finds himself trapped in a double-bind—much like the poet of "Twicknam Garden," who seeks to retreat from feeling altogether ("But that I may not this disgrace / Indure, nor leave this garden, Love let mee / Some senselesse peece of this place bee" [14–16]).

□   □   □

Thus far we have explored the conflict between rhetorics and their enabling vocabularies; it is in meditation, finally, on the nature of the word that we might end this study. The individual word itself bears the weight—or reveals the emptiness, the complexity, the crisis—of communication and understanding. It is the word itself that bends the will, that arouses the senses, that awakens memory, that wounds or heals the soul. It is the word itself that names the world, attempting to wed external phenomena to mental experience; indeed, the word itself gives birth to the world . . . or can cost us the world, when it loses its adequacy and power of reference. And it is the word itself, as the point of intersection of diverse rhetorics, that multiplies and destabilizes meaning. It stands to rea-

son, then, that the problems of rhetoric, of reference, of truth, of
meaning, and of form become ultimately a problem of iteration and
repetition. Thus I conclude with a perspectivist reading of "The
Dreame," a poem that tests and questions the conventions of its
putative genre, the love-dream. "It is a commonplace," Helen
Gardner writes, "among Neo-Platonists that the lover may fashion
in imagination an image of the beloved more beautiful than the
image his senses perceive in her presence." But this imaginary love,
which "overwhelms the spirits and senses to produce a semi-
death," is here joined to "the well-known theme of the sensual love-
dream in which the lover finds in sleep the satisfaction which his
mistress refuses to him waking."[17] Thus Donne transforms "the old
Petrarchan theme of the love-dream" by interrupting the sexual fantasy at its climax.[18] True enough. But more remarkable than the
generic play is the epistemic play between competing realities,
doubts, dreams, and idealities, each articulating a distinctive rhetoric. In "The Dream," then, a lady awakens the poet out of his
dream-state or reverie of love; from this first conscious state, in
which the lady's physical presence actualizes the ideal she represented in the dream, he passes to a second, sadder waking-state, in
which he discovers that the dream or ideal love might never have
been real. He decides in the end, however, to "dreame . . . againe"
or, rather, *to make* this dream his reality, the fantasy now turned into
an act of will. Each of these shifting attitudes describes, I would
argue, a unique episteme or realm of experience that is actualized
by one rhetoric even as it disables another. And thus the poem
contains within itself the capacities, and particularly the tropologies, of the four major rhetorics, whose progression can be observed from stanza to stanza. I emphasize tropology here because
"The Dreame" exemplifies the way words themselves become the
points of intersection of these different rhetorics, the language continuously shifting in meaning and effect.

> Deare love, for nothing lesse then thee
> Would I have broke this happy dreame,
>   It was a theame
> For reason, much too strong for phantasie,
>   Therefore thou wakd'st me wisely; yet

17. *Elegies and Songs and Sonnets*, p. 181.
18. Ibid., p. xxi. On the poem's generic play see also Mario Praz, "Donne's
Relation to the Poetry of His Time," pp. 51–56; and Pierre Legouis, *Donne the
Craftsman*, pp. 75–77.

> My Dreame thou brok'st not, but continued'st it,
> Thou art so true, that thoughts of thee suffice,
> To make dreames truth; and fables histories;
> Enter these armes, for since thou thoughtst it best,
> Not to dreame all my dreame, let's do the rest.
>
> (1–10)

In waking him the lady literally incarnates the dream-image that had given the poet such pleasure in his sleep. The poem thus begins by celebrating the physical presence of a lady so good that "thoughts" of her "suffice, / To make dreames truth; and fables histories," and whose presence therefore does not break but "continue[s]" his dream. Situated within an incarnational rhetoric, this first stanza seeks to affirm the goodness and truth his lady embodies.

Elaborating, seemingly, upon this praise, the second stanza begins with a typically Petrarchan idealization:

> As Lightning, or a Tapers light,
> Thine eyes, and not thy noise wak'd mee;
> Yet I thought thee
> (For thou lov'st truth) an Angell, at first sight.
>
> (11–14)

But in questioning his powers of perception the poem at the same time begins to lose its power of predication, the power to give the lady attributes and a stable identity, literally to fix her in the world (or, rather, the textual space) through adequate words. And such a discovery turns the rhetoric from a celebration of love incarnate to a meditation upon (or, as the poet describes it, a "confession" of) the unspeakability of the lady's divine nature:

> But when I saw thou saw'st my heart,
> And knew'st my thoughts, beyond an Angels art,
> When thou knew'st what I dreamt, when thou knews't when
> Excesse of joy would wake me, and cam'st then,
> I doe confesse, it could not chuse but bee
> Prophane, to thinke thee any thing but thee.
>
> (15–20)

Love becomes an act of religious devotion; but as the poet proceeds in this devotion the lady's spiritual nature, like God's, begins its retreat from language. For "God himself is so unutterable," Donne writes in *Essays in Divinity,* "he hath a name which we cannot pronounce" (p. 23). As Yahweh defeats all attempts at nomination, concealing himself in a shroud of tautology ("I am that I am"), so the beloved cannot be compared or even named; the poet simply blasphemes "to thinke thee"—that is, his beloved—"any thing but thee." Not the name, and not the dream-image, but the lady's physical presence is alone an adequate (self-)representation: in the poet's own words, "thee," tautologically, is but "thee." "Sapho to Philaenis" plays elegant variations upon this theme:

> Thou art not soft, and cleare, and strait, and faire,
> As Down, as Stars, Cedars, and Lillies are,
> But thy right hand, and cheek, and eye, only
> Are like thy other hand, and cheek, and eye
> (21–24)

Language, particularly the metaphoric language of poetic compliment, proves incapable of standing in the lady's place, for metaphor, simile, and synecdoche merely substitute language for being. Acts of nomination fail to incarnate or invoke presence. The word is *not* the thing; the name is not the numen, not the living personality—and even worse, to accept the name in place of the thing is to lose the world, putting language in its place.

The poet falls, then, from incarnationism to a self-conscious and self-effacing, transcendent rhetoric. But while the language is at once denied the powers of identity and presence, surely the tautology itself implies that reality remains a fixed, stable substrate beneath the weak words? The poet can at least repeat "thee," just as one can repeat "God is" even while lacking the ability to say *what* God is, to discover a sufficient predicate. In other words, tautology or self-identity would still seem to confirm the reality of a unique, though ineffable being. As Donne the preacher observes,

> it implies a nearer, a more familiar, and more presentiall knowledge of God . . . when we know how to call God by a Name, a Creator, a Redeemer, a Comforter, then when he consider him onely as a diffused power . . . then when we come to him onely in Negatives, and say, That that is God, which is nothing els. . . . For though it be truly said in the Schoole, that no name can be given to God, *Ejus essentiam adaequatè repraesentans,* No name can reach to the expressing of all that God is. . . . Yet certainly, we could not so much as say, God cannot be named, except we could name God by some name. (*Sermons,* 5:322)

More than a play on words, such paradoxy attempts to assert "presentiall knowledge" of a purely spiritual being. What language cannot name does not, for this reason, fall into oblivion; though absent from (and other than) the word, the existence of transcendent reality is at least asserted, if not affirmed, by a language that is no longer an act of knowing-through-naming so much as a gesturing- or pointing-toward that which lies outside of itself, in a space that language attempts to clear but cannot, itself, inhabit. The third stanza of "The Dreame," however, is denied the possibility even of tautology: "Coming and staying show'd thee, thee / But rising makes me doubt, that now, / Thou art not thou" (13–23). What effect does the figure *ploce,* the doubling of "thee" and "thou," have here if not to double rather than repeat the sense? Does "staying" show the poet that she is "she," that the lady in reality and her dream-ide- alization are one? Or is the lady presented a verbal image of herself, separating and distinguishing the reality from the representation? In other words, is "thee" shown *to be* "thee"? Or is "thee" (as image) shown *to* "thee" (as lady)? Is this an argument over appearance or identity? How can the reader tell? Indeed, subsequent lines in- crease the sense of dualism both in the language and the lady's (self-)identity. In the phrase, "Thou art not thou," the negation affects the words themselves as well as the reality: "Thou" can no longer be repeated, its self-identity denied once the lady's own identity comes under doubt. The referents as well as the words now elude the poet, his faith in a silent though stable reality having turned, suddenly, to an attitude of "doubt" and a rhetoric of nomi- nalist skepticism. Such a lyric, then, reinscribes the problems of truth and reference, presence and absence explored in the verse letter to Rowland Woodward ("If, as mine is, thy life a slumber be"), a poem that seems to claim for itself a transforming power greater than that of Morpheus, the shape-changing god of dreams:

> Never did Morpheus nor his brother weare
> Shapes so like those Shapes, whom they would appeare,
> As this my letter is like me, for it
> Hath my name, words, hand, feet, heart, minde and wit;
> It is my deed of gift of mee to thee,
> It is my will, my selfe the Legacie.
>
> (3–8)

Godlike in its powers, such a text assumes the physical "shape" of its author, taking on his "name" or identity, appropriating his "hand" and "feet," expressing his "heart, minde and wit." Shall we say that the poem "weare[s]" or, perhaps, incarnates the poet, transforming itself into his substance and psyche (his body and blood, as it were)? In fact the sonnet's opening undercuts any asser- tion of presence: "If, as mine is, thy life a slumber be, / Seeme, when thou read'st these lines, to dreame of me, / Never did Morpheus . . ." (1–3). The poem offers no more than a "dreame" of the poet's presence and can only "seeme" to become his "deed of gift." Or, rather, it denies what it simultaneously claims to give: the poet's substantial presence within the textual space. Failing to perform such a sacrament between writer and reader, the poem becomes not a presencing but a promise (and an empty one at that), a testament to the writer's memory that asserts, within its commemorative function, nothing but the poet's own physical absence from the poem, his "death" and need for a Last Will.

"The Dreame," too, falls from celebration to meditation to complaint as each stanza charts the poet's inability to confirm (again, to "fix") the lady's identity as the true and ideal lover, one capable of incarnating his dream of a perfect, lasting love. And yet the poem does not rest, simply, in lament of its failed incarnationism or fall from certitude to doubt. For the final stanza, while remaining pessimistic in tone, offers the possibility that poet and lady together *can make* lasting love a reality, together fashioning a love that will be without shame, fear, or other imperfection:

> That love is weake, where feare's as strong as hee;
>   'Tis not all spirit, pure, and brave,
> If mixture it of *Feare, Shame, Honor,* have.
> Perchance as torches which must ready bee,
> Men light and put out, so thou deal'st with mee,
> Thou cam'st to kindle, goest to come; Then I
> Will dreame that hope againe, but else would die.
> (24–30)

The poet chooses consciously to "dreame that hope againe," inviting lover and reader alike to dream it with him and work toward its realization in the world. Thus sophism provides an alternative to, or at least some compensation for, the poet's initial losses. And yet a second reading might suggest that elements of sophism are present all along. Does the first stanza simply celebrate the lady and love, or does the play between "dreames" and "truth," "fables" and "histories" argue implicitly for constructing such a love, for extending the dream into reality? After all, "To make dreames truth; and fables histories" (8) is precisely the sophist's utopian enterprise. From the beginning, therefore, dreaming becomes the sophist's *apate* or deliberate deception, seeking to make the world after its own (dream-)image.

Thus we return to the same place where this study began, the point of suspension between antithetical conceptions of language, between competing orientations or worldviews. Brought to the intersection of opposing rhetorics, the reader, like the poet himself, is left forever unable to choose with absolute certainty or security—and yet is compelled each moment to do so. For reading itself rests in the choice, and meaning is its consequence. The textual play between incarnationism and transcendence, transcendence and skepticism, skepticism and sophism, sophism and incarnationism creates an interpretive problematic that, if only implicitly, has animated and enabled the history of Donne criticism. Should "The Canonization," "The Good-morrow," "The Sunne Rising" and "A Lecture upon the Shadow" be read as poems that aim at persuasion or the sophist's *apate,* that liberating, playful world-building that requires an act of deception? Or should they be read as self-ironizing texts, texts that point up their own failure to validate argument and affirm truth? Should an interpretation of such poems come to rest, finally, in recognition that truth lies beyond the sureties of language? Or might such poems assert that truth and reality itself are products of language—literally spoken into being? The failure of incarnationism may lead to a smug sort of skepticism; it may also provide opportunities for the sophist's fashioning of new realities. And for the sophist, literature's failure to discover some singular, univocal truth stands in contrast to its triumph over psyche (that is, over the emotions, beliefs, and will of its reading audience).

Over against the polysemy of language is a reader's need to choose a meaning; each reading, moreover, must remain limited in attention and singular in perspective, unfolding in and through time. But nothing prevents criticism from instituting a double or triple reading. Each reading has its own necessity; each suffers, at the same time, from its own blindness, partiality, and acts of exclusion. What, then, prevents a reader from shifting perspectives, preserving each rhetorical possibility—revelling, say, in the poet's confident, demiurgic creation, at the same time recognizing that his new world, recorded in such poems as "The Good Morrow" and "The Dream," remains forever a tissue of words? The *Songs and Sonets* provide compelling reasons, actually, for multiplying perspectives, for we are invited to read these poems as lovers (and different kinds of lovers) as well as critics, as people who at times wish to be persuaded as well as to refute the persuasion. The multiple rhetorics in themselves multiply perspectives and meanings; so too do a reader's own multiple roles.

Surely the discovery of multiple rhetorics enables an equally pluralist, perspectivist criticism. At the same time it should convince us

that all interpretive (indeed, all intellectual) activity remains radically perspectivist, an insight stated over a century ago by Nietzsche:

> How far the perspective character of existence extends or indeed
> whether existence has any other character than this; whether existence
> without interpretation, without "sense," does not become "nonsense";
> whether, on the other hand, all existence is not essentially actively
> engaged in *interpretation*—that cannot be decided even by the most
> industrious and most scrupulously conscientious analysis and self-
> examination of the intellect; for in the course of this analysis the human
> intellect cannot avoid seeing itself in its own perspectives, and *only* in
> these. We cannot look around our own corner.[19]

Literary interpretation describes a special version of this problem.
Readings assume the shape or "perspective forms," as Nietzsche
puts it, of a particular rhetoric—the "corner," as it were, around
which a particular reading or meaning cannot peer. As readers we
typically privilege one specific rhetoric in interpretation, making
each text conform to a particular vision of the world and an understanding of language. Often it does not matter to us whether the
rhetoric we read by even tries to match the rhetoric valorized by the
author and dominant in the text. (If we continue to believe in a
singular rhetoric, how could we even note these different shapes?)
Yet to interpret through the limited perspective of a singular rhetoric only is—like composing in a singular rhetoric—as much a disablement of meaning as it is a facilitation or enablement. As instruments of interpretation the different rhetorics serve each other as
figure-ground. Recognition of multiple rhetorics allows, at least in
part, for a different perspective (a different corner, to return to
Nietzsche's metaphor). And since hierarchies never stay fixed in a
text (deconstruction teaches this: what we consider ground at any
moment of reading becomes figure in the next), the most ambitious
readings might attempt to exploit the potentialities within a range
of perspectives, shifting between orientations or treating them in
rapid alternation, revelling, say, in a speaker's confident, demiurgic
creation of new worlds of value, recognizing at the same time that
these new worlds remain but words. Readings that foster the play
between rhetorics, allowing meanings to oscillate between perspectives, will effectively dash any critic's dream of the univocity of texts
or even of the exclusivity of perspective in interpretation. Readings
and rhetorics, like the *dissoi logoi* of pre-Socratic epistemology, are
forever parasitic, mutually destabilizing, and mutually enabling. To

---

19. Friedrich Nietzsche, *The Gay Science*, p. 336.

interpret by means of a skeptical or deconstructive rhetoric is thus no less valid, and no less reductive, than interpretations premised on an incarnationist (or, to use Derrida's term, a logocentric) rhetoric. Deconstructive insights never fully defeat a text's logocentrism, nor do a text's sophisms ever conjure away all doubt as they attempt to conjure new worlds of experience and value. Regardless of opponents' fears, poststructuralist theories do not really compete with more traditional methodologies for absolute control over a singular meaning, no more than any one rhetoric can ever be named "*the* rhetoric" regulating all discourse; criticisms, like rhetorics, are inherently fragmented visions, perilously reliant upon premises about a language and a reality whose validation must forever remain outside the critical discourse itself. As premises, they are the prior conditions out of which criticism, as a mode of discourse, arises. And discourse can never prove that which it must take for granted. Given their different enabling premises, the readings of various theories are bound to clash, and yet they have inevitably the ability to complement one another, however paradoxical this may seem. Any one theory supplements as much as it negates another's vision, each describing a genuine potentiality within discourse, each bringing its insights to bear on an otherwise silent inscription. Literary theory per se might therefore be restated as a study of the different linguistic, epistemological, and motivational premises (that is, the divergent rhetorics) typically, if implicitly, assumed by the different modes of reading.

This perspectivism, I believe, serves to regenerate as well as complicate the traditional methods and concerns of rhetorical criticism, polysemy arising out of the intersection of multiple rhetorics, those diverse orientations toward language and reality that develop historically (and as we have seen, dialectically: Platonism versus Gorgianism, Thomism versus Augustinianism). And each, in Donne's own time as well as our own, provides a necessary, though never comprehensive, interpretive frame or horizon. Such perspectivism allows us to peer beyond indeterminacy and aporia, the interpretive stumbling blocks of postmodernist criticism, to discover not the chaos of meaning so much as the patterns within (and the predictability of) this multeity. Of course, perspectivism does not solve the problem of authorial meaning or intentionality and it certainly does not reduce texts to a singular, univocal, determinate meaning; it does, however, discover underlying systems of meaning, the polarities of language-attitude and epistemology that make multiple interpretation—or indeed, any interpretation—possible.

CODA

✳✳✳✳

Rhetoric and Form Reconsidered

Human social relations, and love relations in particular, command what seem an infinite range of emotions, motivations, exigencies, and symbolic actions; language, George Puttenham recognizes, is in each case their instrument, as it is the primary instrument of knowledge, of communication, of social reality itself. If love is to thrive, if it is to come into being *as language*—and above all, if it is to achieve expression as literature—its rhetorical exigencies must discover an equal diversity of forms:

> Because love is of all other humane affections the most puissant and passionate, and most generall to all sortes and ages of men and women . . . it requireth a forme of Poesie variable, inconstant, affected, curious and most witty of any others, whereof the joyes were to be uttered in one sorte, the sorrowes in an other, and by the many formes of Poesie, the many moodes and pangs of lovers, throughly to be discovered: the poore soules sometimes praying, beseeching, sometime honouring, avancing, praising: an other while railing, reviling, and cursing: then sorrowing, weeping, lamenting: in the ende laughing, rejoysing and solacing the beloved againe, with a thousand delicate devises, odes, songs, elegies, ballads, sonets and other ditties mooving one way and another to great compassion.[1]

"Praying," "beseeching," "railing," "reviling," "lamenting," "solacing," and "praising" describe various speech-acts of the love poet, rhetorical exigencies underlying the different lyric genres. And thus, while modern theory typically describes genre as a principle regulating a work's internal structures rather than its rhe-

1. *Arte of English Poesie,* pp. 59–60.

torical aims (a work's speech-acts, in other words, its means to affect a reader's understanding, emotions, and will), the Renaissance poet would never view his craft as a choice between these emphases. The literary work, rather, would always *do* as well as *say* something, whether this be "to pleade" (as Puttenham suggests), "to praise," or "to advise." Indeed such aims or *officia* make ancient poets "from the beginning the best perswaders and their eloquence the first Rethoricke of the world."[2] Each aim or function, then, discovers its ideal lyric form. Sir Philip Sidney likewise recommends the different genres for specific functions of instruction, persuasion, praise, and blame: the "bitter but wholesome iambic . . . rubs the galled mind, in making shame the trumpet of villainy," while "the lamenting elegiac . . . would move rather pity than blame." In contrast the lyric poet, "with his tuned lyre, and well accorded voice, giveth praise."[3]

By assuming the orator's powers to teach, delight, and move, the Renaissance poet adopts a thoroughly rhetorical conception of literary form. Of course his schoolmaster had taught him to do just this. In Richard Rainolde's formulary for the grammar school student, *A Booke Called the Foundation of Rhetorike* (1563), model orations in specific prose genres (narrations, moral essays or *chriae*, moral fables, comparisons, descriptions, essays based on praise or blame) are first to be analyzed for their themes, aims, methods of arrangement and appropriate styles, and are then to be re-created in the student's writing. Even the older student, as William Kempe advises, "must observe in authors all the use of the Artes . . . not only every trope, every figure, as well of words as of sentences; but also the Rhetorical pronunciation and gesture":

> And so let him take in hand the exercise of all these Artes at once in making somewhat of his owne, first by imitation; as when he hath considered the propertie of speach in the Grammatical etymologie and syntaxis: the finenesse of speach in the Rhetoricall ornaments, as comely tropes, pleasant figures, fit pronunciation and gesture . . . then let him have a like theame to prosecute with the same artificiall instruments, that he findeth in his author.[4]

In the typically rhetorical vocabulary of Renaissance humanism, Kempe here describes the requisites of the aspiring poet: a devotion to good authors, the careful examination of a model's argument,

---

2. Ibid., p. 25.
3. "Apology for Poetry," pp. 165–66. See also William Webbe, *A Discourse of English Poetrie* (1586), 1:249.
4. *The Education of Children in Learning* (1588), p. 233.

structure, and devices of style, and the decorous use of these "same artificiall instruments" in one's own generic composition.

For the Renaissance, then, genre-concepts arise out of the dynamic matching of form and function—a rhetorical model that directs reading and writing alike, though J. B. Broadbent suggests that "for the Elizabethans rhetoric was synthetic, not analytic," that "a knowledge of the figures and their most appropriate application, learned at school, might help the orator write his speech or the courtier his poem." Renaissance rhetoric, he concludes, "was not intended as a critical or interpretive procedure."[5] The evidence weighs against this. Minturno's and Scaliger's readings of the poets, even E. K.'s commentary on *The Shepheardes Calender*, proceed by means of a rhetorical criticism, and though the Ramist educational reformers reduce rhetoric to tropology exclusively (to "a knowledge of the figures," as Broadbent puts it) nonetheless they, too, teach reading as a mode of rhetorical analysis. To Henry Peacham for example, whose *Garden of Eloquence* is Ramist in organization, a knowledge of rhetorical effects is "so necessary, that no man can reade profitably, or understand perfectlye eyther Poets, Oratours, or the holy Scriptures, without them,"[6] and even Erasmus, one of Ramus's most influential rivals in education theory, stresses the role of traditional rhetoric in the creation, and interpretation, of literary form:

> Now in approaching each work the teacher should indicate the nature of the argument in each particular genre, and what should be most closely observed in it. For instance, the essence of the epigram lies in its pointed brevity. Then he will deal with the theory of wit which Quintilian and Cicero present, pointing out that this literary form takes particular delight in rhetorical exclamations, cleverly thrown in at the end, and thereby startling the reader into remembering their point.[7]

It is to the classical theorists, Cicero and Quintilian especially, that the literature teacher turns for a description of rhetorical effect, and "in the same way," Erasmus adds, "he will be careful to remind pupils of the essential nature of epic poetry, history, the dialogue, the fable, satire, the ode, and the other literary genres." Traditional

---

5. "Milton's Rhetoric," p. 270.

6. *Garden of Eloquence* (1577), sig. Aiii; quoted in Lewalski, *Protestant Poetics*, p. 81.

7. *De ratione studii ac legendi interpretandique auctores*, in *Collected Works*, 24:687–89. The connection of epigram with "rhetorical exclamations, cleverly thrown in at the end" is one that Erasmus makes elsewhere, by the way, in *De Copia*, *acclamatio* being "a climax in the form of an exclamation . . . epigrams end with this" (*Collected Works*, 24:629).

rhetoric thus provides an interpretive procedure as well as a means of literary production.

Admittedly, none of these critics considers the multeity of rhetorics and the potential disparity between rhetoric and genre, the ways language itself complicates and undermines poetic form. For the Renaissance, nonetheless, interpretation situates itself in the dynamic interplay between rhetoric and genre, an interplay modern theory neglects—though there are notable exceptions. Claudio Guillén, for example, describes the heuristic or generative capacity of genre-concepts. "Looking backward," he observes, "a genre is a descriptive statement concerning a number of related works. Looking forward, it becomes above all . . . an invitation to the matching (dynamically speaking) of matter and form," the dynamic relationship between "form" and "matter" paralleling, if not always precisely, the relationships we have charted between rhetoric and genre. For "a preexistent form can never be simply 'taken over' by the writer or transferred to a new work." Rather, Guillén notes, "the task of form-making must be undertaken all over again. The writer must begin again to match matter to form, and to that end he can only find a very special sort of assistance in the fact that the fitting of matter to form has *already* taken place. To offer this assistance is the function of genre."[8] Complementing this outline of a writer's heuristic reliance on genre-concepts is Tzvetan Todorov's linguistic theory, descriptive of a reader's interpretive reliance on a repertoire of genres that "have their origin, quite simply, in human discourse," the linguistic code shared by members of a speech community serving to regulate both the speaker's aims and the audience's understanding.[9] By analogy to speech-acts, then, a reader's linguistic competence (his or her prior knowledge of the literary codes and their range of application) both enables and circumscribes the meaning of each literary text. To pray, to curse, to invite, to name: such speech-acts, derived from social discourse, join with the *officia* of classical rhetoric (to teach, delight, and move) in describing the underlying social/transactional functions of literary discourse, for "the identity of the genre," as Todorov observes, "comes from the speech act that is at its base."[10]

There is, doubtless, great descriptive power in such approaches; none mentioned, however, Renaissance or modern, considers fully

8. *Literature as System: Essays Toward the Theory of Literary History,* p. 111.
9. "The Origin of Genres," p. 169.
10. Ibid., p. 169. Is this not Puttenham's and Sidney's point?

the problem of performance or validation, making them all rather optimistic (if not slightly naive) regarding the status of poetic form. A text may, as Rosalie L. Colie suggests, offer a set of " 'frames' or 'fixes' on the world," mediating between the internal world-of-discourse and external reality.[11] And to that extent it might at least claim to validate its genre, affirming the genre-concept as the means by which it generates and sustains a coherent world-picture. Nonetheless many Renaissance texts, particularly the *genera mista* or "mixed genres" favored by artists like Donne, tend to create a *trompe l'oeil* of representations within the individual work, a multiplication of perspectives that inevitably undermines the easy coherence of a text's description of reality, calling into question the possibility of clear reference and singular, reliable meaning. Poems may, of course, be deliberately "mixed," inviting us to search for their dynamic unity; so expansive a text as *Paradise Lost*, Barbara Lewalski argues, makes just such an invitation, as do Donne's *Anniversaries*.[12] In other texts, though—Donne's "Satyre IV" comes at once to mind—one must attend to the cacophony among forms, and even a "simple" lyric (one uncontaminated, as it were, by mixture or the interlayering of competing genres) must still enact its aims. The problem of genre becomes once again a problem of rhetoric—a problem, in short, of per*form*ance or enactment, one that New Critics and structuralists alike have tended to ignore: Can a text *do* or *be* what it says? The question is poststructuralist, to be sure, but it is one that Renaissance rhetorical theory anticipates (and that Donne himself poses continually, if implicitly, in his writing).

"The Baite," among any number of lyrics, puts such observations to the test, its echo of Marlowe's opening line, "Come live with mee, and bee my love" claiming for the poem a third place in Marlowe's and Raleigh's pastoral sequence, "The Passionate Shepherd" and "Nymphs Reply." Donne's, however, immediately promises "some

11. *The Resources of Kind: Genre-Theory in the Renaissance,* p. 6. Describing genres as so many " 'fixes' on the world" strengthens the implicitly generic focus of Paul Ricoeur's hermeneutic theory, which I shall soon discuss: "what must be interpreted in a text," Ricoeur writes, "is a *proposed world* which I could inhabit and wherein I could project one of my ownmost possibilities. That is what I call the world of the text, the world proper to *this* unique text." For "fiction," Ricoeur suggests, "is the privileged path for the redescription of reality" (*Hermeneutics and the Human Sciences: Essays on Language, Action, and Interpretation,* p. 142). The shape or itinerary of that "path," one might add, is some notion of genre.

12. See "*Paradise Lost* as Encyclopedic Epic: The Uses of Literary Forms," in *Paradise Lost and the Rhetoric of Literary Forms,* pp. 1–24.

new pleasures" (2), calling self-conscious attention to its arguments of seduction and to the genre itself (that is, to the poem's complications upon and divergences from pastoral convention). In Donne's poem, Marlowe's shepherd becomes a fisherman whose arguments ignore time's assault on youth and love, the pastoral's most characteristic theme; equally significant, the fisherman-poet rejects his model's naive, naturalistic praises of the lady for the extravagant hyperboles of Petrarchan compliment. "More then the Sunne" (7) the lady's eyes warm the river, while her beauty eclipses both sun and moon (13–14). In thoroughly unpastoral manner, then, Donne's poet places the lady's beauty above Nature, whereas Marlowe's shepherd attempts to transform her *into* Nature. But more remarkable even than the extravagance of his compliments are their ambivalence. While the fisherman resorts to "treachery," to the deception of fake lures and flies to make his catch, the lady's beauty becomes itself the bait by which she entraps men:

> Let coarse bold hands, from slimy nest
> The bedded fish in banks out-wrest,
> Or curious traitors, sleave-silke flies
> Bewitch poore fishes wandring eyes.
>
> For thee, thou needst no such deceit,
> For thou thy selfe art thine owne bait,
> That fish, that is not catch'd thereby,
> Alas, is wiser farre then I.
>
> (21–28)

Her beauty may not be that of the common courtesan, a painted deception, a false lure. Yet it must still, as live "bait," conceal a hook: the desire that catches the poet, rendering him abject.

As a lyric of unrequited love, "The Baite" turns its ostensible aim, the praise and persuasion of a lady, into a psychological exploration of the poet's own inner turmoil, saying less about the lady than the lover himself. And he is an unwilling lover, one might add, given the melancholy self-incrimination of the last line; in fact the persuasive urgency of the opening "Come live with mee, and bee my love," yields to the plaintive wish, implicit in its ending, that the poet not love at all. The poet's awareness of his own personal folly and of the pains of love thus brings all persuasion and pastoralism itself dangerously close to collapse. Far from playing the conventional role of *pastor* (or *piscator*), Donne's speaker assumes the pose of a Petrarchan lover addressing, in subtly ambivalent terms, an aloof, Petrarchan lady. And this intrusion or contamination of ex-

travagant compliment and complaint into an otherwise pastoral
landscape calls the genre of Marlowe's poem to task. For the fiction
of a thoroughly ideal, thoroughly innocent natural world is at once
stripped away, revealing that the poem and model alike are courtly
performances, self-conscious artistries that are themselves thoroughly fictive. No passionate shepherds live in London. This is not to
say that pastoral simply gives itself over to Petrarchism, transforming
its persuasions fully and without resistance into this other, more
plaintive mode; in "The Baite," rather, Petrarchism destabilizes the
mimetic and thematic elements of pastoral, making the poem a scene
of conflict between competing worldviews and leaving it with no
clearly discernible and consistent attitude toward love (or, for that
matter, toward literary form). Suggestively, the Donne lyric that most
clearly announces its derivative if not parasitic relation to specific past
poems is also most adamant in its refusal to conform to—and thus
confirm or, in a word, validate—its genre. Suspended between two
apparently antithetical linguistic systems, the poem finds itself
unable either to enact its pastoral seductions or to abandon them
entirely for Petrarchan complaint. Simultaneously reliant upon and
critical of its form, "The Baite" takes the question of genre as a theme
in itself, at once the means and the subject of its composition.

And thus, as Clay Hunt observes, Donne "seems generally to
have been unwilling to surrender his personal individuality to the
set patterns of a literary tradition and to undertake to operate, however creatively, within that tradition throughout a poem."[13] He is
right, to a degree. Extending the boundaries of convention and
often testing, straining, subverting genre from within, nonetheless
Donne's poems are thoroughly genre-bound, a creative (and, certainly, a critical) reinterpretation of their enabling forms. Surely,
then, Hunt goes too far in suggesting that Donne "only rarely"
makes "any attempt to formulate that concept of *genre* which was so
normal an initial step in the creative process for most Elizabethan
poets."[14] For whether it is at all possible to write *outside* the boundaries of genre is a question Hunt fails to ask. And yet other of
Donne's readers have erred in the opposite direction, appealing to
genre-concepts as a means to secure some singular, stable, authorially sanctioned meaning.[15] Such appeals ignore the fact that

13. *Donne's Poetry,* p. 13.
14. Ibid.
15. E. D. Hirsch remains the chief spokesperson for such interpretive fun-
damentalism; see his *Validity in Interpretation.*

genre itself must be constituted, either within the textual space or within the writer's (or reader's) heuristic/interpretive activities—activities that are in essence rhetorical and dynamic, inherently open-ended. Poststructuralist theory, moreover, has recently learned to pit rhetoric against form, dissolving a text's apparent unity (its apparent univocity) and denying its claims to become a coherent, self-sufficient system of knowledge, representation, or argument (in short, its claims to self-enactment).[16] Readings can no longer rest secure in the assumption that rhetoric stands in the service of form, giving itself up, fully and faithfully, in the enactment of genre; actually, deconstruction provides a necessary corrective to traditional genre theory's valorization of form over language. But is rhetoric necessarily destructive of form? Must it always defeat, rather than enact, the aims of discourse? Granted, the openness and the surplus of meaning fostered by rhetoric seem thoroughly at odds with traditional conceptions of literary genre. Is it any less reductive forever to valorize rhetoric over form? Is there not always, rather, a dialectical relation between the two?

Astutely, Hayden White describes discourse as a "mediative enterprise," a dynamic interplay between "received encodings of experience" (for which read "genre") and "alternative ways of encoding this reality,"

> some of which may be provided by the traditions of discourse prevailing in a given domain of inquiry and others of which may be idiolects of the author, the authority of which he is seeking to establish. Discourse, in a word, is quintessentially a *mediative* enterprise. As such, it is both interpretive and preinterpretive; it is always as much *about* the nature of interpretation itself as it is *about* the subject matter which is the manifest occasion of its own elaboration.[17]

The dialectic between rhetoric and genre is precisely this "mediative enterprise," and it is within this dialectic that reading and, arguably, all literary tradition is situated. There is no simple resolu-

16. See especially Jacques Derrida, "La Loi du Genre / The Law of Genre." But demonstrating a text's incapacity to do or perform what it says requires, after all, a working conception of form and function; and what does a poststructuralist reading ultimately deny if not the stability and stasis of literary structure? Thus even the critical theories that appear least reliant on genre-concepts (reader-response criticism, for example, or deconstruction) assume the existence of genre-concepts as a premise of their textual operations, even if this assumption is made precisely to deny genre's adequacy.

17. *Tropics of Discourse: Essays in Cultural Criticism*, p. 4.

tion, then, to the problem of genre-concepts. Though involved in literary production, they do not simply reside as elemental presences within a text, nor do they devolve from a system of a priori forms, a system always given in its entirety, regardless of a poet's historical circumstances. Rather, genre-concepts constitute the range of generative strategies available at a given moment to a writer and the corresponding range of interpretive strategies available to a reader. We might be tempted to describe genre as the highest or most general level of intelligibility *within* a literary system; in so doing we would assert the primacy of its heuristic/hermeneutic function. We would still need, however, to describe the means whereby genre achieves intelligibility within any text, serving in the process of its own unfolding to bring meaning to the text itself. A genre might initially "name" the text for a reader (though the necessity of an interpretive entry-point has too often reduced genre criticism to taxonomy).[18] But as I have suggested, the text must also confirm and in some sense validate the genre in a reader's interpretive synthesis of text and meaning. There is no text—no fully intelligible text—without a constituting conception of genre; let me add that there is no genre either, at least no affirmation of genre, without this synthetic activity of interpretation. In contrast, then, to the traditional description of genre as *idea* or as elemental presence within a text (that is, an internal, architectonic structure) one might instead describe it as an itinerary, temporalizing the concept and charting its dynamic unfolding within a text—its movement *through* the text, a rhetorical movement parallel to (in fact dependent upon) a reader's interpretive activity.

Ultimately, therefore, "the function of genre-concepts," as William Elford Rogers suggests, "is to help in articulating, clarifying, and even classifying *interpretations*. Like the mind of the work and the world of the work on which they depend, genres themselves spring into being along with the explicit interpretation of works, and they are themselves interpretable only in terms of the specific interpretations they seem to ground." An adequate theory of genre is thus "no more, and no less, than a theory about *interpretation*, a

18. The following are representative of such taxonomic studies: James J. Donohue, *The Theory of Literary Kinds: Ancient Classifications of Literature*; John F. Reichert, " 'Organizing Principles' and Genre Theory"; Norman K. Farmer, Jr., "A Theory of Genre for Seventeenth Century Poetry"; Paul Hernadi, *Beyond Genre: New Directions in Literary Classification*; Earl Miner, "On the Genesis and Development of Literary Systems"; and Alastair Fowler, *Kinds of Literature: An Introduction to the Theory of Genres and Modes*.

kind of 'metacriticism.' "[19] Writers and readers, texts and meanings are mutually involved in notions of genre. For a genre-concept is the dynamic principle of enablement that initiates and, in part, directs composition and interpretation alike. And it is a dialectical principle, in that the genre-concept itself gets caught up in the rhetorics of interpretation. The interpretive function of genre-concepts does not cease once a writer or reader has named a text and its conventions; the text now works upon the genre-concept itself, testing and reformulating and criticizing it, perhaps confirming it (by performing its aims), perhaps ultimately repudiating it. We might consider "The Good-morrow" and "The Sunne Rising" from this perspective, poems whose very titles identify their thematic genre as the aubade or alba.[20] Does an interpretation of their rhetoric enable and sustain, or must it defeat, the initial genre-concept?

Jonathan Saville describes the scene of their generic precursor, the medieval alba, as

> a universe divided physically into two distinct parts, an enclosed chamber, an *inside*, in which everything of value is to be found, surrounded by a hostile *outside* of much lower value, composed explicitly or by implication of the lady's husband; the watchman; all of society with the exception of the two lovers; [and] all of nature, including the creatures of earth and the astronomical bodies, with all their various movements and processes. . . . The lovers wish to remain together in their inside world, which is the only world that really counts for them. But the outside world, represented by the sunrise and the watchman's announcement, impinges upon the interior world of the chamber of love. The knight must eventually go outside, into the world of lesser value, and he feels this physical exit from the inner world to be a loss of all joy, a separation from all that is good and real. All that sustains him in the moment of separation is the expectation that he will soon

19. *The Three Genres and the Interpretation of Lyric*, p. 75. On the interpretive role of genre concepts see also John T. Shawcross, "Literary Revisionism and a Case for Genre," a response in part to Derrida's deconstruction of class concepts in "La Loi du Genre." Benedetto Croce's *La poesia* ("Poetry," pp. 628–45) remains the classic statement against synchronic, Platonic conceptions of literary form, though see also Eliseo Vivas, "Literary Classes: Some Problems."

20. There are numerous classical precedents, as K. W. Gransden notes: the dawn song "occurs frequently in the Greek Anthology, but its most influential treatment by a classical poet is Ovid, *Amores*, 1.13" ("*Lente, Currite, Noctis Equi:* Chaucer, *Troilus and Criseyde* 3.1422–70, Donne, 'The Sunne Rising,' and Ovid, *Amores* 1.13," p. 159). Medieval precedents occur most often in twelfth century Provençal poetry and in the poetry of Northern France (where, as Jonathan Saville notes, the form is known as the *aube*) and in Middle High German. See Saville's *Medieval Erotic Alba: Structure as Meaning*.

return. . . . For him, as for the lady, the world of true value is nothing
but that single, small, enclosed room; this is the moral center of the
universe; and all around it, up to the very heavens, moves another
world, inferior, deprived, inimical.[21]

On the surface, much of this is suggestive of "The Good-morrow,"
where "love, all love of other sights controules, / And makes one
little roome, an every where" (10–11). Elaborating upon this same
trope, "The Sunne Rising" goes so far as to command the sun to
"Shine here to us, and thou art every where; / This bed thy center
is, these walls, thy spheare" (29–30). Initially, then, both "The
Sunne Rising" and "The Good-morrow" declaim against time, both
the time wasted before their discovery of love and the movement of
time that threatens to separate the lovers, ending their pleasures (of
course, the sun is traditionally an unwelcome guest in the genre, a
"spy" that brings the lovers' typically adulterous relation to light).
But where they diverge markedly from the medieval alba is in their
claim to triumph over temporality, turning their rhetoric from the
traditional complaint or lament to one of celebration.

In "The Sunne Rising," for example, the sun is reduced to a large
cosmic alarm clock, calling the poet back to the daylight world of
education, business, and politics; its task is no more than to "chide
late schoole boyes, and sowre prentices" (5–6), reminding "countrey ants" of their "harvest offices" (8) with the same officiousness
that it tells "Court-huntsmen, that the King will ride" (7). And yet
the poet denies that the sun has power to control the lovers' lives,
the very juxtaposition of "Court-huntsmen" and "countrey ants"
suggesting how little he values the world of business and courtly
ambition, the world he has left for love. The poet thus rejects the
conventions of this genre at the same time that he repudiates his
own initial arguments: no longer chided for invading the lovers'
privacy, the sun is now welcomed into their world as a benevolent
presence, bearing witness to their love and gracing their bedroom
with its splendor. In his address to the sun, then, the speaker of
"The Sunne Rising" can answer his own chiding question—"Must
to thy motions lovers seasons run?" (4)—with a resounding no, for
"Love, all alike, no season knowes, nor clyme, / Nor houres, dayes,
months, which are the rags of time" (9–10). But in claiming to triumph over time, such lyrics more than diverge from convention;
they must also, if implicitly, make a unique and perhaps perilous
claim for the strength of their incarnationist rhetoric—and their suc-

21. *Medieval Erotic Alba*, p. 20.

cess, or failure, to enact their form must rest upon such claims. Rajan, for one, finds at the heart of "The Sunne Rising" an implicit (if naive) belief in "the alchemy of language," one that "can actually transform the world of fact represented by the motions of the sun, and create through rhetoric what cannot be affirmed through logic. That the extravagant hyperbole of the poem asks to be resisted is fairly obvious."[22] It might not be so obvious, actually: such a poem invites our assent, invites us, in fact, to participate in its verbal transvaluation of reality at the same time that it invites our skepticism, our questioning whether such world-building magic is ever more than verbal shamanism. As Murray Krieger observes,

> The poetic gesture as love's gesture may transform the world's ways and its language, but not without undoing them. In its consummations it wins its eschatological victories for the poet-lover, though its reality-bound antagonists—wielding difference, distance, and death—are hardly dissolved. . . . If we are asked to believe in such magic, it is with the tentativeness and skepticism which even a poet-magician like Prospero acknowledges at the close of *The Tempest*.[23]

Thus Krieger alludes to the play between divergent rhetorics, between public celebration and silent, transcendent meditation, between skepticism and the word-magic of sophism, all meeting in the miracle/illusion of poetic language. And the reader is left, finally, to choose. Whatever rhetoric he or she chooses to read by will surely help regulate and systematize the interpretation (giving the interpretation itself, by the way, a greater unity and univocity than the poems themselves could ever possess). Still, if intuitively—if only because I choose to read them in a way that valorizes the rhetorics of belief rather than of doubt, giving myself to such texts and asserting my willingness to be persuaded (though the skeptic would say, "to be deceived")—I find that two particular rhetorics dominate in these poems (at least dominate *my reading* of these poems), an incarnationism that celebrates their nascent love and a sophism that would defend this love against the intrusions of competing rhetorics and value-systems, defend it even at the cost of "truth" or lived experience. In my optimistic reading of these poems, they find (or perhaps *I* find—or privilege) the rhetorics capable of enacting the aims of their genre. How, then, am I to read the more plaintive "Breake of Day," a poem that inverts their *topoi* of praise, denying its own language the power to defeat time and sustain love? Here it is

22. " 'Nothing Sooner Broke,' " pp. 809–10.
23. *Poetic Presence and Illusion: Essays in Critical History and Theory,* p. 24.

the lady who speaks, addressing a man whose excuse for leaving, simply, is " 'tis day" (1). Though not explicitly adulterous, the poet's love is certainly not without its secretiveness: the sunlight, in accordance with tradition, has again become a "spie" (8) that catches the lovers in bed, while the lady has given up her "honor" (11) as well as her heart. And though the middle stanza asserts the powerlessness (or at least the harmlessness) of the sun's light, it cannot establish the strength of the man's love, nor does it empower the lady's language, enabling her in any way to persuade. Unlike the speaker of "The Sunne Rising," she does not chide outsiders like "sowre prentices" and "Court-huntsmen" for their enslavement to time, since her lover is himself such a man. So to the question, "Must businesse thee from hence remove?" (13), the lady provides her own bitter answer: "Oh, that's the worst disease of love, / The poore, the foule, the false, love can / Admit, but not the busied man" (14–16). Neither love nor language has created a new world for the lovers, substituting its own values for the concerns of business. With this failure, "Breake of Day" becomes plaintive, giving blame where a poem like "The Sunne Rising" gives praise to the lady and to the dawning of love.

Once more, it seems that the rhetoric must either validate the genre by enacting its aims, or else the rhetoric will implicitly test, strain, and subvert the form. For discourse, as White suggests,

> throws all "tactical" rules into doubt, including those originally governing its own formation. Precisely because it is aporetic, or ironic, with respect to its own adequacy, discourse cannot be governed by logic alone. Because it is always slipping the grasp of logic, constantly asking if logic is adequate to capture the essence of its subject matter, discourse always tends toward metadiscursive reflexiveness. This is why every discourse is always as much about discourse itself as it is about the objects that make up its subject matter.[24]

A text "will radically challenge" the rules governing its own formation; surely a major rule or "syntactical middle ground" (that is, a *mediating* ground or set of regulating principles) is its own genre-concept. The "metadiscursive reflexiveness" that White ascribes to all discourse necessarily becomes, I would argue, at some point a reflection on the adequacy of a text's genre-concept. Thus the unregulated potentialities within language itself cause a text to turn radically upon its form, questioning its validity, its very status as a

24. *Tropics of Discourse*, p. 4.

reliable and consistent mediating or regulating principle of interpretation.

Like rhetoric, then, genre never remains static in interpretation;
the form itself undergoes a process of restatement as meanings and
expectations are sustained, qualified, undermined, revised. And in
this way genre-concepts change not just between but within literary works themselves: that which gives an initial shape to the text is
inevitably reshaped by the reading experience. The relationship of a
text to its genre-concept is therefore neither stable nor assured, for
genre enables a reader's interpretation of a text that, in some problematic way, constitutes an author's intentions at the same time that
it distorts and exceeds those intentions through the unpredictable
supplementarity of a reader's meanings. As Paul Ricoeur describes
it, a text's meaning

> is rendered *autonomous* with respect to the intention of the author, the
> initial situation of discourse and the original addressee. Intention,
> situation and original addressee constitute the *Sitz-im-Leben* [site-in-life]
> of the text. The possibility of multiple interpretations is opened up by a
> text which is thus freed from its *Sitz-im-Leben*. Beyond the polysemy of
> words in a conversation is the polysemy of a text which invites multiple
> readings. This is the moment of interpretation in the technical sense
> of *textual exegesis*. It is also the moment of the hermeneutical circle be-
> tween the understanding initiated by the reader and the proposals of
> meaning offered by the text. The most fundamental condition of the
> hermeneutical circle lies in the structure of pre-understanding which
> relates all explication to the understanding which precedes and sup-
> ports it.[25]

I would suggest that this "structure of pre-understanding" is no
less than a text's genre-concept, that which provides a reader's
entry point into and itinerary through the text. The genre-bounded-
ness of discourse offers at least a partial means to regulate one's
reading, providing the codes and interpretive frames within which
meaning unfolds in consciousness. And thus genre-concepts offer
"proposals of meaning," though these do not exhaust the range of
possibilities enabled by the various rhetorics. A comparison of readings (my own, say, and Rajan's) would suggest that interpretation
inevitably supplements and exceeds the regulating logic of literary
form.

And Ricoeur points out another problematic relation only partially mediated by genre-concepts. Unlike speech, which claims

25. *Hermeneutics and the Human Sciences*, p. 108.

some living connection with a speaker, no writer remains in complete control of his or her meaning. Once orphaned from the expressive intentionality of its author, a text has no inherent guarantee of communicating this meaning, though it has the capacity to achieve *a* meaning by means of a second interpreting consciousness—in a word, the reader, who chooses a meaning or, more accurately, fashions a meaning and thus appropriates the discourse, making what was initially another's textual space his or her own. All literature reaches out, therefore, to a reader for its actualization, though this meaning is added to a text in a language that differs from its otherwise silent markings or inscription. Indeed, the language of interpretation necessarily differs if it is to escape charges of tautology. For neither repetition nor citation of a word can ensure or stabilize the meaning of that word—the previous chapter sought to demonstrate precisely this. Meaning, after all, is strictly relational: depending upon one's theory of language, words find or fashion a meaning only in relation to physical objects, to mental concepts, or, simply, to other words. (Perhaps, to quote a modern writer, "a rose is a rose is a rose." Without a reader's supplement, though, such repetitions add nothing to knowledge, perception, or experience. Paraphrase, then, is *not* heresy, to deny an (old-)New Critical truism; though parasitic upon the literary text, it is the very life of criticism, the transformation of the written work into a reader's "inner word" or sign.)[26]

Interpretation is always, for this reason, an inherently rhetorical activity of substitution and supplementation. Situated within a particular rhetorical perspective, a reading makes any text intelligible by transcending (in fact, effacing) the original, substituting the reader's own inner word for the textual inscription. Genre-concepts mediate this activity, but these conceptions of literary form do not themselves remain immune to the reformulating, reappropriating activity of interpretation; involved in the meaning of a text, they too undergo a process of reformulation—a rhetorization, as it were, at the reader's hands. Such, at any rate, is the resting point of this present study.

26. The term is Vološinov's (*Marxism and the Philosophy of Language*, p. 39).

BIBLIOGRAPHY

Donne Editions

Coffin, Charles M., ed. *The Complete Poetry and Selected Prose of John Donne*. New York: Random House, 1952.

Gardner, Helen, ed. *John Donne: The Divine Poems*. Oxford: Clarendon Press, 1952.

———, ed. *John Donne: The Elegies and the Songs and Sonnets*. Oxford: Clarendon Press, 1965.

Gardner, Helen, and Timothy S. Healy, S.J., eds. *John Donne: Selected Prose, Chosen by Evelyn Simpson and Edited by Helen Gardner and Timothy Healy*. Oxford: Clarendon Press, 1967.

Gosse, Edmund. *The Life and Letters of John Donne*. 2 vols. Gloucester, Mass.: Peter Smith, 1959.

Grierson, Herbert J. C., ed. *The Poems of John Donne*. 2 vols. 2d ed. London: Oxford University Press, 1938.

Hester, M. Thomas, ed. *Letters to Severall Persons of Honour* (1651). Delmar, N.Y.: Scholars' Facsimiles and Reprints, 1977.

Milgate, Wesley, ed. *John Donne: The Epithalamions, Anniversaries, and Epicedes*. Oxford: Clarendon Press, 1978.

———, ed. *John Donne: The Satires, Epigrams, and Verse Letters*. Oxford: Clarendon Press, 1967.

Peters, Helen, ed. *John Donne: The Paradoxes and Problems*. Oxford: Clarendon Press, 1980.

Potter, George R., and Evelyn M. Simpson, eds. *The Sermons of John Donne*. 10 vols. Berkeley and Los Angeles: University of California Press, 1953–1961.

Shawcross, John T., ed. *The Complete Poetry of John Donne*. Garden City, N.Y.: Archon Books, 1967.

Simpson, Evelyn M., ed. *Essays in Divinity*. Oxford: Clarendon Press, 1952.

Sullivan, Ernest W., ed. *Biathanatos*. Newark: University of Delaware Press, 1978.

Sypher, Francis Jacques, ed. *Pseudo-Martyr*. Delmar, N.Y.: Scholars' Facsimiles and Reprints, 1974.

Primary Texts

Agrippa, Henry Cornelius. *The Philosophy of Natural Magic* (1531). Edited by Leslie Shepard. Seacaucus, N.J.: University Books, 1974.

Aristotle. *The Basic Works of Aristotle*. Edited by Richard McKeon. New York: Random House, 1941.

Ascham, Roger. *The Scholemaster* (1570). In *Elizabethan Critical Essays*, edited by G. Gregory Smith, 1:1–45. Oxford: Clarendon Press, 1904.

Augustine. *On Christian Doctrine*. Translated by D. W. Robertson. Indianapolis: Bobbs-Merrill, 1958.

———. *The Teacher*. Translated by Robert P. Russell. The Fathers of the Church: A New Translation, vol. 59. Washington: Catholic University of America Press, 1968.

Bacon, Sir Francis. *The Advancement of Learning* (1605). Edited by G. W. Kitchin. Totowa, N.J.: Rowman and Littlefield, 1974.

Beroaldo, Phillipo. *Oratio in Principio Lectionis Juvenalis*. In *Reden und Briefe Italienischen Humanisten*, edited by Karl Muellner, pp. 60–63. Vienna: A. Hoelder, 1899. Reprint. Munich: Wilhelm Fink, 1970.

Calvin, Jean. *A Compend of the Institutes of the Christian Religion by John Calvin*. Edited by Hugh Kerr. Philadelphia: Westminster Press, 1964.

———. *Institutes of the Christian Religion*. Edited by John T. McNeill, translated by Ford Lewis Battles. Library of Christian Classics, vols. 21–22. Philadelphia: Westminster Press, 1960.

Casaubon, Isaac. *De Satyra Graecorum Poesi et Romanorum Satira* (1605). Introduction by Peter Medine. Delmar, N.Y.: Scholars' Facsimiles and Reprints, 1977.

Cicero. *Academica*. Translated by H. Rackham. Loeb Classical Library. New York: Putnam, 1933.

Crinito, Pietro. *De Poetis Latinis Libri V*. Lyons, 1561.

Drummond, William, of Hawthornden. *Ben Jonson . . . Conversations with William Drummond of Hawthornden* (1619). Edited by G. B. Harrison. New York: Barnes and Noble, 1966.

Dryden, John. *A Discourse Concerning the Original and Progress of Satire* (1692). In *Essays of John Dryden*, edited by W. P. Ker, 2:15–114. New York: Russel and Russel, 1961.

Erasmus, Desiderius. *Ciceronianus: Or a Dialogue on the Best Style of Speaking*. Translated by Izora Scott. Columbia University Contributions to Education, vol. 21. 1905. Reprint. New York: AMS Press, 1972.

————. *De Copia; De Ratione Studii*. In *Collected Works of Erasmus*. Vol. 24: *Literary and Educational Writings*, edited by Craig R. Thompson. Toronto: University of Toronto Press, 1978.

Fraunce, Abraham. *The Arcadian Rhetoricke* (1588). Edited by Ethel Seaton. Oxford: Oxford University Press, 1950.

Gilbert, Allan, ed. *Literary Criticism, Plato to Dryden*. Detroit: Wayne State University Press, 1962.

Gorgias. "Encomium of Helen." Translated by George Kennedy. In *The Older Sophists*, edited by Rosamund Kent Sprague, pp. 50–54. Columbia: University of South Carolina Press, 1972.

Hall, Joseph. *The Collected Poems of Joseph Hall*. Edited by Arnold Davenport. Liverpool: Liverpool University Press, 1949.

Hillerbrand, Hans J., ed. *The Reformation: A Narrative History Related by Contemporary Observers and Participants*. Grand Rapids: Baker, 1978.

Horace. *Satires, Epistles, and Ars Poetica*. Translated by H. Rushton Fairclough. Loeb Classical Library. Cambridge: Harvard University Press, 1978.

————. *Q. Horatii Flacci, Auli Persii, Iunii Iuvenalis . . . opera . . . .* Basil, 1531.

————. *Q. Horatii Flacci Odarum libri quattuor . . . sermonum libri duo*. Venice, 1520.

————. *Q. Horatius Flaccus: cum commentariis et Enarrationibus . . . .* Lyons, 1597.

Hoskyns, John. *Directions for Speech and Style* (1599?). Edited by Hoyt H. Hudson. Princeton: Princeton University Press, 1935.

Isidore, Bp. of Seville. *Isidori Hispalensis Episcopi Etymologiarum sive Originum Libri XX*. Edited by W. M. Lindsay. Oxford: Clarendon Press, 1966.

Isocrates. *Panegyricus*. In *Isocrates I*. Translated by George Norlin. Loeb Classical Library. Cambridge: Harvard University Press, 1928.

Jerome, St. *Sancti Eusebii Hieronymi Stridonensis Presbyteri Opera Omnia*. Patrologiae Latinae Cursus Completus. Paris: J.-P. Migne, 1877.

Jonson, Ben. *The Works of Ben Jonson*. Edited by C. H. Herford and Percy and Evelyn Simpson. 11 vols. Oxford: Clarendon Press, 1925–1952.

Juvenal. *Juvenal and Persius*. Translated by G. G. Ramsay. Loeb Classical Library. Cambridge: Harvard University Press, 1969.

Kempe, William. *The Education of Children in Learning* (1588). Edited by Robert D. Pepper. Gainesville, Fla.: Scholars' Facsimiles and Reprints, 1966.

Lipse, Juste. *Opera Omnia*. Antwerp, 1614.

Lodge, Thomas. *The Complete Works of Thomas Lodge*. Edited by Edmund W. Gosse. New York: Russel and Russel, 1883.

Longinus. "On the Sublime." Translated by W. Hamilton Fyfe. Loeb Classical Library. Cambridge: Harvard University Press, 1932.

Luther, Martin. *Luther's Commentary on Genesis*. Edited and translated by J. Theodore Mueller. 2 vols. Grand Rapids: Zondervan Publishing, 1958.

Marston, John. *The Poems of John Marston*. Edited by Arnold Davenport. Liverpool: Liverpool University Press, 1961.

Milton, John. *Christian Doctrine*. Translated by John Carey. In *Complete Prose Works of John Milton*, edited by William Alfred, Robert W. Ayers, et al, vol. 6. New Haven: Yale University Press, 1973.

Minturno, Antonio Sebastiano. *L'Arte Poetica* (1564). Edited by Bernhard Fabian. Poetiken des Cinquecento, Band 6. Munich: Wilhelm Fink, 1971.

———. *De Poeta* (1559). Edited by Bernhard Fabian. Poetiken des Cinquecento, Band 5. Munich: Wilhelm Fink, 1970.

Montaigne, Michel de. "Apology for Raymond Sebond." In *The Complete Essays of Montaigne*, translated by Donald M. Frame, pp. 318–457. Stanford: Stanford University Press, 1958.

Parnell, Thomas. *The Poetical Works of Thomas Parnell*. London: William Pickering, 1852.

Peacham, Henry. *The Garden of Eloquence* (1593). Edited by William G. Crane. Gainesville, Fla.: Scholars' Facsimiles and Reprints, 1954.

Persius. *A. Flacci Persii Poetae Satirarum Opus*. Venice, 1482.

———. *A. Persii Flacci Satyrae Sex*. Cologne, 1568.

———. *Flacci Persii Poetae Satyrarum Opus*. Venice, 1485.

———. *Juvenal and Persius*. Translated by G. G. Ramsay. Loeb Classical Library. Cambridge: Harvard University Press, 1969.

Petrarch. *Le Familiari*. Edited by Vittorio Rossi. 4 vols. Florence: C. G. Sansoni, 1932–1941.

———. *Rime, Trionfi, e Poesie Latine a cura di F. Neri, G. Martellotti, E. Bianchi, N. Sapegno*. Milan: Riccardo Ricciardi, 1951.

———. *Sonnets and Songs*. Translated by Anna Maria Armi. New York: AMS Press, 1978.

Petti, Anthony G., ed. *Recusant Documents from the Ellesmere Manuscripts*. Catholic Record Society, vol. 60. St. Albans: Fisher Knight, 1968.

Pico della Mirandola, Giovanni. *Opera Omnia* (1557). 2 vols. Facsimile reprint. Hildesheim: Georg Olms, 1969.

Plato. *The Collected Dialogues of Plato.* Edited by Edith Hamilton and Huntington Cairns. Princeton: Princeton University Press, 1961.

Pseudo-Dionysius. *The Divine Names.* In *Pseudo-Dionysius: The Complete Works,* translated by Colm Luibheid, pp. 47–131. Mahwah, N.Y.: Paulist Press, 1987.

Puttenham, George. *The Arte of English Poesie* (1589). Edited by Baxter Hathaway. Kent, Ohio: Kent State University Press, 1970.

Quintilian. *Institutio Oratoria.* Translated by H. E. Butler. 4 vols. Loeb Classical Library. New York: Putnam, 1920–1922.

Rainold, Richard. *The Foundation of Rhetoric* (1593). Edited by R. C. Alston. Menston: Scolar Press, n.d.

Ricci, Bartolommeo. *De Imitatione* (1541). In *Trattati di Poetica e Retorica del Cinquecento,* edited by Bernard Weinberg, 1:415–49. Rome: Laterza, 1970.

Scaliger, Julius Caesar. *Poetices Libri Septem* (1561). Facsimile reprint. Stuttgart: Friedrich Frommann, 1964.

Seneca. *Ad Lucilium Epistulae Morales.* Translated by Richard M. Gummere. 3 vols. Loeb Classical Library. New York: Putnam, 1917–1925.

Sextus. *Against the Schoolmasters.* Translated by George Kennedy. In *The Older Sophists,* edited by Rosamund Kent Sprague, pp. 42–46. Columbia: University of South Carolina Press, 1972.

Sherry, Richard. *A Treatise of Schemes and Tropes* (1550). Gainesville, Fla.: Scholars' Facsimiles and Reprints, 1961.

Sidney, Sir Philip. "An Apology for Poetry" (1595). In *Critical Theory since Plato,* edited by Hazard Adams, pp. 155–77. New York: Harcourt Brace Janovich, 1971.

Smith, George Gregory, ed. *Elizabethan Critical Essays.* 2 vols. Oxford: Clarendon Press, 1904.

Spingarn, Joel Elias, ed. *Critical Essays of the Seventeenth Century, 1605–1685.* 3 vols. Oxford: Clarendon Press, 1908–1909.

Vadian, Joachim. *De Poetica et Carminis Ratione* (1518). Edited by Peter Schaeffer. Munich: Wilhelm Fink, 1973.

Viperano, Giovanni Antonio. *De Poetica Libri Tres* (1579). Edited by Bernhard Fabian. Poetiken des Cinquecento, Band 10. Munich: Wilhelm Fink, 1967.

Vives, Juan Luis. *Vives: On Education. A Translation of the De Tradendis Disciplinis of Juan Luis Vives* (1531). Translated by Foster Watson. Cambridge: Cambridge University Press, 1913.

Webbe, William. *A Discourse of English Poetrie* (1586). In *Elizabethan Critical Essays,* edited by G. Gregory Smith, 1:226–302. Oxford: Clarendon Press, 1904.

Weinberg, Bernard, ed. *Critical Prefaces of the French Renaissance.* Evanston, Ill.: Northwestern University Press, 1950.

——, ed. *Trattati di Poetica e Retorica del Cinquecento.* 4 vols. Rome: Laterza, 1970–1974.

Wilson, Thomas. *The Arte of Rhetorique* (1553). Edited by Robert Hood Bowers. Gainesville, Fla.: Scholars' Facsimiles and Reprints, 1962.

Secondary Texts

Alcorn, Marshall W., Jr., and Mark Bracher. "Literature, Psychoanalysis, and the Re-Formation of the Self: A New Direction for Reader-Response Theory." *PMLA* 100 (1985): 342–54.

Andreason, Nancy J. C. *John Donne: Conservative Revolutionary.* Princeton: Princeton University Press, 1967.

——. "Theme and Structure in Donne's *Satyres.*" *Studies in English Literature* 3 (1963): 59–75.

Anselment, Raymond A. "'Ascendio Mendax, Descensio Crudelis': The Image of Babel in the Anniversaries." *ELH* 38 (1971): 188–205.

——. *"Betwixt Jest and Earnest": Marprelate, Milton, Marvell, Swift, and the Decorum of Religious Ridicule.* Toronto: University of Toronto Press, 1979.

Austin, J. L. *How to Do Things with Words.* Cambridge: Harvard University Press, 1962.

Bakhtin, M. M. *The Dialogic Imagination: Four Essays.* Edited by Michael Holquist, translated by Caryl Emerson and Michael Holquist. Austin: University of Texas Press, 1981.

Battenhouse, Roy W. "The Grounds of Religious Toleration in the Thought of John Donne." *Church History* 11 (1942): 217–48.

Baumlin, James S. "Decorum, *Kairos,* and the 'New' Rhetoric." *Pre/Text* 5 (1985): 171–83.

——. "Donne's Christian Diatribes: Persius and the Rhetorical Persona of *Satyre III* and *Satyre V.*" In *The Eagle and the Dove: Reassessing John Donne,* edited by Claude J. Summers and Ted-Larry Pebworth, pp. 92–105. Columbia: University of Missouri Press, 1986.

——. "Persuasion, Rogerian Rhetoric, and Imaginative Play." *Rhetoric Society Quarterly* 17 (1987): 33–43.

Baumlin, James S., and Tita French Baumlin. "*Psyche/Logos:* Mapping the Terrains of Mind and Rhetoric." *College English* 51 (1989): 245–61.

Baumlin, Tita French. "Petruchio the Sophist and Language as

Creation in *The Taming of the Shrew.*" *Studies in English Literature* 29 (1989): 237–57.

Beale, Walter H. *A Pragmatic Theory of Rhetoric.* Carbondale: Southern Illinois University Press, 1987.

Bellette, A. F. "The Originality of Donne's *Satires.*" *University of Toronto Quarterly* 44 (1975): 130–40.

Bernard, John. "Orthodoxia Epidemica: Donne's Poetics and 'A Valediction: Of My Name in the Window.'" *South Atlantic Quarterly* 71 (1972): 377–89.

Bewley, Marius. "The Mask of John Donne." In *Masks and Mirrors: Essays in Criticism,* pp. 3–49. New York: Atheneum, 1970.

———. "Religious Cynicism in Donne's Poetry." *Kenyon Review* 14 (1952): 619–46.

Bicknell, E. J. *A Theological Introduction to the Thirty-Nine Articles of the Church of England.* Edited by H. J. Carpenter. London: Longmans, 1957.

Bloom, Harold. "The Breaking of Form." In *Deconstruction and Criticism,* edited by Geoffrey H. Hartman, pp. 1–37. New York: Continuum, 1979.

Bossy, John. "The Character of Elizabethan Catholicism." *Past and Present* 21 (1962): 39–59.

Bozarth-Campbell, Alla. *The Word's Body: An Incarnational Aesthetic of Interpretation.* University: University of Alabama Press, 1979.

Bredvold, Louis I. "The Naturalism of Donne in Relation to Some Renaissance Traditions." *Journal of English and Germanic Philology* 22 (1923): 471–502.

———. "The Religious Thought of Donne in Relation to Medieval and Later Traditions." In *Studies in Shakespeare, Milton, and Donne.* University of Michigan Publications, Language and Literature, 1:191–232. New York: Macmillan, 1925.

Broadbent, J. B. "Milton's Rhetoric." In *Milton: Modern Judgements,* edited by Alan Rudrum, pp. 270–95. London: Macmillan, 1968.

Brodsky, Claudia. "Donne: The Imaging of the Logical Conceit." *ELH* 49 (1982): 829–48.

Bryan, Robert A. "John Donne's Use of the Anathema." *Journal of English and Germanic Philology* 41 (1962): 305–12.

Bueler, Lois E. "The Failure of Sophistry in Donne's 'Elegy VII.'" *Studies in English Literature* 25 (1985): 69–85.

Burgess, Theodore C. "Epideictic Literature." *University of Chicago Studies in Classical Philology* 3 (1902): 89–259.

Burke, John G. "Hermeticism as a Renaissance World View." In *The Darker Vision of the Renaissance: Beyond the Fields of Reason,* edited by Robert S. Kinsman, pp. 95–117. UCLA Center for Medieval and Renaissance Studies, Contributions, vol. 6. Berkeley and Los Angeles: University of California Press, 1974.

Burke, Kenneth. *A Rhetoric of Motives.* New York: Prentice-Hall, 1950. Reprint. Berkeley and Los Angeles: University of California Press, 1969.

Cairns, Francis. *Generic Composition in Greek and Roman Poetry.* Edinburgh: Edinburgh University Press, 1972.

Carey, John. *John Donne: Life, Mind, and Art.* New York: Oxford University Press, 1981.

Cathcart, Dwight. *Doubting Conscience: Donne and the Poetry of Moral Argument.* Ann Arbor: University of Michigan Press, 1975.

Cherwitz, Richard A., and James W. Hikins. *Communication and Knowledge: An Investigation in Rhetorical Epistemology.* Columbia: University of South Carolina Press, 1986.

Clark, Mary T. *Augustine: Philosopher of Freedom.* Tournai: Desclée Company, 1958.

Coffey, Michael. *Roman Satire.* London: Methuen, 1976.

Colie, Rosalie L. *Paradoxia Epidemica: The Renaissance Tradition of Paradox.* Princeton: Princeton University Press, 1966.

———. *The Resources of Kind: Genre-Theory in the Renaissance,* edited by Barbara K. Lewalski. Berkeley and Los Angeles: University of California Press, 1973.

Colish, Marcia L. *The Mirror of Language: A Study in the Medieval Theory of Knowledge.* Lincoln: University of Nebraska Press, 1983.

———. "St. Augustine's Rhetoric of Silence Revisited." *Augustinian Studies* 9 (1978): 15–24.

Collmer, Robert G. "Donne and Charron." *English Studies* 46 (1965): 482–88.

Corder, Jim W. "Varieties of Ethical Argument, With Some Account of the Significance of *Ethos* in the Teaching of Composition." *Freshman English News* 6 (1978): 1–23.

Corthell, Ronald J. "'Coscus Only Breeds My Just Offence': A Note on Donne's 'Satyre II' and the Inns of Court." *John Donne Journal* 6 (1987): 25–32.

———. "Style and Self in Donne's *Satires.*" *Texas Studies in Literature and Language* 24 (1982): 155–86.

Cragg, Gerald R. *Freedom and Authority: A Study of English Thought in the Early Seventeenth Century.* Philadelphia: Westminster Press, 1975.

Crashaw, Eluned. "Hermetic Elements in Donne's Poetic Vision." In *John Donne: Essays in Celebration,* edited by A. J. Smith, pp. 324–48. London: Methuen, 1972.

Croce, Benedetto. "Poetry." Translated by Allan H. Gilbert. In *Literary Criticism: Pope to Croce*, edited by Gay Wilson Allen and Harry Hayden Clark, pp. 627–45. New York: American Book Company, 1941.

Cunnar, Eugene R. "Donne's 'Valediction: Forbidding Mourning' and the Golden Compasses of Alchemical Creation." In *Literature and the Occult: Essays in Comparative Literature*, edited by Luanne Frank, pp. 72–110. University of Texas at Arlington Publications in Literature. Arlington: UTA Press, 1977.

Davis, Robert Con. "Pedagogy, Lacan, and the Freudian Subject." *College English* 47 (1987): 749–55.

Derrida, Jacques. *Dissemination*. Translated by Barbara Johnson. Chicago: University of Chicago Press, 1982.

———. "La Loi du Genre / The Law of Genre." Translated by Avitall Ronell. *Glyph* 7 (1980): 176–232.

———. *Of Grammatology*. Translated by G. C. Spivak. Baltimore: Johns Hopkins University Press, 1976.

———. *Writing and Difference*. Translated by Alan Bass. London: Routledge, 1978.

Descombes, Vincent. *Modern French Philosophy*. Translated by L. Scott-Fox and J. M. Harding. Cambridge: Cambridge University Press, 1980.

Docherty, Thomas. *John Donne, Undone*. London: Methuen, 1986.

Donohue, James J. *The Theory of Literary Kinds: Ancient Classifications of Literature*. 2 vols. Dubuque, Iowa: Loras College Press, 1943.

Eagleton, Terry. *Literary Theory: An Introduction*. Minneapolis: University of Minnesota Press, 1983.

Ebeling, Gerhard. *Introduction to a Theological Theory of Language*. Translated by R. A. Wilson. Philadelphia: Fortress Press, 1971.

Eddy, Y. Shikany, and Daniel P. Jaekle. "Donne's 'Satyre I': The Influence of Persius's 'Satire III.'" *Studies in English Literature* 21 (1981): 111–22.

Egan, James. *The Inward Teacher: Milton's Rhetoric of Christian Liberty*. University Park: Pennsylvania State University Press, 1980.

Ehninger, Douglas. "On Systems of Rhetoric." *Philosophy and Rhetoric* 1 (1968): 131–44.

Elliott, Emory. "The Narrative and Allusive Unity of Donne's *Satyres*." *Journal of English and German Philology* 75 (1976): 105–16.

Elliott, Robert C. *The Power of Satire: Magic, Ritual, Art*. Princeton: Princeton University Press, 1960.

Engnell, Richard A. "Implicatons for Communication of the Rhetorical Epistemology of Gorgias of Leontini." *Western Speech Journal* 37 (1973): 175–84.

Enos, Richard Leo. "The Epistemology of Gorgias' Rhetoric: A Re-Examination." *Southern Speech Communication Journal* 42 (1976): 35–51.

Erickson, Keith, ed. *Plato: True and Sophistic Rhetoric.* Amsterdam: Rodolphi, 1979.

Erskine-Hill, Howard. "Courtiers out of Horace: Donne's *Satyre IV,* and Pope's *Fourth Satire of Dr. John Donne, Dean of St Paul's Versifyed.*" In *John Donne: Essays in Celebration,* edited by A. J. Smith, pp. 273–307. London: Methuen, 1972.

Farmer, Norman K., Jr. "A Theory of Genre for Seventeenth Century Poetry." *Genre* 3 (1970): 293–317.

Ferry, Anne. *All in War with Time: Love Poetry of Shakespeare, Donne, Jonson, Marvell.* Cambridge: Harvard University Press, 1975.

Fiore, Peter Amadeus, ed. *Just So Much Honor: Essays Commemorating the Four-Hundredth Anniversary of the Birth of John Donne.* University Park: Pennsylvania State University Press, 1972.

Flynn, Dennis. "Donne's Catholicism." *Recusant History* 13 (1975–1976): 1–17, 178–95.

———. "Irony in Donne's *Biathanatos* and *Pseudo-Martyr.*" *Recusant History* 12 (1973): 49–69.

Foucault, Michel. *The Order of Things: An Archeology of the Human Sciences.* New York: Random House, 1970.

Fowler, Alastair. *Kinds of Literature: An Introduction to the Theory of Genres and Modes.* Cambridge: Harvard University Press, 1982.

———. "The Life and Death of Literary Forms." *New Literary History* 2 (1971): 199–216.

Freccero, John. "Donne's 'A Valediction: Forbidding Mourning.'" *ELH* 30 (1963): 335–76.

Gadamer, Hans-Georg. *Truth and Method.* New York: Seabury Press, 1975.

Gardner, Helen. "The Argument about 'The Ecstasy.'" In *Essential Articles for the Study of John Donne's Poetry,* edited by John R. Roberts, pp. 239–58. Hamden, Conn.: Archon Books, 1975.

———, ed. *John Donne: A Collection of Critical Essays.* Englewood Cliffs, N.J.: Prentice Hall, 1962.

Geraldine, Sister Mary. "Donne's *Notitia:* The Evidence of the *Satires.*" *University of Toronto Quarterly* 36 (1966): 24–36.

———. "John Donne and the Mindes Indeavours." *Studies in English Literature* 5 (1965): 115–31.

Gransden, K. W. "*Lente, Currite, Noctis Equi:* Chaucer, *Troilus and Criseyde* 3.1422–70, Donne, 'The Sunne Rising,' and Ovid, *Amores* 1.13." In *Creative Imitation and Latin Literature,* edited by David

West and Tony Woodman, pp. 151–71. Cambridge: Cambridge University Press, 1979.

Greene, Thomas M. *The Light in Troy: Imitation and Discovery in Renaissance Poetry.* New Haven: Yale University Press, 1982.

Guillén, Claudio. *Literature as System: Essays Toward the Theory of Literary History.* Princeton: Princeton University Press, 1971.

Guss, Donald L. *John Donne, Petrarchist: Italianate Conceits and Love Theory in the Songs and Sonets.* Detroit: Wayne State University Press, 1966.

Hadas, Moses. *Ancilla to Classical Reading.* New York: Columbia University Press, 1954.

Hagendahl, Harald. *Augustine and the Latin Classics.* Vol. 2, *Augustine's Attitude.* Studia Graeca et Latina Gothoburgensia 20:2. Acta Universitatis Gothoburgensis, 1967.

Hartman, Geoffrey H., ed. *Deconstruction and Criticism.* New York: Continuum, 1979.

———. *Saving the Text: Literature/Derrida/Philosophy.* Baltimore: Johns Hopkins University Press, 1981.

Hernadi, Paul. *Beyond Genre: New Directions in Literary Classification.* Ithaca: Cornell University Press, 1972.

Hester, M. Thomas. "The *Bona Carmina* of Donne and Horace." In *Renaissance Papers, 1976,* edited by Dennis G. Donovan and A. Leigh DeNeef, pp. 21–30. Collection of papers presented at the Southeast Renaissance Conference, 1977.

———. "Donne's 'Hill of Truth.' " *English Language Notes* 14 (1976): 100–105.

———. "Henry Donne, John Donne, and the Date of *Satyre II.*" *Notes and Queries* 24 (1977): 524–27.

———. *Kinde Pitty and Brave Scorn: John Donne's "Satyres."* Durham, N.C.: Duke University Press, 1982.

Hill, Forbes I. "The Rhetoric of Aristotle." In *A Synoptic History of Classical Rhetoric,* edited by James J. Murphy, pp. 19–76. Berkeley and Los Angeles: University of California Press, 1972.

Hirsch, E. D. *Validity in Interpretation.* New Haven: Yale University Press, 1967.

Hughes, Richard E. *The Progress of the Soul: The Interior Career of John Donne.* New York: William Morrow, 1968.

Huizinga, Johan. *Homo Ludens: A Study of the Play-Element in Culture.* Boston: Beacon Press, 1950.

Hunt, Clay. *Donne's Poetry: Essays in Literary Analysis.* New Haven: Yale University Press, 1954.

Husain, Itrat. *The Dogmatic and Mystical Theology of John Donne.* London: Macmillan, 1938.

Ijsseling, Samuel. *Rhetoric and Philosophy in Conflict: An Historical Survey.* Translated by Paul Dunphy. The Hague: Martinus Nijhoff, 1976.

Jahn, J. D. "The Eschatological Scene in Donne's 'A Valediction: Forbidding Mourning.' " *College Literature* 5 (1978): 34–47.

Jones, R. T. "John Donne's *Songs and Sonets:* The Poetic Value of Argument." *Theoria* 51 (1978): 33–42.

Jung, Carl. *Alchemical Studies.* Princeton: Princeton University Press, 1967.

Kahn, Victoria. *Rhetoric, Prudence, and Skepticism in the Renaissance.* Ithaca: Cornell University Press, 1985.

Kennedy, George. *Classical Rhetoric and Its Christian and Secular Tradition from Ancient to Modern Times.* Chapel Hill: University of North Carolina Press, 1980.

Kennedy, William J. *Rhetorical Norms in Renaissance Literature.* New Haven: Yale University Press, 1978.

Kerins, Frank. "The 'Businesse' of Satire: John Donne and the Reformation of the Satirist." *Texas Studies in Literature and Language* 26 (1984): 34–60.

Kernan, Alvin B. *The Cankered Muse: Satire of the English Renaissance.* New Haven: Yale University Press, 1959. Reprint. Hamden, Conn.: Archon Books, 1976.

Khanna, Urmilla. "Donne's 'A Valediction: Forbidding Mourning'— Some Possible Alchemical Allusions." *Notes and Queries,* n.s., 17 (1970): 404–5.

Kinneavy, James L. *Greek Rhetorical Origins of Christian Faith: An Inquiry.* New York: Oxford University Press, 1987.

Kinsman, Robert S., ed. *The Darker Vision of the Renaissance: Beyond the Fields of Reason.* UCLA Center for Medieval and Renaissance Studies, Contributions, vol. 6. Berkeley and Los Angeles: University of California Press, 1974.

Knox, Norman. *The Word Irony and Its Context, 1500–1755.* Durham, N.C.: Duke University Press, 1961.

Krieger, Murray. *Poetic Presence and Illusion: Essays in Critical History and Theory.* Baltimore: Johns Hopkins University Press, 1979.

Lanham, Richard. *Literacy and the Survival of Humanism.* New Haven: Yale University Press, 1983.

———. *The Motives of Eloquence: Literary Rhetoric in the Renaissance.* New Haven: Yale University Press, 1976.

Lauritsen, John R. "Donne's *Satyres:* The Drama of Self-Discovery." *Studies in English Literature* 16 (1976): 117–30.

Legouis, Pierre. *Donne the Craftsman: An Essay upon the Structure of the Songs and Sonnets.* New York: Russel and Russel, 1962.

Lein, Clayton D. "Theme and Structure in John Donne's *Satyre II.*" Comparative Literature 32 (1980): 130–50.

Leishman, J. B. *The Monarch of Wit: An Analytical and Comparative Study of the Poetry of John Donne.* London: Hutchinson, 1951.

Lewalski, Barbara K. *Donne's Anniversaries and the Poetry of Praise: The Creation of a Symbolic Mode.* Princeton: Princeton University Press, 1973.

―――. *Paradise Lost and the Rhetoric of Literary Forms.* Princeton: Princeton University Press, 1985.

―――. *Protestant Poetics and the Seventeenth-Century Religious Lyric.* Princeton: Princeton University Press, 1979.

―――, ed. *Renaissance Genres: Essays on Theory, History, and Interpretation.* Harvard English Studies 14. Cambridge: Harvard University Press, 1986.

Lewis, C. S. "Donne and Love Poetry in the Seventeenth Century." In *John Donne: A Collection of Critical Essays,* edited by Helen Gardner, pp. 90–99. Englewood Cliffs, N.J.: Prentice Hall, 1962.

McCanles, Michael. "The Dialectical Structure of the Metaphysical Lyric: Donne, Herbert, Marvell." In *Dialectical Criticism and Renaissance Literature,* pp. 54–117. Berkeley and Los Angeles: University of California Press, 1975.

―――. "Mythos and Dianoia: A Dialectical Methodology of Literary Form." In *Literary Monographs,* edited by Eric Rothstein, 4:3–88. Madison: University of Wisconsin Press, 1971.

Malloch, A. E. "John Donne and the Casuists." *Studies in English Literature* 2 (1962): 57–76.

―――. "The Technique and Function of the Renaissance Paradox." *Studies in Philology* (1956): 191–203.

Manley, Frank. "Formal Wit in the *Songs and Sonnets.*" In *That Subtle Wreath: Lectures Presented at the Quatercentenary Celebration of the Birth of John Donne,* edited by Margaret W. Pepperdene, pp. 5–27. Atlanta: Agnes Scott College, 1972.

Marlies, Mike. "Doubt, Reason, and Cartesian Therapy." In *Descartes: Critical and Interpretive Essays,* edited by Michael Hooker, pp. 89–113. Baltimore: Johns Hopkins University Press, 1978.

Marotti, Arthur F. *John Donne, Coterie Poet.* Madison: University of Wisconsin Press, 1986.

Mazzeo, Joseph A. *Renaissance and Seventeenth Century Studies*. New York: Columbia University Press, 1964.

Medine, Peter. "Isaac Casaubon's *Prolegomena* to the *Satires* of Persius: An Introduction, Text, and Translation." *English Literary Renaissance* 6 (1976): 271–98.

Meiland, Jack W., and Michael Krausz, eds. *Relativism: Cognitive and Moral*. Notre Dame: University of Notre Dame Press, 1982.

Miller, Clarence H., and Berrey, Caryl L. "The Structure of Integrity: The Cardinal Virtues in Donne's *Satyre III*." *Costerus* I (1974): 27–46.

Miller, J. Hillis. "The Critic as Host." In *Deconstruction and Criticism*, edited by Geoffrey H. Hartman, pp. 217–53. New York: Continuum, 1979.

Miner, Earl. *The Metaphysical Mode from Donne to Cowley*. Princeton: Princeton University Press, 1969.

———. "On the Genesis and Development of Literary Systems." *Critical Inquiry* 5 (1979): 339–53, 553–68.

Moore, Thomas V. "Donne's Use of Uncertainty as a Vital Force in *Satyre III*." *Modern Philology* 67 (1969): 41–49.

Murphy, James J., ed. *A Synoptic History of Classical Rhetoric*. Berkeley and Los Angeles: University of California Press, 1972.

Neel, Jaspar. *Plato, Derrida, and Writing*. Carbondale: Southern Illinois University Press, 1988.

Nietzsche, Friedrich. *The Gay Science*. Translated by Walter Kaufmann. New York: Vintage Books, 1974.

Orgel, Stephen. "The Renaissance Artist as Plagiarist." *ELH* 48 (1981): 476–95.

Palisca, Claude. "*Ut Oratoria Musica:* The Rhetorical Basis of Musical Mannerism." In *The Meaning of Mannerism*, edited by Franklin W. Robinson and Stephen G. Nichols, pp. 37–65. Hanover, N.H.: University Press of New England, 1972.

Perelman, Chaim. *The Realm of Rhetoric*. Notre Dame: University of Notre Dame Press, 1982.

Peter, John Dermond. *Complaint and Satire in Early English Literature*. Oxford: Clarendon Press, 1956.

Pieper, Joseph. *Silence of St. Thomas: Three Essays*. Translated by John Murray and Daniel O'Connor. New York: Pantheon, 1957.

Pigman, G. W., III. "Imitation and the Renaissance Sense of the Past: The Reception of Erasmus' *Ciceronianus*." *Journal of Medieval and Renaissance Studies* 9 (1979): 155–77.

———. "Versions of Imitation in the Renaissance." *Renaissance Quarterly* 33 (1980): 1–32.

Pirsig, Robert. *Zen and the Art of Motorcycle Maintenance.* New York: Bantam, 1974.

Popkin, Richard H. *The History of Scepticism from Erasmus to Descartes.* New York: Harper, 1964.

Poulakos, John. "Rhetoric, Sophists, and the Possible." *Communication Monographs* 51 (1984): 215–26.

———. "Toward a Sophistic Definition of Rhetoric." *Philosophy and Rhetoric* 16 (1983): 35–48.

Praz, Mario. "Donne's Relation to the Poetry of His Time." In *A Garland for John Donne, 1631–1931,* edited by Theodore Spencer, pp. 51–72. Cambridge: Harvard University Press, 1931.

Quinn, Kenneth. *Latin Explorations: Critical Studies in Roman Literature.* London: Routledge, 1963.

Quint, Dennis. *Origin and Originality in Renaissance Literature: Versions of the Source.* New Haven: Yale University Press, 1983.

Rajan, Tilottama. "'Nothing Sooner Broke': Donne's *Songs and Sonets* as Self-Consuming Artifacts." *ELH* 49 (1982): 805–28.

Ramage, Edwin S., David R. Sigsbee, and Sigmund C. Fredericks. *Roman Satirists and Their Satire: The Fine Art of Criticism in Ancient Rome.* Park Ridge, N.J.: Noyes Press, 1974.

Reichert, John F. "'Organizing Principles' and Genre Theory." *Genre* I (1968): 1–12.

Richards, I. A. *The Philosophy of Rhetoric.* New York: Oxford University Press, 1965.

Ricoeur, Paul. *Hermeneutics and the Human Sciences: Essays on Language, Action, and Interpretation.* Edited and translated by John B. Thompson. Cambridge: Cambridge University Press, 1981.

Roberts, D. H. "'Just Such Disparity': The Real and the Representation in Donne's Poetry." *South Atlantic Bulletin* 41 (1976): 99–108.

Roberts, John R., ed. *Essential Articles for the Study of John Donne's Poetry.* Hamden, Conn.: Archon Books, 1975.

Rockett, William. "Donne's Libertine Rhetoric." *English Studies* 52 (1971): 507–18.

Rogers, William Elford. *The Three Genres and the Interpretation of Lyric.* Princeton: Princeton University Press, 1983.

Romilly, Jacqueline de. *Magic and Rhetoric in Ancient Greece.* Cambridge: Harvard University Press, 1975.

Rorty, Richard. *Philosophy and the Mirror of Nature.* Princeton: Princeton University Press, 1979.

Ross, Malcolm Mackensie. *Poetry and Dogma: The Transfiguration of Eucharistic Symbols in Seventeenth Century English Poetry.* New Brunswick, N.J.: Rutgers University Press, 1954.

Rudnytsky, Peter L. "'The Sight of God': Donne's Poetics of Transcendence." *Texas Studies in Literature and Language* 24 (1982):
185–207.

Sackton, Alexander. "Donne and the Privacy of Verse." *Studies in
English Literature* 7 (1967): 67–82.

Saville, Jonathan. *The Medieval Erotic Alba: Structure as Meaning.*
New York: Columbia University Press, 1972.

Schmitt, Charles B. *Cicero Scepticus: A Study of the Influence of the
"Academica" in the Renaissance.* The Hague: Mouton, 1972.

Searle, J. R. *Speech Acts: An Essay in the Philosophy of Language.*
Cambridge: Cambridge University Press, 1969.

Seigel, Jerrold E. *Rhetoric and Philosophy in Renaissance Humanism:
The Union of Eloquence and Wisdom, Petrarch to Valla.* Princeton:
Princeton University Press, 1968.

Selden, Raman. *English Verse Satire, 1590–1765.* London: George
Allen and Unwin, 1978.

———. "John Donne's 'Incarnational Conviction.'" *Critical Quarterly* 17 (1975): 55–73.

Shawcross, John T. "Literary Revisionism and a Case for Genre."
Genre 18 (1985): 413–34.

Sherwood, Terry G. *Fulfilling the Circle: A Study of John Donne's
Thought.* Toronto: University of Toronto Press, 1984.

Slights, Camille Wells. *The Casuistical Tradition in Shakespeare, Donne,
Herbert, and Milton.* Princeton: Princeton University Press, 1981.

Sloane, Thomas O. "The Crossing of Rhetoric and Poetry in the
English Renaissance." In *The Rhetoric of Renaissance Poetry*, edited
by Thomas O. Sloane and Raymond Waddington, pp. 212–42.
Berkeley and Los Angeles: University of California Press, 1974.

———. *Donne, Milton, and the End of Humanist Rhetoric.* Berkeley and
Los Angeles: University of California Press, 1985.

———. "The Persona as Rhetor: An Interpretation of Donne's *Satyre
III.*" *Quarterly Journal of Speech* 51 (1965): 14–27.

Smith, A. J., ed. *John Donne: Essays in Celebration.* London: Methuen, 1972.

———. "Theory and Practice in Renaissance Poetry: Two Kinds of
Imitation." *Bulletin of the John Rylands Library* 47 (1964): 212–43.

Snyder, Susan. "Donne and DuBartas: The *Progress of the Soule* as
Parody." *Studies in Philology* 70 (1973): 392–407.

Solmsen, Friedrich. "The Aristotelian Tradition in Ancient Rhetoric," *American Journal of Philology* 62 (1941): 35–50, 169–90.

Sonnino, Lee Ann. *A Handbook of Sixteenth Century Rhetoric.* New
York: Barnes and Noble, 1968.

Spencer, Theodore, ed. *A Garland for John Donne, 1631–1931.* Cambridge: Harvard University Press, 1931.

Stanwood, P. G., and Heather Ross Asals, ed. *John Donne and the Theology of Language.* Columbia: University of Missouri Press, 1986.

Stein, Arnold. "Donne and the Satiric Spirit." *ELH* 11 (1944): 266–82.

———. "Donne's Harshness and the Elizabethan Tradition." *Studies in Philology* 41 (1944): 390–409.

———. "Donne's Obscurity and the Elizabethan Tradition." *ELH* 13 (1947): 98–118.

———. *John Donne's Lyrics: The Eloquence of Action.* Minneapolis: University of Minnesota Press, 1962.

Steiner, George. *After Babel: Aspects of Language and Translation.* New York: Oxford University Press, 1975.

Stringer, Gary. "Learning 'Hard and Deepe': Biblical Allusion in Donne's 'A Valediction: Of My Name, in the Window." *South-Central Bulletin* 33 (1974): 227–31.

Struever, Nancy S. *The Language of History in the Renaissance: Rhetorical and Historical Consciousness in Florentine Humanism.* Princeton: Princeton University Press, 1970.

Summers, Claude J. and Ted-Larry Pebworth, eds. *The Eagle and the Dove: Reassessing John Donne.* Columbia: University of Missouri Press, 1986.

Szasz, Thomas. *The Myth of Psychotherapy: Mental Healing as Religion, Rhetoric, and Repression.* Garden City, N.Y.: Anchor Press, 1978.

Tebeaux, Elizabeth. "John Donne and the Problem of Religious Authority: 'Wranglings That Tend Not to Edification.'" *South Central Bulletin* 42 (1982): 137–43.

Thomas, Keith. *Religion and the Decline of Magic.* New York: Scribner's, 1971.

Tillich, Paul. *The Dynamics of Faith.* New York: Harper and Brothers, 1956–1957.

Tjarks, Larry D. "Donne's 'Loves Usury' and a Self-Deceived Persona." *Southern Quarterly* 14 (1976): 207–13.

———. "Recurrence and Renascence: Rhetorical Imitation in Ascham and Sturm." *English Literary Renaissance* 6 (1976): 156–79.

Todorov, Tzvetan. "The Origin of Genres." *New Literary History* 8 (1976–1977): 159–70.

Tuve, Rosemund. *Elizabethan and Metaphysical Imagery: Renaissance Poetic and Twentieth-Century Critics.* Chicago: University of Chicago Press, 1947.

Untersteiner, Mario. *The Sophists*. Translated by Kathleen Freeman. New York: Philosophical Library, 1954.

Vickers, Brian. "Analogy versus Identity: The Rejection of Occult Symbolism, 1580–1680." In *Occult and Scientific Mentalities in the Renaissance*, edited by Brian Vickers, pp. 95–163. New York: Cambridge University Press, 1984.

———. *Classical Rhetoric in English Poetry*. Edinburgh: R. D. Clark, 1970.

———. "The *Songs and Sonnets* and the Rhetoric of Hyperbole." In *John Donne: Essays in Celebration*, edited by A. J. Smith, pp. 132–74. London: Methuen, 1972.

Villeneuve, François. *Essai sur Perse*. Paris: n.p., 1918.

Vitanza, Victor. "Critical Sub/Versions of the History of Rhetoric." *Rhetoric Review* 6 (1987): 41–66.

Vivas, Eliseo. "Literary Classes: Some Problems." *Genre* I (1968): 97–105.

Vogel, Arthur A. *Body Theology: God's Presence in Man's World*. New York: Harper and Row, 1973.

Vološinov, V. N. *Marxism and the Philosophy of Language*. Translated by Ladislav Matejka and I. R. Titutnik. Cambridge: Harvard University Press, 1986.

Walter, Otis. "Plato's Idea of Rhetoric for Contemporary Students: Theory and Composition Assignments." *College Composition and Communication* 35 (1984): 20–30.

Waswo, Richard. *Language and Meaning in the Renaissance*. Princeton: Princeton University Press, 1987.

Weinberg, Bernard. *A History of Literary Criticism in the Italian Renaissance*. 2 vols. London: University of Chicago Press, 1961.

West, David, and Tony Woodman, eds. *Creative Imitation and Latin Literature*. Cambridge: Cambridge University Press, 1979.

White, Harold O. *Plagiarism and Imitation during the English Renaissance*. Cambridge: Harvard University Press, 1935.

White, Hayden. *Tropics of Discourse: Essays in Cultural Criticism*. Baltimore: Johns Hopkins University Press, 1978.

White, James Boyd. *When Words Lose Their Meaning: Constitutions and Reconstitutions of Language, Character, and Community*. Chicago: University of Chicago Press, 1984.

Wiley, Margaret L. *The Subtle Knot: Creative Scepticism in Seventeenth-Century England*. Cambridge: Harvard University Press, 1952.

Williamson, George. *The Donne Tradition: A Study in English Poetry from Donne to the Death of Cowley*. New York: Noonday Press, 1930.

———. "Strong Lines." In *Seventeenth Century Contexts*, pp. 120–31. Chicago: University of Chicago Press, 1960.

Witke, Charles. *Latin Satire: The Structure of Persuasion*. Leiden: E. J. Brill, 1970.

Wright, George T. "The Personae of Donne's Love Poems." *Southern Quarterly* 14 (1975): 173–77.

Yates, Francis A. *Giordano Bruno and the Hermetic Tradition*. Chicago: University of Chicago Press, 1964.

Zively, Sherry. "Imagery in John Donne's *Satyres*." *Studies in English Literature* 6 (1966): 87–95.

INDEX